Morgan Park

Morgan Park

DULUTH, U.S. STEEL, AND THE FORGING OF A COMPANY TOWN

Arnold R. Alanen

With Photographs by Chris Faust

University of Minnesota Press
Minneapolis • London

Portions of this book previously appeared in these publications by Arnold R. Alanen: "Sixty Years of Transition in a Planned Company Town, with a Portrayal of Current Resident Evaluations," in *The Behavioral Basis of Design, Book 1: Selected Papers*, Peter Suedfeld and James A. Russell, eds. (Stroudsburg, Penn.: Dowden, Hutchinson, and Ross, Inc., 1976), 185–92; "Morgan Park: U.S. Steel and a Planned Company Town," in *Duluth: A Bicentennial Collection*, Rick Lydecker and Lawrence J. Sommer, eds. (Duluth: American Revolution Bicentennial Commission, 1976); "The Rise and Demise of a Company Town," *Professional Geographer* 29 (February 1977): 32–39; *Pines, Mines, and Lakes: A Field Guide to the Architecture and Landscapes of Northeastern Minnesota* (Madison: Department of Landscape Architecture, University of Wisconsin–Madison and Vernacular Architecture Forum, 2000).

Published in cooperation with the Center for American Places, Santa Fe, New Mexico, and Staunton, Virginia. www.americanplaces.org.

Copyright 2007 by the Regents of the University of Minnesota

Photograph gallery copyright 2007 by Chris Faust

Published by the University of Minnesota Press
111 Third Avenue South, Suite 290
Minneapolis, MN 55401-2520
http://www.upress.umn.edu

Library of Congress Cataloging-in-Publication Data

Alanen, Arnold R. (Arnold Robert)
    Morgan Park : Duluth, U.S. Steel, and the forging of a company town / Arnold R. Alanen ; with photographs by Chris Faust.
       p.   cm.
    Includes bibliographical references and index.
    ISBN: 978-0-8166-4136-9 (hc : alk. paper)
    ISBN: 978-0-8166-4137-6 (pb : alk. paper)
    1. Company towns—Minnesota—Duluth—History.   2. City planning—Minnesota—Duluth—History.   3. United States Steel Corporation—History.
    4. Steel industry and trade—Minnesota—Duluth—History.   I. Title.
    HN80.D88A53 2007
    307.76'709776771—dc22
                                                          2007042110

Printed in the United States of America on acid-free paper

The University of Minnesota is an equal-opportunity educator and employer.

15 14 13 12 11 10   10 9 8 7 6 5 4 3 2

In memory of John R. Borchert (1918–2001)
Regents Professor of Geography
University of Minnesota

My academic mentor and friend,
who encouraged me to write about
the landscape and geography
of "home"—northeastern Minnesota.

CONTENTS

Photographs of Morgan Park by Chris Faust follow page 174

ACKNOWLEDGMENTS

The manuscript for this book was written in Madison, Wisconsin, some 350 miles from Morgan Park and Duluth. Since anyone who writes a detailed history about a particular place must be thoroughly familiar with that locale, I spent considerable time in northeastern Minnesota doing research over the past seven years. (This was just two years less than the total time required to construct both the steel plant and the community!) Some of the costs involved in these activities were defrayed by a grant from the Graduate School of the University of Wisconsin–Madison, while a small stipend from the Vernacular Architecture Forum, provided just prior to the organization's meeting in Duluth in 2000, contributed to the redrafting of several Morgan Park house plans and elevations. A grant from the Graham Foundation for Advanced Studies in the Visual Arts was crucial in that it allowed me to acquire and utilize many of the historic photographs that illustrate Morgan Park's evolution, and to hire landscape photographer Chris Faust, who, in 2002, provided several contemporary images of the community used in this book.

I am indebted to a number of other organizations for the services they provided, and several staff members affiliated with those institutions deserve special thanks; some of them, in fact, welcomed the completion of this book as much as I did. The Northeast Minnesota Historical Center (NEMHC) at the University of Minnesota Duluth, which holds the largest archival collection of written and visual Morgan Park materials, served as my most important information source. Patricia Maus, the curator at NEMHC, kindly devoted much of her time and energy to this project. At the Duluth Public Library, Kris Aho and David Ouse always greeted me warmly when I appeared in their building, even if they knew the library's photocopying equipment would soon be in constant use. In St. Paul, the Minnesota Historical Society provided an invaluable service by allowing me to borrow hundreds of reels of microfilm that I could then peruse in Madison. For the past thirty-three years my colleagues in the Department of Landscape Architecture at the University of Wisconsin–Madison have always been supportive of my primary research and teaching program:

cultural landscape studies, the history of the built environment, and cultural resource preservation. All of these interests are represented here.

While engaged in writing I quickly discovered that many of the manuscript's details required verification and clarification, something that could be undertaken only in Duluth and Morgan Park. I was not, however, readily able to accomplish such a task because of distance constraints and the demands of a full academic schedule. Fortunately, I was able to overcome this hurdle because two Duluthians came forward and provided voluntary research assistance from 2004 onward. Maryanne Norton's research skills and generous spirit are well known to many people who have explored and documented Duluth's history and architecture, but I'm quite certain that my requests were more demanding and problematic than those posed by other investigators. Because of her willingness to track down and substantiate countless facts, both mundane and complicated, the story of Morgan Park that unfolds on these pages is much richer and more complete. Mike Flaherty, a former resident of Morgan Park who has lived in five different concrete-block houses located throughout the community, spent many hours on my behalf in Duluth's City Hall, where he found various building and demolition permits that allowed me to explain the architectural evolution of the community with greater accuracy and insight. Both Maryanne and Mike reviewed early drafts of the entire manuscript, and Richard Hudelson of the University of Wisconsin–Superior, an expert on the working-class experience in Duluth, cogently commented on those sections that dealt with labor history.

Within Morgan Park, Nancy Thompson, a resident since 2000, kept me informed about current community changes and events, and introduced me to several long-time citizens I later interviewed. Two of those individuals, John Howden and Al Bothun, offered intimate knowledge about life in Morgan Park extending back to the 1910s and 1920s. Other former and current residents (Isobel Olson Rapaich, Paul and Sally Solomon, Bill and Sue Majewski, Isabel and Bob Davey, June Bothun, Barbara Isaacson East, Don Long, and Vonna Mae and Elmer Malinen) kindly responded to my many inquiries. The Reverend Peter Bagley located archival information dating to the early formation of Morgan Park's United Protestant Church, including comments by one of the community's most outspoken critics, the Reverend J. W. Kuyper. Despite the demands they encountered while working within a very busy Morgan Park middle-school environment, librarian Karen Isensee and principal Mitch Clausen provided access to former *Parktorian* high school yearbooks and historical materials.

Over the span of several years, three of my former graduate students—George F. Thompson, Michael Koop, and Frank Edgerton Martin—accompanied me on visits to Morgan Park; their perceptive observations have always forced me to think more deeply and clearly about the design and planning features that distinguish the community. As the founder of the Center for American Places, George Thompson has facilitated the publication of hundreds of books about the landscape and geography of the United States. When he and I toured Morgan Park in 2000, George saw the potential for a book about the design and planning history of the community, and he encouraged me to pursue such a project; I am pleased that the book is being published in cooperation with the Center for American Places. Michael Koop, a long-time employee of the Minnesota Historical Society's State Historic Preservation Office, demonstrated his considerable field documentation skills as we reviewed and sorted out Morgan Park's array of housing designs and forms during our preparations for the 2000 meeting of the Vernacular Architecture Forum. Comments by landscape historian and writer Frank Martin made me take note of the small but important details of landscape design that still remain in Morgan Park. In 2003 Frank was entrusted with a considerable collection of archival materials that came from the former Morell and Nichols partnership, the landscape architecture firm responsible for the planning of Morgan Park during the early twentieth century. The materials originally had gone to Gregory Kopischke, a landscape architect who had been documenting the firm's work; following his untimely death in 2002, the records were transferred to Frank, and then to the Northwest Architectural Archives at the University of Minnesota.

Most of the graphics, as well as the majority of written sources used to document the Morgan Park story, are located in public archives. In addition, a number of individuals kindly provided me with images and reference materials, or noted where they could be found. I thank Robert (Bob) Berg, Christine Carlson, John Gregor, Robert Harder, Karin Hertel McGinnis, John Isle, Donald Kress, Dale Lewis, Robert Silberman, John Strongitharm, and Lori Trifilette for this assistance. My cousin, Arvo William Alanen, identified and dated the vintage vehicles that are evident in some historic photographs. While working on the book it was my good fortune to employ Lynette Neitzel, a professional digital enhancer, who improved the clarity and quality of many images during her tenure as a graduate student in our department. Minneapolis architect Robert Gerloff redrafted several of the house plans and elevations found in chapters 4 and 6, as did former undergraduate students Tamara Larson and Kassie Martine; Kassie also prepared the maps.

My association with the University of Minnesota Press has been fruitful and rewarding. Acquisitions editor Todd Orjala contacted me in 2001, asking if I might prepare a manuscript about the Morgan Park community and nearby steel plant. During the 1920s our respective grandparents were heavily involved in the formation of Finnish cooperatives in eastern Aitkin County, Minnesota; therefore, it is appropriate that their grandsons would have this opportunity to collaborate on another project more than three-quarters of a century later. Andrea Patch at the University of Minnesota Press deserves accolades for her patience in coping with an author who always wanted to refine one more chapter or add another image to the manuscript. Linda Lincoln improved the manuscript through her careful copy-editing, while Laura Westlund and Rachel Moeller ushered it through the production process. Finally, Denise Carlson prepared the index.

Lynn Bjorkman, my wife, an architectural historian and preservation planner who also is interested in company towns and landscape history, has been my helpmate throughout the entire time I was engaged in writing this book. She offered both editorial assistance and insights when I had difficulty finding the correct words for a particular statement or paragraph, and on visits to Morgan Park she worked with me in documenting the community's current features.

In sum, this book clearly demonstrates that writing itself may be a singular and even solitary task, but the results build on the contributions of many others.

PREFACE

Today tourism is a major "industry" in Duluth. Each year an estimated 4.5 million visitors spend as much as $400 million in the Zenith City. Here they marvel at the stunning vistas of Lake Superior visible from the city's steep hillside, gather at the waterfront and watch ships pass under the Aerial Lift Bridge, and shop and spend money in the renovated stores and restaurants of Canal Park.

Tourism was already evident in Duluth by the late nineteenth century, but from the 1870s to the 1970s this was a city based on heavy industry and shipping activities. Most of the industrial district has always been situated behind the natural breakwater of Minnesota Point; from there it stretched to the southwest along the shoreline of the St. Louis River, reaching as far as the neighborhood of New Duluth (Figure P.1). Concentrated along the harbor and industrial district was a labyrinth of docks and waterways that, by the 1950s, comprised nineteen square miles, with almost fifty miles of water frontage and seventeen miles of dredged channels.[1] At various times this zone supported numerous enterprises that have subsequently disappeared: saw milling, shipbuilding, metal forging, paint manufacturing, food processing, furniture making, appliance manufacturing, and other ventures. Some were very successful, many were short-lived.

Today, relatively few examples of industrial activity are scattered along sections of Duluth's waterfront: two huge ore docks, where iron-ore freighters are filled with the mineral wealth of northeastern Minnesota; five grain elevators and other storage sites, where ships bearing the flags of many nations both deliver and take on bulk and containerized products; and a paper mill, built during the 1980s, where the majority of the "supercalendared" paper used in the nation's magazines and advertising inserts is manufactured today.

From 1915 to 1972, the largest single employer in this industrial zone, and all of greater Duluth, was a manufacturing complex built and operated by the U.S. Steel Corporation and its subsidiaries. U.S. Steel's Duluth operations—which once produced steel, wire, fence posts, nails, and cement—were reduced to rubble by the late 1990s, but for almost six decades the plant's belching smokestacks stood for local and regional economic prosperity.

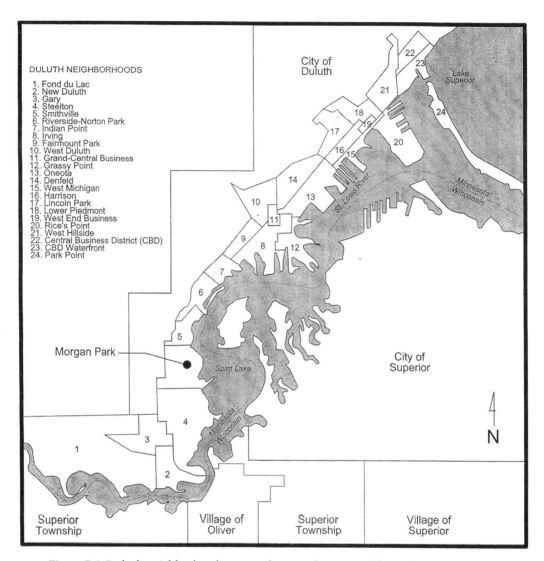

DULUTH NEIGHBORHOODS

1. Fond du Lac
2. New Duluth
3. Gary
4. Steelton
5. Smithville
6. Riverside-Norton Park
7. Indian Point
8. Irving
9. Fairmount Park
10. West Duluth
11. Grand-Central Business
12. Grassy Point
13. Oneota
14. Denfeld
15. West Michigan
16. Harrison
17. Lincoln Park
18. Lower Piedmont
19. West End Business
20. Rice's Point
21. West Hillside
22. Central Business District (CBD)
23. CBD Waterfront
24. Park Point

Figure P.1. Duluth neighborhoods, proceeding southwestward from the central business district along the St. Louis River to Morgan Park and beyond, 2006. Adapted from information supplied by Duluth's Department of City Planning; cartography by Kassie Martine.

The former U.S. Steel site is reached from downtown Duluth by traveling five miles south along the I-35 corridor to the Grand Avenue exit, where one goes toward the southwest. Little evidence of former industrial enterprise survives along Grand Avenue. Vacant and abandoned land now occupies several of the places that once accommodated these activities, but the predominant image is of gas stations, motels, fast-food establishments, taverns, other commercial enterprises and services, and an occasional church.

Farther along the route the buildings give way to trees and vegetation. Serving as a backdrop for much of the roadway are numerous streets and avenues, each lined with vernacular dwellings that have housed several generations of Duluth's working-class families. A few places and features serve as distinctive landmarks: the Lake Superior Zoo, with its granite outcroppings and structures that date back to the 1930s New Deal era; distant views of Spirit Mountain or Brandon's Peak, a sacred site for the local Ojibwe; and occasional glimpses of the St. Louis River.

Three miles later one arrives at the former U.S. Steel site. A high cyclone fence surrounds the vacant tract, currently filled with brush and areas of crumbling concrete. Just east and north of the former industrial area is the residential community of Morgan Park, the only remaining vestige of U.S. Steel's once-dominant presence. Here, from 1913 to 1922, U.S. Steel developed a model company town for the families of about five hundred skilled workers, technical personnel, and managers. No more than 15 to 25 percent of the total steel plant workforce was ever housed in Morgan Park, but the model town's well-constructed houses, pleasing landscape features, sophisticated physical plan, and numerous community facilities represented U.S. Steel's commitment to early twentieth-century "welfare capitalism" in Duluth.

Nearby, at the intersection of Grand and Eighty-eighth Avenue West, a small sign identifies the primary entrance to the community. After you pass under a historic railroad viaduct, an English Gothic-style church appears on the horizon. A number of Morgan Park's residences—most spreading out to the east and south—can be seen from the vantage point offered at the churchyard. Here, an observer will recognize the presence of both single- and multiple-family dwellings, many located side by side. Other viewers familiar with architectural history will notice hints of the Prairie style, especially the long, sloping roofs with pronounced overhangs. Upon venturing farther into the community, everyone will notice the distinctive singular building material that distinguishes Morgan Park: concrete. This is, in fact, a community where the majority of buildings were constructed of concrete blocks. Some residents have subsequently covered the exterior walls of their houses with wood, metal, or vinyl siding, and others have enclosed or removed original porches and entrances; nonetheless, the underlying uniformity of styles and materials embodied in the original design is still evident throughout the majority of Morgan Park's buildings.

Whether considering Duluth, northeastern Minnesota, or the entire state, the histories of both the steel plant and the Morgan Park community are important, interesting, and unique. The story of these two intertwined entities—the manufacturing facility and the model town—is the focus of this book.

The volume begins with an introductory chapter that places Morgan Park within the context of other model company towns in the United States and the Lake Superior mining region from the early nineteenth century to World War I. Following this introduction, the volume is divided into four parts with thirteen chapters.

Part I, "A Steel Plant and a Company Town, 1907–1915," has four chapters, two of which discuss the factors that culminated in the decision to build a manufacturing facility in Duluth, as well as the many difficulties encountered during steel plant construction. The ensuing two chapters consider efforts to house steelworkers and their families, first in nearby communities and neighborhoods such as Gary and Oliver, then in Morgan Park; the fourth chapter gives special attention to the planning and development of the community as a model town, focusing primarily on the landscape and architectural design considerations that distinguished the town's formative years.

Part II, "Working and Living in Morgan Park, 1916–1929," begins with a consideration of the relative prosperity achieved at the steel plant from World War I through the 1920s. Following this discussion, the further physical development of Morgan Park is addressed, and life in the community is portrayed at a time when U.S. Steel's prosperity supplied residents with the services and amenities that defined it as a model town.

Part III, "From Despair to Prosperity, 1930–1945," begins with two chapters that look at the extremely difficult situation encountered during the 1930s, a decade when the steel plant typically operated on an intermittent basis, and when beleaguered workers, both in Morgan Park and elsewhere in Duluth, felt fortunate to find part-time employment. These chapters are followed by a discussion of the complete turnaround that occurred when the nation's need for steel products skyrocketed during World War II; the section concludes with a consideration of the issues that residents encountered when ownership of Morgan Park's housing stock was transferred from corporate to individual control.

Part IV, "Closing a Steel Plant but Preserving a Community, 1946–2006," serves as an epilogue for the book. It begins with an overview of the manufacturing facility from 1946 until its traumatic closing in the 1970s. The subsequent and concluding chapter focuses on the community during the same years, but also carries the story up to the present, a period characterized by a growing appreciation for Morgan Park's history and design legacy.

Although I am a native of northeastern Minnesota, I did not visit Morgan Park until I spent two years, during the early 1960s, as an undergraduate student on the campus of the University of Minnesota Duluth. I was, however, well aware of the steel plant before living in Duluth, having heard it described on many occasions by my steelworker cousin, Kauko Pursi. He had emigrated from Finland in 1938 at the age of seventeen to work on my family's Aitkin County farm, located sixty miles west of Duluth. Shortly after becoming an American citizen, Kauko volunteered for service in the U.S. Army Air Forces, serving as a medic during the World War II years. Following his military discharge, Kauko found employment at the steel plant, where, for more than a quarter-century, he seldom missed a day of work because of illness or injury. Throughout the 1950s he came to our farm, where he helped us with haymaking activities during the busy weeks of summer. Working alongside him I became familiar with the annual rhythms of a steelworker's life. Because of the many strikes that marked the decade, he often had spare time to help us. And even when there were no strikes, a lengthy vacation schedule afforded him additional time for farm work. When I complained about the sauna-like heat that enveloped us as we pitched hay or lifted bales inside the barn loft, Kauko said it was nothing compared to the temperatures he experienced at the steel plant. "That's where one does a real man's work," he informed me in his eastern Finnish dialect.

After leaving the University of Minnesota Duluth, I became aware of Morgan Park's distinctive origins, first as an undergraduate architectural studies major at the Twin Cities campus of the University of Minnesota, and then during the late 1960s and early 1970s, when I studied planned communities as a graduate student in the Department of Geography. My advisor, Professor John R. Borchert, encouraged me to continue this line of research in my future academic career, something I have done to the present. Upon joining the faculty at the University of Wisconsin-Madison in 1974, I received a small grant to conduct a survey of residents in Morgan Park and the nearby community of Gary only a few years after the steel plant's closing. Although I employed many of the survey findings in articles that were published later in the decade, I have now gone back to the original data and mined it for additional information, which is incorporated into the last two chapters of this book.[2]

For more than two subsequent decades, my contact with Morgan Park was limited to occasional visits and the reading of accounts that appeared in the *Duluth News-Tribune*. In 2000, however, I once again had reason to look closely at Morgan Park, this time as the author of a field guide for the annual meeting of the Vernacular Architecture Forum (VAF), a multidisciplinary organization of scholars and field professionals interested in studying and preserving examples of "ordinary" architecture and landscapes in North America.[3] The two days of field excursions that occurred as part of the 2000 meeting included several places in Duluth, as well as on Minnesota's Iron Range and along the North Shore of Lake Superior. The Morgan Park stop, however, was clearly a highlight. The VAF members' observations and discussions regarding the significance of the community's buildings, plan, and landscape design again piqued my curiosity and interest. Shortly thereafter I began working on a volume that would cover the one hundred years of history associated with both the steel plant and the Morgan Park community.

Because of my long-time familiarity with Morgan Park, I first believed the manuscript would be brief and could be completed relatively quickly. I was mistaken. Instead, after beginning work, I soon realized there was much more to the Morgan Park story than I had originally thought. And now, after a total of five years of research and writing, I know there are still many more stories of this place and its people yet to tell.

INTRODUCTION
MODEL COMPANY TOWNS IN AMERICA, 1800–1914

Company towns have been part of the fabric of American life since the early nineteenth century, or about one hundred years before Morgan Park emerged in northeastern Minnesota. Some of these places are identified as "model towns," "model villages," or "model cities" because of their unique attributes: innovative physical designs that utilized the talents of professional architects, landscape architects, planners, and engineers; and social programs that provided a menu of benefits for workers and their families. The intention of these offerings was not necessarily altruistic, however, for model towns were primarily intended to attract skilled and dependable workers who would be contented, efficient, and less likely to engage in strikes and labor disorder.

America's nineteenth-century company towns were typically managed in a highly paternalistic manner, which meant the sponsoring industrialists or corporations sought to control employee behavior, both in the workplace and the home. Two well-known model towns serve as bookends for the century: Lowell, Massachusetts, and Pullman, Illinois. Industrialization was introduced to America at Lowell and several smaller New England mill villages during the early years of the century, whereas Pullman, the site of an infamous 1894 labor conflict, stands as one of the nation's clearest examples of paternalistic excess and malevolence. But by the early twentieth century, many industrialists and corporate managers were searching for a middle ground, often termed "welfare capitalism," that could accommodate the mutual needs of the workers and employers. Morgan Park is one of several pre–World War I company communities that demonstrate the application of these middle-ground principles.

From Lowell to Pullman

Small mill villages began appearing in New England at the beginning of the 1800s when textile operators recruited workers and their families to small manufacturing properties. By the 1820s, as new textile mills were constructed in larger towns and cities, the owners began staffing their facilities with young, single women from New England. The mill owners provided a range of programs and services in these towns—including highly regulated boardinghouse and dormitory accommodations, art and literary groups, and compulsory Bible-reading classes—all intended to assuage the qualms of the women and their parents about living and working in an industrialized environment. Despite the seeming benefits, most were part of what planning historian Margaret Crawford calls a "total organization of production" that ultimately subjected the female employees "to complete industrial discipline."[1]

Lowell, the best known of these planned communities, was founded in 1812. By 1839, an impressed European observer reported that besides boardinghouses, Lowell displayed "numerous little wooden houses painted white, with green blinds, very neat, very snug, very nicely carpeted, and with a few small trees around them, or brick houses in the English style. . . . Here are all edifices of a flourishing town in the Old World, except the prisons, hospitals, and theatres" (Figure I.1). Other noteworthy examples of New England paternalism were Hopedale and Ludlow, Massachusetts; South Manchester, Connecticut; Peace Dale, Rhode Island; and Fairbanks Village, Vermont. As noted by architectural historian John Garner, the New England region displayed "some of the first experiments in American town

Figure I.1. Boardinghouses on Dutton Street, with one of the textile mills in the background, Lowell, Massachusetts, 1848. Delineated by O. Pelton. Courtesy of Lowell Historical Society.

planning and management," and served as "a proving ground for later industrial settlements." The Lowell planning and organizational model ended by the 1860s, when recent European immigrants who demanded few of the original amenities replaced the Yankee female mill workers.[2]

Because the United States was overwhelmingly an agricultural nation until the Civil War, relatively few manufacturing settlements developed outside of New England during the first half of the nineteenth century. But as the economy became more industrialized from the 1860s onward, numerous new towns sprang up in several areas of the country. These towns, nevertheless, did not necessarily display a singular organizational pattern or layout. According to Crawford, "Each industrial district established its own standards for working conditions and community life that shaped a characteristic physical and social order."[3] Throughout this period, the paternalistic practices of employers could be either onerous or benevolent. At best, workers and their families were provided with adequate, low-cost housing and medical services; at worst, they were subjected to strict discipline and arbitrary rules.

The arduous conditions that characterized many corporate environments contributed to worker unrest that was increasingly evident by the 1870s, no more so than during the "Great Upheaval" of 1877—the nation's first mass labor strike. It was concern over such labor issues that led railway sleeping car manufacturer George R. Pullman, in 1880, to develop a model village on vacant land south of Chicago. The community, named for Pullman himself, was envisioned as a place where the industrialist could provide improved living conditions for his workers while simultaneously exerting control over their actions and deportment.[4]

Architect Solon Spenser Beman and landscape architect Nathan F. Barrett designed a community that reflected George Pullman's belief in the "commercial value of beauty." The red brick, American Queen Anne–style buildings, along with a compact grid plan, an artificial lake, and numerous small parks, provided the community with a clear sense of urbanity (Figures I.2 and I.3). The infrastructure, much of it planned by civil and sanitary engineer Benezette Williams, was considerably advanced for the time. Some of the treated sewage was recycled, while the remainder was applied to nearby farm fields owned by George Pullman; storm water runoff was discharged into nearby Lake Calumet through a separate system of cobblestone gutters. Early observers commented favorably on the appearance and organization of Pullman, although some, such as economist Richard Ely, offered a more cautionary interpretation. "The citizen is surrounded by constant restraint

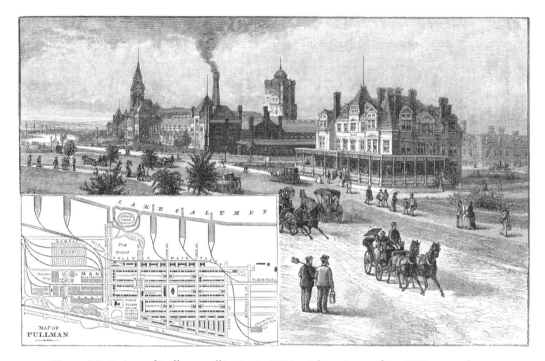

Figure I.2. A view of Pullman, Illinois, in 1884, with an inset of its 1885 town plan. The Pullman Palace Car Works, the community's major manufacturing facility, is on the left; the Florence Hotel is on the right; and a section of the community's formally designed landscape is in the foreground. From Richard T. Ely, "Pullman: A Social Study," Harper's New Monthly Magazine *70 (February 1885).*

and restriction," wrote Ely in 1885. "[E]verything is done for him, nothing by him." Pullman, Ely concluded, was "un-American."[5]

By 1893, Pullman's 12,600 residents made it the nation's largest company town. But then in 1894—a year marked by major labor strikes in the steel mills of Homestead, Pennsylvania, the silver mines of Coeur d'Alene, Idaho, and elsewhere—an embittered conflict broke out in the Pullman factory. The strike, which lasted from May to July, was linked in no small part to the high rents, wage reductions, and rigid regulations imposed by George Pullman. Despite the presence of more than fourteen thousand police, state militia, and federal troops who were deployed to maintain order, considerable rioting and bloodshed ensued. After the strike ended, public and judicial opposition to the heavy-handed paternalism exposed by the 1894 strike contributed to rapid changes in the organization and management of other American company towns. In 1898, one year after George Pullman's death, the Illinois State Supreme Court ruled that ownership of all property in a single town

Figure I.3. Pullman's row houses provided factory workers and their families with small but well-built residential quarters. From Ely, "Pullman: A Social Study."

or city "was opposed to good public policy and incompatible with the theory and spirit of our institutions."[6] Ten years later Pullman's tenure as a company town had ended, although the residential and institutional buildings that still remain make it one of Chicago's most distinctive neighborhoods.

Beyond Pullman

Because of the negative publicity associated with Pullman, other industrialists quickly questioned the underlying principles and practices that were part of its relatively brief history. Already in 1895, the Apollo Steel Company hired the nation's best-known landscape architect, Frederick Law Olmsted Sr., to develop a plan for the steel-manufacturing town of Vandergrift, Pennsylvania, located about thirty miles northeast of Pittsburgh. The picturesque plan and curvilinear street pattern, along with the company's individual home ownership program (albeit for skilled workers and managers only), were seen as improvements over Pullman (Figure I.4). Olmsted's plan was unfortunately considered too expensive, however, and subsequent development differed very little from most company towns.[7]

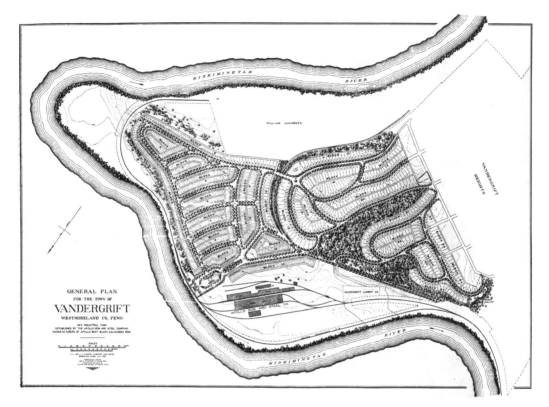

Figure I.4. Unlike most company towns, the 1885 plan for Vandergrift, Pennsylvania, with famed landscape architect Frederick Law Olmsted Sr. as the designer, was distinguished by its picturesque qualities. From Arthur C. Comey and Max S. Wehrly, "Planned Communities," Part 1 of the National Resources Committee, Urban Planning and Land Policies, Volume 2 of the Supplementary Report of the Urbanism Committee to the National Resources Committee *(Washington, D.C.: U.S. Government Printing Office, 1939).*

An even greater departure from traditional paternalism occurred from 1905 to 1907 at Gary, Indiana. Here, just east of Chicago, the U.S. Steel Corporation developed a massive manufacturing complex on an eleven-square-mile site positioned midway between the iron-ore mines of Minnesota and the coalfields of Pennsylvania and West Virginia. While U.S. Steel reportedly poured $80 million into the initial development of Gary, most of the financial outlay was devoted to the construction of a modern steel-manufacturing center, a port, and railroads. Company engineer A. P. Melton's plan for Gary was far from inspired, revealing an interminable street grid that had no more than a few areas designated for parks and

Figure I.5. The plan for the large industrial city of Gary, Indiana, revealed little in the way of progressive planning, but some of the early housing, designed in 1906 (and shown here in 1923) by the Chicago architectural firm of Dean and Dean, received positive reviews. In 1913 Dean and Dean would begin designing similar housing for the model village of Morgan Park, Minnesota. Courtesy of Calumet Regional Archives, Indiana University Northwest.

public facilities. According to planning historian John Reps, the layout of Gary differed very little from the speculative plats produced by nineteenth-century town promoters. Some housing areas of Gary displayed relatively progressive design features, but U.S. Steel executives essentially sought to avoid any comparison with Pullman (Figure I.5). Therefore, they promoted speculative commercial and residential development in Gary, which meant that "short-run economic objectives prevailed over modern, aesthetic, and effective planning." Although the city's 2000 population of about 103,000 residents represents a significant decline from the peak figure of 178,000 in 1960, Gary still serves as America's largest corporate-sponsored town.[8]

Welfare Capitalism and the "New" Company Town

Gary notwithstanding, the Progressive Era of the late 1890s and early 1900s did lead to noticeable transformations in the nation's company towns. Among the industrial betterment programs proposed by reformers were those that featured "welfare capitalism" or "welfare work"—defined as "any service provided for the comfort or improvement of employees which was neither a necessity of industry nor required by law."[9] Employees were provided with home-ownership programs, health care and life insurance plans, stock investment options, limited retirement benefits, workplace safety improvements, and even home economics classes for the wives and daughters of workers. After 1900, the National Civic Federation, a fervent anti-socialist organization that attracted numerous industrialists to its ranks, promoted many of the programs. Among the members of the National Civic Foundation was Elbert Gary, U.S. Steel's chairman of the board. As summarized by Richard Hudelson and Carl Ross, Gary believed that America's business leaders "had an obligation to work together, to avoid the dangers of ruinous competition, and to replace the anarchy of the market with intelligent planning."[10]

Among the welfare provisions were proposals to develop model villages for workers. While these planned communities gave capitalists highly visible opportunities to express their versions of social awareness, the new settlements also provided design professionals with possibilities to develop well-planned workers' communities and environments. Because of their notable design qualities and the role the communities played in decentralizing local industry and housing and in easing urban congestion, Margaret Crawford termed these places the "new" company towns.[11]

By the early 1900s American model villages often incorporated contemporaneous design styles as part of their architecture and planning. Several used some of the design concepts associated with the City Beautiful, a turn-of-the-century American planning movement that sought to make civic beauty a common cause, and that often featured axial roads and formally designed areas for civic centers, city halls, schools, and churches. The housing and services that several European industrialists provided for their workers also inspired some of the model villages and social welfare programs that emerged on the American side of the Atlantic. Among the European examples were the towns and programs of the Krupp steel-manufacturing enterprise by Essen, Germany; the projects of various Swedish mining and manufacturing companies; and the nineteenth-century British model villages of

Bournville, Saltaire, and Port Sunlight. It was the English garden city, however, that most directly influenced America's early twentieth-century model villages.[12]

The garden city idea is associated with Ebenezer Howard, an English clerk and social reformer whose book, *Tomorrow: A Peaceful Path to Real Reform* (later republished as *Garden Cities of Tomorrow*), received worldwide attention when it appeared in 1898. Concerned about the crowded and unhealthy conditions that lower-income people encountered in England's expanding urban areas, Howard sought to marry city and country through the development of garden cities—new towns of thirty thousand to fifty thousand people that would be separated from the central city and each other by an agricultural greenbelt.[13]

In 1903, renowned town planners Raymond Unwin and Barry Parker designed the garden city of Letchworth, located north of London. American planners soon familiarized themselves with plans and photographs of Letchworth that appeared in various professional publications. Some garden city proposals, such as joint land ownership, were deemed too radical for America, but the physical design ideas found a receptive audience among planners. They were attracted to the garden city "as a new ideal," even though the American communities typically emerged as garden suburbs and garden villages, rather than as complete towns. A review of several American industrial communities, made in 1921 by Massachusetts landscape architect and town planning consultant John Nolen, led him to conclude that none met all the criteria of the best English garden communities. Nevertheless, Nolen did observe that each of the industrial towns in his assessment, including Morgan Park, displayed at least some similarity with the English examples.[14]

Among the model industrial villages that borrowed some design concepts from garden city planning was Fairfield, Alabama, developed in 1910 by the Tennessee Coal and Iron Company, a U.S. Steel Corporation subsidiary. Located eight miles from downtown Birmingham and at the center of coal, iron ore, and limestone deposits, Fairfield is considered an example of "the new forces of American site planning" emerging at this time. Boston landscape architect George H. Miller's plan displayed an axial road that focused on a formally developed civic center, while the majority of residential areas were organized in gridiron blocks of limited length. The Craftsman-style one-story bungalows and two-story duplexes—typically with varied porches, dormers, protruding eaves, and shingled surfaces—differed noticeably from the majority of American company towns and their row upon

*Figure I.6.
A bungalow and
garden, renting
for twenty dol-
lars a month in
the white sec-
tion of Fairfield,
Alabama, 1917.
Courtesy of
Library of
Congress.*

row of uniform residences (Figure I.6). Later additions to the community "were largely carried out by outside speculative interests with no regard for the original plan either in relation to the street system, the character of the development, or the objectives of the founders." By the 1930s Fairfield had become a highly segregated community: whites resided in the original model village, whereas African Americans were relegated to poorly planned, speculatively built housing districts.[15]

Chickasaw, also in Alabama, offers another example of the racial divide that characterized many company towns in the American South (Figure I.7). Built six miles outside of Mobile by a U.S. Steel subsidiary engaged in shipbuilding, the corporation was unapologetic in describing the town site: "It is divided distinctly into two sections, white and colored," noted a 1920 publication. Housing densities in the black section were twice that of the white district, and blacks resided in dwellings with two, three, and four rooms, whereas whites were accommodated in units with four, five, and six rooms. In addition, the African American village was situated immediately adjacent to the shipbuilding works, with its attendant noise and pollution.[16]

Other "new" model towns of the pre–World War I era are Goodyear Heights in Akron, Ohio; Indian Hills in Worcester, Massachusetts; and Torrance, near Los Angeles, California. Also in the group is Morgan Park, which first appeared on the outskirts of Duluth in 1913. Morgan Park, none-

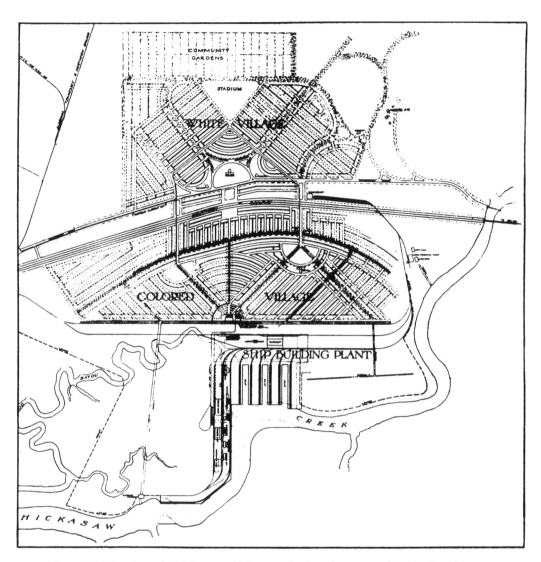

Figure I.7. The plan of Chickasaw, Alabama, displayed separate districts for African American and white residents. From U.S. Steel Corporation, Bureau of Safety, Sanitation, and Welfare, Bulletin No. 7 *(December 1918).*

theless, was not the first example of corporate town planning in the expansive Lake Superior mining district spreading out to the east, north, and west of Duluth. That designation belongs to Michigan's "Copper Country," where mining began during the 1840s. Morgan Park, however, is even more closely linked to two model company towns—Gwinn, Michigan, and Coleraine, Minnesota—both constructed as part of early twentieth-century iron-ore mining ventures.

Corporate Paternalism in the "Copper Country"

The first companies that extracted copper ore in the far northern reaches of Michigan's Upper Peninsula during the mid-nineteenth century encountered numerous challenges. None was more problematic than the question of supplying laborers with housing and provisions for the five or six months of the year that Lake Superior was icebound. The considerable forethought and planning required to satisfy these restrictions eventually evolved into a highly paternalistic system that saw the mining firms exert considerable power over residents and local governments. "No more completely controlled paternalism has ever existed in this country," commented historian V. H. Jensen in 1950.[17]

Since most early mining developments were financed by investors based in Boston and the eastern United States, the incipient Copper Country settlements displayed some of the trappings of New England villages and company towns: a clear separation between settled areas and the surrounding wilderness, a common area for the grazing of domestic animals, orthogonal street layouts, and small houses of uniform size and dimension. Already in 1856 a correspondent for the *Mining Magazine* of London reported that the settlement of Clifton, Michigan, had been so successfully planned and organized it could serve as a model for mining enclaves elsewhere in the world. Housing, gardens, recreation, and access to sunshine were available in Clifton, noted the correspondent, and disorderliness and drunkenness reportedly had been eliminated.[18]

No other copper firm approached the paternalistic offerings of the Boston-based Calumet and Hecla Mining Company (C&H), headed by the stern industrialist and scientist Alexander Aggasiz. By the early twentieth century, C&H had built and leased 1,200 houses in Copper Country (Figure I.8). It also had accomplished the following: constructed an armory and school buildings; donated land for a YMCA; erected and equipped a hospital, as well as a large library filled with books in many European languages; developed and operated community water and sewer systems; and granted land and subsidies to numerous religious organizations.[19]

Some observers claimed that because of these benefits, Copper Country miners willingly worked for lower wages than they could have received in the American West. "It is the kind of paternalism that kills unionism and in one generation builds out of foreigners, ignorant of Anglo-Saxon institutions, citizens that any community can be proud," reported the *Engineering and Mining Journal* in 1911. Just two years later, however, a strike organized

Figure I.8. Uniform housing designs, such as these saltbox residences provided by the Calumet and Hecla Mining Company for its workers in Ahmeek, Michigan, depicted here in 1914, were characteristic of many American company towns. Courtesy of Michigan Technological University Archives and Copper Country Collections.

by the Western Federation of Miners led to major confrontations between laborers, who stated they were poorly paid and forced to work under dangerous conditions, and company executives who adamantly opposed union recognition. The strikers ended their work stoppage in April 1914, but received no concessions from the companies.[20]

By 1942, when Copper Country miners were given legal authority to organize labor unions, most of the district's high-grade ore had been depleted. C&H closed its local operations in 1969, which led to a further erosion of the population numbers and economic vitality that already had been set in motion following the 1913–14 strike. The population of the greater Calumet community, the key mining center in the district, fell from an estimated thirty thousand people in 1910 to fewer than eight thousand by 2000.[21] Today, Calumet serves as the headquarters for Keweenaw National Historical Park, which interprets the origins and evolution of America's first bonanza mining district.

Welfare Capitalism for Iron-Ore Miners

The successful commercial extraction of iron ore commenced in different areas of northern Michigan, Wisconsin, and Minnesota from the 1850s through the early 1900s. Unlike the Copper Country, however, the iron-mining companies did not have adequate financial resources to provide their employees with significant services and amenities. This pattern would change following the national financial panic of 1893, when a few large companies seized control of the region's ore-production facilities.

Mather, Manning, and Gwinn

Among the major firms that emerged in the post-1893 period was the Cleveland-Cliffs Iron Mining Company (CCI), headed by William Gwinn Mather from 1891 to 1931. It was Mather, more than anyone else, who moved beyond paternalism and introduced welfare capitalism to the entire Lake Superior mining district—even though most CCI operations were found in northern Michigan. Mather adopted his ideas from several sources, including observations he made while inspecting company-sponsored programs in Europe. "Relief and pension funds, health service, good housing, workingmen's life insurance associations, co-operative distributive stores, schools of all kinds, schemes of recreation, etc.," Mather wrote, "have been fostered in a wonderful degree by some employers, principally in Europe, to further the good and prevent the bad conditions."[22]

Shortly after returning from a European sojourn in 1893, Mather established a visiting nurse program at CCI and offered prizes to residents who displayed the most attractive home yards and gardens. Between 1905 and 1909 he organized a welfare department that supervised CCI's medical, housing, and improvement programs; developed a company pension plan for employees; and formed a mine safety department. Later, Mather provided his employees and their families with clubhouses that offered bowling alleys, showers, reading rooms, swimming pools, and recreation halls. Several hospitals were also provided in "consideration of the importance of providing the best of facilities for the handling of those cases which are the results of the hazard of the [mining] business"; an expanded visiting nurse program offered prenatal care for expectant mothers and instruction in sick care, hygiene, and sanitation.[23]

In 1906–07, Mather commissioned Massachusetts landscape architect Warren H. Manning, a well-known town planner, to design the model company town of Gwinn in a remote mining district of northern Michigan. Envisioning Gwinn as "a verdant isle among the pines," Manning called for the preservation of heavily wooded "reservations" or natural greenbelts that surrounded the town site. All of this, predicted a reporter for the *Detroit Free Press,* would allow the company's laborers to "make more of the outdoor life which they need, as their work in the mines keeps them for most of the day where sun and fresh air can never penetrate." The Gwinn plan revealed several City Beautiful features, most notably three radial streets that served as "important road vistas" for major public buildings (Figure I.9). Manning also provided Gwinn with a common—an open-space feature characteristic of New England.[24]

When compared to the residences that would develop in Morgan Park one decade later, Gwinn's company housing was quite modest. CCI initially built fifty-five duplexes for lower-income workers and eighteen single-family units for managers and supervisors; individual residents constructed eighty-two houses (Figure I.10). Six buildings formed the small commercial district, and four public buildings and four churches were situated elsewhere in the community.[25]

CCI began disposing of its residential properties during the economic depression of the 1930s, and ended local mining operations in 1946. Although

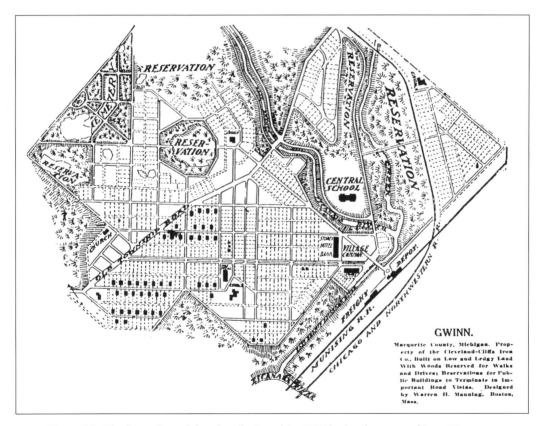

Figure I.9. The formality of the plan designed in 1907 by landscape architect Warren H. Manning for the small model town of Gwinn, located on the Marquette Iron Range of northern Michigan, contrasted with the surrounding wooded area. From Detroit Free Press, *March 15, 1908.*

Figure I.10. An overview of a residential area in Gwinn, Michigan, about 1910. Two churches appear in the distant background. Author's collection.

the economic future for Gwinn appeared bleak at this time, the cold war brought new life to the area during the 1950s, when a large U.S. Air Force base, K. I. Sawyer, was constructed just a few miles from the community. Gwinn's population peaked at 2,350 residents in 1990, but the closing of the air base later in the decade contributed to declines in local employment and economic opportunities that still plague the community to this day.[26]

The architectural appearance of Gwinn has changed over the past century, but its origins are still reflected in the town plan, the common, the landscape reservations, and the name of the high school athletic teams, the "Model Towners." The integrity of the physical features, as well as the community's ties to William Mather and Warren Manning, were recognized in 2001, when the Gwinn Model Village Historic District was listed in the National Register of Historic Places.[27]

Coleraine: Company Town Planning in Northeastern Minnesota

Like Gwinn, the planning and development of the model company town of Coleraine, Minnesota, occurred during the early twentieth century. Unlike Gwinn, however, no notable landscape architect or town planner was involved in Coleraine's initial development. Instead, it was John Greenway, an engineer and executive for the Oliver Iron Mining Company, who assumed primary responsibility for planning and supervising this northeastern Minnesota model village.

As built, Coleraine displayed several well-designed structures and a few City Beautiful elements. The major planning feature was a formal avenue that linked the community park and its ornate floral displays to a school for elementary, junior and senior high school students, as well as junior college students (Figure I.11). Potential businessmen were required to demonstrate evidence of good "citizenship" before Greenway allowed them to establish commercial enterprises. This practice, one observer contended, ensured that Coleraine only had "stable, virile men who have the interest of their town at heart." Greenway also hoped to eliminate the "saloons, gamblers [and] wantons" that he despised in typical mining towns. Coleraine did, in fact, have just one tavern, whereas the adjacent community of Bovey had twenty-two in 1907. While Greenway may have cast an unfavorable eye

Figure I.11. The City Beautiful features of Coleraine, a model town that emerged on the western section of Minnesota's Mesabi Iron Range in 1906, were clearly defined by the axis that connected the formally designed community park in the foreground and the school in the background. From U.S. Steel Corporation, Bureau of Safety, Sanitation, and Welfare, Bulletin No. 7.

upon the neighboring community, Bovey's citizens regarded their town as a "safety valve" for Coleraine, a place that "couldn't survive anyway if it didn't have a fast-paced nearby village where its residents could let off a little steam."[28]

Coleraine's history as a company-controlled community ended many decades ago, unlike most of the nearby mines, which closed during the 1960s; the population of 1,100 recorded in the year 2000 has, nevertheless, remained remarkably constant for almost a century. The most visible features of Coleraine's model town legacy are its buildings, seven of which are listed in the National Register of Historic Places.[29]

Gwinn and Coleraine never received the level of financial investment that would later occur at Morgan Park. Likewise, neither of the two communities ever displayed the quality of planning, housing, infrastructure, and community services that U.S. Steel provided in its Duluth model town. Gwinn and Coleraine, however, stand out as two of the earliest efforts to implement the principles of welfare capitalism in the Lake Superior region, and they paved the way for Morgan Park, described by architectural historian Katherine Eckert as "the most important example of corporate town planning in the Lake Superior area."[30]

PART I

A Steel Plant and a Company Town, 1907–1915

The Duluth plant has been more than five years in building, but now that it is completed it is said to be the most modernly equipped steel plant in the world.

—*Wall Street Journal,* November 15, 1915

Concrete block houses, paved streets and alleys, beautiful landscape gardening, and complete provision in all things for comfort and convenience make Morgan Park stand out among all industrial homesites.

—*Duluth News Tribune,* August 27, 1915

1. THE ECONOMICS AND POLITICS OF IRON ORE AND BIG STEEL

Duluth's residents rejoiced in April 1907 when they heard that a steel plant would be constructed in their city. With financing supplied by the U.S. Steel Corporation, America's first billion-dollar organization, Duluthians believed their city was on the verge of becoming the "Pittsburgh of the Northwest."[1] The decision to build in Duluth, however, occurred only after U.S. Steel officials and Minnesota politicians had entered into a complex courtship that started somewhat demurely at the turn of the twentieth century, but then became extremely tumultuous during the first three months of 1907. The early April marriage forged between the two parties occurred only when U.S. Steel's tremendous financial power and commensurate need for Minnesota iron ore were pitted against the state's ability to levy taxes on the corporation's immense mineral holdings.

U.S. Steel: An Overview

When U.S. Steel was incorporated in 1901 under the bylaws of the state of New Jersey, it immediately became the world's largest industrial enterprise. Formed through the amalgamation of several steel and iron ore companies, U.S. Steel secured ownership to 213 manufacturing plants located in five states, and some one thousand miles of rail lines. Of greatest importance to Minnesota at the time was the fact that U.S. Steel controlled well over one-half of the 104 mines operating in the state. Following the merger, U.S. Steel's presence in Duluth was immediate. Two major U.S. Steel subsidiaries were already headquartered in Duluth: the Oliver Iron Mining Company, which ran the corporation's extraction operations in Minnesota and the entire Lake Superior district; and the Pittsburgh Steamship Company, which operated the corporation's fleet of Great Lakes ore boats. Also in the city were the headquarters for both the Duluth, Missabe & Northern (DM&N) and Duluth and Iron Range (D&IR) railways, which had ore docks in Duluth and Two Harbors, and huge iron-ore distribution and rail yards in nearby Proctor.[2]

British economic historian and geographer Kenneth Warren has linked the genesis of U.S. Steel to two major factors in the nation's early twentieth-century economic system: a "trend toward concentration," which resulted in the establishment of large business units; and the combination of varied industries into "trusts." For the steel industry this meant that "iron making, steel production, and rolling and finishing operations were . . . commonly combined at a single site." Or, as Carnegie Steel Company president Charles Schwab stated a year before U.S. Steel's formation, concentration and combination in the steel industry were based on the principle that "the greatest economy would result from having one mill make one product, and make that product continuously."[3]

When Schwab became U.S. Steel's first president in 1901, Judge Elbert Gary was selected as chairman of the corporation's executive committee. Gary served as chief executive officer, whereas Schwab, as president, "was to see that the orders of the executive committee were carried out by the subsidiaries." When Schwab attempted to implement an operating plan that proposed drastic reductions in the executive committee's influence, Gary immediately opposed his colleague's actions. Because of their personalities and philosophical differences, Schwab resigned as president in 1903; William Corey, Schwab's former associate at Carnegie Steel, replaced him. Corey departed U.S. Steel in 1911 and was followed by James Farrell, who remained as president until 1932. It was Gary, however, who effectively ran U.S. Steel until his retirement as chairman in 1926. Included in "Judge Gary's umbrella" was an edict to preserve stability in the steel industry by maintaining a pricing structure that favored older manufacturing centers over a simpler, geographically based system. The clearest evidence of this practice was the "Pittsburgh Plus" pricing system, which calculated all transportation costs for finished steel, no matter where it was produced in the nation, as if the manufacturing had occurred in the Pennsylvania city.[4]

Gary's critics also claimed he was "emotionally distant" from the majority of U.S. Steel workers because he so strongly supported a wage system that gave preference to managers and skilled employees over common laborers; likewise, single men were often the last to be hired, but the first to be laid off—especially those regarded as the least skilled or least efficient workers. Whatever Gary's personal sentiments, there is little doubt that common laborers received a very small proportion of the huge revenues generated by the corporation. From 1902 to 1916 wages for these laborers increased very slightly, from twenty cents to twenty-six cents per hour, while the length of the average workweek grew from 67.5 hours to

68.5 hours. Additional evidence of Gary's defiant attitudes occurred in 1909, when he shut down eight U.S. Steel plants rather than reducing prices for the company's products, resulting in significant hardships for workers and local merchants. Gary opposed the termination of both the twelve-hour workday and Sunday work; he was biased against "new immigrant" laborers from Eastern and Southern Europe, even though they were a vital part of the corporation's workforce; and he adamantly opposed the formation of unions, as evidenced by his failure to consider the requests of laborers during strikes and periods of labor unrest.[5]

Elbert Gary had many detractors, but even some of them agreed that his leadership was essential for guiding the gigantic corporation through a number of difficult situations. He was the "impressive public face" of the corporation and of the entire American steel industry. The paternalistic, steady-state management style that Gary pursued for a quarter of a century, however, did not serve U.S. Steel very well after his retirement in 1926, something that became clearly evident during the Great Depression of the 1930s.[6]

U.S. Steel's first chairman also made most of the major decisions concerning the development of a manufacturing plant in Duluth. While the facility may have been a relatively small unit situated a considerable distance from the nation's major manufacturing centers and from U.S. Steel's New York City headquarters, Gary and several members of his executive board spent considerable time visiting Minnesota during the years the plant was being planned, built, and put into operation. Many visits were linked to the unique political, economic, social, and technological issues that U.S. Steel faced in Duluth. These problems ranged from Duluth's cold weather to efforts by Minnesota politicians to increase the tax rates on U.S. Steel's vast mineral holdings situated throughout the state's Iron Range.

Minnesota's Iron Range

U.S. Steel's manufacturing facility might have been planned for Duluth, but it was the iron-ore deposits of the Iron Range that were actually responsible for the plant's emergence. The meaning and importance of the U.S. Steel–Iron Range relationship were based on the simple arithmetic of supply and demand: 60 percent of the company's iron ore was derived from the district in 1901, a figure that grew to 75 percent by 1910.[7] Without U.S. Steel's significant dependence on Minnesota ores, the corporation, quite simply, could not have been induced to build a major manufacturing operation in Duluth.

The Iron Range, located in the northeastern region of the state, includes three districts or ranges: the Vermilion, Mesabi, and Cuyuna. The Vermilion shipped its first ore in 1884, followed by the Mesabi in 1892 and the Cuyuna in 1911. The Mesabi quickly emerged as the largest source of iron ore in both the Lake Superior mining region of northern Michigan, Wisconsin, and Minnesota, and throughout the entire United States. By 1910, the Mesabi produced close to thirty million gross tons of iron ore—70 percent of all iron ore mined in the United States, and almost 25 percent of the world's output.[8]

Shortly after the Mesabi opened, taxes derived from its ore deposits provided local governmental officials with revenues that funded a host of municipal projects and programs. Nowhere was this more evident than in Hibbing, where the city's budget totaled $2.4 million in 1921—almost a ninefold increase over 1913. Hibbing mayor Victor Power was the best-known Iron Range official who used tax revenues to fund a host of programs, including athletic and recreational activities, mothers' clubs, night schools, well-baby clinics, music and drama organizations, community doctors and nurses, and relief projects for out-of-work miners. The most visible examples of this munificence were the public buildings that appeared in Hibbing, especially its city hall, auditorium, and a $4 million school that served as the educational "jewel" of the Mesabi and the entire state. Virtually every community on the Iron Range displayed similar, albeit smaller and less ornate, examples of municipal and educational buildings.[9]

While Iron Range communities benefited directly from the iron-ore deposits situated within their borders, Minnesota officials also realized that the state could use "the immense power given to it by its possession of the largest domestic iron-ore deposits to stimulate its own wider economic and social development."[10] This recognition would have a direct bearing on the construction of a steel-production facility that finally opened in Duluth in late 1915.

Early Iron and Steel Operations in Duluth

Duluth's U.S. Steel plant would be, by far, the largest industrial facility ever established in the city. It was, however, preceded by a number of small iron manufacturing ventures that developed from the 1870s to the 1890s. These operations were spawned by railroad-construction activities in northeastern Minnesota, but all were short-lived. They included a manufacturing plant that produced two hundred Northern Pacific Railroad cars in 1872, and the Duluth Iron Car Company, organized in 1888, which fabricated railroad cars until the World War I years. The first effort to make charcoal iron was undertaken by the Duluth Blast Furnace Company in 1874. This action was accomplished by importing iron ore from northern Michigan's Marquette Iron Range and firing the ore with charcoal derived from pine burned in pits located just outside of Duluth and at Mahtowa in adjacent Carlton County. The Iron Bay Company initiated a more ambitious venture in 1889, but it failed during the national financial panic of 1893. The most successful enterprise was the Zenith Furnace Company, which opened in 1902. This complex eventually included a blast furnace, a coal dock, and sixty-five coke ovens located on eighty acres of land along St. Louis Bay. The company produced pig iron, was active in the wholesale coal trade, and sold by-products such as ammonia gas, coal gas, and coal tar. Later purchased by the Interlake Iron Corporation, the facility served as the northernmost merchant pig iron plant in the United States until it closed permanently in 1962.[11]

Once the prodigious extent of the Mesabi's iron-ore reserves was established, numerous recommendations were made to construct a steel plant in Duluth. The facility was envisioned as an integrated manufacturing operation, one that would assemble all the raw materials needed for steel making—iron ore, coal, and limestone—and convert them into coke, pig iron, and steel at a single site. The recommendation was based on the premise that rather than shipping all of Minnesota's iron ore to manufacturing plants in the eastern United States, some of it should be converted into steel in Duluth. The city's advantages went beyond proximity to the Mesabi, for the city was also poised at the head of navigation on the Great Lakes and served as the terminus for several major rail lines. In 1907 author Herbert Casson asked why these factors had not yet contributed to the development of a steel plant in either Duluth or nearby Superior, Wisconsin. "The Pittsburgh Vikings sail up to the iron ranges and carry off the loot—millions of dollars' worth every summer week," Casson exclaimed. "And all the while, for some reason which no outsider can understand, the men of Duluth and Superior . . . have been satisfied to run errands and quarrel, like a couple of messenger boys."[12]

Proposing and Opposing a Tonnage Tax

Ultimately, it was not the economic geography of Duluth that contributed to the construction of a fully integrated steel plant within the city. The facility was, in fact, "the price the United States Steel Corporation would eventually have to pay to maintain good relations with the state that controlled the price of its iron ore." During a special session of the Minnesota legislature in early 1902, Representative Jacob F. Jacobson of Lac Qui Parle County in far southwestern Minnesota introduced a bill that would have imposed a five-cents-per-ton tax on all iron ore mined in the state. Although the bill was passed by the house, it was "slaughtered" in the senate.[13]

Five years later the tonnage tax became such a politically volatile issue that it dominated the thirty-fifth session of the legislature. In mid-January 1907, legislators adopted a resolution that claimed taxes derived from the state's privately owned mineral lands were "insignificant and out of all proportion to their true and actual value." The resolution also called for the formation of a joint house and senate committee to determine the actual value of the mineral resources, and make "recommendations for additional laws as they may think necessary for the full protection of the rights of the State in and to said mineral lands." Several legislators inferred that the bill should have two quid pro quo elements: a tonnage tax on all exported ore that would be added to the existing ad valorem tax and a provision to rescind the new tax if any company agreed to establish a steel manufacturing enterprise in the state.[14]

Since the proposed legislation was clearly targeted at U.S. Steel, corporate officials wasted little time in responding to the threat. Immediately after the legislative resolution was introduced, U.S. Steel's Finance Committee prepared an internal memorandum that it didn't release to the public for another five weeks. Included in the memorandum was a brief statement, noting that "a substantial plant for the manufacture of iron and steel [will] be constructed and operated in the vicinity of Duluth, Minnesota, provided it is practicable and reasonably profitable." A three-member executive committee headed by Elbert Gary was then appointed "to make an exhaustive study of the question."[15]

U.S. Steel's public pronouncements, nevertheless, continued to list Duluth's disadvantages as a steel-production center: labor shortages, restricted markets, and a lack of coal resources. The city's politicians, newspaper editors, and business leaders quickly rebutted these assertions, alleging that the shortage of coal was but a minor hindrance since it could be transported on empty ore carriers returning to Duluth, and that a more-than-adequate labor supply and market would be provided by the steady movement of new people into the area.[16]

Throughout February, as U.S. Steel's special committee assessed its options, state legislators continued their work on the tonnage tax bill. The two Republican politicians from western Minnesota who sponsored the legislation, Representatives Rufus Jefferson of Bingham Lake (a former Duluth resident, and one of the first men from St. Louis County to volunteer for Civil War duty in the Union Army during the early 1860s), and Henry Bjorge of Lake Park, reported that the specific intention was to give "the state a tax on ore taken away from the state and, also, to remit that tax under conditions that will induce manufacturing of the ore within Minnesota." Jefferson claimed that the bill would lead to the development of a huge manufacturing complex in Duluth, and ultimately result in a city with a half-million residents.[17]

The proposed tax was strongly opposed by the vast majority of Iron Range officials and residents. Their opposition was based on the fear that additional taxation might impede the exploitation of lower-grade ores on the Iron Range, thereby jeopardizing the financial status of local communities. Public meetings convened throughout the Iron Range from early to mid-February allowed local citizens to express these sentiments to state politicians. A meeting organized by the Eveleth Businessmen's Association expressed concern over the "dire possibilities" of the proposed tax amendment; "an enthusiastic mass meeting of citizens" in Chisholm voiced opposition to the tax; and Hibbing's citizens submitted a resolution to the state legislature that protested "against the enactment of an iron tonnage tax law."[18]

In downstate Minnesota, the *Minneapolis Tribune* expressed a more cynical view, claiming "the excitement in the official circles of St. Louis County over an imaginary tonnage tax on iron ore mines confirms the theory of alliance between the steel trust and local officialdom." Such an arrangement, asserted the newspaper, meant that the steel trust paid "nearly all the taxes in that region as it controls nearly all the voters." The *Duluth News Tribune* mounted a counterattack against the claims, stating that the implications were false and represented an insult to St. Louis County officials and citizens. The Duluth editors took great pains to point out that steel interests neither paid all taxes, nor controlled local politics in the region. "This county is not a rotten borough of the steel corporation," asserted the *News Tribune*, "which does not seek to control it politically or otherwise, nor could it do so if it wished."[19]

As the rhetoric mounted throughout the state, Duluth's Commercial Club invited nine legislators to participate in a train tour of the Iron Range. The group was met by large delegations of citizens in each of the nine towns they visited. The reception at Ely—where one thousand flag-waving school children welcomed the salons—was especially memorable. School superintendent C. L. Newberry addressed the gathering, stating that any change in taxation would jeopardize the city's educational system and thereby affect the many children who came from non-English-speaking homes. A similar reception greeted legislators in Virginia, the home of Lafayette Bliss, president of the League of Range School Superintendents. Bliss appealed to the legislators and "to the humanity of the people of the state," beseeching them "to save these schools and communities from a law which could only be passed in ignorance of the evils it would work."[20] Local officials throughout the Iron Range gave several reasons for their opposition to the proposed legislation, but the perceived impact that increased iron-ore taxes would have on the mining district's network of public schools trumped all the others.

Despite the strong antitax sentiments they had observed, most legislators apparently still favored the imposition of such a levy because they believed it would "force the steel trust to establish smelters and foundries in this state." The tenor of the debate changed abruptly on March 1, however, when U.S. Steel's Finance Committee released its January 22 internal memorandum, stating that a steel plant would be built in Minnesota—"provided it is practical and will be reasonably profitable." Shortly thereafter, Elbert Gary and other U.S. Steel executives traveled to Duluth, where they met with the Commercial Club and local legislators, looked at potential steel plant sites in western Duluth, and inspected a nearby hydroelectric facility at Thomson on the St. Louis River. Despite the singular attention Duluth was receiving, Superior's *Leader-Clarion* asserted that the plant would be constructed in Wisconsin because U.S. Steel officials needed a site with excellent shipping facilities and large areas of level, developable land. "These they can get in Superior," declared the editor. "Such a site cannot be had for love or money in Duluth." Despite his predictions, one day after Gary's committee completed its visit, all pronouncements indicated that "a favorable report" would be issued on behalf of Duluth.[21]

On March 25, the House Committee on Taxes and Tax Laws voted to impose a tonnage tax of five cents on all iron ore mined in the state. Within a week, U.S. Steel submitted a letter to Minnesota house speaker Lawrence Johnson, affirming the company's decision to build a manufacturing facility in Duluth that would include "a blast furnace, blooming mill, steel rail mill, shape mill, two bar mills, by-product coke oven, coal docks, shops, cement plant, etc., six open furnaces." Johnson was also assured that work on the plant would commence "as soon as the plans are finished and will be pushed to completion as rapidly as possible." Then, on the afternoon of April 2, house representatives engaged in four hours of spirited debate over the tax bill, which began with Representative Jefferson's insinuation that "every-

Figure 1.1. When local officials and residents learned of U.S. Steel's decision to construct a manufacturing plant in Duluth, they were certain the city would become a major metropolis and manufacturing center. From Duluth News Tribune, April 2, 1907.

body in St. Louis County is cowed into abject submission to that hideous octopus [i.e., U.S. Steel]." Representative A. J. Rockne, from the southeastern Minnesota town of Zumbrota, made a forceful rejoinder to Jefferson, remarking that legislators needed to consider the people of St. Louis County "with a view to doing justice to them." Representative John Saari of Sparta, a community on the eastern Mesabi Range, protested against intimations that the county was a "vassal of the steel corporation"; his constituents were just as independent as Minnesotans residing elsewhere in the state, Saari contended. At 6:30 that evening, the bill was defeated in the house by a vote of fifty-eight against and fifty-one in favor (Figure 1.1).[22]

As soon as U.S. Steel was assured of the tax bill's fate, corporate officials secured options on land located in southwestern Duluth. Superior residents who had hoped to attract the plant now consoled themselves with dreams of "the hundreds of new factories and dozens of new railroads" that would emerge in their city, and of the "thousands of . . . workmen [who] will live on this side of the bay." Although these grandiose projections were never realized, U.S. Steel did, in fact, quickly incorporate a separate subsidiary organization in Wisconsin: the Interstate Transfer Railway Company.[23] By late 1909 the company would begin constructing a bridge and rail line that, by the summer of 1910, connected the steel plant site to Superior's harbor and docks.

Observers interpreted the reasons for U.S. Steel's favorable decision in various ways, though few commentaries were as blunt as those offered by the *Duluth News Tribune,* which once alleged that the tax was intended to "penalize the corporation for its rape of the mineral wealth of the state." Superior's *Leader-Clarion* was almost as blunt in its description, claiming "the state of Minnesota held a club with which it could beat out the brains of the steel corporation, in the shape of a tonnage tax on ore, and the state of Minnesota has compelled the steel corporation to locate its mill at Duluth." The *New York Times* gave a more reasoned response, reporting that two major factors were responsible for U.S. Steel's action: substantial gains in construction activity throughout the western states and the supposition that proximity to the Mesabi Range would offer a 75 percent savings in iron-ore transportation costs. Another account termed the arrangement between U.S. Steel and the state of Minnesota a "gentleman's agreement"—the exchange of a steel plant for an agreement not to impose unfavorable legislation. C. R. Rusk, writing on behalf of Duluth's Commercial Club, noted that the steel plant proposal had inspired a "loyal feeling" in northeastern Minnesota, which might even extend to other sections of Minnesota. The *Minneapolis Journal* remained skeptical, alleging that Duluth officials had "timed their dancing to the piping of the [steel] trust." The unusual nature of the Minnesota arrangement was also noted by a Pittsburgh correspondent for London's *Iron and Coal Trades Review,* who reported that U.S. Steel had chosen to build the plant for a reason never before considered by any American iron and steel manufacturer: "to quiet the uneasiness of the people" who lived in one state.[24]

Dreams for Duluth

Duluth's backers greeted U.S. Steel's decision and the legislative action with unabashed enthusiasm. An early April editorial headline in the *Duluth Evening Herald* declared that residents had witnessed a monumental moment in the history of their city and region: the removal of the "tonnage tax menace" through legislative fiat. "The action of the house in defeating the bill to place a tonnage tax on the iron ore production of the northern part of the state," exulted the *Herald,* "sweeps away the last serious threatened obstacles to the great and assuredly glorious future progress not alone of St. Louis county but of every portion of the section in which iron ore has been found or may be found hereafter." Claims were made that "Greater Duluth" would arrive in a day, rather than after "long years of slow growth," and that increases in business would bring "prosperity of the most brilliant kind." Such prosperity, Duluth's promoters contended, offered the city immunity from future national economic recessions and provided the impetus for the total settlement and development of St. Louis County as a premier agricultural district. Duluth's *Labor World* weighed in with a similar observation, stating that because of the population growth that would follow steel plant development, "the day is not far distant when the Duluth district will be as famous for its cereal products as it is now for its mineral wealth."[25]

Population projections made by various organizations and individuals were equally buoyant. Some prognosticators even predicted that Duluth's 1907 population of about 75,000 people would double to 150,000 by 1910, and then double again over the next decade, reaching a total of 300,000 by 1920. (Actual figures for 1910 and 1920 were 78,465 and 98,915 residents, respectively.) To others, it was only logical that the Duluth plant and the gigantic U.S. Steel complex emerging at Gary, Indiana, would be linked: "Gary being within a few miles of the center of the population of the country will be pushed forward to gigantic proportions in the manufacture of semi-finished and finished materials, while Duluth will become the great pig iron making district and a great factor in making heavy steel products." Mayor Marcus Cullum's 1907 address to his constituents also fore-saw unlimited possibilities for Duluth: "The future of our city looks big with events," Cullum exulted. "The unbelievers of the

Figure 1.2. Duluth Evening Herald *cartoonist Coleman Naughton illustrated the optimism of Duluth Mayor Marcus Cullum as he viewed the city's future from the perspective of 1907. From* Duluth Evening Herald, *March 15, 1907.*

past become credulous, the credulous expectant, the wise convinced, that here shall be built a city in this great Northwest—a great, throbbing, vital center that shall give and shall receive. . . . I believe that I can pledge the people that we will give to their service the best that is in us, and do away with partisan strife and personal bickering, and join the press and the public in one harmonious effort to advance the city to her manifest destiny." A few days after Cullum made his speech, *Duluth Evening Herald* cartoonist Coleman Naughton depicted the mayor peering through a telescope at the Duluth of the future, a city distinguished by large downtown skyscrapers and a harbor filled with boats and ships (Figure 1.2).[26]

Despite the optimism, actual work on the steel plant moved ahead with what seemed like glacial hesitancy to Duluth residents. No less an authority than Elbert Gary asserted that the Duluth works would operate by 1909, but not even U.S. Steel's chairman could foresee the obstacles that delayed the onset of construction activities to late 1909 and early 1910, and he certainly could not have predicted the outbreak of war in Europe in 1914, which stalled final work on the plant for another eight months. Steel production finally began in Duluth in late 1915.[27]

2. BUILDING A STEEL PLANT: RECESSION, INDECISION, AND WAR

In mid-June 1907, U.S. Steel formed the Minnesota Steel Company as a subsidiary organization that would oversee the land acquisition, construction, and eventual operation of its Duluth manufacturing operations. All of Minnesota Steel's officers held executive positions with U.S. Steel, which meant that major decisions regarding the emerging facility were made in the corporation's New York City headquarters. Several officials, however, moved to Duluth, where they supervised the day-to-day activities associated with steel plant construction and management. The most important of these early executives was George L. Reis, who served as Minnesota Steel's first vice president and general manager.[1]

Minnesota Steel had purchased more than one thousand acres of land in the southwestern area of Duluth by late June. The property was undeveloped at the time, but in 1889 portions had been designated as "Spirit Lake Park," one of many subdivisions touted for sale during the city's great real estate boom of 1888–93, once described as a period "when men fought for the privilege of buying town lots in the suburbs" (Figure 2.1). The national economic depression of 1893 quickly brought an end to further speculation at Spirit Lake Park, the same fate that befell other subdivisions situated throughout southwestern Duluth and Superior.[2]

By 1907 several purchasers who still held title to properties in Spirit Lake Park had died; others were residing outside of Duluth, some even in Europe. It was not until early January 1909 that Minnesota Steel finally tracked down all the owners and secured title to the last parcels. Included as part of the acquisition were two and one-half miles of St. Louis River shoreline, which had an expansive area of water along the riverway called Spirit Lake. Although the 1,250 acres of land had been appraised at only $29,500 in 1906, Minnesota Steel undoubtedly paid more than this figure by the time all the properties were secured.[3]

Land acquisition posed only a small problem compared to other issues that postponed construction activities for the subsequent two years: a nationwide economic recession that began in October 1907, the "special climatic

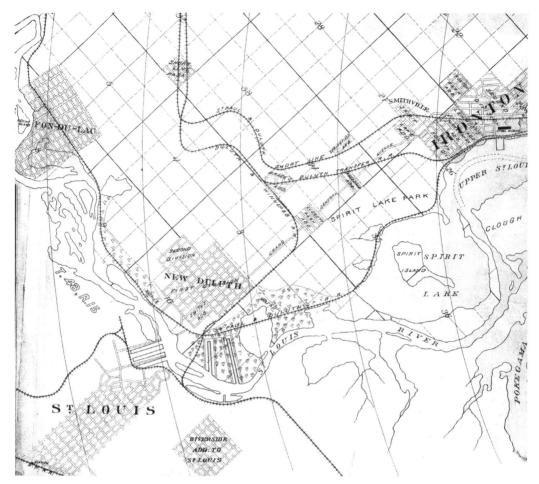

Figure 2.1. Most of the acreage that U.S. Steel's subsidiary, the Minnesota Steel Company, purchased for its future operations was once part of Spirit Lake Park, an unsuccessful real estate venture of 1889. From Index and Outline Map of the City of Duluth, St. Louis County, Minn., and Vicinity, with July 1893 Supplement *(Philadelphia: Fred K. B. Roe, 1890); courtesy of Northeast Minnesota Historical Center.*

conditions" that demanded solutions before steel could be produced in Duluth's "high-latitude location," and continued efforts by Minnesota legislators to impose a tonnage tax on U.S. Steel's iron-ore mining operations. Another telling reason for the delay may have been, as Kenneth Warren has surmised, the corporation's lack of "enthusiasm" for its Duluth venture. U.S. Steel's internal documents concerning the project remained rather circumspect, even after the decision was made to build in Minnesota. A brief notice in the corporation's 1907 annual report simply stated that U.S. Steel had "purchased a site containing about 1,580 acres (of which 300 acres are now submerged) located in St. Louis County, Minnesota, ten miles from the center of Duluth, on which it is proposed to construct a moderate sized iron and steel plant. . . . The plans for the scope and construction of the steel plant have not yet been developed." The corporation's public face, on the other hand, generally offered a more upbeat view of Duluth's potential as a steel-manufacturing center. A September 1907 article in the *Engineering and Mining Journal* reported that U.S. Steel officials believed the Duluth works had a "very promising" future, so much so that the facility might eventually "rival any plant it now has or is erecting." Two reasons were given for this optimism: Duluth's hinterland had not yet experienced large-scale railroad construction, and the city was economically better equipped to supply the steel-production requirements of its immediate region than were factories located in more distant places, such as the Chicago–Gary district.[4]

Much of the initial delay certainly may be attributed to the financial panic of October 1907, which led to a nationwide steel-production decline that extended throughout much of 1908. When U.S. Steel's net 1907 earnings fell from $17 million in October to $10.5 million in November and then to $5 million in December, the corporation obviously was reluctant to invest in new facilities. (The recession also had a dramatic impact on the Iron Range, where total ore shipments declined from almost thirty million gross tons in 1907 to eighteen million in 1908.) Some preliminary plans were approved for the proposed manufacturing site in February 1908, but vice president Reis gave a somewhat measured response when reporting on these actions. "While the plans in general, as prepared by us, have been approved," he stated, "there yet remains a very great deal of detail work yet to be done before actual building operations can begin, as is the case with all large undertakings of a similar nature."[5]

The Tonnage Tax Again

The envisioned steel plant continued to receive attention from several national newspapers in late 1908, but Duluth's business leaders were more concerned about the present, not the distant future. In October, with the state election approaching, fifty-three of the city's prominent citizens endorsed Republican gubernatorial candidate Jacob F. Jacobson on the front page of the *Duluth News Tribune,* favoring him over the incumbent, Democrat John A. Johnson. Two days later another endorsement listed the names of one hundred and sixty additional Duluth supporters. Even though Jacobson, as a state representative in 1902, had led the charge to impose a tonnage tax, Duluth's business community believed he would veto such a bill if he became governor. The *Tribune* maintained its support even though Johnson announced that he did not favor a tonnage tax. The *Duluth Evening Herald*, on the other hand, strongly supported Governor Johnson, terming him "honest and sincere" and "an ideal campaigner"; the newspaper was elated when Johnson handily won reelection in November 1908.[6]

In late January 1909 the cat-and-mouse game that pitted politicians and officials from northeastern Minnesota against those from elsewhere in the state flared up once again. A state house resolution was quickly introduced that called for the appointment of a five-member legislative committee to determine if U.S. Steel and its subsidiaries "have not been paying their just proportion of the taxes." Although the resolution failed, Representative Bjorge, as he had done in 1907, then submitted another bill in February 1909, this one calling "for an act imposing a tonnage tax on all iron ore mined and shipped from lands situated in the State of Minnesota." The bill was intended to increase the tax on ore shipments by five cents per ton, a fee that would have greatly increased U.S. Steel's annual financial outlay to the state's coffers.[7]

St. Louis County's house delegation quickly prepared a "Brief Against the Tonnage Tax Bill." The report cited a letter from an independent steel manufacturer who claimed that some companies might consider building plants in Superior or Ashland since Wisconsin's tax laws were more favorably disposed toward corporate interests. Duluth attorney and iron-ore magnate Chester Congdon, who had been elected as a Republican to the house only a few months earlier, submitted the "Brief" in mid-February. Congdon and his St. Louis County political colleagues warned that prospective iron and steel facilities might "be driven into Wisconsin by adverse legislation."[8]

Despite this opposition, the house passed the tax bill on March 17 and sent it on to the senate. Public opposition developed quickly throughout northeastern Minnesota. The city's Catholic and Episcopal bishops, along with Trevanion Hugo, chairman of Duluth's Commercial Club and mayor of the city from 1900 to 1904, made plans to inform the senate that the "tonnage tax is robbery." Simultaneously, a committee of Mesabi Range mayors drafted a letter for circulation among legislators, bluntly stating that the bill would "confiscate our homes, destroy our means of livelihood and wipe out the results of years of patient toil."[9]

In early April, Duluth's Commercial Club invited twenty senators to participate in a train tour of northeastern Minnesota, where they could hear mining town residents "protest against the measure that strikes at their home, their commercial life, their churches and their schools." Departing from St. Paul just before midnight, the salons' train arrived in Duluth the next morning, and members of the Commercial Club joined them. The train then proceeded along the Duluth, Missabe and Northern Railroad's tracks to Coleraine, located at the western end of the Mesabi. Before returning to Duluth on late Saturday afternoon, the entourage ventured as far east as the city of Virginia; along the way they toured mines and listened to the pleas of civic leaders and mining officials. A Duluth reporter who accompanied the group was optimistic in his assessment of the outcome, observing that "from the time the senators first sighted the outer workings of the gigantic Canisteo mine at Coleraine until they saw the shadows from the east envelope the ramparts of the great Virginia open pit . . . at nightfall, they were intensely interested and appeared to be profoundly impressed."[10]

Duluth Mayor R. D. Hoven made a final attempt to stymie passage of the bill on the morning of April 7, when he placed an announcement in the *News Tribune* asking several hundred men to join him on a railway journey to St. Paul that would culminate in a large demonstration at the capitol building. Three hundred men from Duluth and the Iron Range joined Hoven at the depot early that afternoon. Upon arriving in St. Paul the men assembled at the Ryan Hotel, donned blue ribbon badges emblazoned with the words, "No Tonnage Tax," and then departed "in a long column, by twos, [and] proceeded like a small army to march on the capitol." There they cheered Representative Congdon as he gave a forceful and lengthy speech that didn't conclude until one hour before midnight. Congdon appealed directly to legislators who came from places other than northeastern Minnesota. "We of St. Louis County and northeastern Minnesota live in a barren, a bleak country," Congdon declared. "We have iron ore, cold weather, and men but we have not the rich agricultural lands that you have in southern Minnesota." The Duluth millionaire addressed his legislative colleagues directly, asking them to consider the following question: "What is the encouragement for a corporation to invest millions in this state in such a manufacturing industry when the state discriminates against it in tax legislation?"[11]

Despite Congdon's best intentions, the tonnage tax bill narrowly passed the senate on April 16. All the hopes of northeastern Minnesotans were now pinned on Governor Johnson. Thousands of letters and telegrams soon arrived on the state executive's desk from constituents residing throughout the region. Meanwhile, Duluth's church congregations asked for divine intervention in guiding the governor's decision. The Reverend W. E. Harmon of St. Peter's Swedish Episcopal Church issued a prayer, asking God to "rule the heart of Thy servant, the governor of this state, that he, knowing whose minister he is, may above all things seek Thy honor and glory [and] the safety, welfare and prosperity of Thy people." Duluth's Catholic bishop, the Right Reverend J. D. Morrison, was much more direct with his telegraphed instructions, leaving no question as to what he hoped the governor would do: "In the name of the people of Northeastern Minnesota, whose welfare is vitally affected, I beg your excellency to veto the tonnage tax bill," wrote Morrison. The Reverend Campbell Coyle of the First Presbyterian Church also requested assistance, but gave the deity some latitude in making the decision: "May God guide the governor and cause him to act justly, no matter where the blow shall fall," Coyle entreated.[12]

Johnson vetoed the bill on April 20, giving four reasons for his decision: the bill was "a more or less uncertain and ill-digested experiment, not fully understood even by its friends, and intensely feared by the sections of the state to which it specifically applies"; it would "strike a severe blow at the development and prosperity" of northeastern Minnesota; it could cause "sectional hatred, which may disrupt and endanger the future best development" of the state; and because the current system of taxation had been successful "in securing revenue from the iron ore properties."[13]

After Johnson acted as the bill's "executioner," Duluth's citizens "fairly danced for joy" in the city's streets, engaging in festivities likened to a Fourth of July celebration or a "Broadway in Old New York on New Year's night." Some streets and avenues were described as being "almost impassable," with people "jammed up against buildings, wedged into corners and poked in the ribs until they were breathless." Throughout the revelry the participants cheered their governor, crying out in unison: "Who's all right?" The response, quite obviously, was: "Johnson!"[14]

U.S. Steel may have once again avoided the tonnage tax bullet, but a Superior newspaper cautioned that it was time for the corporation "to do something more than talk." If not, warned the newspaper, "two years hence there may not be a man like John A. Johnson to stand between the two ends of the state of Minnesota." Indeed, U.S. Steel officials recognized that future state executives might not be as favorably disposed to their interests as Johnson, a possibility that was underscored by his death just five months later. "As the governorship is not a life job, it looked well to the Steel Corporation to go ahead with the plant," reported the *Iron and Coal Trades Review* in its summary of these actions.[15]

Inaction to Action at the Steel Plant Site

Despite U.S. Steel's statements, only limited work was evident at the future plant site for much of 1909. In fact, most of the related construction activity was occurring elsewhere: excavations for a thirty-mile-long rail link to Adolph, where iron ore from the Mesabi Range, beginning in 1915, would be diverted southward to the blast furnaces (Figure 2.2); expansion of the docks and harbor facilities at Superior to accommodate building materials arriving on Great Lakes carriers; and construction of a belt line railway south of Superior, including a bridge to cross the St. Louis River, which divided Minnesota and Wisconsin.[16]

By August 1909, Congdon had become so concerned about the seeming lack of activity that he wrote to U.S. Steel officials, inquiring about the status of the Duluth project. The corporation's financial committee responded in September, stating that even though they might not be able to promote the project "strictly as a manufacturing and commercial proposition," they recognized "that the Corporation is committed to the building of a plant." Therefore, the committee recommended the construction of a $10 million facility, a two-fold increase over the amount that had been projected two

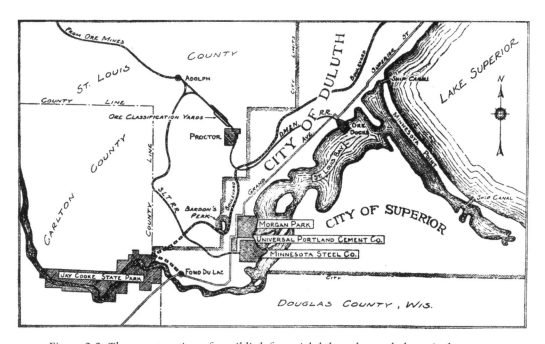

Figure 2.2. The construction of a rail link from Adolph to the steel plant site began in early 1909; eventually iron ore from the Mesabi Range would be shipped along the tracks. Courtesy of Northeast Minnesota Historical Center, Pamphlet 650, ca. 1925.

years earlier. The *Iron and Coal Trades Review* succinctly summarized the reasoning behind this decision: "The Corporation is up to the point where it must quit work or build a plant. It chooses the latter."[17]

Indications of U.S. Steel's new level of commitment were evident by October, when Congdon, with the authorization of Elbert Gary, wrote a letter to Duluth's newspapers, calling attention to the twenty-three engineers and draftsmen working diligently on plans and detailed specifications for the plant's initial unit. Congdon also noted U.S. Steel president William Corey's surprise that Duluthians had any doubts about the corporation's commitment to the project. According to Congdon, Corey believed that in the immediate aftermath of the 1907 panic, "it seemed unwise to expend millions of dollars to construct a plant, when half of the capacity of the other plants was unused." But, with business conditions having improved by late 1909, he explained that U.S. Steel "can now use this plant as soon as it is completed."[18]

Sustained efforts were made to ready the grounds for construction: more trees and brush were removed, ravines were filled in, railroad tracks were laid down, and engineering plans were drawn for a road to the steel plant site. In November, Minnesota Steel let out bids for the purchase of construction cranes and equipment, which were moved to the site late in the year. The *News Tribune* greeted these actions with enthusiasm, claiming that the city was clearly emerging as a "natural gateway" to a large region that would soon include millions of people, rather than just hundreds of thousands.[19]

Congdon and Corey predicted that all steel plant construction would be completed by late 1910. Both men may have been very successful businessmen, but in this case they clearly were not clairvoyants. It soon was obvious that the plant's opening would be delayed because of numerous technical problems that bedeviled the engineers working in Duluth's Board of Trade Building. Of concern were "the special operating conditions" posed by northeastern Minnesota's rigorous winter weather. Various solutions were developed to cope with the problems. One report noted that some water and sewer lines were placed as many as thirty feet below the surface to facilitate rapid drainage and to avoid freezing during the winter. The mill buildings were constructed of two-piece concrete blocks so that continuous air passage could occur within the walls; and a steam-heated "sweat house" was designed to thaw out frozen iron ore. Crews working on the site during the four most intense months of winter were also "compelled to build fires to thaw out the ground ahead of the shovels, and to keep the concrete in shape for working."[20]

Figure 2.3. By February 1910 construction of the bridge that would span the St. Louis River had commenced in Wisconsin and was extending toward Minnesota. The first trains crossed the upper level of the bridge in early September 1910, but the lower level was not accessible to vehicles and pedestrians until July 1917. Courtesy of Northeast Minnesota Historical Center, S2386B3f2.

Simultaneously, construction of the rail link between Superior and the plant site was proceeding at a rapid pace. In late 1909 tracks were being laid from Superior's harbor toward the Pokegema River, a small waterway located four miles east of the St. Louis River. By February 1910 the Pokegema had been crossed, and one month later four hundred men, including several underwater divers, were driving piles for a double-decked bridge that eventually passed over the St. Louis River and the extensive marsh on the Minnesota side of the waterway (Figure 2.3).[21]

In March, a correspondent reported that the steel plant site revealed "a tremendous skeleton" of its future appearance. The cement block plant and powerhouse were nearing completion, and excavations for the sewer lines were proceeding. On the other hand, the proposed conversion of the St. Louis River into a major transportation corridor for larger ships was not making progress, despite the fervent hopes of Duluth's residents. In March 1910, Duluth's U.S. Representative Clarence Miller and Minnesota's U.S. Senator Knute Nelson sought federal funding for a survey that would look at the feasibility of dredging and deepening the St. Louis River channel between Duluth's ore docks and the steel plant site. (Only excursion boats and small vessels were able to reach Spirit Lake.) The plan, however, was squelched when Minnesota Steel vice president Reis "threw cold water" on the proposal when he informed federal engineers that the manufacturing plant would require neither direct water access to Lake Superior nor any adjacent docking facilities for many years. Instead, Reis reported that the importing of supplies and raw materials and the exporting of manufactured steel could occur by way of rail connections that extended to and from Superior's harbor. Reis concluded his letter with a statement that left no doubt as to his sentiments: "I could not personally recommend the expenditure of the government of any money for this purpose on the ground that it is necessary to the operation of the proposed plant until the necessity arises."[22]

The *Duluth News Tribune* issued a heated disclaimer, stating that the newspaper was "disgusted" by the letter, exclaiming that Reis had been "exceedingly discourteous," that he had engaged in a "harmful" action, and that he had "proved himself disloyal" both to Duluth and U.S. Steel. In fact, the newspaper even recommended that the corporation "should administer needed discipline to its steel plant representative." The *Superior Telegram*, however, was quite pleased with the pronouncement, smugly claiming that Duluthians should have realized the rocky features of the St. Louis River channel ruled out any deepening of the chasm. "The people of Duluth would have seen this impossibility long ago if their eyes had not been blinded by their own interests," wrote the *Telegram*'s editor.[23]

Duluth's residents found consolation when warmer weather arrived and construction activities expanded. In April, Minnesota's new governor, Adolph Eberhart, along with a small entourage of people, trekked through the construction zone. Much of Eberhart's time was spent "slipping, leaping . . . and often stepping into marshy ground" as he made his way through a "jungle" of brush to view the framework for the structure that would soon span the St. Louis River.[24]

Minnesota Steel filed its plan with Duluth's city building inspector in early May 1910, requesting permission to erect forty-eight structures, all constructed of concrete and steel, and accommodating machinery termed "the best of its kind." Although the permit was not issued until late August, construction work was already well under way by July. The first structure was the "stately" powerhouse, with a smokestack that stood 175 feet high. By late July the first excavations for the open-hearth furnace building were visible, and a huge mixer to grind out material for "great masses of concrete" was about ready to operate. The thousands of concrete blocks that were formed each day by another machine provided ample work for masons employed at the site. Just six weeks after excavation work began, superstructures for the plate mill, forge works, and a blast furnace were visible. Also nearing completion by this time were the primary trunk sewers that emptied directly into Spirit Lake, including one trench with "the proportions of a fair sized canal." In early September 1910, the upper deck of the 1,900-foot-long bridge over the St. Louis River opened to train traffic, and the belt-line railroad to Superior's harbor facilities was completed; soon, large quantities of structural steel and other construction materials were arriving by rail at the busy plant site. All of the activities, predicted two of Superior's well-known "old settlers," meant that a manufacturing complex eventually would extend thirty miles eastward from their city to Iron River, Wisconsin; and also grow forty miles northeastward from the plant site until reaching as far as the Lake Superior port of Two Harbors, Minnesota. Each of these places, the two optimists envisioned, would be "striving to outdo its neighbor with smoke and noise."[25]

Terming the actions that had occurred between April 1907 and August 1910 as "the most tedious part of a great work of this character," the *Duluth Herald* listed the "preliminaries" that had demanded so much time and attention: "The site had to be bought from a far-scattered multitude of owners; land had to be condemned for lines of railroad to carry the ore to the plant and the finished product to the docks and warehouses, and these lines had to be built; permission had to be secured from the government to bridge the St. Louis River; and the bridge had to be built; the ground had to be prepared for the foundations of the buildings, and the foundations had to be built." With completion of the plant virtually guaranteed, the newspaper assured its readers that the greater Duluth area was "as pregnant with possibilities" as it had been when U.S. Steel made its initial announcement in 1907.[26]

A Steel Plant Emerges

By early 1911, the construction site was populated by a "small army" of four hundred laborers engaged in "digging, building and fitting things together." Most of the workforce consisted of common laborers, but some skilled recruits were also arriving from Gary, Indiana. A network of rail lines crossed the property, which allowed a fleet of locomotive engines to move equipment around the site and to transport the cement "soup" produced by the "hungry" concrete mixer. All of the work progressed despite a thick blanket of snow that covered the ground. Much of the "heavy concrete work" for the two massive structures that would house the open-hearth and blast furnaces was completed by March.[27]

At the same time in St. Paul, Representative Bjorge and a few of his colleagues were working on another version of a tonnage tax bill that they planned to introduce in the 1911 session of the Legislature. With the steel plant now a virtual certainty, few Duluth officials and citizens gave much attention to the measure. Strong opposition obviously came from most Iron Range communities, but as the *Labor World* noted, citizens who lived elsewhere in the state gave little thought to the tonnage tax. "Only the politicians down there [in southern Minnesota] talk about it, and they use it largely for political effect," stated the newspaper. On March 16, when the bill was put to a vote in the house, Chester Congdon once again mounted a spirited critique that reportedly "shattered the arguments of the authors of the bill with volley after volley of pertinent facts and possible disastrous results if the bill were enacted into law." Congdon's arguments prevailed, and the measure was handily defeated by a vote of seventy to forty-eight.[28]

As work on the facility progressed, the Duluth Commercial Club arranged a May 1911 excursion for several hundred of the city's businessmen (no women were invited) to assure skeptics about the considerable progress being made at a construction site "destined to become one of the greatest steel manufacturing plants in the world." The men who toured the site were most impressed by the massive scale of the equipment, buildings, and infrastructure. "The sewers are big, the shops are big—there is an air of bigness about everything," noted one reporter. Since many of the men "stood awed by the possibilities for the future," it was believed that they now would "lay their future business plans on more pretentious lines."[29]

Throughout much of 1911 U.S. Steel officials also made several trips to Duluth, where they inspected the emerging manufacturing facility and spoke to local civic groups. One September visitor was James Farrell, who arrived shortly after becoming president of the corporation. Farrell addressed members of the Commercial Club at the Kitchi Gammi Club, a facility that catered to the city's business elite. Acknowledging that the plant's development had been deferred in the past, Farrell pointed out that the delays had resulted from "much patient study of conditions" related to marketing and manufacturing. Farrell concluded his remarks with words that must have warmed the hearts of Duluth's business elite. "As practical men of affairs you will agree that closed factories and idle workmen spell misery and disaster to any community," intoned Farrell. "We should plan our work so that progress will be steady until the maximum of efficiency has been attained." Accompanying Farrell was E. J. Buffington, president of the Illinois Steel Company, another U.S. Steel subsidiary. Buffington informed listeners that the local manufacturing plant would be a success because of Duluth's two distinctive advantages: "the cost of assembling the raw material and the cost of distributing the finished products in the direction of demand"—namely, the vast region that stretched westward from Duluth to the Great Plains and beyond.[30]

In November 1911, when the *Iron Age* published a plan of the envisioned steel plant complex (Figure 2.4), the publication concluded that the Duluth project could very well benefit from the experience gained at U.S. Steel's gigantic complex at Gary, Indiana, and might even become "the most modern and economical in operation of any steel works yet built." Of note were the concrete blocks used to construct the buildings' walls, which contrasted with the sheet metal previously employed at other steel plants. Plans were also under way to develop a manufacturing plant for converting by-product slag into cement.[31]

While early construction activities at the steel plant complex might have proceeded more slowly than Duluthians had anticipated, they certainly could console themselves with the progress that occurred throughout 1912. An April description of the construction site termed it "a rumbling din of electric drills and compressed air hammers interspersed with the shouts of busy laborers," while other accounts commented on the "skeletons of immense buildings" waiting to be filled in with concrete blocks and the image of smokestacks "that loom up against the sky." The financial panic that affected the country during late 1907 and most of 1908 was now considered a positive occurrence since it gave U.S. Steel officials greater time to revamp their original proposals and expand the project. Indeed, as W. A. McGonagle, the public affairs committee chairman for the Duluth Commercial Club noted one year earlier, Duluth was fortunate because the plant's completion "was delayed pending the perfecting of new processes of steel manufacture." Optimism was evident everywhere, extending from Duluth to the New York headquarters of U.S. Steel. The comments of steel corporation officers never approached the hyperbole of city promoters, but corporation president Farrell made an uncharacteristically unrestrained comment in April 1912 when he stated that the new plant would serve as "the forerunner of enterprises which, in time, will make Duluth one of the world's greatest manufacturing centers." Further confirmation of U.S.

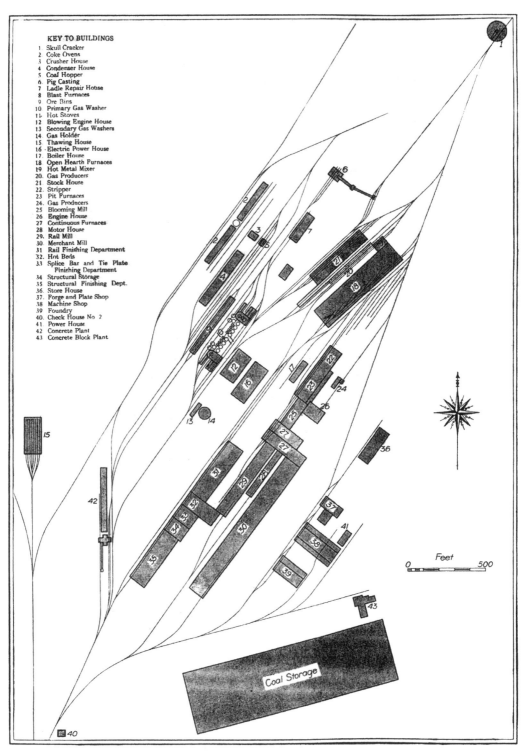

Coal Storage

Feet
0   500

Figure 2.4. The layout of buildings at the steel plant site was illustrated in a major iron and steel publication of 1911. From Iron Age *(November 30, 1911).*

Steel's commitment occurred in June, when an additional $6 million was allocated to complete the plant."[32]

Throughout the initial years of construction activity, any person seeking work could stroll directly onto the steel plant grounds and join the employment line. In 1912, however, unimpeded access to the property was curtailed when a large, "extremely opaque fence" emerged around the manufacturing operation. During that year, Albert Solomon, a former police sergeant from Buffalo, New York, who had arrived in Duluth two years earlier to work at the construction site, was hired to supervise the watchmen guarding the grounds; soon he would be designated as Morgan Park's chief of police. Also an accomplished amateur photographer, Solomon took pictures that offer the best illustrations of early steel plant history (Figure 2.5).[33]

As 1913 dawned, attention predictably focused on the state capitol building once again, where the "tonnage tax twins," the ubiquitous Henry Bjorge and his house colleague, Thomas Frankson of Spring Valley, prepared another bill that sought greater revenues from Minnesota's iron-ore shipments. Since Chester Congdon no longer served in the house, Republican Representative Cleon T. Knapp of Chisholm led the tax opponents' charge. As a mid-February vote on the bill approached, onlookers anticipated the debate that would precede the balloting: "Bjorge is expected to open the firing," said one reporter; "then will come Knapp with as exhaustive a survey as has ever been delivered in all the tonnage tax battles." To bolster Knapp's arguments, the Range Ministers Association forwarded a strongly worded

Figure 2.5. The construction of one of the two blast furnaces that would eventually be part of the steel plant complex was clearly under way by 1913. Photograph by Albert Solomon. Courtesy of Northeast Minnesota Historical Center, S2366, vol. 1, "Plant Construction and Departments."

communication to legislators in St. Paul. "We protest against the passage of the bill because it discriminates against the northern part of the state," wrote the religious leaders; "it is an enemy of the iron industry; it originated in jealousy; it follows class legislation; it is partial and sacrifices industrial activity and success to an unjust and unequal system." Whether or not the ministerial outrage influenced any legislators, the bill was again defeated in the house, this time by a margin of six votes. The achievement was marked by the *Duluth News Tribune's* pithy observation: "The beast is dead once more and may it stay dead as well as damned for the good not only of this section but of the whole state of Minnesota."[34]

Throughout this time, noticeable progress was evident at the steel plant site. In late February 1913, when seventy-five to eighty rail cars loaded with construction materials arrived, the occasion was termed an example of U.S. Steel's "evident desire to bring its Duluth plant to the producing stage at as early a date as possible." In April a Duluth-based steel executive reported that significant efforts were being made "to push our plant to completion just as fast as money and men can do it." During the month Governor Eberhart made another visit to Duluth and the construction site. Eberhart gave several speeches during his brief stay in the city, reporting that serving as state executive allowed him to perform an especially pleasant task: spreading the word throughout Minnesota "that in Duluth, the word 'steel' does not mean 'steal.'" In May a group of superintendents who supervised U.S. Steel operations in places as distant as Birmingham, Alabama, and Joliet, Illinois, also inspected the Duluth venture, intending "to become fully informed on its structural advantages." President Farrell brought additional favorable news on a July 1913 trip to Duluth, when he announced that the total financial outlay for U.S. Steel's plant would now reach $20 million—almost four times more than predicted six years earlier.[35]

When writing for the *Herald* in 1913, J. E. Rockwell reported that any visitor would find it difficult to "grasp the immensity" of the structures, such as the nearly completed merchant mill, which was just over one thousand feet long (Figure 2.6). Rockwell also observed that because of Duluth's favorable summer climate, future steel plant employees could work efficiently throughout the year. "There are no long spells of oppressively hot weather in Duluth," he stated, "when men fall fainting and exhausted from the heat, and when it is a physical impossibility to keep production any place near its normal."[36]

Later in the summer a "throng" of approximately eight hundred Superior men and women, many of whom had received a half-day civic holiday from

THE MERCHANT MILL BLDG.
STEEL PLANT, DULUTH, MINN.

Figure 2.6. By 1913, the walls and roof were in also place for the merchant mill, which was more than one thousand feet long; production would begin three years later. Author's collection.

the city's mayor, along with one hundred Methodist ministers from throughout Wisconsin sailed to Morgan Park on the excursion steamer *Columbia*. After arriving at the Spirit Lake dock the men marched in double file to the plant site, where they toured the emerging structures. (Since women once again were barred from the grounds, they stayed onboard the vessel.) The men's "expressions of wonder at the magnitude of the plant were so unanimous as to almost be a chorus," noted one account. Of particular interest were the blast furnaces, "the mammoth chimneys of which towered hundreds of feet in the air." In 1914 more than one hundred members of the Minnesota Master Plumbers' Association toured the property, as did thirty representatives of the American Society of Mechanical Engineers. Impressed by the "stupendous size of the Duluth establishment," the engineers termed it equal to any steel plant in Pittsburgh or the eastern United States. The level of development and optimism evident throughout Duluth even awed the *Minneapolis Journal*, which had initially opposed the steel plant.[37]

Claims were also made that Minnesota Steel had employed great effort to avoid accidents, so much so that "even the most daring fate-tempter could hardly badly injure himself." Nonetheless, the men who worked there faced constant threats to life and limb. This fact became strikingly evident in September 1913, when a gas tank exploded while several men were using a torch to place a tire on a locomotive wheel. Three workers—Andrew Mazak, Carl Rusch, and Charles Simpson—were killed, and three others were injured. Although a temporary hospital building was located at the construction site, the accident proved so serious that the men were transported to downtown Duluth; because of the seriousness of the men's injuries and the bad road conditions, however, they spent up to two hours being moved to the hospital by ambulance.[38]

Despite the tragedy, work at the plant continued at a steady pace, even as iron and steel experts continued to debate the economic rationale for building such a facility in Duluth. An *Engineering and Mining Journal* correspondent termed the plant "an important departure from our established practice of many years, which has been that it is better to carry the iron ore to the fuel than the fuel to the ore." Francis Stacey, writing in the *World's Work,* noted that hauling coal over long distances to a manufacturing site might have appeared "curious" to most people, but asserted that the practice was indicative of new "economic laws" that promoted efficiency in business. To Stacey the emergence of a Duluth steel plant was an illustration of "Pittsburgh moving west."[39]

By May 1914, Duluth's citizens were looking to the future, with some considering the "ceremonial occasion" that could mark the plant's opening. In August, however, the assassination of Archduke Ferdinand in a remote district of the Austro-Hungarian Empire not only transformed the landscapes of Europe into battlefields, but also changed America's business and industrial climate virtually overnight. The sudden shift in demands for war-related materials led to the immediate shutdown of construction operations at the Duluth plant. No major work would occur at the site over the next eight months.[40]

Visionary Celebrations and a Belated Opening

During the winter of 1915, many Duluthians who viewed the "esoteric gloom" of the silent steel plant site reportedly were "writhing in curiosity" about its future. Finally, on the last day of March, word was received that "work on the Minnesota steel plant [would] be resumed." According to one official, the sudden resumption of activities was not necessarily tied to increased wartime demands, but rather because U.S. Steel was "concerned about the future." Almost immediately, 800 men gathered at the plant gate, hoping to find employment. Since transportation services were so woefully inadequate, at least 150 men who found work walked four miles to the job site, labored for ten hours, and then hiked back to their homes.[41]

When Governor Winfield Hammond toured the site in late April, the size of the operations impressed the state executive, although he expressed surprise at "so much modern machinery lying here idle and not bringing any returns on its investment." In early July 1915, after corporate officials predicted that steel production would begin on the first day of November, leaders of Duluth's Commercial Club proposed that the grand opening be marked by a massive celebration, including a huge banquet, speeches by prominent individuals, a band concert, and evening fireworks. The *Duluth News Tribune* immediately gave its enthusiastic support to the plans, calling for the decking of the entire city with flags and bunting, speeches by national and local steel officials, a banquet in one of the steel plant's immense buildings, "and a final procession through avenues of red lights and bombs, skyrockets and roman candles." Mayor William Prince recommended that if the events were of "sufficient magnitude," the city should designate November 1 a civic holiday. Also offering support were officials of Superior's Rotary and Commercial clubs; one prominent Superiorite who spoke to the clubs' members envisioned "pithy addresses by local and national experts"—such as geologist Charles Van Hise, president of the University of Wisconsin—all of whom would speak about the history, settlement, and future of the Duluth-Superior region. A farmer from Twig, a small community located fifteen miles northwest of downtown Duluth, wrote that rural groups in northeastern Minnesota should also give their support because of the steel plant's contribution to local land value gains.[42]

The *News Tribune* then began asking its readers for ideas about how to mark the occasion. Duluth's citizens certainly did not lack for creativity when responding to the request. One suggestion called for a flotilla of vessels, including freighters and tugs, which would proceed through the ship canal into St. Louis Bay as far as the iron-ore docks. Another submission recommended a "monster barbeque" at one of Duluth's lakeshore parks, followed by a "water fete" in Lake Superior. One Duluthian pictured a parade to represent the city's industrial and institutional life—"all fire equipment and fire fighters, the entire police force, city officials, a representation of leading citizens, school children and young people and floats typifying all business concerns and civic organizations." Calling for a "steel pageant," another respondent recommended that "as much steel should be crammed into the parade as possible." One entrant wished to see a procession of "the national guard, United Spanish War Veterans, Sons of Veterans, naval militia, high school cadets, uniform ranks of fraternal orders and members of other semi-military organizations." A recommendation was also made to shoot fireworks out of an airplane flying over the harbor, while the most optimistic submission raised the possibility of going to the nation's chief executive: "Why not invite President Wilson?" one man asked.[43]

In mid-August, however, the Commercial Club declared that any celebration should be delayed until the spring of 1916, because it would give more time to plan for "the greatest event of the city's history and one that will attract the attention of the continent." The committee also reasoned, quite correctly, that better weather conditions prevailed during spring than in early November.[44] Ultimately, the plant did not produce steel until early December, one month later than had been predicted, and no further mention of a celebration appeared. No parades would fill the streets, no bands would blare out military marches, no speakers would orate in the city's meeting halls, no fireworks would light the night-time sky, no banquets would fill the stomachs of Duluth's denizens, no water festivals would play out in the harbor, no flotilla of boats and ships would gather in Lake Superior and St. Louis Bay, no civic holiday would close the city's offices and businesses, and no U.S. president would visit the city.

While the celebratory fervor dissipated as quickly as it had risen, activities at the steel plant site continued unabated throughout the summer and fall of 1915. By July the size of the construction force approached one thousand workers. Many crews were put on a seven-days-a-week schedule that began at 7:00 in the morning and ended at 8:30 in the evening. Smaller-sized crews worked throughout the night. (Many years later, one former employee would claim that only two excuses were allowed for missing work during this period: "to attend one's wedding or one's own funeral.") To transport the workers, the Northern Pacific Railroad placed additional passenger cars on trains running between Duluth and the steel plant.[45]

The first coal and limestone were shipped by rail from Duluth's docks to the bustling construction site in early August, and by the end of the month 150 carloads of coal were arriving daily. The coal began to be dried out in several of the plant's ninety-six coke ovens, and in late October coke was produced for eventual use in the blast furnaces. Work on the ten open-hearth furnaces was rushed, given that the interior walls of each unit had to be dried out for several weeks before being lined with bricks. Chief engineer K. C. Hoxie lit a ceremonial wood fire in one of the furnaces, an action later repeated by other company officials in the nine remaining open hearths.

Following this, the bricks were dried by gas flames that approached three thousand degrees Fahrenheit. In early November the first trainload of fifty-five railway cars, each filled with fifty tons of iron ore excavated from the Clark, Sharon, and Spruce mines on the Mesabi Range, appeared at the site. Some 1,500 tons of Cuban manganese ore for the manufacture of specialty steel were also shipped to the plant. Over the next weeks additional train-loads of ore were directed toward the plant—the vanguard for a countless stream of ore cars that would arrive over the next six decades.[46]

Duluth's citizens obviously were pleased that the steel plant was nearing completion during the final weeks of 1915, but voices of discontent ema-nated from Superior, where residents expressed frustration that vehicular traffic still could not pass over the bridge that spanned the St. Louis River. In fact, it had been five years since the first train crossed the bridge, but Minnesota officials had subsequently failed to complete the western road approach to the overpass. "They [Duluth officials] build a ramp to let us down into the swamp," fumed a frustrated Superior businessman, C. A. Erhart, "and then they build a fence across it for fear we might use it and get drowned in the bog." Superior's "enemies are the people of Duluth," Erhart exclaimed, because they hoped to delay passage over the bridge for as long as possible. Occasionally during the winter months, when horses were used to pull loads of supplies across the frozen St. Louis River, the ice gave way and the animals drowned. No wonder that Superior officials were eager to make the twenty-six-foot-wide roadway accessible to vehicles and the flanking six-foot-wide sidewalks open to pedestrians. To make their point, in September 1915 members of Superior's Rotary Club engaged in a "novelty" event by holding a picnic on the unfinished span. Finally, later that year, the Superiorites pleaded their case to the U.S. War Department. A favorable decision was rendered during the spring of 1916, but the Duluth approach would not be completed until July 1917.[47]

While the bridge issue may have consumed Superior's officials and news-papers, Duluthians and Minnesota Steel executives gave it scant notice until the War Department's resolution of 1916. Instead, virtually all attention in Duluth was devoted to the anticipated opening, which kept being pushed back because of small problems encountered at the plant; these setbacks ranged from the failure of some equipment to arrive on schedule to the amount of time required to place brick linings in the open-hearth furnaces.[48]

Even as the delays extended into November, daily commentaries in the city's newspapers provided readers with a torrent of incorrect predictions about the imminent plant opening. No single issue, however, was more inaccurate than the *Duluth Herald* for November 24. Emblazoned across the entire front page of the newspaper was a bold headline—"Making Steel in Duluth"—asserting that on the previous evening, one of the blast furnaces had been "blown in" with a "rip and roar." The *Herald* reported that most of the region's steel officials had witnessed the event, but their attempts to cheer the occasion had been "lost in the roar of the fiery rush of compressed air through the monster furnace." The front page of the *Wall Street Journal* published a similar erroneous account, claiming that "yesterday, the first blast furnace was lighted."[49]

Minnesota Steel officials immediately issued a disclaimer, stating that the *Herald*'s report was "absolutely without foundation." The *Duluth News Tribune*, ever willing to point out its rival's error, noted that even the technical information in the *Herald*'s account was incorrect. Blast furnaces produce pig iron, pointed out the *Tribune*, whereas open-hearth furnaces manufacture steel. The following day the *Herald* sheepishly reported that production had been delayed because of a conveyor car malfunction. The newspaper concluded its qualification by pointing to the secrecy that surrounded all operations. "The minor officials at the plant are completely muzzled by orders from headquarters," claimed the *Herald*, and "the same policy of secrecy is maintained at the head office of the company."[50]

Given the unrealized expectations of November, perhaps it is not surprising that production of the first mould or "heat" of pig iron, which occurred on December 1, received little attention from journalists. In fact, the auspicious occasion garnered no more than a one-paragraph notice on the fourth page of the *News Tribune*, and was relegated to the seventeenth page of the *Herald*. Instead, it was war reports from such places as Saloniki, Bulgaria, Montenegro, Germany, France, and other overseas locations that dominated Duluth newspaper headlines in December 1915 and for the subsequent three years.[51]

Throughout this time, Duluth's steelmakers continued to experiment with the proper formula of iron ore, coke, and limestone required for the manufacture of high quality pig iron. On December 11, the plant produced its first steel when the open hearth's molten metal was poured into ingot moulds. The steel ingots then went to the rolling mill for reheating and compression into narrow, long slabs, or "blooms." Two days later the blooms were forwarded to another mill so they could be rolled into billets approximately two inches by four inches in dimension. The billets were clipped into various lengths for storage or shipment, and eventually converted into milled products such as rods, wire, and nails. Since Duluth's merchant mill would not be completed for several more months, the first billets were sent to fabrication plants in Gary, Indiana. The crew that guided the first train out of Morgan Park on December 15 cheered as the engine and railway cars departed on the southward journey.[52]

The opening of the manufacturing facility may not have been as auspicious as its resolute backers and promoters had once anticipated, but after employees had worked every day for several weeks in a row, Christmas Day finally gave them time to enjoy a twenty-four-hour respite from their labors. The majority of Duluth's citizens also found new reason to rejoice during the 1915 holiday season: after eight and one-half years of fits and starts, a functioning steel-manufacturing facility was finally operating within the city's boundaries.

3. NEIGHBORHOOD HOUSING FROM GARY TO OLIVER

Duluth's steel plant would not operate until late 1915, but by 1909–10, several hundred construction laborers working at the future manufacturing site required housing. The need for residences grew steadily as work progressed over subsequent years.

The first sixty company-built houses opened in the model town of Morgan Park during the spring of 1914; nonetheless, even when just over five hundred units were available by 1922, no more than 15 to 25 percent of the corporation's permanent workforce found accommodations in the model village. Thus, most employees resided in Duluth's older neighborhoods, or acquired new housing in recently developed subdivisions located close to the manufacturing facility. Virtually all workers settled on the Minnesota side of the St. Louis River, though some of the most ambitious real estate schemes were found in adjacent Wisconsin.

Early Communities, Neighborhoods, and Subdivisions

Initially, most new housing for steel plant construction workers was built on vacant lots in communities and settlements platted southwest of downtown Duluth during earlier years of the city's history. The oldest communities included Fond du Lac, originally established as a fur-trading post in 1820, incorporated as a separate village in 1857, and annexed by Duluth in 1895; and the townsite of Oneota, platted in 1856 and absorbed by the Village of West Duluth in 1888. Both Oneota and West Duluth were then annexed by Duluth in 1894. Numerous speculative subdivisions—Spirit Lake Park, Ironton, New Duluth, Bay View Heights, and others—were promoted from 1888 to 1893, a period once defined as a time when "platting lands, selling lots and making money was Duluth's chief industry."[1]

Spirit Lake Park, intended as a "fine residence suburb" with large lots and a mile of waterfront along the St. Louis River, was platted by a syndicate of seven Duluth, Milwaukee, and Chicago men in 1889 (see Figure 2.1). Most of Spirit Lake Park's 352 acres of land were cleared during the following year, but after the investors determined that "conditions rendered it premature," the plat was not filed in the county courthouse. The land holding was sold to the Minnesota Steel Company in 1907.[2]

A plat for the adjacent subdivision of Ironton (now Riverside) was also filed in 1889. Although the promoters made strong efforts to ensure Ironton's success, the nationwide "Big Panic" of 1893 led to the failure of this enterprise, an outcome that obviously served as a "great disappointment" to its investors.[3]

The evolution of New Duluth, however, most clearly illustrates the economic boom-and-bust phenomena that define the 1888–93 era. When New Duluth's lots became available in October 1890, investor C. E. Lovett termed it "the most remarkable sale ever held in the Northwest." Since each purchaser was limited to two lots, several speculators concocted a "brilliant scheme" that had surrogate buyers, "toughs of the worst kind," stand in line and then acquire the properties for their sponsors. With so many buyers cramped into the overcrowded sales office, the shortage of air caused some participants to faint as they waited; one man, according to reports, even died shortly after the event. Nonetheless, the sale was deemed a great success, and within two years several docks that emerged along the marshy banks of the St. Louis River were attracting sawmills, furniture and refrigerator factories, sash and door manufacturers, and iron and brass foundries to New Duluth. Houses, store buildings, hotels, and churches were also emerging quickly. Despite this auspicious start, the nationwide panic of 1893 brought an abrupt end to further development and only a few firms survived the economic calamity. Although New Duluth had been incorporated as a separate village in October 1891, the rapid decline in tax revenues and population numbers that occurred after 1893 led to its merger with Duluth two years later.[4]

Only months after U.S. Steel made its April 1907 decision to construct a manufacturing plant, the once "practically dead" and "deserted village" of New Duluth was reportedly "coming to life." Although money was being invested in houses that hadn't "sheltered a human being for many years," it was not until 1909–10 that construction workers began searching for lodging in New Duluth's residences and boardinghouses. Most early laborers lived in either West Duluth or downtown Duluth and commuted by train to and from the construction site. During the summer months some workers boarded excursion boats that embarked from the Duluth harbor for points along the St. Louis River, including a dock on Spirit Lake. A few years later a boardwalk connected central New Duluth and the steel-plant gates.[5]

Some new subdivision and land development activities occurred proximate to the plant site shortly after 1907, but these pursuits were limited in number and scale, and often consisted of little more than the rearrangement of lots in an existing plat. Among the first real estate agents who promoted land and housing sales close to the steel plant site was T. W. Wahl. In late 1908 Wahl predicted that the initial residential and commercial development generated by steel plant development would occur between downtown Duluth and the manufacturing facility. Quite conveniently, Wahl had lots for sale in two places—the old Ironton subdivision and the more recently platted Spirit Lake (both part of the Riverside and Smithville neighborhoods today)—that extended to the northeast from the plant site and toward downtown. A handsome, well-illustrated brochure emphasized the two subdivisions' attributes: attractive settings, which made both developments the "most beautiful places" in the area, and "ideal" locations, which would allow workers to live within walking distance of the steel plant. Certainly not forgotten was the investment potential afforded by the two subdivisions. "It goes without saying that those who buy property there are going to make the profits," declared Wahl. "It is also self evident that those who invest now will make the largest profits." In 1909, an Eveleth realty firm, Barge and Perham, was serving as the Wahl Company's representatives on the Iron Range. Soon Wahl would claim that because his holding was flanked by a hill on one side and water on the other, many lots were similar to some of the most valuable properties in downtown Duluth. Three years later the realty company, now called Wahl and Messer, was touting the proximity of Spirit Lake to the new model town.[6]

Gary, Minnesota: Speculation on the Steel Plant Border

The most widely promoted subdivisions were situated within the new community of Gary, named for U.S. Steel's Elbert Gary. Duluth realtor Andrew Volk's announcement for the first subdivision came out in 1910. Soon, advertisements for Gary appeared throughout the Iron Range and in local foreign-language publications, such as Duluth's *Sosialisti*, a newspaper read by Finnish-American workers. The Finnish-language notice extolled Gary's attributes and noted that its namesake in Indiana had become a city of 47,000 people in just eight years.[7]

From 1911 to 1914 other developers filed plats for three additional Gary subdivisions. All wrapped around the western and southern sections of the steel plant, though the majority of development actually occurred in the southern section of Gary (Figure 3.1). In May 1913 Volk disposed of his unsold lots to a syndicate of Chicago and Minneapolis investors headed by Duluth realtor Alfred Kuehnow; the new owners immediately consolidated with the Gary Land Company to form the largest real estate firm in western Duluth (Figure 3.2). Volk reportedly garnered $350,000 for the transaction, "a good-sized fortune" according to the *Duluth Herald*. (Another report put the price at $236,000.) Volk's financial success was considered a favorable omen for other developers, who were just beginning "to realize the profits which are eventually to be theirs." By December 1913 the Gary Land Company had sold virtually all of the 577 lots it purchased seven months earlier. Nonetheless, fewer than half the lots were developed over the next two years, and by the time the steel plant opened in late 1915, only 214 housing units had been constructed in Gary.[8]

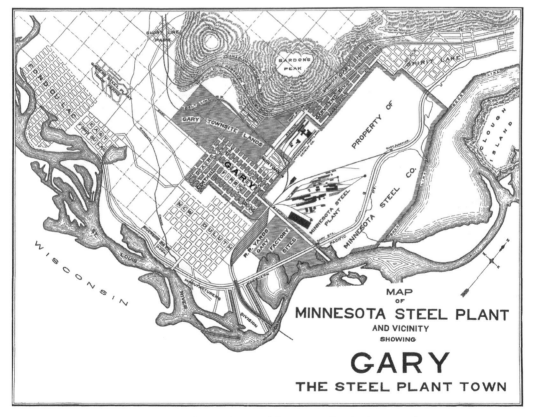

Figure 3.1. Between 1910 and 1914, most of the vacant land adjoining the Minnesota Steel Company's western and southwestern property lines was platted into lots for new subdivisions that formed the settlement of Gary. From Steel Plant Investment Co., "Map of Minnesota Steel Plant and Vicinity Showing Gary the Steel Plant Town," ca. 1916. Courtesy of Northeast Minnesota Historical Center, S3150, 4:99.

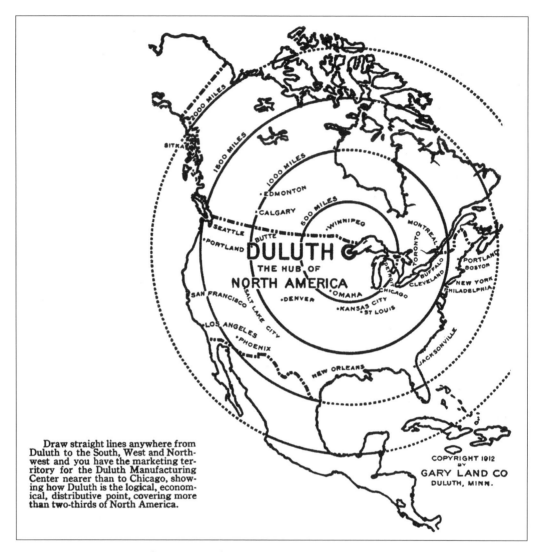

Figure 3.2. In 1912 the Gary Land Company attempted to attract real estate investors by highlighting the location of Duluth and the steel plant—at the center of North America. The map failed to note that much of Duluth's market area was sparsely populated. From Gary Land Company, "Duluth's Mammoth Steel Plant." Courtesy of Northeast Minnesota Historical Center, Pamphlet 651.

Somewhat surprisingly, real estate developers in Duluth and Gary welcomed U.S. Steel's May 1913 announcement that hundreds of residences and a model town were envisioned for workers who otherwise would have participated in the private housing market. As perceived by local civic leader Julius H. Barnes, most realtors now believed that U.S. Steel's decision demonstrated its "faith in Duluth as a producing and distributing point in the steel business." Likewise, the *Duluth Herald* stated that developers owning properties in neighborhoods bordering the St. Louis River would experience a "boom" in real estate sales. "That there will be enough for all is the general sentiment," wrote the newspaper.[9]

"Things are happening fast in Duluth," reported realtor Watson S. Moore in 1913. To him, U.S. Steel's housing decisions meant "more business for everybody, increased opportunities for business, new business enterprises coming to the city and greatly increased real estate activity." Andrew Volk, who had filed the original Gary plat in 1910, described the "jubilant" mood of local realtors following U.S. Steel's 1913 announcement—"undoubtedly one of the best things that ever could happen to that end of the city."[10]

By this time, Gary had more than seven miles of graded streets, a bank, a public school, two lumberyards, hotels, bakeries, stores, two telephone companies, and numerous residences. Despite the apparent progress, conditions were far from idyllic. Gary may have had an elementary school by September 1913, but it was nothing more than a one-room portable building that housed seventy-five to eighty students. Cracker boxes, each used by two students sitting side by side, served as seats. Throughout the winter a single wood-burning stove that emitted heat "spasmodically" meant children sitting at the front of the room were excessively hot, while those at the back found themselves "shivering during most of the session." The arrival of warmer weather in May sometimes sent the temperature in the unventilated building as high as eighty-eight degrees Fahrenheit. Conditions in nearby New Duluth were somewhat better, but the local school was so overcrowded that the student overflow was accommodated in a rented store building. Despite these problems, the situation did not improve until September 1915, following the dedication of the Harriet Beecher Stowe School in New Duluth, "constructed in accordance with the latest ideas in architecture."[11]

A few sources claimed that Gary's residences were "built in a very substantial manner"; nonetheless, Duluth building inspector R. R. Grant was kept busy turning down construction permits submitted to his office, many for houses sited on lots only thirty feet wide. Despite Grant's efforts, many rental units constructed in Gary from 1911 to 1913 were far from adequate. Men who lived in boarding and rooming houses were often "crowded in every available corner," sleeping in cramped quarters with insufficient light and ventilation. One rooming house had a basement filled with so much water that health officials termed it a navigable "young lake"; many boarding and rooming houses were fire hazards, such as one facility used by immigrant Montenegrins, which burned to the ground in 1913—fortunately without any loss of life. Other workers, some with wives and children, lived in tar-paper shacks, where they subsisted "in the scantiest manner." After an August 1913 inspection, Dr. H. E. Webster, Duluth's director of public health, reported that as many as ten to twenty foreign-born people might be crowded into a room only ten feet by twenty feet in size. The housing shortage was so acute that by the summer of 1913 "a village of tents" provided the only accommodations for many of Gary's recent arrivals.[12]

Inspections conducted by Duluth's mayor and city health officials in August determined that Gary's lack of sewers contributed to "cess pools, puddles of water about the dwellings and yards saturated with slops from kitchens and wash basins, all of them prolific of flies and odors which breed sickness and discomfort." The only drinking water came from shallow "scooped out" wells. The officials observed cow stables and chicken coops located next to houses and hotels, manure piles and privies situated by cisterns, and commercial and residential districts filled with "overpowering stenches." A clogged wooden trough under one avenue discharged filth at both ends. Another account described a bakery where "flies divided their activities between the interior and piles of garbage on the outside"; nearby was an overcrowded and extremely dirty rooming house with an interior washbasin that emptied "into an open pool just outside the room where the dough is kneaded." One family with three children even shared their house with a cow. In early October 1913 as many as ten cases of typhoid, two resulting in death, were attributed to Gary's "filthy spots." Terming Gary "a danger center," health officials concluded that the problems would not be resolved "until effective means of carrying off waste [were] provided."[13]

The "pale, anemic children, living in indescribable dirt and ignorance" most certainly were distressing to Duluth officials who viewed conditions in Gary. To them, the community was "a citadel of filth due to ignorance, apathy or disregard of the rudiments of sanitation and civic decency." The moral climates in Gary and New Duluth were also of concern, so much so that in 1914 Duluth's City Council adopted a resolution putting an end to saloon applications in both places.[14]

For years, woeful road conditions bedeviled anyone who traveled to or from either Gary or New Duluth. In April 1913 Alfred Kuehnow complained that it was "utterly impossible" to reach the two neighborhoods and the steel plant site "without danger of becoming mired in the mud." Not only was the road "a disgrace to the city," exclaimed Kuehnow, but Duluth was also "criminally negligent" for failing to exercise adequate supervision over the construction contractor. By August the "gulch" had become so deep and torturous that vehicles were forced to "bump, jump, slide and wriggle" up and down its steep slopes. When the gap was finally repaired in August 1914, the community celebrated as Kuehnow was the first person to drive his automobile over the "big fill." Nevertheless, at times in 1915 one section of the route between Ironton and Smithville still remained impassable, which meant that jitney passengers had to disembark at either neighborhood, walk for a block and a half, and then board another jitney. No wonder that members of the recently formed Gary Improvement Club were anxious "to further the many interests which are insistently demanding attention."[15]

Despite the less-than-desirable conditions, realtor Volk predicted that the city of Duluth would soon provide Gary with its necessary services. The typhoid epidemic was quickly halted in October 1913 after city officials ordered Gary's residents to boil their drinking water and when local citizens "cleaned up [the] filthy places as well as possible." Within two months garbage collection was offered in the community, and work on a sewer system that served both Gary and New Duluth began in early 1915; later in the year a water tank appeared on Gary's horizon, and the roadway between New Duluth and downtown Duluth was paved (Figure 3.3). Most claims about Gary's future may have been grossly exaggerated— including forecasts that the community would eventually have fifty thousand people—but Volk's prediction about the extension of Duluth's city services to the settlement was one of only a very few predictions that ultimately proved accurate.[16]

Subdivision Promotion in Wisconsin

Extensive residential promotion also occurred in and proximate to Superior throughout the time the steel plant was under construction. Superior actually was no stranger to iron- and steel-manufacturing operations, since some small ventures had preceded Duluth's new plant by several years. The earliest efforts began in 1888 when the West Superior Land and River Improvement Company promoted the development of a steel production unit along the city's lakefront. One year later the organization had attracted a pipe manufacturer, the West Superior Iron and Steel Company, to the site. The facility prospered until 1893, but the national economic panic of that year led to bankruptcy and closure. In 1900 the United States Cast and Steel Company, a major manufacturer of iron and steel drainpipes and culverts, purchased the facilities. This operation closed for good in 1911, however, once concrete began replacing iron as a material for culverts. When many

Figure 3.3. Looking north along the main street of Gary, Minnesota, in 1916. In the foreground is the Central State Bank, established in 1913; Charles G. Strand's tavern, built in 1914, is in the immediate background. Both buildings, which remain in Gary today, are located along Commonwealth Avenue, just north of its intersection with Gary Street. Courtesy of the Oliver (Wisconsin) History Project, Abbott Family Collection.

of the buildings were being dynamited in 1917, an observer ruefully noted that the "blasts are demolishing the very thing that a quarter of a century ago promised greatness to that section of the city of Superior." The last three structures were razed in 1936.[17]

When the West Superior Iron and Steel Company facility opened in 1889, a nearby residential area called the "Steel Plant District" was laid out for the purpose of housing skilled workers. In 1902, a large section of nearby land previously donated to the city of Superior received the name of Billings Park, as did the residential section. When Duluth's steel plant decision was made public in 1907, Superior realtors immediately promoted the potential investment benefits of Billings Park lots. The ads claimed that the neighborhood was located only a few miles from the proposed plant, but far enough away to avoid any negative consequences. "The smoke and dust thrown off from the blast furnaces," noted one advertisement, "make it not only undesirable but almost impossible to live within several miles of the plant."[18] People unfamiliar with the local transportation network likely failed to realize, however, that no road or bridge yet provided direct access between Superior and the future steel works. In fact, the actual trip from Billings Park to the construction site approached twelve miles, including a required trip through the downtowns of both Superior and Duluth. Billings Park eventually became one of Superior's largest and most desirable neighborhoods, but its growth was due to the development of the downtown and harbor district.

Vehicles and pedestrians could not cross the St. Louis River via a bridge until July 1917, but a flurry of subdivision platting started south of Superior in 1910—the year that trains first made their way over the span. These subdivisions were laid out along the "belt line," the name for the railway that linked the steel plant and Duluth's rail system to Superior's harbor and the iron-ore docks at Allouez, an industrial suburb located east of the city (Figure 3.4). After crossing the bridge into Wisconsin, the belt line curved southeastward to a point about two miles below Superior's southern boundary, where it then headed toward the northeast and Allouez.

Superior's boosters listed several objectives for the belt line: to ensure that every railroad entering the head of the lakes district would intersect with the new system; to connect the steel plant with U.S. Steel's docks; to make some fifteen miles of territory accessible for additional manufacturing operations; and to furnish inexpensive sites for further town-site development. A clear example of Superior's optimism was the Harding Purchase, a 1,500-acre tract of riverfront property "held in reserve for large industrial plants." One attempt to secure an industrial operation for the Harding Purchase was undertaken in late 1915 by Thomas Wahl when he sought to attract a branch of the Ralston Steel Car Company to Superior; however, the Columbus, Ohio, manufacturer of pressed steel freight cars chose not to locate on the Harding tract.[19]

Pittsburgh, the first Wisconsin subdivision associated with the steel plant, emerged south of Superior in 1910; it was termed "the new steel city of the West" by developers, as well as "one of the best real estate bargains ever offered at the head of the lakes." Carnegie, the second subdivision, was one of the most ambitious promotional schemes ever envisioned as part of

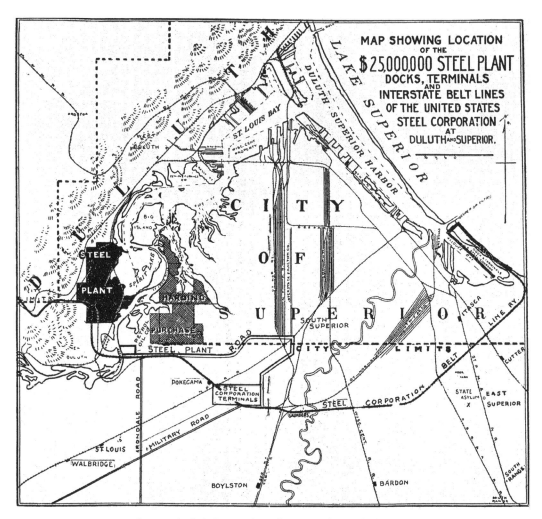

Figure 3.4. Completion of a belt-line railway between the steel plant site and Superior's harbor and docks in 1910 was accompanied by considerable real estate speculation in Wisconsin. From Rufus Stephenson and Co. (Superior), "Keep Your Eye on the Steel Plant and Belt Line Acres," ca. 1909. Courtesy of Northeast Minnesota Historical Center, Pamphlet 652.

steel plant activities in Duluth (Figure 3.5). At the end of 1910 promoters asserted that the sale of Carnegie's lots had "gone forward in amazing fashion and . . . led all the others in the good opinion of investors." Less than two years later notice was given that because of the significant demand for residential and commercial locations, thirteen new subdivisions had been added to Carnegie. Advertisements for the entire Carnegie tract, now portrayed as the sole area of desirable and easily developable land available along either side of the St. Louis River, pointed to its advantages over any nearby subdivision emerging in Minnesota:[20]

They [future purchasers] would not want to construct their homes or live on the east or north side of the plant, which is so rough and rocky they can scarcely climb over it. They surely could not try to build a city on the very limited amount of ground to the west and southwest of the plant, right in the midst of the smoke, gas, fumes and soot which will constantly be blown over this location by the ever prevailing northeast winds.[21]

Declaring that astute individuals who acquired lots in the new subdivision would escape any pollution produced by the steel plant, Carnegie's promoters asserted that purchasers were securing land of "no average proportions."[22]

Alas, virtually no development occurred in either Carnegie or Pittsburgh.

The lack of activity was evident by 1913, when a prospective movie theater operator from Illinois who visited Carnegie learned that no other theaters existed in the subdivision; in fact, "he couldn't find anything else there." Limited development occurred in most of the other plats—Air Line Division, Belt Line Acres, Parkside, Riverside Addition, Steel Industry Tracts, Steel Plant Acres, Steel Plant Belt Line Harbor, Steel Plant Garden Tracts, and Sunnyside/Sunnyside Gardens—laid

Figure 3.5. This section of an advertisement for the residential subdivision of Carnegie, Wisconsin, platted southwest of Superior in 1910, illustrates the envisioned magnitude of the steel plant. Despite the smoke shown in the advertisement, promoters claimed that Carnegie would be pollution-free because of its favorable location. From Great Northern Land Company, "Carnegie," ca. 1911. Courtesy of Northeast Minnesota Historical Center, S3150, 1:41.

out just south of the belt-line railway. Some of these developments included small land tracts where it was envisioned that steelworkers could raise fruits, vegetables, chickens, and one or two cows. Advertisements for Steel Plant Acres and Belt Line Acres, both platted in 1910, declared that the loamy soil was "open and practically cleared, absolutely free from stone and growing up to timothy and clover."[23]

When the Heimbaugh and Spring Company of Duluth and Superior began promoting its six-hundred-acre Sunnyside Gardens holding south of the belt line in 1914, those who purchased a ten-acre parcel also received a free lot in the nearby townsite of Sunnyside. After clearing one acre of land each buyer received, free of charge, three thousand strawberry, one thousand raspberry, fifty currant, and fifty gooseberry plants from the company. The soil was of such high quality, asserted the company, that only "a pretty poor specimen" of a man would not be able to raise a family on a truck farm, or fail to realize an annual income of at least one thousand dollars from the sale of produce. Soon the company was claiming that new residents were "rapidly transforming the wild land into comfortable homesteads." After one season at Sunnyside Gardens, August Van Weil was reported to have garnered $1,090 from three acres of strawberries, rutabagas, and potatoes; strawberries from W. D. Terry's two-acre field were marketed in Superior for $1,500, while a Mr. Harty received $1,000 from a single acre of strawberries. With Superior and Duluth located nearby, workers were reminded that their free time could be used profitably: "They can go out to their farm in the morning," declared one advertisement, "work all day and be back home the same night." Heimbaugh and Spring claimed that within two years after the lots had been put up for sale, 150 families were engaged in land clearing; nevertheless, there is no evidence that more than a few truck gardeners ever succeeded at Sunnyside Gardens.[24]

The sole Wisconsin subdivision that achieved a modicum of success was Oliver, platted in 1910 at the eastern approach to the bridge over the St. Louis River. A. R. Anderson operated the Oliver Townsite Company out of an office in downtown Duluth. Like Pittsburgh and Carnegie, the original twenty-acre Oliver plat was situated proximate to the large land area that once constituted the subdivision of St. Louis, an unsuccessful townsite venture that had been laid out in 1892, abandoned in 1896, and then subjected to mortgage foreclosures until 1910 (see Figure 2.1).[25]

The Oliver plat was surrounded by subdivisions associated with Pittsburgh and Carnegie, and named for Henry Oliver, the founder and former president of Duluth's Oliver Iron Mining Company—the nation's largest producer of iron ore when U.S. Steel absorbed it in 1901 (Figure 3.6). Advertisements

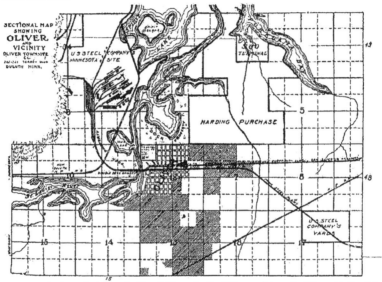

Figure 3.6. For several years the attributes of Oliver, Wisconsin, were touted in newspaper advertisements throughout northeastern Minnesota and northwestern Wisconsin. From Duluth Herald, *May 26, 1913.*

proclaimed Oliver's "high, dry, stoneless and absolutely desirable building sites," as well as its advantages over other settlements in the area, especially sufficient distance from the steel plant's undesirable "smoke, soot, gas, fumes, odors and cement dust." By 1913, when Oliver displayed graded streets and sidewalks, telephone service, a lumberyard, and twenty-two buildings, including a post office, a school, houses, saloons, and three hotels, developer Anderson claimed that the population would reach thousands within a few years. One year later Oliver was incorporated as a 1,400-acre village that encompassed Carnegie and some twenty subdivisions located proximate to or along the belt-line railway. Despite the optimism, Oliver's official census count never exceeded 250 residents from 1920 to 1990, though it did reach 358 in 2000.[26]

4. THE EMERGENCE OF A MODEL COMPANY TOWN

Public notice of U.S. Steel's intentions to build a model company town on the distant outskirts of Duluth appeared in May 1913, but earlier signs indicated that the huge corporation was planning a community for its workers. In January 1909, the *Duluth Herald* noted that U.S. Steel eventually would build a new town for several thousand people next to the manufacturing plant, while a March 1910 account in the *Duluth News Tribune* gave a more explicit description of the corporation's intentions: to provide a model town, complete with "strictly modern homes, beautiful as to architecture and commodious of arrangement, business houses, paved streets, a perfect sewer and lighting system, and halls for public meetings and places of amusement."[1] Three more years passed, however, before full-scale planning activities commenced.

Intentions and Objectives

When U.S. Steel spokespersons publicized their model town intentions in May 1913, they provided a rationale for expending considerable corporate resources on the construction of such a community. Much of their reasoning was based on the slum-like conditions found in many other steel manufacturing cities, described as "cheap shacks without proper sanitary provisions being thrown together by speculators." The distance from the steel plant to the built-up areas of Duluth was also considered a significant impediment in attracting an adequate workforce. "It is impossible to induce experienced workmen to move their families to Duluth until they come and look over the ground themselves," reported one official. "When they find no available houses with modern conveniences at a fair rental, they return. It is believed that if they find comfortable, new dwellings ready for their families at a fair rental, they will remain and be content to make Duluth their home."[2]

The trade journal *Iron Age* voiced a similar viewpoint, noting that much of northeastern Minnesota's labor force was seasonal in that railroad construction, Great Lakes shipping, and open-pit mining all came to a standstill during the winter months. To ensure that the steel plant had a dependable, year-round labor force, the publication agreed that a sizeable proportion of workers required housing displaying "a higher standard of excellence than has been attempted elsewhere." Or, as U.S. Bureau of Labor analyst Leiffur Magnusson wrote in 1918: "Buying land merely for its plant, erecting that plant, and leaving the housing of its working force to exploitation of private landholders, would have proved a shortsighted industrial policy."[3]

Providing some workers with a model town quite unlike anything else in the Duluth area meant that U.S. Steel was committing itself to a course of action that demanded considerable corporate attention and resources over the next three decades. The initial planning and building of such a town required the skills and talents of town planners, landscape architects, architects, engineers, contractors, and construction workers, and the subsequent management of the enclave called for the inputs of carpenters, painters, masons, gardeners, fire protection and police workers, clerks, managers, recreation directors, and social work and medical professionals.

Anthony Morell and Arthur Nichols: Creating and Implementing a Town Plan

Before U.S. Steel publicized its model town intentions, the corporation hired a Minneapolis landscape architecture and town planning firm, Morell and Nichols, to prepare a detailed physical plan for what would become Morgan Park (Figure 4.1). The senior member of the firm, Anthony Urbanski (1875–1924), was born and educated in France; after immigrating to the United States sometime around 1902, he adopted his mother's surname, Morell. He then began working for the well-known New York City landscape architect, Charles Leavitt Jr. Also joining the Leavitt firm in 1902 was Arthur Nichols (1880–1970) of Massachusetts, who, during that same year, had received the first degree in landscape architecture awarded by the Massachusetts Institute of Technology. Before the two men left the Leavitt firm in 1909, they worked on several major projects, including the design of John D. Rockefeller Sr.'s estate in Pocantico Hills, New York, and the plan for Monument Valley Park in Colorado Springs, Colorado. Both men also gained considerable familiarity with Duluth, since one of Leavitt's major clients was Chester Congdon, the Minnesota iron-ore magnate who served as a key state legislator during the early years of steel plant promotion. From 1902 to 1909 Morell and Nichols prepared and implemented the landscape design for "Glensheen," Congdon's large Duluth estate that fronted on Lake Superior.[4]

Figure 4.1. Landscape architects Arthur Nichols (left) and Anthony Morell at the time they were engaged in the planning of Morgan Park from 1913 to 1922. Courtesy of Northwest Architectural Archives, Morell and Nichols papers.

In 1909 the two men departed Leavitt's firm and moved to Minneapolis, where they established the Morell and Nichols partnership, Minnesota's earliest and best-known landscape architecture firm. In addition to Morgan Park, the two landscape architects pursued a number of other projects in Duluth, most notably designs for several bridges and sections of Skyline Drive, a lengthy scenic parkway that overlooks Lake Superior; and the plan for Morley Heights, a residential community sponsored by Duluth's Marshall-Wells Hardware Company. The firm also worked on commissions throughout Minnesota, among them landscape designs for several large estates in the Minneapolis area, and site plans for parks, subdivisions, resorts, cemeteries, schools, hospitals, sanitariums, asylums, and prisons. Two other Morell and Nichols projects that had some similarity to Morgan Park, albeit on a considerably smaller scale, were the mining settlement of Verona, Michigan, situated between Bessemer and Wakefield on the eastern Gogebic Iron Range; and the agricultural colony of Ojibwa in northern Wisconsin. They also pursued projects in North and South Dakota, Iowa, and elsewhere in the United States and Canada. Nichols continued to operate the firm after Morell's untimely death in 1924, and even maintained the name of Morell and Nichols, Inc., until his retirement from full-time practice in 1953 at the age of seventy-three.[5]

Immediately after arriving in Minneapolis, both men established affiliations with several public agencies in Minnesota. Morrell was a member and secretary of the Minneapolis Planning Commission, and Nichols, as early as 1909, began serving as a consultant landscape architect to Minnesota's State Board of Control, an affiliation that continued until 1935. In 1910 he entered into a productive relationship with the University of Minnesota that did not terminate until 1952. He worked as a consultant to the Minnesota Highway Department (1932–40) and Minnesota Department of Conservation (1953–60), and prepared the 1944 plan for the Minnesota State Capitol Approach in St. Paul. Nichols also served as a vice president of the American Society of Landscape Architects in 1928, an indication of the professional esteem he had already achieved by this time. Nichols died in Rochester, Minnesota, in 1970 at the age of ninety.[6]

A City Beautiful in a Garden

Sometime before April 1913, Morell and Nichols formulated a conceptual plan for the model town that utilized a topographic survey that U.S. Steel engineers had prepared several years earlier. The landscape architects' plan displayed a schematic arrangement of curvilinear streets, along with possible locations for a few buildings (Figure 4.2). In late April a brief *New York Times* notice incorrectly placed the model town at Carnegie, the unsuccessful subdivision that had been platted in Wisconsin three years earlier. One month later, when U.S. Steel confirmed its model town intentions, the *Times* interpreted the information correctly, reporting that the community would be a "parked town" with tennis courts and clubhouses, and basements and bathrooms in every dwelling unit. The *Duluth Herald* provided the most detailed information, giving readers a basic sketch of two major features that eventually would characterize the community: an entry boulevard and a clubhouse (Figure 4.3). One day after the sketch appeared the *Herald*'s editorial page described the future community in idyllic but functional terms: "There will be light and air for all; and there will be yards for the children to play in and for the housewives to make gardens in. Workers in the steel plant will not merely exist—they will live." Simply called the "model town" or "model city" over the subsequent year, the community was given the name of Morgan Park in June 1914 to honor J. Pierpont Morgan, the primary financial backer of U.S. Steel.[7]

Throughout the summer of 1913, Morell and Nichols worked on a detailed physical plan for Morgan Park as workers cleared the future townsite—described as "a tangled area of brush, stumps and second-growth timber." The two landscape architects experimented with different design details,

Figure 4.2. Morell and Nichols submitted this schematic proposal for the model town that would be built immediately north of the manufacturing facility. From part of an original topographic survey made by U.S. Steel engineers in 1910 and revised by Morell and Nichols in early 1913. Courtesy of Northeast Minnesota Historical Center, S2386B3of7.

but the overall layout and arrangement of the plan remained constant and clearly mirrored their preference for the City Beautiful. Although the physical aspects of turn-of-the-century City Beautiful planning are usually associated with monuments and civic centers for large urban areas, some of the design principles—"emerald parks, sinuous parkways, [and] graceful trees flanking parked boulevards"—were also applied to small cities and

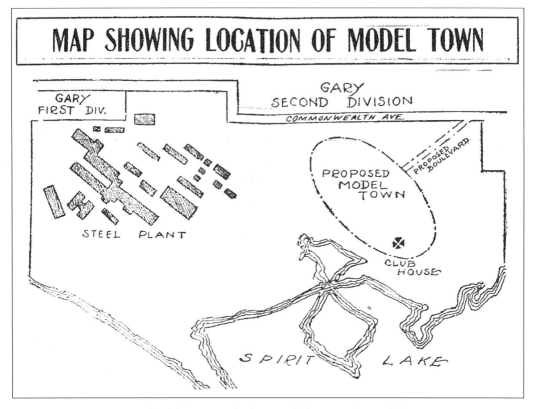

Figure 4.3. An initial public notice of what would become the model company town of Morgan Park featured two of its important elements: an entry boulevard and a clubhouse. From Duluth Herald, *May 14, 1913.*

towns such as Morgan Park. To Morell and Nichols, the City Beautiful was the "greatest and most important factor" that merited consideration in any visionary planning exercise.[8]

To carry out their version of City Beautiful planning at Morgan Park, the landscape architects called for the filling in of several small ravines that traversed the site. This action transformed the area into a relatively flat plateau that overlooked Spirit Lake and the St. Louis River, and allowed them to realize "the most desirable street plan"—a modified grid with a combination of rectilinear, curved, and radial roadways (Figure 4.4). The majority of curvilinear streets reflected the natural configuration of the terrain, especially at the northeastern end of Morgan Park where the roadways, according to the *American Architect,* served "as a logically suggested artistic form that would show the natural profile of the lake shore and its ravines" located forty feet below. Only a few curved roads were "made for their own sake."

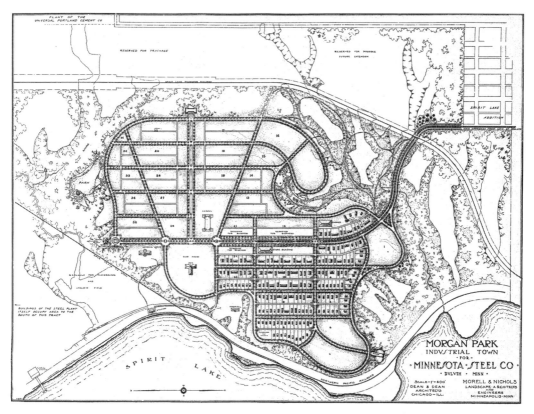

Figure 4.4. The initial plan for Morgan Park, prepared by Morell and Nichols in 1913, illustrates the overall street pattern and detailed arrangement of houses in the eastern neighborhood. Also shown is the site for the clubhouse and Minnesota Steel's office building; the location of the school, as well as the function of the boulevard that extended west of the clubhouse (the latter would be modified in subsequent plans). Author's collection; copy available at Northwest Architectural Archives, Morell and Nichols papers.

By November 1913 a local reporter claimed that U.S. Steel had clearly demonstrated its "determination to build a city second to none of corresponding size in the world."[9]

Two radial or diagonal streets, each with a seventy-foot-wide right-of-way, angled westward from the future clubhouse grounds and expressed the plan's formal City Beautiful elements. The radials also accentuated the visual and social importance of the school and clubhouse. The 1913 plan had a linear boulevard located between the two radials, with the school located just outside the eastern radial. By 1915, however, the plan was modified so that the former boulevard space could accommodate the school and a short street (Figure 4.5).

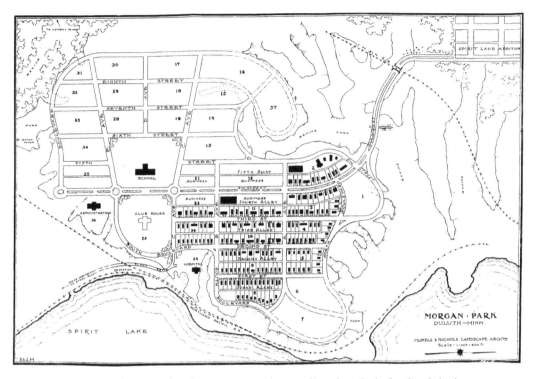

Figure 4.5. In the 1915 plan for Morgan Park, Morell and Nichols finalized the location of the school. The envisioned boulevard that had extended west of the clubhouse in the 1913 plan was now converted into a short street that began at the upper edge of the school property. The street names and numbers were changed to their current usage in 1930. Author's collection; copy available at Northwest Architectural Archives, Morell and Nichols papers.

The major roadway that entered the community offered another formal element for Morgan Park. The gently curved parkway passed through a portion of one residential neighborhood and then continued directly to the south, where it bordered a second neighborhood before terminating at the steel plant gates. Flanking the parkway were the future sites for Morgan Park's institutional facilities: two churches that would anchor the community's eastern and western borders; the office and laboratory building for Minnesota Steel; a clubhouse; a school; and a commercial building with stores, shops, and offices. The entire parkway, 80 feet wide, included a 22-foot-wide boulevard for the pair of streetcar tracks that eventually ran down both of the outer edges; each set of tracks was paralleled on its far side by 16-foot-wide paved roadways, 7.5-foot-wide grass medians, and 5-foot-wide sidewalks. A U.S. Steel publication summarized the corporation's satisfaction with both the aesthetic and practical properties of the road network. "The street layout presents an interesting combination of straight, curved and radial streets," observed the writer. "The long, winding approach and the encircling drives and occasional curved streets made necessary by local conditions give a pleasing variation from the more economical rectangular blocks which occupy the center of the town."[10]

"Hunkyville" and "Pig Pen"

All of Morgan Park's residential development occurred in two areas of the community that, for purposes of discussion, will be identified as the eastern and western neighborhoods. Community residents seldom used these or any geographically based identifiers; instead, they defined the neighborhood where they did *not* live as the "other side." Also employed were two local vernacular terms, "Hunkyville" and "Pig Pen." Hunkyville, a somewhat pejorative term derived from "Bohunk," referred to the lower-income western neighborhood. Many steel towns, including Gary, Indiana, included a neighborhood called Hunkyville, which was largely populated by Eastern Europeans. Since Morgan Park had few Eastern European residents, the western neighborhood was termed Hunkyville because of its lower-income status. The etymological origins of the more upscale Pig Pen, or eastern neighborhood, have been lost, though the name may have emerged as a sardonic response to Hunkyville.[11]

The neighborhood streets throughout Morgan Park had 50-foot-wide rights-of-way, which included a 22-foot-wide pavement; two grassy medians, each 8.5 feet wide; and two 4.5-foot-wide sidewalks paralleled each street. The backyard alleys had rights-of-way and pavements that were 16 feet and 8 feet wide, respectively. Since the electric and telephone lines for the model town were situated underground and beneath the grassy terrace located between the street curb and the sidewalk, only relatively few poles, some with ornamental features, were required for the streetlights and electrically powered streetcars. Two wells supplied drinking water, while river water was used for lawn sprinkling, toilets, and fire protection; the water lines were buried beneath the grassy median strip that separated the street curb and the sidewalk. Separate sanitary and storm sewers were buried under the alleys, a practice that was "expected to do much to keep the town free from contagion." The water and sewer lines were placed as many as eighteen feet below the surface—much deeper than was typical for the area—in response to Duluth's severe winter climate and to facilitate drainage from all areas of

Morgan Park into the St. Louis River. (The depth of the excavations caused considerable difficulty when the water and sewer lines required repair and replacement ninety years later.) The sewers that serviced both the Morgan Park community and the steel plant discharged directly into Spirit Lake and the St. Louis River. Anticipating governmental opposition for its sewage disposal practices already in 1913, Minnesota Steel made plans to provide a large underground septic tank; it was never built, and untreated sewage continued to flow into the river until 1960.[12]

Morell and Nichols may have been proponents of the City Beautiful, but their proposal for Morgan Park also displayed vestiges of another contemporary planning concept, the city in a garden or, as it was commonly termed after 1900, the garden city or garden suburb. At Morgan Park the most visible aspects of garden city planning were the community's decentralized location, environmental setting, and landscape design features. Located well outside Duluth's built-up areas and surrounded on three sides by undeveloped land covered with pine, spruce, aspen, birch, and maple trees, Morgan Park was publicized as a community within "natural park areas." Spirit Lake and the St. Louis River formed Morgan Park's eastern boundary, while steep, tree-covered ravines separated the community from neighboring Smithville to the north, and other ravines offered a barrier between the model town and the steel plant to the south. Several high bluffs to the west and northwest were located well outside Morgan Park's boundaries, but even they provided a "commanding and picturesque" backdrop for the community. Sites for two major parks, one located at the far northeastern corner of the community and the other along its southern boundary, were provided in the Morell and Nichols plan, while small playgrounds were situated throughout the community.[13]

Developing the Eastern Neighborhood

As Morell and Nichols were working on their overall Morgan Park proposal, they also prepared a detailed site plan for the first grouping of residences in the eastern neighborhood, or "Pig Pen." Most of the land surveys were completed by July 1913, and some initial site work began on the last day of the month. Contractors were invited to submit bids for a project that had several specifications and requirements: the excavation and trenching of 100,000 cubic yards of earth, the laying of some seven miles of water and gas lines and five miles of sewer lines, and the placement of seventy-three manholes and seventy-four intakes. Duluthians George R. King and John

Lundquist were awarded the $125,000 contract in early August, and they completed their work in 1914. When nine Duluth officials visited the site in September 1913, Mayor William Prince reported that only "the most modern ideas" of city planning were being followed throughout the model town (Figure 4.6).[14]

Morgan Park's roadways were still termed "as yet in poor condition" by late May 1914, but shortly thereafter the Butler-Coons Company of Hibbing received a contract to begin paving the streets, alleys, sidewalks, steps, and curbs (Figure 4.7). Owen Brainerd, a consulting engineer from New York City, supervised the work, most of which was finished by October 1915. (Macadam paving had originally been proposed, but concrete was recommended for reasons of longevity and ease of maintenance.) Morgan Park's

Figure 4.6. The Butler-Coons Company of Hibbing graded the streets and sidewalks in Morgan Park's eastern neighborhood in 1913 and 1914; shown here is Edward Street, looking to the east from its intersection with Eighty-seventh Avenue West. Author's collection; copy available at Northwest Architectural Archives, Morell and Nichols papers.

Figure 4.7. After crews completed the grading of the eastern neighborhood, concrete was used to pave the streets and sidewalks and to construct curbs and steps; here the men are paving a section of Eighty-eighth Avenue West. Author's collection; copy available at Northwest Architectural Archives, Morell and Nichols papers.

engineers were among the first in the country to use "one-course concrete" for curb and sidewalk construction. Rather than forming the base of typical "lean" concrete, which employed a rich course of cement and sand only as topping, the Morgan Park formula used a single base of concrete that provided sufficient surface mortar for increased strength and "maximum resistance to wear."[15]

The eastern neighborhood plan displayed four parallel north-south streets, and four perpendicular east-west avenues. All single-family houses were located around the periphery of the neighborhood, while the multi-family dwellings were placed at the center and along Morgan Park's primary entrance drive. The majority of residences were set back thirty feet from the street, with an equal distance separating most dwelling units from their neighbors. Wherever feasible, the houses were sited as close as possible to their northern lot lines so as to "offer the maximum amount of space on its south side for the growth of flowers, grass and shrubbery." Sufficient space was also available at the rear of each housing unit for a kitchen garden.[16]

The grading plans and design details for the streets, boulevards, and front yards that Arthur Nichols prepared and supervised reflected the professional training he had received in both landscape architecture and civil engineering at the Massachusetts Institute of Technology. Nichols certainly was well versed in the utilitarian properties of road engineering—grading, paving, alignment, profiles, cross sections, drainage, and maintenance—but he gave greatest attention to the aesthetic and landscape design features of roadways. As Nichols once stated, highway and roadway planning required consideration of "certain definite landscape objectives, all of which would bring construction more closely into harmony with the total terrain."[17]

Nichols's proposals for the residential blocks often incorporated turf-covered, sloped terraces and lawns that reflected the site's natural contours—especially the steep grades that overlooked Spirit Lake (Figures 4.8, 4.9). Today, the terraces and lawns are basically intact and remain as distinctive landscape features.

The "parked town" appearance of the neighborhood was further enhanced by the planting plan. The landscape architects retained many of the existing trees, and also recommended "a thorough planting scheme of [additional] trees and shrubs throughout the community." All together, the proposal called for the planting of 1,500 trees and 5,000 shrubs. The conifers in the planting list included balsam fir, white spruce, Colorado blue spruce, dwarf mountain pine, white pine, and American arborvitae, while the deciduous specimens included sugar maple, cut-leaved maple, white birch, wild blackberry, American ash, Lombardy poplar, Carolina poplar, American mountain ash, and American elm. The plan also called for thirty-nine varieties of deciduous shrubs, six types of bush roses, and six different species of vines.[18]

To make "the place a beauty spot," about one hundred men began leveling, grading, and seeding the neighborhood's lawns, terraces, and boulevards in April 1915. Once it was realized that no single nursery could provide the 5,000 shrubs and 1,500 trees, the orders were spread out among numerous suppliers. The largest shrub groupings were placed in trenches, with the individual trees being planted in holes dug in the terraces between the sidewalks and streets. Duluth's newspapers commented favorably on the improvements made from 1913 through 1915, noting that the "barren

Figure 4.8. Landscape architect Arthur Nichols prepared and supervised the grading plans that were developed for the terraces and sloped lawns in several areas of Morgan Park, most notably this section of Eighty-fourth Avenue West, looking north, in August 1916. Courtesy of Northeast Minnesota Historical Center, S2366B7f2.

spot on top of the hill overlooking the river" had become "one of the most desirable places in the city" (Figure 4.10).[19]

Outside of Duluth, a writer for *Illustrated World* (the predecessor of today's *Popular Science* magazine) said that at Morgan Park U.S. Steel had "wandered out into the wilderness, made a little clearing, and established a complete, self-contained community." R. V. Sawhill of the *Iron Trade Review* was enthusiastic about Morgan Park's landscape features. "Excellent work by the landscape architects has enhanced its natural beauty," he reported in September 1915, "and the use of wide, winding boulevards, lined with rows of maple, elm and ash trees will in a few years make the streets resemble natural parkways." Charles MacKintosh, writing in the Minnesota State Art Commission's journal, was even more laudatory: "With all this

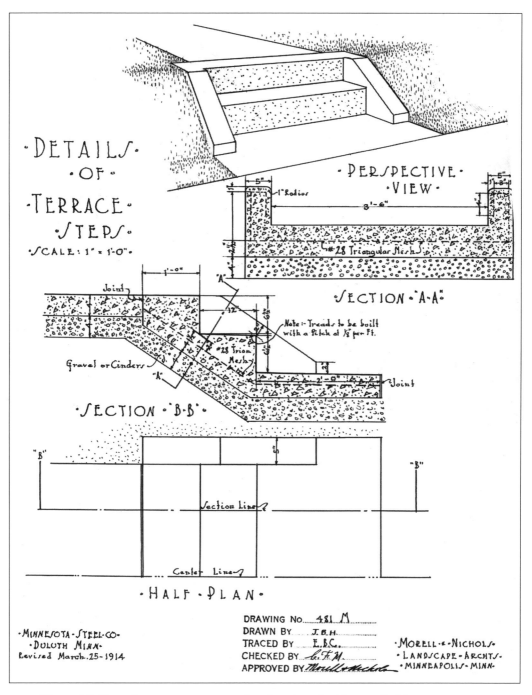

·DETAILS·
·OF·
·TERRACE·
·STEPS·
·SCALE: 1" = 1'-0"·

·PERSPECTIVE·
·VIEW·

1" Radius
3'-6"
5"
5"
#28 Triangular Mesh

·SECTION·A-A·

Joint
1'-0"
12"
Note: Treads to be built with a Pitch at ⅛ per Ft.
#28 Trian. Mesh.
Gravel or Cinders
"A"
1'-0"
Joint

·SECTION·B-B·

"B"
"B"
Section Line
Center Line

·HALF·PLAN·

·MINNESOTA·STEEL·CO·
·DULUTH·MINN·
Revised March.25-1914

DRAWING No. 481 M
DRAWN BY J.B.H.
TRACED BY E.B.C.
CHECKED BY C.F.M.
APPROVED BY Morell & Nichols

·MORELL·&·NICHOLS·
·LANDSCAPE·ARCHTS·
·MINNEAPOLIS·MINN·

Figure 4.9. One of numerous construction drawings for Morgan Park's terrace steps, prepared under the supervision of Arthur Nichols. Courtesy of Northwest Architectural Archives, Morell and Nichols papers.

Figure 4.10. Once the basic features of the planting plan were evident, observers praised the design skills of landscape architects Morell and Nichols. The wires on Eighty-eighth Avenue West were for electrically powered streetcars; the photograph, looking south, was taken in August 1916. Courtesy of Northeast Minnesota Historical Center, S2366B7f2.

greenery—sloping lawns, twining vines, ambitious shrubs and trees—and with its curving and well paved streets, avenues and boulevards, the little community soon will have the appearance of an old New England village rather than of a very young and very new Western townlet!"[20]

George and Arthur Dean: Architects of Industrial Housing

All of Morgan Park's housing, as well as most of the community buildings, were designed by the Chicago architectural firm of Dean and Dean. George Robinson Dean (1864–1919), the principal partner, began his career in the Chicago office of Shelpley, Rutan, and Coolidge, a Boston-based architectural firm. In 1893 he joined his brother, engineer Arthur Randall Dean (1869–1949), forming a partnership that was headquartered in Chicago's

Steinway Hall. For several years thereafter, George Dean interacted with Frank Lloyd Wright, one of the nation's most prestigious architects. Wright, in fact, referred to the "comradeship" he enjoyed with George Dean and several other young Chicago designers who were then engaged in creating architecture that might become the "New School [i.e., style] of the Middle West."[21]

In 1906, the Dean and Dean firm received a commission from the Gary Land Company to prepare residential designs for a subdivision associated with the U.S. Steel manufacturing complex then under construction along northwestern Indiana's Lake Michigan sand dunes. As they would do at Morgan Park seven years later, the architects developed prototypical designs for several house types at Gary, most characterized by their Prairie-style features: wide eaves, broad gables, low-pitched roofs, and banks of windows (see Figure I.3). Shortly after George Dean's unexpected death of pneumonia in late 1920, the *Western Architect* of Chicago gave him special credit for his residential design work at Gary. The journal commended Dean, saying that instead of following "the previous common practice of building rows of shacks, all on the same plan and design," he had "introduced an individuality of design and a town plan in arrangement that has since set the pace for similar erections throughout the country." The architectural practice continued to operate until 1922, which allowed Arthur Dean and the firm's employees to complete their contractual work at Morgan Park.[22]

The ABCs of Housing: All Built of Concrete

George Dean visited Duluth in late May 1913, and during June and July he and his employees, who were sequestered in Duluth's Wolvin Building, finalized proposals for Morgan Park's first housing units. By August plans were in place for 170 residential buildings that included 350 housing units. (Structural inadequacies later led to the razing of one single-family unit.) Apparently the firm completed its Morgan Park work so quickly by adapting some of the earlier designs that had been developed for Gary, Indiana.[23]

Although the residential designs for several houses at both Gary and Morgan Park were similar, there were some differences in the building materials used at the two locations. Frame, brick, concrete, and stucco predominated at Gary, whereas the majority of Morgan Park's houses were constructed of concrete blocks, with stucco often applied to the exterior surfaces. The *Duluth Herald* quickly gave its approval to the housing proposals for Morgan Park, reporting that "the construction is to be thoroughly modern . . . and the variety of construction promises to prevent monotony."[24]

Building with Hydro-Stone at Morgan Park

The mass production of concrete blocks in North America began in 1900, the year that Harmon Palmer received a patent for the invention of a cast-iron machine for fabricating the blocks. Prior to this time masonry homes were considered too expensive for moderate-income people, but once the molding machines became available, concrete blocks were touted as a building material that might allow everyone to live in a masonry residence. By 1907 at least one hundred firms were producing similar machines, and in 1910, over one thousand companies were manufacturing concrete blocks in the United States and Canada.[25]

Concrete blocks were fashionable for several reasons, but primarily because they offered "a cheap, quick, and easy alternative to more traditional materials." By the 1930s, however, their popularity had declined. The masons who lifted and laid the blocks, which could weigh as much as one hundred pounds apiece, often found them prohibitively heavy; furthermore, the introduction of relatively inexpensive masonry veneering during the 1920s meant that builders could cover a wood-frame house with a thin outer layer of brick or stone. The widespread use of cinder blocks, which also appeared during the 1920s, provided a lightweight replacement for blocks made of concrete.[26]

By 1904–5, Duluthians were submitting numerous orders for concrete block residences. The city's building contractors and residents continued to assess the possibilities of concrete-block construction over the next several years, though it was only at Morgan Park where they could observe an entire town being built of the material.[27]

In July 1913 the Minnesota Steel Company issued a call to building contractors, asking them to bid on Morgan Park's first 170 concrete-block residential buildings. Responses arrived from points as distant as Chicago, New York, and Pittsburgh, but Duluth contractor George Lounsberry received the contract for the project, which approached one million dollars.[28]

The concrete blocks were formed at the construction site with a hand-operated machine developed and marketed by the Hydro-Stone Company of Chicago (Figure 4.11). Hydro-Stone blocks were T-shaped, which meant they could be used to construct either "one-piece" or "two-piece" walls (Figure 4.12). When used in a one-piece wall, the single projecting interior "lug" on each block acted like a concrete stud, to which furring and lath could be attached, followed by the application of fiber plaster. A two-piece wall, formed by two rows of staggered and reversed double-lugged blocks that faced inward to create continuous hollow chambers within the wall, offered

Figure 4.11. The Hydro-Stone Company of Chicago, as revealed by this 1920 advertisement, highlighted the concrete blocks that its machines had fabricated for the construction of Morgan Park's buildings. From Harvey Whipple, ed., Concrete Houses: How They Were Built *(Detroit: Concrete-Cement Age Publishing Company, 1920).*

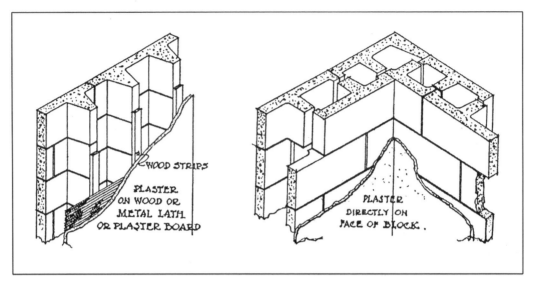

Figure 4.12. The Hydro-Stone Company illustrated how its concrete blocks could be employed to form one- and two-piece block walls. Adapted from Whipple, Concrete Houses.

a smooth surface on both exposed sides that could then be covered directly with plaster or stucco. The basements for the first group of houses in Morgan Park's eastern neighborhood were built using two-piece walls set on concrete footings situated five and one-half to six feet below grade line, while the upper floors were constructed of one-piece exterior walls (Figure 4.13).[29]

The workers who produced blocks at Morgan Park's construction site shoveled Portland cement, sand, water, and gravel or stone aggregate into the Hydro-Stone machine; after the material was tamped down, a lever was tripped to release the newly formed block. The blocks were stacked in a curing shed, then sprinkled with water for several weeks as they dried. Overall, 700,000 blocks were produced for the first group of houses.[30]

Constructing an entire neighborhood of uniformly colored and textured concrete blocks might have given Morgan Park the appearance of a place filled with concrete boxes, but early observers gave the community's appearance high marks (Figure 4.14). The *Illustrated World* offered a straightforward compliment, noting that "the houses do not look as though they had been made by machinery," whereas concrete expert Harvey Whipple was more effusive, terming the Hydro-Stone blocks used at Morgan Park "distinctive" because they offered "a feeling for architectural uses" and provided an "attractive surface for finished wall surfaces." Likewise, the

Figure 4.13. A one-piece concrete block wall for a residence under construction in the eastern neighborhood, September 15, 1915. Photograph by Albert Solomon. Courtesy of Northeast Minnesota Historical Center, S2366, vol. 4.

American Architect identified Morgan Park as a community of "considerable interest," given that concrete blocks and stucco had been employed throughout the community. The journal noted that the use of a single material at Morgan Park had not resulted "in the monotony usual in most instances," but actually provided considerable variety—"and the whole esthetic result is much to be commended."[31]

Residential Designs

From August 1913 to August 1915, as many as six hundred men employed by the Lounsberry Company carried out the full range of tasks associated with home-building activities in the eastern neighborhood. After the crews laid

Figure 4.14. An overview of Morgan Park under construction in 1914 or 1915. Author's collection; copy available at Northwest Architectural Archives, Morell and Nichols papers.

the concrete block walls, they poured solid concrete floors and covered them with hardwood flooring, applied plaster and tinting to interior surfaces, framed doors and windows, finished rooms with birch trim, constructed rafters and ceiling joists, creosoted and applied cedar shingles to the roofs, wired and plumbed rooms, and painted doors, windows, and baseboards. Twenty dwellings were ready for occupancy by March 1914, with the first residents moving into the community on the last day of the month. Most of the 349 units would be occupied by late 1916 and early 1917.[32]

The Dean and Dean firm provided a total of thirteen different designs for the first single-family and multifamily structures that emerged in Morgan Park (Figure 4.15). The seventy-nine single-family dwellings included thirty houses that had five rooms, thirty-nine with six rooms, and ten with eight rooms. The ninety multifamily buildings (270 dwelling units) included fifty-five duplexes (110 units) and ten structures with four apartments (40 units), each with four or five rooms; fifteen four-family row houses (60 units) with four rooms; and ten six-family row houses (60 units) with five rooms.[33]

House Type	Structures	Rooms/Unit	Dwelling Units
Single Family	30	5	30
Single Family	39	6	39
Single Family	10	8	10
Duplex	20	4	40
Duplex	35	5	70
Fourplex	10	4/5	40
Four-Unit Row House	15	4	60
Six-Unit Row House	10	4	60
Total	169	4.7	349

Figure 4.15. Houses completed in Morgan Park's eastern neighborhood, 1913–17. From Leiffur Magnusson, "A Modern Industrial Suburb," Monthly Review of the U.S. Bureau of Labor Statistics 6 (April 1918).

Single-Family Dwellings

Nine different designs were developed for the seventy-nine single-family residences that materialized in Morgan Park from 1913 to 1915. Six of the nine, however, represented three pairs of plans with reversed floor layouts. Several features typically associated with Prairie School designs distinguished the structures. "The houses were clean, modern, integrated family units," stated one observer very familiar with the Dean and Dean firm. "[O]pen rooms and generous banks of windows completed the simple, unified character of each house, while family living areas flowed into each other eliminating dark, wasteful hallways."[34] Even though the house plans were rather simple rectangular boxes, their pitched roofs, broad gables, and wide eves gave further indication of Prairie-style influences.

Casual observers probably did not realize that a rather limited palette of house plans was used at Morgan Park. The designers offered an impression of architectural variety by alternating different house types along the community's streets; another observer stated that the apparent diversity occurred because "only one [house] of a given pattern can be seen from any one point of view" (Figures 4.16, 4.17). The overall architectural result was praised in a 1915 metal workers' journal, which commented that when considering "external arrangement there is sufficient variation in size, in the contour of roofs, the staining of shingles and arrangement of porches to

Figure 4.16. Architectural variety was provided along the roadways of Morgan Park's eastern neighborhood by alternating housing types, roofline forms, and the size and style of entry porches. Shown here, in July 1917, is a view of Eighty-sixth Avenue West, looking south of its intersection with Edward Street. Courtesy of Northeast Minnesota Historical Center, S2366B7f2, photograph 15256.

Figure 4.17. Floor plans for the smallest detached residence in Morgan Park, identified as house type 15. Adapted from Magnusson, "A Modern Industrial Suburb"; redrafted by Kassie Martine.

dissipate that monotony of appearance characteristic to a large number of homes of similar floor plan."[35]

The thirty five-room houses were based on four designs, though in reality these were two paired plans. Pronounced saltbox roofs and an open veranda that spanned the entire front facade distinguished the simplest pair, both identified as plan 15 (Figures 4.18, 4.19). The front entrance opened into a small vestibule that offered access to the living room as well as to the stairs leading up to the second floor. Behind the living room were the dining room and a kitchen and pantry. A small covered porch was attached to the rear of the house. The second floor had two bedrooms, a bathroom, and three closets. These houses, and all of the single-family residences, had full basements that offered space for a furnace, laundry facilities, and storage.[36]

Two other "twinned" designs, 15-E and 15-F, were also used for several five-room single-family houses (Figure 4.20). Each plan was virtually square in form, with either an open veranda or an enclosed porch spanning most of the front facade. The vestibule provided access to a small reception and stair hall that offered access to the living room on one side and the kitchen at the back of the house. Archways connected the hall and living room, as well as the dining and living rooms; the fireplace was placed at a forty-five-degree angle within the living room. A pantry and porch extended to the rear of the kitchen. Two large bedrooms, along with a bathroom and several closets, composed the second floor.[37]

The thirty-nine single-family houses with six rooms followed either a 16-E, 16-F, 16-G, or 16-H plan; again, 16-E and 16-F were reversed layouts, as were 16-G and 16-H. The floor plans for 16-E and 16-F were basically square, whereas plans 16-G and 16-H were rectangular. All included a porch—either a full front, portico front, or a two-thirds front—facing the street (Figures 4.21, 4.22). The first-floor layouts were relatively similar to those for 15-E and 15-F, but their somewhat larger dimensions provided second-floor space for one additional bedroom. The dwellings displayed either a hip or gable roof, with some having a jerkinhead form (a gable end that was "clipped" at an angle). Stucco was applied to the upper-floor exteriors of several residences.[38]

The ten eight-room houses built in Morgan Park followed one of three plans identified as 18-D, 18-F, and 18-H. The most common type, 18-H, was a two-story bungalow with a sloping gable roof and a front dormer. The roof that faced the street sloped downward to the first floor, whereas the back roof only covered the second floor. The large roof overhang and pronounced roof slope gave these dwellings an especially pronounced Prairie-style appearance.[39]

Figure 4.18. One example of house type 15 displayed a distinctive saltbox roof, 1917. From "Morgan Park, Minn.: An Industrial Suburb for the Minnesota Steel Company—Dean and Dean, Architects," American Architect 113 (June 1918).

Figure 4.19. The appearance of house type 15 could be changed quite noticeably by modifying the roof forms, ca. 1917. From "Morgan Park, Minn."

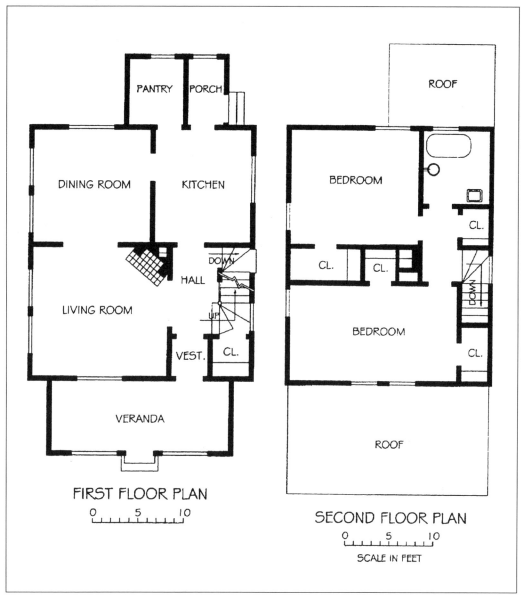

FIRST FLOOR PLAN

PANTRY PORCH

DINING ROOM   KITCHEN

HALL

DOWN

LIVING ROOM

UP

VEST.   CL.

VERANDA

0   5   10

SECOND FLOOR PLAN

ROOF

BEDROOM

CL.

CL.   CL.

DOWN

BEDROOM

CL.

ROOF

0   5   10
SCALE IN FEET

Figure 4.20. House type 15-E had five rooms but somewhat more interior space than type 15. Adapted from Morgan Park Company, The New Houses in Morgan Park *(Duluth: Morgan Park Company, 1917). Courtesy of State Historic Preservation Office, Minnesota Historical Society; redrafted by Tamara Larson.*

Figure 4.21. Elevations and floor plans for house type 16-F, a six-room residence. Adapted from James Alexander Robinson, The Life and Work of Harry Franklin Robinson, 1883–1959 *(Hong Kong: Hilross Devel. Ltd., 1989). Copy provided courtesy of Northeast Minnesota Historical Center; redrafted by Robert Gerloff.*

Figure 4.22. Elevations and floor plans for house type 16-G, a six-room residence. Adapted from Robinson, The Life and Work of Harry Franklin Robinson; *redrafted by Robert Gerloff.*

Multifamily Dwellings

The multifamily dwellings included duplexes, four-unit apartment buildings, and row houses. The fifty-five duplexes (110 units) formed the largest grouping. Twenty duplex buildings, plans 24-A and 24-B, had units with four rooms each, while thirty-five structures, plans 25-A and 25-B, incorporated five rooms. Rectangular in form and two stories high, each building had a basement. The first floor of both the four- and five-room units were designed with a living room, kitchen, and rear porch; the second floor of the five-room units had three bedrooms, one more than the four-room residences. All duplexes had a gable roof pierced by two prominent chimneys (Figure 4.23). Located at the corner of each front facade was a portico, supported by two concrete piers, which covered the entrance to both duplex units. A flat deck and balustrade marked the second level.[40]

The design for the ten four-unit apartment buildings, identified as plan 445-A, provided forty dwelling units. Square in plan, each building had two units with four rooms, and two with five rooms. The exteriors revealed a

Figure 4.23. This duplex, with four rooms per unit, is distinguished by its entry porticos and second-floor balustrade, 1917. From "Morgan Park, Minn."

pronounced hip roof, four chimneys, and a central ventilation shaft. The entrance porticoes, placed at the center of the front entrance, had large concrete piers that supported a two-story porch (Figure 4.24).[41]

Rounding out the array of multifamily structures were twenty-five rowhouse buildings with a total of 120 dwelling units. Fifteen buildings (plan 44-A) had four independent side-by-side units with four rooms each: a living room and a kitchen/dining room on the first floor, and two bedrooms and a bathroom on the second (Figures 4.25, 4.26). Two sloping roofs, each covering two units, extended over the front porches of the building; the rear porches were of similar design. The most prominent feature of these buildings was the dominant central gable, which punctuated the roof of the front facade. The ten row house buildings with six units each (plan 62-A) also exhibited an accentuated central roof gable, but had three rather than two front and back porches. Because of the linear form of the row houses, Morgan Park's residents called them "sheepsheds."[42]

Figure 4.24. The apartment buildings with four units, as seen here about 1917, are still identified by their massive two-story entry porches, four chimneys, and a central ventilation shaft. From "Morgan Park, Minn."

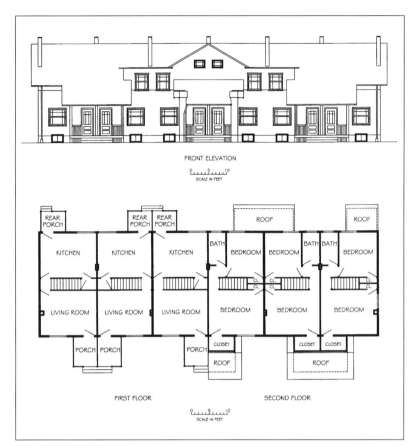

FRONT ELEVATION

SCALE IN FEET

REAR PORCH | REAR PORCH | REAR PORCH

KITCHEN | KITCHEN | KITCHEN

BATH | BEDROOM | BEDROOM | BATH BATH | BEDROOM

ROOF | ROOF

LIVING ROOM | LIVING ROOM | LIVING ROOM | BEDROOM | BEDROOM | BEDROOM

CL. CL. | CL. CL. | CL. CL.

PORCH PORCH | PORCH | CLOSET | CLOSET CLOSET

ROOF | ROOF

FIRST FLOOR | SECOND FLOOR

SCALE IN FEET

Figure 4.25. Floor plans and front elevation for a six-unit row house, each with four rooms. Three first-floor units are depicted on the left, while three second-floor units are on the right. Adapted from Magnusson, "A Modern Industrial Suburb"; redrafted by Kassie Martine.

Figure 4.26. View of a four-unit row house, ca. 1917. From "Morgan Park, Minn."

Residential Dormitories and Other Buildings

Besides the family residential units, several other structures were evident in Morgan Park at the time of the December 1915 steel plant opening. Among these buildings were four concrete-block boardinghouses, all constructed by the George Lounsberry Company for a total of $20,000. Separated from the residential area by a transverse alley and fence, the four buildings initially housed seventy-four clerical and technical workers, most of them unmarried. Collectively known as the Nenovan Club (or "NE-no-van"), the largest building was a three-story structure with forty-four rooms (Figure 4.27). The other three, all two stories high, had eighteen, eleven, and eight rooms respectively; later, the smallest building would be designated for female employees.[43]

A complex gable/jerkinhead roof and six jerkinhead dormers capped the largest building, which was T-shaped in plan; a wood-frame entrance portico provided access to the structure. Two of the other dormitories had a centrally positioned wood-frame entry portico; a gable roof topped one of these buildings, whereas the other utilized a hip roof with dormers. No in-

Figure 4.27. The three-story Nenovan boarding house, viewed from the northwest in 1918. Courtesy of Northeast Minnesota Historical Center, B7f5, photograph 15050.

formation is available about the smallest dormitory, which was demolished in 1935–36.[44]

The first floor of the main dormitory had two rows of sleeping rooms placed along a central corridor, and separate quarters for the manager (Figure 4.28). A kitchen and general dining room accommodated the Nenovan's tenants, as well as roomers who lived in private homes. The kitchen and dining room also served as a restaurant where other residents of Morgan Park could order meals. Two years after the Nenovan opened, a Duluth realtor claimed that its facilities should be called "club rooming houses," not boardinghouses. Especially impressed by the dining opportunities, the realtor exclaimed, "the men are not in their rooms between meals, but live as they would in any private club." Similarly, a new resident of the Nenovan Club described his accommodation as "a warm, light room, immaculately clean, with good looking furniture," and affordable at a price he "had learned to think was entirely out of style."[45]

The administrative building for Minnesota Steel, which housed the company's main offices and laboratories, opened during the fall of 1915. Once again it was George Lounsberry who received the construction contract for the concrete-block and reinforced concrete structure, which cost $100,000

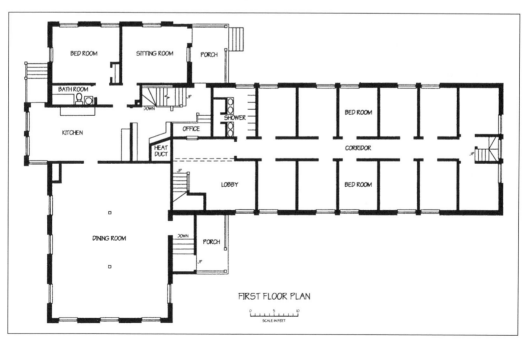

Figure 4.28. First-floor plan of the three-story Nenovan boarding house. Adapted from Magnusson, "A Modern Industrial Suburb"; redrafted by Robert Gerloff.

Figure 4.29. The administrative operations and laboratory functions of the Minnesota Steel Company were located in the large administrative building, shown here on April 5, 1915, a few months before its official opening. Courtesy of Northeast Minnesota Historical Center, S2366B7f6.

to build and equip (Figure 4.29). The imposing two-story 70-by-120-foot building was sited along the eastern side of Morgan Park's major entry road and just outside the steel-plant entry gates.[46]

Since the school building would not open until late 1916, as many as one hundred elementary students were taught in one of the residential duplexes for almost two years. Junior and senior high students attended school in New Duluth. Excavations for the hospital commenced in October 1915, and a small postal station opened in early November.[47]

Early Residents and Sojourners

Morgan Park's first residents, who moved in on March 30, 1914, were steel plant brick works superintendent John McLimans, his Canadian-born wife, Emmy, and their four daughters. They were quickly followed by several other families, including electric power supervisor Charles Sampson, his wife, Mary, and their two children; assistant timekeeper James Aird and his wife, Margaret; and police chief Albert Solomon, his wife, Ida, and their three children, two of whom also worked at the steel plant.[48]

The estimated two to three hundred people who occupied sixty houses by May 1914 were supplemented by a "big influx" of fifty families who arrived one month later. An even larger contingent of some one hundred "skilled mechanics" and their families were scheduled to move from Duluth to Morgan Park in October 1915, but their arrival was delayed for a few weeks because of virtually impassable local road conditions. As 1915 drew to a close, Morgan Park's population approached six hundred people.[49]

In June 1915, when a group of state politicians visited Morgan Park, they viewed the steel plant's "great buildings and furnaces," as well as the "fashionable new residence section." Few Duluthians, however, had been able to visit the model town while it was under construction. To acquaint citizens with the incipient community, Duluth's Commercial Club arranged an August 1915 excursion on the tour boat *Columbia*. Although prospective sightseers were informed that visits to the steel plant would not be possible "because of the rush of preparation for its opening," they were assured that a trip to "a wonderful industrial village" was on the program. While there they would view "concrete block houses, paved streets and alleys, beautiful landscape gardening, and complete provision in all things for comfort and convenience." This trip, nevertheless, differed from the May 1911 visit when hundreds of men toured the steel plant construction site. The 1915 excursion served as an equal opportunity venture for everyone—"especially ladies" (Figure 4.30).[50]

The more than five hundred people who paid twenty-five cents each for the outing were amazed and pleased with what they observed. One

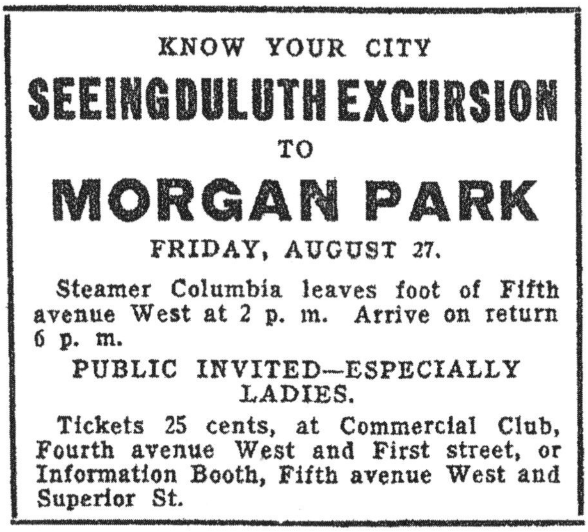

KNOW YOUR CITY

SEEING DULUTH EXCURSION

TO

MORGAN PARK

FRIDAY, AUGUST 27.

Steamer Columbia leaves foot of Fifth avenue West at 2 p. m. Arrive on return 6 p. m.

PUBLIC INVITED—ESPECIALLY LADIES.

Tickets 25 cents, at Commercial Club, Fourth avenue West and First street, or Information Booth, Fifth avenue West and Superior St.

Figure 4.30. Duluth's women were encouraged to tour Morgan Park in August 1915. From Duluth News Tribune, *August 26, 1915.*

woman proclaimed Morgan Park's well-constructed houses, paved streets, and highly maintained lawns were like those of "a fashionable residence addition," while another believed the apartments were an improvement over those in downtown Duluth. Two months later seven St. Paul officials spent a day inspecting Morgan Park. Upon completing the tour, Mayor Winn Powers stated that he had "never before seen anything to compare with this." It was the "entire housing scheme," along with the "careful thought and exhaustive analysis" given to all facets of community development, which were most impressive to Powers. To him it was "almost impossible" that all of the development had occurred within the span of just two years.[51]

Additional construction would occur in Morgan Park over the next seven years, but by the end of 1915, the community displayed many of the outward trappings of a model company town: a clearly articulated plan, well-designed and constructed housing, extensive landscape design treatments, modern sanitary services, and an emerging group of community buildings. It was, proclaimed one Duluth publication, a place that had "none of the squatters' shacks, goat alleys and poverty streets, tenements and two-shift boarding houses, incident to some large manufacturing industries." Much more subtle, however, were the management policies, some probably only vaguely understood by people not associated with Morgan Park. One important practice was explained to the five hundred Duluthians who toured the community in August, namely, that not a single house in Morgan Park could be sold because "steel company officials want the model city for their employees, alone." Otherwise, predicted the officials, the houses "might get into the hands of men who would [then] exact exorbitant rentals from the workmen."[52] Ownership of the housing stock would, in fact, remain as the most evident facet of corporate control at Morgan Park for almost thirty more years.

PART II

Working and Living in Morgan Park, 1916–1929

Even the steel mill on the high ground beyond the intervening valley, its tall stacks rising against an unfamiliar background, is a picture that would yield much to the stroke of Pennell's crayon.

—*Iron Age* 97, January 6, 1916

This is certainly a clean place.

—Comments by delegates from the Minnesota League of Municipalities when visiting Morgan Park in 1916

5. STABILITY AND PROSPERITY FOR U.S. STEEL

Despite its relatively small size and isolated location, the steel plant at Morgan Park was influenced by numerous events that played out on a national and global stage from 1916 through 1929. The period began with millions of European troops engaged in seemingly endless and senseless trench warfare, and concluded almost a decade and a half later with a world poised on the edge of a major economic depression. The first three years of the plant's existence, from 1916 through 1918, were characterized by high employment and production figures that would not be approached until another war engulfed the world a quarter century later. Steel output throughout the 1920s was not quite as gaudy as what had been experienced during the initial years of manufacturing activity, and the early part of the decade even included a brief period when the entire facility was shut down because of a nationwide economic recession. Overall, however, the 1920s were a period of relative stability and prosperity for Morgan Park and Duluth.

Manufacturing Armaments during Wartime

At the dawn of 1916, Minnesota Steel's recently opened but still unfinished plant remained a beehive of activity. It now employed 1,735 men in manufacturing activities and an additional 75 in the office and laboratory. Since the merchant mill remained under construction, the steel plant's billets and blooms were shipped to Gary, Indiana, and Joliet, Illinois. Meanwhile, the "blowing in" of the second blast furnace at Morgan Park occurred on February 19, 1916, an event marked by a ceremony that saw master mechanic Louis Reis apply a small torch to some oil-soaked wood and coke placed inside the new unit. (Reis quickly made his way up the ranks of the Minnesota Steel Company, eventually serving as president for almost five years.) After this symbolic occasion, cigars were distributed among the blast-furnace workers, who then cheered the company officials in charge of the project. Pig iron production also increased when the number of functioning open-hearth furnaces expanded from four to eight between January and May, and eventually to ten over subsequent months. The *Iron Age*, which

typically limited its discussions and articles to technical and engineering issues, was uncharacteristically effusive when describing the manufacturing
plant's early appearance: "The steel mill on the high ground beyond the
intervening valley," enthused the journal, "its tall stacks rising against an
unfamiliar background, is a picture that would yield much to the strokes of
Pennell's crayon."[1]

In early 1916, financial analysts anticipated that the Duluth works would
"soon become an important factor in the corporation's organization"; despite the optimistic prognostications, the production of blooms was delayed
for several weeks when a power plant engine exploded into pieces, narrowly
missing several workers. Machinists from the Allis-Chalmers Company in
the Milwaukee area quickly arrived at Morgan Park, where they made patterns of the destroyed parts that were then fabricated in their Wisconsin
factory. By early May, Minnesota Steel was putting out some 1,200 tons of
steel per day.[2]

Even though most of the plant was completed by May, Duluth officials
insisted that Minnesota Steel submit an application for a supplementary
building permit, "in order to have the building records show a complete
and accurate account of all improvements in the city." The city granted
the $7 million permit quickly. The merchant mill finally opened in June
1916, which meant that blooms and billets could now be converted locally
into bars, flats, rounds, and squares (Figure 5.1). The output was used by
American manufacturing firms, many engaged in the production of military ships, vehicles and ammunition. The British and French governments
were ordering rails, refrigerator cars, and boxcars made in America, and
European military forces consumed large quantities of steel armaments, especially shrapnel. The *Washington Post*'s earlier prediction that the Duluth
plant would turn out "steel bullets" for the war effort was confirmed later
in 1916, when its entire output was purchased for use in Europe. Significant
amounts of iron ore were consumed during this period; approximately
582,000 tons were shipped to the Morgan Park plant in 1916, followed by
704,000 tons in 1917.[3]

Situated just southwest of the steel manufacturing complex, and opening
in 1916, was the Universal Portland Cement Company plant, a facility that
converted slag generated by the steel-making process into cement. When
the fourth kiln was completed in mid-September, the plant's 350 to 400 employees could turn out 4,000 barrels of cement daily. "We can ship every
barrel that we produce," reported Ray Huey, the general superintendent of
the unit until his retirement in early 1943. An electrical engineer with a de-

Figure 5.1. The steel plant, sometime between 1915 and 1920. Photograph by Kurt Florman; courtesy of Karin Hertel McGinnis (copy available at Northeast Minnesota Historical Center, S2386B14f21).

gree from the Illinois Institute of Technology, Huey termed his facility "the acme of the art of cement making." It included the region's first "electrical precipitating devices," which supposedly reduced the "dust nuisance" that the production process generated.[4]

Visitors continued to inspect the plant during the summer of 1916, including two professors and six Chinese students from the Massachusetts Institute of Technology who "watched the process of steel manufacture." Five hundred people attending the Minnesota Retail Grocers Association convention in Duluth toured Morgan Park in July. The two hundred women convention-goers were entertained and given tours of the community, and each received a bouquet of flowers during the visit. The three hundred men were divided into groups of fifty, each group led by two guides "who managed to keep the crowd well together."[5]

In June 1917, residents from throughout the Duluth-Superior region marked the opening of the automobile section of the bridge that connected Wisconsin and Minnesota. Despite the rainy day, which made the roads muddy and almost impassable in some places, many people drove their automobiles on a circuit that started in Duluth and continued to Morgan Park and Gary, then over the new bridge to Oliver, South Superior, and Superior before returning to Duluth via the Interstate Bridge that connected the two cities. One month later Oliver and Superior residents organized a bridge celebration that featured decorations and a wire-walking exhibition, all of which attracted more than one thousand people, who participated "in song, dance and general good fellowship." By November Oliver's boosters were asserting that within a year their community would "throw off the swaddling clothes of a village and enter into the sisterhood of cities."[6]

Locating and Managing a Labor Force during Wartime

At the beginning of 1916, Minnesota Steel determined that 697 (40 percent) of the 1,735 workers it employed in manufacturing operations had been born in the United States. The 1,038 foreign-born men included 356 "old immigrants" from those areas of Western and Northern Europe (and Canada) where migration began during the early to mid-nineteenth century. This group of steelworkers consisted of 117 Swedes, 70 Canadians, 49 Norwegians, 49 Britons, 30 Germans, 22 Irish, and 19 men from four other countries. The 687 "new immigrants," on the other hand, were from areas of Eastern and Southern Europe that contributed significantly to the waves of people who arrived in the United States from the 1890s to 1914. The 440 South Slavs formed the largest group—185 identified as "Austrians" or "Slavs," 121 as Croatians, 48 as Slovenians, 27 as Serbians, 26 as Bosnians, 18 as Montenegrins, and 15 as Dalmatians. Following the South Slavs were 72 Italians, 45 Russians, 42 Poles, 27 Greeks, 21 Hungarians, 19 Finns, and 21 men representing five other nationalities.[7]

The jobs performed by the men were strongly correlated with their ethnic backgrounds. Of the 357 men employed in the blast and open-hearth furnaces and the coke ovens—the most difficult and dangerous jobs at the plant—only 9 percent were old immigrants, 28 percent were of American birth, and 63 percent were new immigrants. The South Slavs alone filled four of every ten of these jobs. Another 492 men worked as common laborers in the steel plant yard; 266 (54 percent) were new immigrants, 116 (24 percent) were American-born men, and 110 (22 percent) were old immigrants.

Of the remaining 896 steel plant workers—many of whom held skilled and semiskilled jobs in the electrical department, machine shop, rolling mill, and on-site office—467 (55 percent) were born in America, while the remaining 408 workers (45 percent) were divided almost equally between old and new immigrants.[8]

The war years from 1916 to 1918 were characterized by a nationwide shortage of workers, which meant that Minnesota Steel officials often experienced difficulties in securing an adequate labor force. As word of steel plant job opportunities spread, prospective laborers streamed to the facility from elsewhere in Minnesota, from other American states, and from Europe (Figure 5.2). As revealed by the composition of the total workforce in 1916, the largest contingent was made up of South Slavs, some of whom began arriving during the early phases of steel plant construction and settled

primarily in Gary and New Duluth. Other workers were recruited directly from other areas of the United States, including more than one hundred African Americans, many from the South, who began arriving later in 1916; they were viewed by Minnesota Steel officials as men willing to work for lower wages than white employees, and less likely to strike and join labor organizations.

Figure 5.2. During the early years of steel plant history, workers checked in and out of small employment "towers." Shown here, on March 17, 1921, is watchman George Comer. Courtesy of Northeast Minnesota Historical Center, S2366.

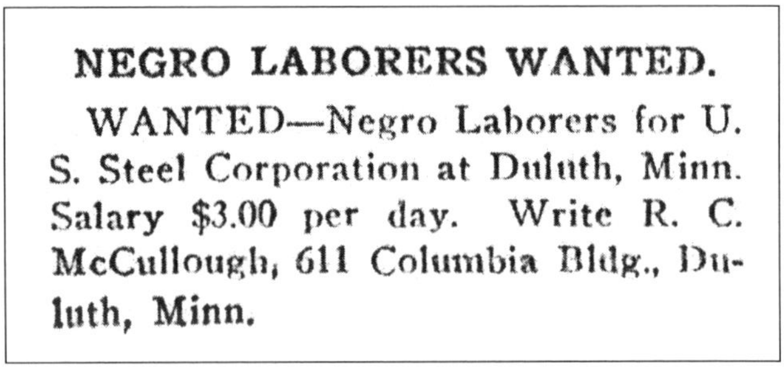

Figure 5.3. A Minneapolis African American newspaper included an advertisement for steelworkers in 1916. From Twin City Star *(Minneapolis), June 3, 1916.*

NEGRO LABORERS WANTED.

WANTED—Negro Laborers for U. S. Steel Corporation at Duluth, Minn. Salary $3.00 per day. Write R. C. McCullough, 611 Columbia Bldg., Duluth, Minn.

Other blacks made their way to Morgan Park after the *Twin City Star,* a Minneapolis African American newspaper, printed a brief June 1916 advertisement that noted "Negro laborers" could receive three dollars per day at the steel plant (Figure 5.3). Nine months later, when rumors circulated that more African Americans would be hired, a Minnesota Steel executive "emphatically denied" the report, stating that their numbers would remain steady.[9]

By November 1917, seven months after America's entry into the war, thirty-four former steel plant employees were serving in the armed forces, a number that grew over the subsequent year. Actually, as early as July Minnesota Steel officials were anticipating that a significant number of steelworkers would eventually leave for military service; therefore, they decided that hiring women for office work was "inevitable." From that point on, until the war's end sixteen months later, plans were made to hire as many as two hundred female office and clerical workers. Their superior performance would result in the continued employment of women as office employees for the remainder of the plant's existence. And twenty-five years later, during World War II, women would be employed in all facets of steel manufacturing.[10]

The battles of World War I may have been fought outside the United States, but the period is also noted for the domestic hysteria that led to hostile conditions for several groups and individuals. The teaching of German language and culture ended in many American schools by 1918, including those in Duluth. The city's teachers also had to sign a loyalty oath, which made each instructor "a special government informer of suspected treason either in the schools or in the vicinity of them."[11]

Even more onerous was the animosity experienced by people perceived to have radical, socialist, or pacifist sympathies. Some "slackers," a pejorative term applied to men who sought to avoid military service, received extremely brutal treatment, none more so than Olli Kuikkonen (often misspelled Kinkkonen), a Finnish immigrant who was tarred and feathered and then lynched in mid-September 1918 by a Duluth vigilante group, the

Knights of Labor. When his body was discovered in October, Duluth's coroner alleged that Kuikkonen had been shamed into committing suicide because he had earlier renounced his American citizenship. The *Duluth News Tribune* concurred, purporting that the "kindest thing" that could be done about the "Judas" who "went out and hanged himself" was to forget him.[12]

Another heinous act occurred less than two years later when a mob of several thousand frenzied men lynched three African American circus workers who had been accused of raping a white woman in Duluth. A 1979 assessment of the tragedy by Mike Fedo argued that the lynching was at least partially precipitated and carried out by white men from the western area of Duluth who resented U.S. Steel's importation of African American workers. Hudelson and Ross acknowledge the value of Fedo's study in unearthing and interpreting information about the incident and tragedy, but point out that other factors undoubtedly were more important than resentment over jobs. They conclude that the lynching was primarily a product of racism. With African Americans often regarded as "alien beings" in the nation's racial order, their position "left them vulnerable to injustices both violent and nonviolent."[13]

Adding fuel to the ill will of the times was the antisedition bill that Governor Jacob Burnquist proposed to the Minnesota Legislature in early 1917. Passed in April, the bill placed severe limitations on the activities of individuals and organizations deemed anti-American. Considered one of the most insidious legislative acts in state history, the bill authorized the creation of the Minnesota Commission of Public Safety, an institution that had unprecedented and virtually unrestricted authority to inflict conformity on ethnic populations. Because of its arduous and politically inflammatory powers, the commission was disbanded in late 1920.[14]

Since large numbers of foreign-born, nonnaturalized men were employed in industries such as steel production, many manufacturers feared that these workers might engage in seditious and destructive acts. In southwestern Duluth, where the largest number of the city's foreign-born population lived, immigrant groups and organizations were encouraged to participate in "patriotic parades," and were also encouraged to "impress the government with their patriotism" by signing resolutions that could be forwarded to President Woodrow Wilson. When thirty Serbians from Gary volunteered for service in their national army in May 1917, the men were feted at a banquet and accompanied to Duluth's railroad depot by a parade and band.[15]

Special "Americanization" programs were initiated in many industries, including the steel plant at Morgan Park. In February 1917 Minnesota Steel officials ordered all immigrant laborers who had not yet taken out their first citizenship papers to do so immediately. The directive was justified as a "precautionary" measure that would "insure the safety of the plant in case of hostilities with Germany and to protect in every measure possible contracts which are now being filled at the plant." Those workers who failed to obey the edict were informed they might "jeopardize their positions." The response was immediate. Over the next few days a "rush" of 158 employees filed citizenship applications with the Clerk of the District Court in Duluth; one steel plant official even claimed that 912 more workers would soon follow. At the steel plant itself, discussions of the war were forbidden, an action that supposedly met with "little or no personal friction among the men."[16]

Concerns about sabotage also led to the hiring of as many as twenty-five private detectives and watchmen, who guarded the steel plant's buildings, bridges, and rail lines "against any depredations that might be committed by reckless sympathizers of a foreign enemy." (More guards were stationed at Duluth's harbor and transportation facilities.) Minnesota Steel's guard force was expanded later in 1917, reportedly "to see that no German sympathizer or spy gets a chance to blow up the Morgan Park plant." Attired in military-like uniforms, the "highly paid and well-armed special agents" guarded the steel plant night and day, denying admittance to anyone not directly associated with Minnesota Steel's operations (Figure 5.4). In May a "self-appointed committee" of patriotic steelworkers secured donations for the purchase of a twenty-by-forty-foot American flag that they placed on a one-

Figure 5.4. Duluth News Tribune *cartoonist Ray D. Handy depicted the "opaque fence" that surrounded the steel plant during World War I and one of the armed guards who patrolled the grounds. From* Duluth News Tribune, *June 17, 1917.*

hundred-foot-tall pole located atop one of the plant buildings. Only some members of the workforce could observe the dedication, however, since the public was not allowed on the grounds. The residential community was also placed under guard during special events, such as the school dedication in March 1917. One woman who attended the ceremonies recalled that with "armed soldiers in and around the place everywhere . . . the whole air [was] charged with excitement and fear."[17]

Pittsburgh Plus Revisited

Many Duluthians believed that eventually several significant by-product manufacturing plants would emerge adjacent to the steel-production facility. Initially, however, U.S. Steel officials expressed little enthusiasm for any further expansion. Despite the great demand for steel during the war years, these officials still expressed concern over the "disappointing" nature of the plant's early production history. Economic historian-geographer Kenneth Warren has observed that the corporation decided not to pursue any immediate expansion because of the restricted demand for steel in the twelve states that formed Duluth's sparsely settled agricultural hinterland— Minnesota, Iowa, North and South Dakota, Nebraska, Kansas, Colorado, Montana, Wyoming, Idaho, Oregon, and Washington—along with northern Wisconsin and Michigan and western Canada. Duluthians, however, felt that the market for locally produced steel would improve only if the Pittsburgh Plus pricing system were modified. U.S. Steel executives strongly opposed any change, fearing that "it would break up a system that bolstered the competitiveness of centers of production of far more importance to its overall success."[18]

Members of the Duluth Real Estate Exchange issued an August 1917 proclamation that called for the removal of the "discrimination that now exists against Duluth as compared to other places where steel plants are located." The statement concluded with an assertion that Duluth had not yet received those "advantages which should accrue to the city by reason of the manufacture of steel at this port." The Real Estate Exchange issued a further declaration in October, this one demanding improvements at the steel plant so its products could be used by Minnesota manufacturers.[19]

Later in the year representatives from several city organizations formed the General Steel Base Price Committee of Duluth, which presented its case to the American Iron and Steel Institute's Committee on Steel and Steel Products, headed by Elbert Gary. When the plea was rejected, a local member addressed Gary directly, informing him that the decision was "a keen disappointment to the Duluth people." Seven months later, Gary and several U.S. Steel executives arrived in Duluth for a series of meetings with local officials. Gary was greeted at the railroad depot by a long-time acquaintance, Billy Sunday, the famed evangelist, who was conducting a religious crusade in the city. U.S. Steel's chairman then engaged "in frank and somewhat extended conversations" with Duluth officials. When asked about the fairness of calculating transportation costs for Duluth's products as if they had originated in Pittsburgh, Gary replied that the city had been designated the primary basing point simply because it was the best location for steel manufacturing in the United States. Local officials in other American cities had also requested designation as basing points, Gary claimed, but after making thorough investigations of the nation's steel-pricing system, their findings always led to a similar conclusion: "it is just as desirable to have one basing point as to have a gold standard."[20]

During his discussions, Gary clarified U.S. Steel's long-term views about the Duluth plant. "It is my opinion, but it is not a promise," the industrialist ventured, "that if patience is exercised by Duluth, if you wait for the development of this country, the time may come when these mills and more like them may be utilized to the further advantage of this community." After being asked if consideration was actually being given to the expansion of operations at Morgan Park, Gary coyly replied with the same litany of answers that U.S. Steel officials always offered when listing Duluth's shortcomings: the unfavorable climate, the need to haul fuel and supplies over considerable distances, and the city's limited market area. Further development at Duluth, Gary warned his audience, would not take place unless U.S. Steel were "guaranteed protection" in maintaining the existing pricing system.[21]

Other cities followed Duluth's lead in agitating for a change in the Pittsburgh Plus system. Duluthians also received support from an organization with an unwieldy title, the Western Association of Rolled Steel Consumers for the Abolition of Pittsburgh Plus. A Duluth member of the organization posed a question to U.S. Steel officials that, once again, must have reminded them of the political power Minnesota could muster because of the state's rich ore deposits. Pointing out that the state supplied 80 percent of the nation's iron ore, the Duluth manufacturer asked: "[D]oesn't it really seem unreasonable for us to pay the freight on this ore clear to Pittsburgh and back to Minnesota, and be charged the Pittsburgh plus price?"[22]

Despite his reservations about Duluth, Gary undoubtedly sensed that several issues raised by city officials could find support in the Minnesota

Legislature. Therefore, in July 1918 Gary approached Duluth officials with an offer: a limited expansion by U.S. Steel at Morgan Park in exchange for a guarantee not to push ahead with the basing point issue. If local officials agreed, Gary intimated that the corporation might construct a wire mill, a nail mill, a tinplate works, and a sheet mill, "all up to the standard of our usual developments." U.S. Steel's chairman assured local officials that "should it subsequently be found necessary to abolish the Pittsburgh plus freight base," Duluth would "benefit in an industrial way in any changes that may be made."[23]

Gary may have promised to build the new mills, but an official decision was not immediately forthcoming—undoubtedly because of a rapid decline in the demand for local steel products following the signing of the November 1918 Armistice. In April 1919, when word about the possible closing of operations at Morgan Park appeared in local newspapers, as well as in the *New York Times* and the *Wall Street Journal,* Gary was asked if the manufacturing unit, "one of the [corporation's] high cost plants," might close. Gary's response was typically brusque and inconclusive. "If it is true you can get the news from up there [in Duluth]," he replied. George Reis, Minnesota Steel's seventy-two-year-old vice president and general manager, spoke up immediately, assuring Duluthians that the plant wouldn't close, although he did admit that the company had "found it necessary to reduce our working force and from indications we will continue the reduction." Just one month later, 1,700 of 3,300 workers were furloughed. Although steel company officials hoped to avoid any further curtailment of operations, they acknowledged that future development would be based on market demands for semifinished steel.[24]

Wishing to find some way of capitalizing on their significant investment at Morgan Park, U.S. Steel officials launched an investigation to determine which finished products might be most marketable in Duluth's geographically expansive, but sparsely populated hinterland. Another rail mill certainly was not the answer. Since major railroad construction had ended in the United States by the time the Morgan Park rail mill was completed in early 1916, it produced little, if any, steel track. Instead, the mill was later converted into a facility that manufactured blooms and billets—semifinished commodities that did not generate as much revenue as fully finished products, such as rails.[25]

Finally, in September 1919, U.S. Steel decided to initiate another construction program at Morgan Park. The envisioned facilities were intended to manufacture wire and small plates and shapes—products that officials believed were most marketable throughout Duluth's market region. The timing of the notice, however, was not especially auspicious. America's steel industry was involved in its first major strike, and just over a year later the nation would be mired in a deep economic recession. Despite Gary's claims that the new mills would emerge in "jig" time, the opening did not take place until summer 1922.[26]

No Strikes Here

In late June 1916, representatives of the Industrial Workers of the World (IWW), termed "strike agitators" by Minnesota Steel officials and Duluth's newspapers, stood at the Gary entrance to the steel plant. From this relatively safe point they handed out information and literature, much of it written in languages other than English, about the IWW and its efforts to create "one big union." Minnesota Steel reported that while they had "no fear" of a strike, "special officers" on the lookout for agitators would arrest anyone who ventured onto company property.[27] The IWW would soon be engaged in an especially bitter strike on the Iron Range, but the steel plant was not struck.

In September 1919, America's steel industry was shaken by a massive work stoppage that began after leaders of the National Committee for Organizing Iron and Steel Workers issued a strike call. The National Committee, however, chose to concentrate its resources in the country's major steel production centers, and did not strike in either the Duluth or Birmingham, Alabama, districts. The 1919 strike call was accompanied by twelve demands, which ranged from requests for an eight-hour workday to improved wages, though the right to unionize was considered especially crucial. As many as 367,000 steel-manufacturing employees departed their jobs by the end of September, but four months later, after the refusal of steel company executives to honor the strikers' demands, the organizers authorized any remaining participants to return to work. The strike leaders' concession statement expressed their frustrations with the four-month-long experience. "The Steel Corporation," noted the telegraphed message, "with the active assistance of the press, the courts, the Federal troops, State police and many public officials, have denied the steel workers their rights of free speech, free assemblage and the right to organize, and, by this arbitrary and ruthless misuse of power, have brought about a condition which has compelled the national committee for organizing iron and steel workers to vote today that the active strike phase of the steel campaign is now at an end."[28]

Not only had the strikers failed to gain any concessions, but they had also suffered grievously during the four months. Some twenty of their colleagues were killed by federal troops, marshals, and agents; collectively, the strikers lost between $87 and $112 million in wages; and those who returned to work were forced to give up their union cards. Elbert Gary expressed no remorse over the actions he and his fellow executives had pursued, alleging that the steel industry was saved from "the closed shop, Soviets, and the forcible distribution of property."[29]

Since the strike had no easily observable consequences within the ranks of Minnesota Steel's workforce, conservative and mainline newspapers such as the *Duluth News Tribune* and *Wall Street Journal* touted this phenomenon as evidence of the local workers' lack of interest in unions. "There are no union organizations at the Minnesota steel plant and no open attempt at organization . . . has been made there," asserted the *News Tribune,* and the *Journal* reported that "no men went out on strike . . . for the reason that no unions are organized at the Duluth plant." When a local steelworker was questioned about whether he and his colleagues should join the walkout, the employee reportedly replied: "Why should we strike?" Another worker stated that Minnesota Steel's employees had "nothing in common" with the national strike organization. "We are not organized," he noted. "It is their own affair and if they can put the strike over, it is their business." Once it became obvious that local workers would not participate in the strike, the *Duluth Herald* also weighed in with its approval. "The general attitude among the men at the Minnesota Steel Company's plant at Morgan Park is one of satisfaction as to the present conditions," stated the *Herald,* "and they show no desire to strike or to stop work, even for a short time."[30]

Despite these assertions, there is clear evidence that Minnesota Steel officials were concerned about the possible strike actions of their employees. Shortly after the strike commenced elsewhere in the country, the *Labor World* commented on Minnesota Steel's labor practices: "When it is known that a workman is identified with a union, be it far remote from the steel industry, he is summarily discharged. Particularly is this true with relation to the Duluth plant [at Morgan Park]." During and after the national walkout, newspapers considered radical or subversive were banned from Morgan Park, including *Truth,* published by the Scandinavian Socialist Federation in Duluth. "Not one copy of our paper is allowed to go into Morgan Park," lamented Jack Carney, the Irish editor of *Truth,* who reported that workers and residents did not dare have the publication sent to their homes "for fear they might lose their jobs." Henry Schultz, a resident of Cumberland,

Wisconsin, located about eighty miles south of Superior, voiced similar sentiments when he visited Morgan Park in early October 1919. Although the "beauties" of Morgan Park impressed Schultz, especially the "fine living conditions, the cheap rent, high wages and every convenience for social activities and sport," he also noted the dissatisfaction expressed by many employees, "largely because no discussions of anything pertaining to the work or organizations of any kind are permitted. Agitators are fired the moment they open their mouths."[31] Indeed, the workforce employed at Morgan Park would need to wait more than a quarter century before they engaged in their first strike action.

The composition of Minnesota Steel's labor ranks changed somewhat in September 1920, when a contingent of workers seldom seen in Duluth—150 Spanish-speaking men—was brought to Duluth. Although the *Labor World* surmised that the new employees had arrived from Spain, they almost certainly were Mexicans. The account intimated that the company was "trying out Spanish labor at Morgan Park, and if it proves satisfactory many more Spanish laborers will be brought here to take the places of southern Negroes who leave here every season at the beginning of cold weather." The *Labor World's* reporter even inferred that additional Spanish laborers might eventually replace Morgan Park's African American and Slavic workers,

> . . . [who] have been getting too independent since the war and are asking [for] higher wages and shorter hours, even going so far as to talk unionism. It is held by the Steel Trust's employment agents that the Spanish workmen will be easy exploiting at low wages for some years yet, and they will not take readily to the American workers' ways, not at least until they shall have earned sufficient money to bring their families here, after which some time will elapse before their wives and children will climb to American standards. The period of submission and the process of change to the American way will take fully 10 years.[32]

The account failed to mention, however, that African Americans were not necessarily departing the steel plant because of cold weather. A much more plausible reason, forwarded by Hudelson and Ross, is that after the lynchings of June 1920, the social and cultural "climate" of Duluth became much less friendly for African Americans. Nevertheless, the *Labor World* concluded its discussion with a claim that Duluth was experiencing its "first taste of . . . cheapest labor, brought here to work for the biggest and richest corporation on earth." John Howden, who was eleven years old in 1920, remembered that "the Mexicans did hard labor, mostly shovel work." Apparently they were dismissed before or by June 1921, when the steel plant shut down during the depths of a national recession. At that time, 1,400 of the plant's 1,700 workers were transferred to construction jobs at the steel plant and the Morgan Park community, but apparently few, if any, of the 150 Spanish-speaking laborers were included. Very little is known about the experiences of these men during their brief tenure in Morgan Park, other than that they resided in Minnesota Steel's labor camp, and that efforts were made to provide them with English-language night school classes in early 1921.[33]

Following the unsuccessful strike of 1919, the steel industry's "arbitrary personnel, compensation, and disciplinary practices remained intact." Although organized labor realized very few gains during the 1920s, some observers noted the underlying discontent experienced by much of the nation's industrial workforce. Future U.S. President Herbert Hoover, who visited the steel plant in 1920 while on a tour of mining and industrial areas in northern Minnesota and Michigan with four hundred fellow members of the American Institute of Mining and Metallurgical Engineers, certainly did not advocate for a change in the status quo. On the other hand, one nationally prominent person voiced concern over labor conditions while on a 1923 speaking engagement in Duluth—the "lady muckraker" and investigative journalist Ida Tarbell. Well known for her early twentieth-century exposé of John D. Rockefeller and the Standard Oil Company, Tarbell spoke on the topic of "Industrial Unrest" to the Duluth Business Women's Club. Informing her audience that few workers understood the purpose of their labor within the American industrial system, Tarbell exclaimed: "What a dreadful, deadening thing!" Strongly opposed to the typical twelve-hour workday of the 1920s, "one of the big causes for unrest," Tarbell recommended that each laborer "have a voice in his work." Nevertheless, the journalist was no fan of labor unions. A union is too similar to the military, contended Tarbell, who instead called for "shop councils" made up of representatives from labor and management. Such councils, Tarbell believed, would provide forums "for the intelligent discussions of wages, hours, conditions, grievances or personal problems." Many companies, including U.S. Steel, eventually instituted shop councils or company unions, but they were rejected by the rank and file, said local labor organizer Earl Bester, because "they didn't give the people any collective bargaining or collective authority."[34]

Workers Caring for Workers and Families

Very little union activity may have occurred at Morgan Park during its early history, but steel plant employees assisted one another by participating in self-help organizations. Shortly after the plant opened, workers employed in its various departments formed "sunshine clubs." These clubs, similar to others established elsewhere in American steel mills, initially set aside small amounts of money to purchase flowers for ill and injured workers, as well as the families of employees who died from natural causes or work-related accidents.[35]

The monetary resources of Morgan Park's sunshine clubs were tapped many times, especially during the wartime years, when workers' lives and limbs were threatened by the intensity of steel-production activities. In 1916 alone, at least six men died at the plant. The first death, in February, was that of Oswald Gauthier, a twenty-two-year-old crane operator, crushed to death between a crane and a wall of the open-hearth building. Immediately after the accident, company officials issued a statement claiming that Gauthier had been killed because he disobeyed orders by exiting the crane on the wrong side of its cupola. Three months later, in May, three men were killed in separate incidents in one thirty-eight-hour period. First was Oscar E. Peterson, an eighteen-year-old electrical department laborer who died instantly on a Saturday afternoon when he fell into a rail car and was buried under several tons of iron ore. Next was twenty-four-year-old Jan Drogvic, struck and killed by lightning as he and several other workers approached the plant's western gate after finishing the Sunday day shift. Third was Christ Hansen, a forty-three-year-old machinist, crushed by a crane after a careless fellow worker started the machine during the early morning hours of the subsequent Monday. The carnage continued into July, when thirty-eight-year-old Gust Nelson, an "unknown laborer," was run down by a switch engine as he was working on railway tracks that linked Morgan Park and Gary. Late in the year, Ralph Cosen was struck and killed by a moving crane.[36]

By early 1918, Morgan Park's sunshine clubs had consolidated into one association, the Good Fellowship Club, an organization with numerous altruistic objectives: "If a member should become sick and is unable to have proper attention," reported W. H. Clark, the organization's first president, "the Good Fellowship Club will provide a doctor and nurse, and see that he receives every attention possible, and, again, if anyone should be in such a position that his family is not receiving [a] proper amount of nourishment, it is the object of the Good Fellowship Club to see that his family is supplied with clothing, groceries, etc., or in other words, it is the object of the Good Fellowship Club to do all in its power to help those who are in need of help." The club also assisted members who needed help in paying insurance policies, in having garnishments removed, and in getting credit extended. Similar Good Fellowship Clubs were organized in many of U.S. Steel's manufacturing plants.[37]

In December 1917 a "Relief Committee" began reviewing assistance requests from steelworkers living throughout Duluth. Twenty-five inquiries, most from employees residing outside of Morgan Park, were considered during the initial two months. The first request was from Charles Geving, a laborer who had been unable to work for a month because of heart problems. Geving's family—a wife, eight children (five under fourteen years of age), and an elderly mother-in-law—was living on the $1.50 per day that a sixteen-year-old son earned at a menial job. The committee voted to provide the family with $25 of assistance, along with $5 to purchase Christmas toys and candies for the children. Another relief case involved W. W. Johnson, who worked in the open-hearth building as a night labor foreman and was bedridden at home after suffering a stroke. Johnson's sixty-five-year-old wife requested his transfer to the hospital because of her inability to care for him. The Relief Committee gave its strong approval to the petition, emphasizing that the case was "a very needy one."[38]

In 1918, the final year of World War I, most Good Fellowship Club members joined the Red Cross as an expression of their support for the "boys over there." Funds were also allocated to provide twenty-five needy families with Christmas dinners, and to purchase toys for the children. The third community Christmas party sponsored by the Good Fellowship Club in 1919 attracted 1,500 children from Morgan Park, Gary, and New Duluth (Figure 5.5). A few days later, children from Duluth's three orphanages were entertained at a separate party. The Good Fellowship Club sponsored its initial community picnic during the summer of 1919, an event that attracted 2,000 people to the Morgan Park baseball field (Figure 5.6). In 1928, a total of 4,500 people attended the event. The orphanage children were also invited to all of the picnics.[39]

While the club's executive committee expressed interest "in getting the foreign element to attend [the picnics]," similar consideration was not given to African Americans. When discussing whether or not to extend an invitation to the "Colored Folks," the entire committee voted "in favor of eliminating them . . . and that they be given a picnic at a later date."[40]

Figure 5.5. Some of the 1,500 children from Morgan Park, Gary, and New Duluth who attended the 1919 Christmas party, an annual event that was first organized by members of the Good Fellowship Club in 1917. Courtesy of Northeast Minnesota Historical Center, S2366B8f4.

Once the Good Fellowship Club's membership and treasury grew, requests for assistance increased. Most significant was a loan program that provided emergency funds, usually $50, to help club members meet unexpected bills. When boardinghouse resident H. Stedman was hospitalized in 1918, deductions for rent and company store purchases left him with only $7 that could be forwarded to his wife and three children in Minneapolis. The Relief Committee agreed that Stedman be provided with a loan "until he can get on his feet for a new start." Not all loan applications were so poignant, as indicated by John Hardy's request for $50 to purchase a cow. In the very most needy cases the loan was often changed into an outright gift. After forgiving the debts of four members who had received loans ranging from $5 to $290 in 1922, the committee noted that the cancellations should

Figure 5.6. For many years the annual summer picnic, here depicted in 1920, was one of the most anticipated events sponsored by the Good Fellowship Club. Courtesy of Northeast Minnesota Historical Center, S2366b817aa, photograph 16921.

not be regarded "as uncollectible nor as charity, but merely to show the goodwill of the Good Fellowship Club in assisting their members in case of dire need or when in trouble."[41]

Chasing Prosperity during the 1920s

In 1919 steel corporation officials claimed that the new Morgan Park mills would be completed quickly, but building permits were not issued until July of the next year. The decision to go forward with two mills—one for rods, the other for wire—was made in spite of a noticeable postwar decline in the demand for the steel plant's manufactured products. During the span of a few months in early 1919, the plant's employee numbers were reduced from 3,300 to 1,600 workers. By April reports were circulating in New York financial circles about a "substantial curtailment in operations" at the Duluth works, or possibly closing the facility "in the very near future for lack of business." Ultimately the plant would operate at no more than one-third of its capacity for the next two years. The merchant mill shipped only 108,000 tons of finished steel products in 1920, and of this, a mere 28,000 tons went to states in Duluth's market area. By way of comparison, the Illinois Steel Company, another U.S. Steel subsidiary, actually sent 8,000 more tons of steel to Minnesota than the Morgan Park facility shipped to all of its destinations in 1920.[42]

The deep national recession of the early 1920s had a deleterious impact on the entire American steel industry. The demand for steel products dipped noticeably during the fall of 1920, and then spiraled downward until late 1921. After the nationwide output of steel had fallen by one-half from October 1920 to March 1921, wage reductions were imposed throughout the industry. In May, Elbert Gary announced that the average annual wage for a U.S. Steel laborer, which had reached an all-time high of $2,173 in 1920, would be lowered to $1,639. In late October 1921, only one-half of the nation's steelworkers were employed, most on a part-time basis. Overall production at U.S. Steel Corporation plants fell from 21.6 million net tons in 1920 to 12.3 million net tons in 1921—the lowest figure the firm had experienced since the depression year of 1908.[43]

The situation at Morgan Park reflected the nationwide trends. Following U.S. Steel's May 1921 decision, the hourly rate for a common laborer fell from forty-six cents to thirty-seven cents. Conditions only worsened in June, when the entire facility was shut down. Although 1,700 laborers suddenly lost their jobs, 1,400 of them were put to work on the many construction jobs underway at the wire mills and in Morgan Park's residential areas (Figure 5.7).[44]

The initial reasoning that had led U.S. Steel officials to authorize a manufacturing plant in Minnesota—the avoidance of additional iron ore taxes—was also rendered moot in 1921. A tonnage tax bill had passed the house in the 1917 session of the Minnesota Legislature, although it was defeated in the senate. Then, in 1919, a bill passed, but Governor Burnquist vetoed the measure. In 1921 another bill was introduced, this one calling for a 6 percent tax on the net value of all ore mined in Minnesota. The bill passed overwhelmingly in both houses of the Legislature and was signed into law by the new governor, Jacob Preuss. (In his January inaugural message, Preuss pledged that if the bill were passed he would approve it since the Minnesota Republican Party platform, "upon which I was elected, declares for a fair and equitable tonnage tax.") After staving off tonnage tax legislation for fourteen years, the ever-vigilant efforts of northeastern Minnesota's politicians had finally been stymied.[45]

Figure 5.7. When the steel plant shut down for almost a year in June 1921, some 1,400 unemployed steelworkers were transferred to construction jobs throughout Morgan Park. These men, shown on August 8, 1921, are working on the new wire mill that opened in July 1922. Photograph by Albert Solomon; courtesy of Northeast Minnesota Historical Center, "Wire Mill Construction," S2366, Vol. 2.

New Mills, New Dreams

Neither the passage of the tonnage tax nor the closing of the Morgan Park steel plant curtailed construction of the new rod and wire mills, which opened on July 5, 1922. Unlike 1915, when daily newspaper coverage was devoted to progress at the steel plant, rather little notice was bestowed on the emerging rod and wire mills. The lack of recognition is surprising, given that the mills would utilize much of the steel produced by the plant's furnaces, all of which had been idle for close to a year.

In anticipation of the mills' opening, one blast furnace began working at half capacity in February 1922. Soon, that furnace and five open hearths were fully operational; the second blast furnace was blown in by mid-October, and production activities at the merchant mill and the new wire and rod mills were well underway. Employees who lived in Morgan Park were the first to be rehired, followed by others from the western districts of Duluth; soon 1,200 workers were engaged in the reinvigorated manufacturing operations. More good news arrived in late August when U.S. Steel announced that all of its common laborers would receive a 20 percent wage increase. Over the next several months the plant operated at 60 percent of capacity and occasionally exceeded this figure.

The new mills, which embodied "the most advanced principles of construction and equipment," were built of structural steel and had walls of concrete blocks formed on the site; saw-tooth-type roofs with large expanses of glass topped both buildings. The rod mill was attached to the existing merchant mill, while the wire mill, which quickly emerged as a dominant feature on the steel plant landscape, was located three hundred yards distant.[46]

The rod mill produced round bars that were transferred to the wire mill in three-hundred-pound bundles. A complex set of operations, supervised by skilled "wire drawers," converted the bars into wire. After the wire had been galvanized, much of it was transformed into the three hundred varieties of nails produced by 183 machines that spewed out several hundred nails per minute (Figure 5.8). The nails were then packed into wooden kegs

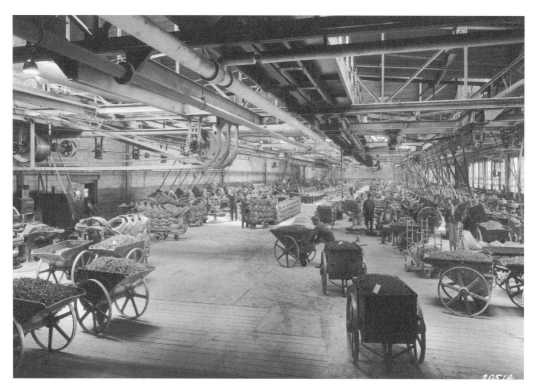

Figure 5.8. An interior view of the nail mill in 1924, two years after it opened. Courtesy of Northeast Minnesota Historical Center, S2386B30f7.

crafted in the plant's cooperage department. Another fifty machines produced barbed wire, while fourteen more manufactured woven wire.[47]

During the summer of 1924, numerous repairs were made to the plant, and new machinery for the manufacture of steel fence posts was installed in the merchant mill. The "steel arrow type posts," which could be fabricated at the rate of about one per second, were designed with a special stiffness that allowed them to be driven into the ground without holes. Many posts were packed with lengths of woven wire and shipped in specially designed railway cars to agricultural markets in the western United States. The posts were also touted for their ability to withstand brush fires, to serve as supports for snow fences and signs, and to ground lightning strikes, which might provide protection for cattle huddled against fence wires during thunderstorms. Fence-post manufacturing quickly emerged as a key factor in the plant's overall production picture. During the latter half of 1924, when the entire Morgan Park plant experienced a short-term drop to 35 percent of capacity, only the fence post–fabricating unit generated any orders—so many, in fact, that two shifts of workers were employed in the merchant mill. "If it had not been for this," reasoned the *Duluth News Tribune*, "the mill would have been closed entirely."[48]

Even as economic conditions improved during the latter half of the 1920s, other data illustrate the market problems still encountered at Morgan Park. The total finishing capacity of the merchant, rod, and wire mills now approached 220,000 tons annually, but this figure was noticeably lower than the 360,000 tons that had been predicted some ten years earlier. Chairman Gary again commented that failure to reach the original goal was linked to Duluth's relatively high manufacturing costs for finished steel products, which exceeded those of Gary and Pittsburgh by 38 and 13 percent, respectively. Likewise, during the 1920s the steel ingot capacity of Morgan Park's open-hearth furnaces was not expanded beyond the 540,000 net annual tons that had been available when the facility opened. At Gary, by contrast, the annual net capacity of U.S. Steel's plant increased from 3.4 million to 4.9 million tons during the 1920s, a gain of about 30 percent.[49]

Meanwhile, the vagaries of the Pittsburgh Plus price system continued to receive attention in several steel production centers. Finally, in 1924, after the Federal Trade Commission had conducted several years of steel price hearings, the Pittsburgh Plus system was rescinded. Duluth officials quickly seized on the ruling, hoping it would "immediately open the way to the creation of a real steel industry at the Head of the Lakes instead of just a steel plant." Nevertheless, U.S. Steel officials delayed any action on

Pittsburgh Plus, eventually selecting only a few additional cities as basing points. Chicago became the base for determining the price of steel manufactured in Duluth, but this action did little to benefit Morgan Park. Wire manufactured at the plant was still priced at two dollars more per ton than in most other manufacturing cities. Another fifteen years would pass before Duluth became a true basing point for steel products.[50]

Managing a Steel Plant

During the 1920s steel corporation officials often revealed two different faces when commenting on and evaluating their Morgan Park venture. This practice was especially noticeable once they realized that the merchant, rod, and wire mills could usually meet regional market demands by operating at no more than 60 percent of capacity. The officials continued to make public pronouncements touting Morgan Park's attributes and potential, but they also shared internal documents among themselves that raised questions about the plant's profitability and viability.

Perhaps no official could better see the glass both half full and half empty than Samuel Sheldon, a Massachusetts Institute of Technology graduate, former baseball player, and U.S. Steel official who became the first general superintendent of the Minnesota Steel Company and the Morgan Park plant in 1913, and was then named vice president and general manager in 1920. In early 1923 Sheldon informed readers of the *Duluth Herald* that the recently opened rod and wire mills supplied "the finished products required by the great agricultural states of the West and Southwest. Location is favorable from the standpoint of distribution, especially for the products of its wire mill, situated as it is in the heart of a great consuming territory."[51] Sheldon, nevertheless, could be considerably more circumspect when describing the plant's shortcomings to his fellow U.S. Steel officials. These concerns were apparent in a 1925 letter that summarized the company's first decade of experience in a remote manufacturing district:

> In this particular institution we have to be very careful. Good men are scarce and stabilized men are scarce. . . . We have always been obliged to train men for every new operation we undertake. The principle was laid down in the early years of the property and we had to have men that could do more than one thing. In other words it has always been the practice here to take construction gangs on new departments and train them for operations. Naturally this policy was followed out in the

erection of the wire mill. As a matter of fact during the boom times during the war we had 3,500 men in our employ and a careful analysis showed that only 366 had ever worked in any part of a steel works before or in any of its appurtenances. In other words in round numbers 3,200 were trained here. . . . The wire mill when running full has 572 men and I think we have only three wire drawers who did not learn the business here.[52]

Most of the 572 wire drawers that Sheldon mentioned joined the workforce when the wire mills opened. Many of these men arrived from areas of rural Minnesota, and some from elsewhere, including a few African Americans who journeyed to the steel plant from the South. One was George A. Cox, a black laborer who departed his childhood home in Thomasville, Mississippi, during the early 1920s (see Figure 10.5). The twenty-two-year-old Cox began working for Minnesota Steel in 1923, eventually becoming a crane operator. Three of his brothers would also find positions at the plant, and by the 1940s his son was a steelworker, too. Cox would later report that all five members of the family "like to work . . . at the steel plant." Around 1928 another Mississippian, Lew Wiley (Wyley), joined the steel plant workforce. An African American from a rural village close to the Mississippi River delta, Wiley eventually became an electric operator in the steel plant, and would be a strong labor union supporter.[53]

Because of his image as a colorful, complex, and opinionated personality, Samuel Sheldon overshadows the more anonymous and bland supervisors who succeeded him at Morgan Park over subsequent decades (Figure 5.9). Termed the "Wild Bull of the Pampas" by some employees, Sheldon issued a steady stream of edicts to his office staff, several of which sought to regulate trivial aspects of personal appearance and behavior. In 1926, after abruptly decreeing that all female employees should wear an office uniform over their street clothing that did not "extend less than six inches below the knee," Sheldon warned that any failure to follow the policy would "result in discharge." Notwithstanding his assertion, the general manager was forced to admit, one year later, that the regulation was not being followed completely; therefore, Sheldon informed his assistants that in the future they should "please tell the ladies to go back and wear what I told them." Then in 1929 Sheldon ordered the stationery managers in each Minnesota Steel Company office to retrieve pencil stubs from all employees before issuing a new one. "It is not the intent to plaster Duluth and the families of our employees with our pencils or pencils for their own enjoyment," he dictated.

Figure 5.9. Following Samuel B. Sheldon's death in 1929, a plaque in the company's main office building commemorated his role as president and general manager of Minnesota Steel. The structure was demolished during the 1970s. Photograph by the author, 1971.

"They are to be used for business and for nothing else. They should take care of them just as they do their own property and if they don't they better."[54]

While Sheldon's practices might be considered relatively harmless personality quirks, he was a very stern anti-unionist who did not hesitate to rid the steel plant of workers who expressed more than a passing interest in labor organizations. In 1921 Iver Felde, an experienced steelworker, was fired after attending a union meeting in one of Duluth's labor halls. Felde's mistake, according to Jack Carney's description in *Truth*, was doing nothing more than listening to what a speaker had to say. "The spies spotted him," reported Carney. "They reported their discovery. The head of Felde went off for attending a meeting at Workers Hall and for listening to a lecture on what the workers must do to free themselves."[55]

Sheldon acted again in 1928 when a small group of steel plant employees attending a "Crane Operators Ball" in Duluth's Woodman Hall discussed the Amalgamated Steel, Iron, and Tin-Metal Workers union. Even though no union cards were signed at the gathering, Sheldon and his associates quickly fired twelve of the men. All were rehired two months later, but with the proviso that they would be "blacklisted" if their union activities continued. Included in the group was Earl Bester, who would successfully organize a local union at the steel plant in 1936. The son of a Michigan copper miner from England who had been blacklisted during a major strike in 1913–14, Bester eventually filled a variety of major union roles throughout northeastern Minnesota, ranging from local president to district director.[56]

Prosperity Achieved

Other than the wartime era, the latter years of the 1920s were among the most successful in Morgan Park's early history. In 1927 the *Wall Street Journal* reported that the nail mill was engaged full time, with "good bookings for its products"; requests for steel fence posts were "substantial," and the merchant mill was filling special orders, including "steel markers for use on the highways over the West." Throughout this period Duluth's residents maintained their hope that U.S. Steel would enlarge its Morgan Park operations. When U.S. Steel President Farrell visited Duluth in September 1928, his first trip to the city in ten years, local officials once again asked if the corporation had any local expansion plans. "We are not contemplating any immediate expansion in Duluth," stated Farrell, "but the plant . . . is showing a steady growth in business, and we are as anxious to expand its operations as the people of Duluth are to have us."[57]

Farrell's recognition of a "steady growth in business" certainly was not illusory. While the plant had generally operated at 35 to 80 percent of its capacity from 1924 to 1928, it approached the 100 percent production level by April 1929. Employee numbers may not have been as high as those reached during the wartime years, but 2,700 workers now labored round-the-clock producing steel, and another 400 staffed the cement plant. Because of the demands for wire, "the heaviest in company history," the *Wall Street Journal* reported that U.S. Steel was giving consideration to the enlargement of its merchant mill at Morgan Park.[58] The stock market crash that occurred just one month later, however, brought an immediate end to these plans.

The overall prosperity and level of activity that prevailed at the Morgan Park steel plant from 1916 to 1930 were unfortunately accompanied by a commensurate decline in the environmental quality of the St. Louis River. When recalling the 1920s, former Duluth city engineer John Wilson wrote that untreated waste from the steel plant "had the most pronounced effect upon the river of anything found elsewhere." (Sewage from the Morgan Park community also emptied directly into the river.) "The blackened condition of the shore line could be seen from the boulevard, green life was absent where contact was made with the water," stated Wilson; "even the bottom muds had little life of any kind." Wilson noticed that the oily tar separated as it entered the water, and the resulting surface film reflected "all the colors of the rainbow," simultaneously forming "a black mat on the bed of the stream." This meant, he concluded, that any presence of poisonous substances such as carbolic acid and cyanide was "a very decided element as far as the development of a nuisance was concerned." Similarly, when Minnesota health officials evaluated pollutants in the river from 1927 to 1930, they reported that anyone having "intimate contact with the water or deposits of sludge" would face a public health risk.[59] Ironically, the environmental situation would soon improve, for within a year after the national stock market crash of October 1929 the steel plant entered into a long period of quiescence and emitted little pollution.

Meanwhile, the uncertain economic conditions of late 1929 were exacerbated at Minnesota Steel when Samuel Sheldon died unexpectedly of heart problems at the age of sixty-one. Immediately after his November death, the *Duluth News-Tribune* eulogized Sheldon as "an able, fair, and likable executive, as well as a practical manufacturer of iron and steel products." Acknowledging that he may have been a "bluff, outspoken" man who had the "habit of calling a spade a spade," the *Tribune* also identified Sheldon as "whole-hearted, honest, and sincere," totally "unassuming" in his interactions with people, and someone who never sought "the limelight of publicity." To the *New York Times,* Sheldon was, above all, a "noted steel man."[60]

At the conclusion of the 1920s, steelworkers and Morgan Park's residents faced a decidedly unpredictable future. Almost a decade and a half of general prosperity would soon end, and the erstwhile general manager and president of Minnesota Steel no longer served at the organization's helm. The most traumatic period in the steel plant's relatively brief manufacturing history was about to begin.

6. THE COMPLETE COMPANY TOWN

Morgan Park was home to about six hundred people at the beginning of 1916. To resident and visitor alike, the most obvious feature that distinguished the embryonic community was "the extensive use of concrete for municipal purposes, as well as for all the dwellings." Despite the almost universal application of concrete, a material generally considered drab, harsh, dull, and massive, visitors were impressed with Morgan Park's "attractive appearance." Delegates from the Minnesota League of Municipalities who toured Morgan Park in 1916 gave a succinct summary of their impressions: "This is certainly a clean place," they observed. One year later a Japanese housing specialist who visited Morgan Park was "quite pleased" with the community. Duluth's citizens were also "amazed and pleased" by what they saw at Morgan Park; local realtor C. R. Stowell wrote that this "modern industrial town site . . . may well excite the admiration of the landscape architect, the builder, the planter [planner] of subdivisions, [and] the city builder."[1] Once the community's housing program was completed in 1922, followed by the maturation of the trees, shrubs, and vines during the remainder of the decade, praises for Morgan Park were sung even more enthusiastically (Figures 6.1, 6.2).

The period from 1916 to 1930 marked the time that Morgan Park functioned as a complete company town, a place where residents were provided with numerous amenities, conveniences, and services. When visiting Duluth in June 1916, U.S. Steel housing specialist C. L. Close reported on the corporation's plans to make Morgan Park "the most perfect and ideal industrial city in the world." Close also asserted that "nothing was to be spared, either time, money or skill, in producing at the Minnesota Steel plant and environs, the greatest city of idealism the country has ever seen."[2] While Close certainly offered an overly optimistic view of Morgan Park's future, U.S. Steel did commit considerable financial resources to the community over the next one and a half decades. The services and features, however, would not come without a price. As Morgan Parkers learned, residing in a company town meant that a paternalistic sponsor and landlord often managed their lives on a daily basis.

Figure 6.1. As plants and vegetation matured in Morgan Park, the community's appearance received compliments from both residents and nonresidents. This view is of Eighty-eighth Avenue at its intersection with Beverly Street in August 1916. Courtesy of Northeast Minnesota Historical Center, S2366B7f2.

More Houses, More Residents

With as many as 3,500 workers employed at the steel plant during the World War I era, a serious housing shortage developed throughout Morgan Park and its environs. In April 1916, local real estate agents claimed that the population of Gary and New Duluth had increased by 40 percent in six weeks. "Everything that is fit to live in has been taken," the agents reported, "and there are houses in which two families are living although they were built but for one." Even the opening of Fairmount Park, a new neighborhood situated between downtown Duluth and Morgan Park, did not solve the housing dearth, which continued through the summer and into autumn. "There are jobs and positions galore in Morgan Park," noted an October account, "but the problem facing officials there now is to take care of the families of the men who are employed in that locality. Every available house has been put into use, but these are not enough."[3]

Figure 6.2. A view looking west along Eighty-fourth Avenue West in July 1917 depicts a typical residential street scene with terrace, sidewalk, a slightly elevated front yard and lawn, and residence. Courtesy of Northeast Minnesota Historical Center, S2366B7f3.

Meanwhile, in Morgan Park the interiors of the most recently completed houses were being painted during the summer of 1916. Although the Morgan Park Company allowed residents to choose from a limited range of colors, more expensive paint and materials could be employed—but only if the resident paid "the difference between the standard price and the cost of the special work." Minnesota Steel officials, however, were more concerned about the housing shortage and began making plans for further residential building in April 1916, and again in early 1917.[4] A temporary labor camp was also built along the southwestern border of the community in 1917, and more permanent housing was constructed in 1918 and 1922. Unlike the dwellings constructed for skilled workers and their families from 1913 to 1915, the subsequent housing programs served a broader spectrum of employees, ranging from lower-income laborers to highly salaried managers.

Lower-Rent Housing in the Western Neighborhood

In 1916 planning began for Morgan Park's western neighborhood, or "Hunkyville." The initial section, "Block 33," served as the site for the first grouping of lower-rent residences in Morgan Park (Figure 6.3). The building permits for these residences, as well as for several other buildings already completed or under construction in the community—the Nenovan boardinghouses, the hospital, and the store building—were approved in May 1916. A number of existing trees were soon transplanted from Block 33 to the yet-to-be-developed clubhouse and hospital grounds; construction of the streets and buildings began in August 1916 and was completed by June 1917. The residential buildings included ten row houses or terrace houses with forty-two dwelling units, as well as three dormitories for 116 laborers. Steel company officials reported that the new housing would "rent at a

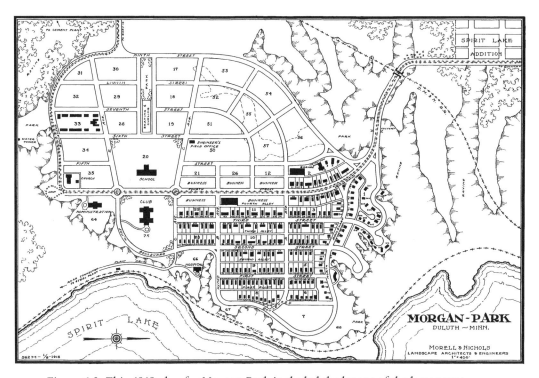

Figure 6.3. This 1918 plan for Morgan Park included the layout of the lower-rent district in Block 33, designed by Morrell and Nichols in 1916–17. Similar site plans would be implemented for Blocks 34 and 35 soon thereafter. The linear area of open space west of the school was now designated to serve as a park in summer, and as a curling rink with an ice-covered slide in winter; these recommendations were carried out for a few years only. Author's collection; copy available in Northwest Architectural Archives, Morell and Nichols papers.

lower cost" and was "designed to meet the demands of the lower paid employees of the plant."[5]

Landscape architects Morell and Nichols called for Block 33's houses to be arranged around a centrally located open space or courtyard designated for gardens and children's recreational activities (Figures 6.4, 6.5). In a somewhat condescending gesture to the residents, the small piece of ground situated between the dwellings and each alley was covered with gravel rather than being planted with grass because company officials "believed that it will not be kept up and hence may prove unsightly."[6]

Leiffur Magnusson, a former Duluth teacher and Rhodes Scholar candidate at the University of Minnesota who had joined the U.S. Department of Labor as a library cataloguer in 1910, prepared a lengthy report about Morgan Park in 1918. When appraising the western neighborhood, Magnusson wrote that rather than arranging the terrace houses into "ordinary continuous rows, extending unbroken for a whole block, as found in larger cities," they had been

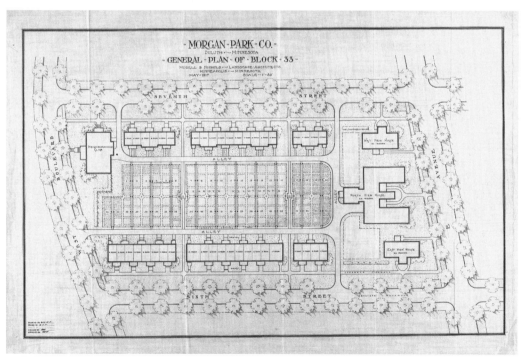

Figure 6.4. Site plan for Block 33, with proposed garden layouts in the central area, May 1917. Linear groupings of row houses flanked the eastern and western sides of the block, three boardinghouses were located along the northern side, and the Neighborhood House was situated at the southwestern corner. North is to the right. Courtesy of Northwest Architectural Archives, Morell and Nichols papers.

Figure 6.5. Gardens in the central area of Block 33, fall 1918. Today this area is filled with garages and storage buildings. From U.S. Steel Corporation, Bureau of Safety, Sanitation, and Welfare, Bulletin No. 7.

organized into "short rows or groups" with four to ten units each. Each building served as "a symmetrical architectural unit," noted Magnusson, which gave it "none of the monotony of the ordinary row of houses."[7]

Unlike the concrete-block houses previously built in Morgan Park's eastern neighborhood, the row houses in Block 33 were constructed of frame and boards and covered with plaster or stucco. Two of the buildings had four housing units each, one had six, another had eight, and two had ten. The four-unit terraces had multigabled roofs, including a centrally placed gable that rose upward to the building's third level. Open or enclosed porches, each serving two units, were placed at both the front and rear. The six- and eight-unit buildings were relatively similar to the four-unit structures, though they had an additional central porch and a higher middle gable. The ten-unit structures were more massive, and had two prominent three-story gables that provided additional space in four of the third-floor units. Only eight dwellings had basements.[8]

Of the forty-two dwelling units, twenty-six had four rooms, two had five rooms, and fourteen had six rooms. The four-room dwellings included a living room and a kitchen/dining room on the first floor, two bedrooms on the second, and a bathroom and storage space in the attic (Figure 6.6). The kitchens were large enough for use as dining rooms (Figure 6.7). Some of the five- and six-room dwellings had a partition wall and a door situated between the kitchen and dining room, and included either one or two additional bedrooms. Monthly rents ranged from $10 to $18.75 per dwelling. Boarders were discouraged, but it was recognized that some residents in the five- and six-room dwellings might rent out a bedroom to secure additional income.[9]

The floors were constructed of reinforced concrete, and except for the eight units with basements, all were raised slightly above grade level to maintain dryness and avoid frost and freezing problems. Interior walls were covered with plaster and a special washable fabric. Since the residences had such minimal storage space, the kitchen walls were even designed so they might be employed "to the greatest extent possible for storage of food, utensils, and china, and

Figure 6.6. Located in the foreground of this August 1920 photograph, looking south along Ninetieth Avenue West in the western neighborhood, is the entrance to a four-unit residence; to its immediate left is an eight-unit residence. The water tower and steel plant are in the background. Courtesy of Northeast Minnesota Historical Center, S2366B8f7aa.

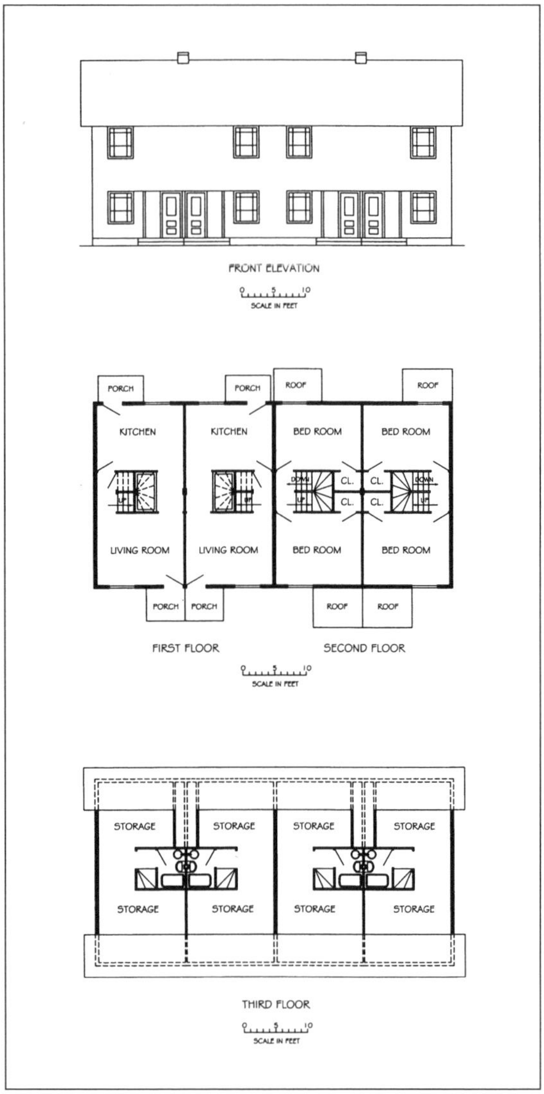

Figure 6.7. Elevation and floor plans for a four-unit residential building, each with four rooms, in the western neighborhood. A kitchen and living room are on the first level, two bedrooms are on the second, and a bathroom and storage space are in the attic. Adapted from Magnusson, "A Modern Industrial Suburb"; redrafted by Kassie Martine.

thus conserve floor space for other purposes." Heat was provided either by a first-floor stove or a basement furnace; a coal bin was placed on each rear porch. The *American Architect* commented that latticework would be placed along the backside of the porches so as to screen the "usual objectionable and untidy appearance of such porches, resulting from their general use as storage and 'catch all' places for ice boxes, washing machines, dishpans and other kitchen and household appliances."[10]

The West View, East View, and North View boardinghouses, also built of frame and boards and covered with stucco, were sited along the northern side of Block 33; relatively large areas of open space surrounded all three buildings, and a transverse or perpendicular alley and fence separated them from the row houses. The first floor of each building had a dining room, as well as a recreation room located immediately above on the second floor. All were designed with surveillance in mind, a not uncommon practice in company-managed boardinghouses of the nineteenth and early twentieth centuries. The outside entrance to each building was "so arranged that every person entering the dining room or recreation room must pass the custodian's office."[11]

The second phase of the western neighborhood's building program was initiated in 1920 when two additional blocks, identified as 34 and 35, were developed. (A plan for Block 32 was never implemented.) The organization of both was quite similar to that of Block 33, with the housing arranged around "a large [central] square for recreational or park purposes." Unlike Block 33, however, where all the dwellings were multifamily units, some single-family residences and duplexes emerged in the two newer blocks. Twenty-four structures, all constructed of frame and boards and covered with stucco or plaster, offered a total of seventy-three lower-rent dwelling units, each with a basement. Five of the new buildings were single-family houses with either six or seven rooms, nine were duplexes, and the remaining ten had four, six, or eight units, each with either four or six rooms (Figure 6.8). Not included in the total was the Catholic church rectory.[12]

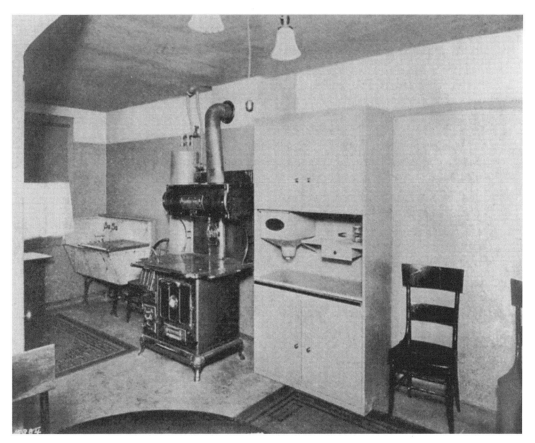

Figure 6.8. A kitchen in one of the lower-rent dwellings in the western neighborhood, 1918. In the far left corner is a combination sink and laundry tub. From Magnusson, "A Modern Industrial Suburb."

Figure 6.9. A view, looking south in 1922, of the recently completed housing and buildings that compose Blocks 34 (right) and 35 (left) in the western neighborhood; Hilton Street runs from east to west in the foreground. The steel plant looms in the background; two landmarks are the Catholic church and the water tower. Courtesy of Northeast Minnesota Historical Center, S2366B7f1.

The completion of Blocks 34 and 35 in 1922 brought an end to the company-sponsored housing program in Morgan Park's western neighborhood. When combined with Block 33, a total of thirty buildings that offered 115 single-family and multifamily residences was now available in the neighborhood, as well as dormitory rooms for 116 men (Figure 6.9).

Labor Camp

Minnesota Steel had provided a number of its construction laborers with temporary bunkhouses and a mess hall as early as 1913. The buildings in this camp, "rough structures with tar paper exteriors," were dismantled in 1917 because of their "insanitary and inadequate" condition. They were immediately replaced by a "modern sanitary camp," located just west of the lower-rent western neighborhood (Figure 6.10).[13]

The new camp housed three to four hundred laborers, most of whom would be involved in the construction of the wire mills, the Protestant church, and new residences over the next several years. Four large bunkhouses—two for winter, the other two for summer—served as the camp's sleeping quarters; they were sometimes termed "Mexican houses" by local residents (Figure 6.11). Nearby were two smaller bunkhouses—one for construction

Figure 6.10. Morgan Park labor camp, 1917. Courtesy of Northeast Minnesota Historical Center, S2386B14f21.

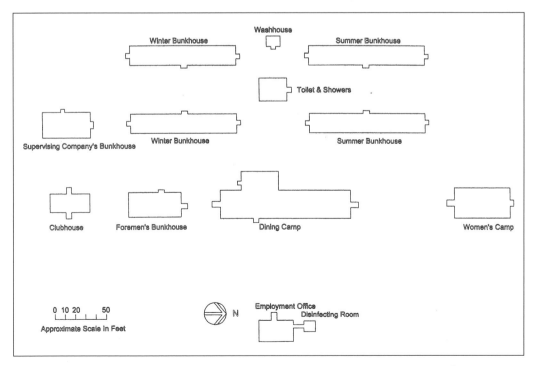

Washhouse

Winter Bunkhouse

Summer Bunkhouse

Toilet & Showers

Supervising Company's Bunkhouse

Winter Bunkhouse

Summer Bunkhouse

Clubhouse

Foremen's Bunkhouse

Dining Camp

Women's Camp

0 10 20   50

Approximate Scale in Feet

N

Employment Office

Disinfecting Room

Figure 6.11. Plan of the labor camp, 1917. Derived from Magnusson, "A Modern Industrial Suburb"; redrafted by Kassie Martine.

Figure 6.12. Mess hall in the labor camp, August 1917. Courtesy of Northeast Minnesota Historical Center, S2366B8f 7aa.

foremen, the other for employees of the Knudsen and Ferguson company, which managed the camp. A separate dormitory housed ten female domestic workers. Also located in the camp were a common mess hall, a clubhouse, and an employment office. The mess hall kitchen had its own bake shop, which produced "all the bread, pastry, and cake used in the camp" (Figure 6.12). A concrete block stable for twelve horses, forty by forty feet in size, was also built at the camp in early 1920.[14]

Despite its temporary status, the camp was touted as having "all modern conveniences," such as furnaces, showers, electric lights, and running water. The buildings were torn down sometime by the late 1920s or early 1930s, thereby eliminating a district of Morgan Park once described as "erected and furnished in a manner to excite the admiration of all who visit the community."[15]

"Silk Stocking Row"

Residential construction also occurred in Morgan Park's eastern neighborhood during much of 1917 and 1918. In early 1917 the Minnesota Steel Company commissioned the Dean and Dean architectural firm to prepare designs for a number of single-family residences in Blocks 1 and 6. The architects developed twelve basic residential designs for a total of forty-six residences, all intended to house a portion of Minnesota Steel's supervisors, managers, and salaried workers. Late in the year, as most of the dwellings approached completion, eligible workers were invited to apply for the housing unit of their choice. The Morgan Park Company reviewed the requests in mid-January 1918, and successful applicants began moving into the dwellings soon thereafter.[16]

The thirty houses in Block 1, sometimes identified as "Silk Stocking Row" by residents who lived elsewhere in the community, clearly represented Morgan Park's most exclusive and prestigious district (Figure 6.13).

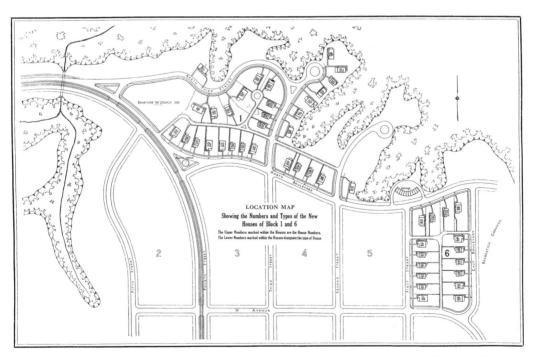

Figure 6.13. Plan for Blocks 1 and 6 in the eastern neighborhood, prepared by Morell and Nichols in 1917. Block 1, which housed Minnesota Steel's executives, managers, and professional employees, became Morgan Park's most exclusive district. Block 6 completed the development of the eastern neighborhood. From Morgan Park Company, The New Houses in Morgan Park.

The "artistic" site plan prepared by Morell and Nichols utilized the nearby ravines and dense tree cover as a backdrop for the homes, which made it "a residential park with winding streets." The two designers organized the residences to "obtain the most attractive view from the living and dining room windows"—a practice that one local observer described as building houses "on an angle rather than destroy[ing] any of the trees now standing." Also of note were two culs-de-sac, both of which served several houses situated along the northern border of Block One.[17] A conventional linear street would have resulted in the removal of many existing trees, and lessened the organic relationship with the adjacent park-like area.

Sixteen houses were also built in Block 6, which adjoined Block 1. The development of this block, located in the far northeastern corner of Morgan Park, completed the "build out" of the eastern neighborhood. Once again, Morell and Nichols prepared a site plan for the block that displayed the same landscape design features—most notably the sloped, grass-covered lawns—that had been employed some four years earlier in the neighborhood.

Designing the Residences: Architect H. F. Robinson

The new housing designs for Morgan Park's eastern neighborhood, and undoubtedly some of the lower-rent residential buildings in Blocks 34 and 35, were overseen by Henry (Harry) Franklin Robinson, one of the key architects employed by the Dean and Dean company from late 1916 through 1922. Before joining the firm at age thirty-three, Robinson had already acquired impressive professional credentials with three of Chicago's best-known architects: Frank Lloyd Wright and the husband-wife team of Walter Burley Griffin and Marion Mahoney.

Immediately after graduating from the University of Illinois in 1906 with a degree in architectural engineering, Robinson joined Wright's studio, located in the Chicago neighborhood of Oak Park. When Wright departed on a three-year-long European sojourn in 1908, Robinson accepted a position with Griffin and Mahoney. The two, both former Wright employees, became architectural celebrities in 1914 when they won an international competition for the new capital city of Canberra, Australia. Robinson, however, had already rejoined Wright in 1911, after the master architect returned from Europe. With Wright ensconced at Taliesin, his home and studio in Spring Green, Wisconsin, Robinson was rehired to manage Wright's Chicago office.[18]

In 1916 Robinson left Wright for the last time, this time because of a bitter salary dispute—a not uncommon reason for the departure of several architects employed by Wright over many years. Robinson then moved to the Dean and Dean firm, where he served as the chief draftsman and supervised as many as twenty employees. He continued working with the firm following George Dean's death in 1919, remaining there until the office closed in late 1922. During these three years the design work for Morgan Park was completed. Robinson then established his own private practice in Chicago, but in 1934, during the depths of the Depression, he found employment with the federal government's Public Housing Authority (PHA). Robinson continued working for the PHA until retiring in 1955 at the age of seventy-one; he died four years later.[19]

Under Robinson's supervision, the Dean and Dean firm prepared twelve different single-family residential designs for Blocks 1 and 6; nine additional designs were the reverse or "mirror image" of another plan. Of the forty-six dwellings, eight were true bungalows—two with five rooms and six with seven rooms. The remaining thirty-eight dwellings, several identified as "bungalow types," included a single five-room unit, fifteen with six rooms, seven with eight rooms, and nine with nine rooms (Figure 6.14). Most were

Figure 6.14. Architectural rendering of house type 18-F, one of several residential designs with Prairie-style characteristics that Henry Robinson of the Dean and Dean firm prepared for the Morgan Park managers' district in 1917. From "Morgan Park, Minn."

equipped with sunrooms, enclosed front and rear porches, fireplaces, vegetable cellars, French doors that connected the sunroom and living room, and "electric fixture plugs in floors, baseboards and wall fixtures."[20]

The simplest of the house plans, two "twins" identified as 16-E and 16-F, were quite similar to the earlier layouts of 15-E and 15-F. The porches for both houses, one the reverse of the other, spanned two-thirds of the front facade and opened into a vestibule and stair hall. The living room was located along one side of the hall, while the dining room and kitchen were placed at the rear of the house. Unlike 15-E and 15-F, however, where two large bedrooms were located on the second floor, the plans for 16-E and 16-F displayed three smaller bedrooms.

One plan, identified as 16-J, is indicative of one "bungalow type" house (Figure 6.15). Entry to the seven-room residence occurred from a porch, which opened into the reception hall. Three open arches allowed the interior spaces of the house to flow from the reception hall to the living room, dining room, and alcove. Flanking these three rooms were a bedroom, the kitchen, and a pantry. The fireplace was put between two windows situated along one long wall of the living room. The second floor of the house, basically square in plan and divided into two bedrooms and a sewing room, was centered over the rectangular lower story. The broad roof planes that

Figure 6.15. Floor plans and elevations for house type 16-J, a six-room residence. Adapted from Robinson, The Life and Work of Harry Franklin Robinson; *redrafted by Robert Gerloff.*

extended over the residence made it one of the clearest examples of a Prairie style–influenced house in Morgan Park.

The somewhat elongated plans for 17-A and 17-B had seven rooms (Figure 6.16). Both plans, one the reverse of the other, incorporated front porches with open and enclosed sections. Entry into the house was by way of the open porch, which led into a vestibule and a large reception and stair hall; the enclosed porch had French doors that provided access to the living room. The open arch between the reception hall and living room allowed the entire space to serve as one large room. A pantry at the rear of the house connected the kitchen and dining room. The second floor included a central hall that accessed four bedrooms.

One of the largest houses, plan 19-A, had nine rooms and was two and one-half stories high (Figure 6.17). The rectangular plan included a porch with both open and enclosed sections. French doors opened from the enclosed porch into the living room, which had a large fireplace, while the adjacent dining room could be closed off by sliding doors. The floor plan was similar to those for several of Morgan Park's smaller houses in that the open arch between the living room and reception hall allowed the two rooms to function as a single expansive space. Another similarity was the rear pantry that connected the kitchen and dining room. The second floor had four bedrooms and a bathroom, while the attic included two additional bedrooms and a bathroom.

Figure 6.16. Floor plans for house type 17-B, a seven-room residence. Adapted from Morgan Park Company, New Houses in Morgan Park; *redrafted by Kassie Martine.*

Figure 6.17. Floor plans and elevations for house type 19-A. The nine rooms made it one of the largest residences in Morgan Park. Adapted from Robinson, The Life and Work of Harry Franklin Robinson; *redrafted by Robert Gerloff.*

One other plan, 19-B, also was a two-and-one-half story, nine-room "bungalow-type" residence (Figure 6.18). Its most distinguishable exterior feature was the prominent sloping roof with dormers. Besides a kitchen, living room, and bathroom, the first floor of these houses had an enclosed porch and alcove, a combination sitting/dining room, and two bedrooms. The second floor, intended for as many as eight female roomers, had four large bedrooms (each with two large closets) and a bathroom.

With the conclusion of Morgan Park's residential construction program in 1922, the community had 246 buildings, which provided houses for 510 families. A total of 216 buildings with 395 residences distinguished the east-

FIRST FLOOR PLAN

SECOND FLOOR PLAN

FRONT ELEVATION

SIDE ELEVATION

Figure 6.18. Floor plans and elevations for house type 19-B. This nine-room residence was designed to accommodate four roomers on the second floor. Adapted from Robinson, The Life and Work of Harry Franklin Robinson; *redrafted by Robert Gerloff.*

	Number of buildings	Number of units
Eastern neighborhood		
Built 1913–15	170	349
Built 1917–18	46	46
Western neighborhood		
Built 1915–17	6	42
Built 1921–22	24	73
Total	246	510

Figure 6.19. Family residential buildings and units in Morgan Park, 1922. From Morgan Park Company response to Arthur C. Comey and Max S. Wehrly, "Harvard School of City Planning, Questionnaire to Public Officials of Model Community Developments," 1936 (Frances Loeb Library, Graduate School of Design, Harvard University).

ern neighborhood, while the western neighborhood accommodated the remaining 30 structures and 115 residences (Figure 6.19). Temporary housing for several hundred mostly unmarried employees was also provided in the Nenovan Club, the labor camp, and the North View, East View, and West View boardinghouses. No more housing, either permanent or temporary, would emerge in Morgan Park for twenty-five more years.

A Store and a School, but No Saloon: Morgan Park's Community Buildings

Early visitors may have been pleased with what they observed at Morgan Park, but the dearth of institutional and commercial services during the community's formative period did pose some inconveniences for residents. In May 1916, one new resident wrote a satirical letter to the *Duluth News Tribune* noting how pleasant it was to live in a "restricted neighborhood" that didn't allow cows, chickens, stables, or saloons. But, as he pointed out, the inconveniences of living in a community without a store posed several problems. What does one do, he asked, "when no tobacco can be found in the house, when the cream jug breaks and one has to drink black coffee and put syrup on the oatmeal, when the bread unexpectedly runs out, when a lemon is five miles away, or when unanticipated dinner guests suddenly appear and no berries are available? In our eagerness to avoid a business district," the correspondent wrote, "we had put ourselves in a place where there were no business conveniences. As though to avoid kitchen smells we built the kitchen a quarter mile from the dining room." But the writer was well aware that the needed services would arrive in due time and that he lived in a rather special place. "For an excellent and not too ornate example . . . of planning, see once more Morgan Park," he commented, "the only Duluth suburb that was really planned." Indeed, just two months later Morgan Park would boast a company store and a hospital, and by the end of the year the school had opened. In a few years a clubhouse, two churches, and several smaller buildings would emerge.[21]

Since U.S. Steel funded most of Morgan Park's public buildings, either entirely or partially, company officials gave considerable attention to the design, function, and management of the structures. While the close attention of a corporate sponsor could result in higher-quality design and improved construction materials, some activities and functions deemed objectionable for moral, sanitary, or economic reasons were excluded from the community altogether. Taverns, saloons, and prostitution were banned from "the little city within a city," and no union or labor hall would ever be found in Morgan Park (Figure 6.20).

A Company Store and a Little More

The construction of Morgan Park's company store began in 1915, but U.S. Steel officials did not spell out their retail philosophy to residents and Duluth merchants until early 1916. At this time an announcement appeared in

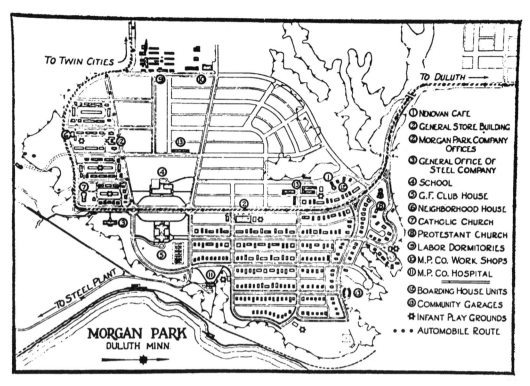

Figure 6.20. The overall pattern of development revealed at Morgan Park in 1922 would remain basically unchanged for the next thirty years. Courtesy of Duluth Public Library.

Duluth's newspapers, stating that a company store was necessary in Morgan Park because of its isolated setting and distance from downtown Duluth. Steel corporation officials explained that it was "very necessary that residents of the village be provided with the means of obtaining promptly and conveniently the most important household necessaries, especially those which must be purchased from day to day." Those items included meats and groceries, clothing, boots, shoes, hats, caps, haberdashery goods, furniture, household utensils, drugs, small hardware, "and such other things as may be found in an up-to-the-minute general store in any large village in the rural sections of Minnesota."[22]

Because of Morgan Park's limited population size, the officials also reasoned that several "small stores of miscellaneous character would find it difficult to supply the needs of the village with benefit to themselves or with satisfaction to the community." Nevertheless, Duluth's Retail Merchants' Association expressed immediate opposition, claiming that U.S. Steel was not establishing the store for profit reasons, "but to add to the comfort of its employees." Expressing the most vociferous opposition was Isaac Freimuth, who, in 1883, had founded what later became Duluth's first department store. Alleging that "a company store is the most obnoxious thing on earth," Freimuth and several other retail merchants requested a conference with U.S. Steel officials, hoping to convince them that the company store plan should be canceled.[23]

Despite the opposition, U.S. Steel's company store intentions prevailed. The Lounsberry Company constructed the two-story structure, 98 by 188 feet in size, which was built of concrete blocks and topped by a hip roof (Figure 6.21). Groceries, meats, clothing, hardware, pharmaceuticals, and home furnishings were sold on the first floor, while the upper level had private offices and shops occupied by the Park State Bank, a barber, a millinery, doctors, and a dentist (Figure 6.22). A branch of the city library opened in the building in early 1917, but it was moved to the school in May of that year. During subsequent years the proprietors and functions of the small

Figure 6.21. The Lake View Building, ca. 1916, accommodated stores, shops, and medical offices. Courtesy of Northeast Minnesota Historical Center, S2366B7af9, postcard collection.

Figure 6.22. Interior view of the hardware and dry goods store in the Lake View Building, August 1916, one month after it opened. Courtesy of Northeast Minnesota Historical Center, S2366B79f8.

shops and offices changed quite often; nonetheless, the company store remained a community mainstay well into the 1930s.[24]

The grand opening of the Lake View Building (also called Lakeview) in July 1916, intended "to get the public interested in the new store to arouse enthusiasm," employed special guides, who led visitors through the facilities. Charles Helmer's orchestra provided music for the event, which concluded with an evening dance in the building. Subsequent annual spring openings presented the store "in gala attire," with "fascinating accessories, new models, and up-to-date trimmings," as well as "late fashions and attractive materials." An alcove in the store was also used for exhibits, such as two hundred recent photographs of Morgan Park that were put on display in May 1917.[25] During the store's early years, a new Ford Model TT truck was used to make deliveries throughout Morgan Park and its surrounding area (Figure 6.23).

Figure 6.23. After the grocery store opened in the Lake View Building in 1917, deliveries were made with a Model-TT Ford truck, shown here in August 1920. Courtesy of Northeast Minnesota Historical Center, S2366B7af9.

In 1916, when the annual meeting of the Minnesota Retail Grocers Association meeting was held in Duluth, two hundred women toured the store in the Lake View Building, expressing "much interest in the arrangement and the up-to-date manner of handling goods." Two years later a new worker who had just secured a room at the Nenovan Club remarked on the goods and items available in the grocery store: "Here [are] no regiments of baked beans, flanked by dry looking salt meats," exulted the recent resident. "No. Here an up-to-the-minute stock, the reddest of meats, and the freshest and crispest of vegetables—an inviting place to enter." But there was even more, he exclaimed, for under a single roof there was a drug store, a dry goods store, a shoe repair shop, and a bank—"and everything so reasonable—that must be the slogan of this town."[26]

Accommodating Children and Adults: A School and a Clubhouse

The two most heavily used community buildings in Morgan Park were the school and the clubhouse. Confirmation of the two buildings' aesthetic and symbolic significance was evident in the original town plan, which placed them at opposite ends of a major east-west axis. Expansive areas of open space, with ornate garden and planting displays, provided an impressive setting for both buildings.

Preliminary designs for the school were prepared by the Duluth architectural firm of Kelly and Williams in early 1916. Although the facility was under the jurisdiction of Duluth's board of education, Minnesota Steel provided considerable financial support for its construction. The firm's officials also recommended that the architects make several changes to the initial proposals: to lengthen the building by thirty-six feet; to add two classrooms; to modify the placement of windows so as to allow more light to penetrate into the school; to make two of the building facades symmetrical; and to apply "faced brick" on the rear side of the school. The board voted to accept the changes, but only if "the steel plant will share the added expense."[27]

The building permit for a $116,000 concrete-block structure, incorporating the approved design changes, was issued in February 1916. Construction of the two-story building proceeded so quickly that students were able to move in by December (Figure 6.24). Almost 21,000 square feet of space were provided in the T-shaped, two-story school, which had fifteen classrooms (some identified by the names of famous educators, such as Maria Montessori), two administrative offices, four manual training rooms, two rooms for cooking and sewing classes, a library, a small gymnasium, and an auditorium with a stage and balcony. Tennis courts, a football field, and a running track were provided outside the building.[28]

The official dedication occurred in March 1917, when some 1,500 people attended a festive event where A. E. Bishop, the Boston-based editor of the *Journal of Education*, served as the keynote speaker. The program also included tours of the new facility, musical presentations, exhibits of children's schoolwork, and the showing of movies taken in the schools of Gary, Indiana. After greeting visitors in a formal reception line, the dignitaries were taken on an inspection trip of the hospital, the Lake View Building, and the Nenovan Club. Since it was wartime, the heavily armed guards who had been hired to protect the steel plant closely scrutinized each person arriving at the ceremony.[29]

In May 1916 Morgan Park residents and the plant's steelworkers received

Figure 6.24. Morgan Park school, looking toward the southwest, about 1920. Courtesy of Northeast Minnesota Historical Center, S2366B7f9.

word that a clubhouse would be built across from the school on an eight-acre tract of land. Eventually, U.S. Steel would invest $153,000 in the 158-by-258-foot building and its equipment, though wartime labor shortages delayed the opening to early 1918.[30]

The first story of the stucco-covered, concrete-block building, designed by the Dean and Dean architectural firm, was raised a half level above grade to allow natural lighting and ventilation to reach into the recesses of the basement. The footprint for the clubhouse—four wings grouped around a central core—also revealed the architects' efforts "to insure the greatest amount of sunlight and air and an unobstructed view from all windows." Exposed concrete buttresses supported the building's side walls, as well as the red tile roof that topped the structure. Labor analyst Leiffur Magnusson expressed satisfaction with the clubhouse design, noting that it "conforms to the general architecture of the community" (Figure 6.25).[31]

One clubhouse portal provided entry to the youth section, while another entrance had a large enclosed observation porch that offered a panoramic

Figure 6.25. The Good Fellowship Club building, about two years after it opened in early 1916. Courtesy of Northeast Minnesota Historical Center, S2282b1, postcard collection.

view of Morgan Park and its residential districts, hospital grounds, company office building, the St. Louis River valley, and in the distant background, the steel plant. Most visible were the outdoor recreational facilities—courts for handball, volleyball, basketball, and tennis, and greens for lawn bowling and croquet—as well as the formal gardens and plantings.[32]

Within the building a central vestibule extended to an auditorium and separate men's and women's sections, each with a lounging room that afforded "an unobstructed view in three directions through wide high windows." The main auditorium, seating 480 people, had a large stage equipped with "all conveniences." Located in the basement were a gymnasium, a handball court, an elevated running track, a twenty-by-sixty-foot swimming pool with a diving board, a billiard room, a photography darkroom, a cafeteria, three bowling lanes, and three separate locker and shower rooms (Figure 6.26). Good lighting, emphasizing "simplicity and harmony," enhanced the color scheme throughout the building.[33]

In January 1918 almost three thousand people attended the clubhouse dedication, where they toured the building, heard musical offerings, and

Figure 6.26. The gymnasium and its elevated running track in the Good Fellowship Club building, January 1918. Courtesy of Northeast Minnesota Historical Center, S2366B7f1.

engaged in social dancing. About two weeks later a card party for more than two hundred people marked the "first big social affair" in the clubhouse. Sponsored by members of Morgan Park's Anti-Monotony Club, the gathering raised funds for the Red Cross.[34]

A Hospital on a Hill

With Morgan Park situated a considerable distance from major medical facilities in downtown Duluth, Minnesota Steel officials realized that a nearby hospital was necessary to serve ill and injured employees. Therefore, a thirty-two bed facility, built and equipped for $50,000, opened in 1916 at a location with a direct view over Spirit Lake and the St. Louis River valley. Upon completion it was termed "one of the most nearly complete in the Northwest in the matter of equipment," including the "latest medical and surgical appliances."[35]

Once again, it was the Lounsberry Company that received the construction contract for the concrete-block hospital. The gabled roof and long eves that extended over the four-story rectangular building gave it a basic Prairie-style appearance (Figure 6.27). The treatment and patient rooms were located on the second and third floors, as were the two operating rooms, and the two solariums with their expansive areas of glass that faced toward the south (Figure 6.28). The fourth floor served as a nurses' dormitory, while the lower level housed the kitchen, a laundry, storage areas, housekeeping rooms, and an ambulance garage.[36]

Figure 6.27. The Morgan Park hospital, looking toward the northeast, ca. 1916. Courtesy of Northeast Minnesota Historical Center, S2386B14f21.

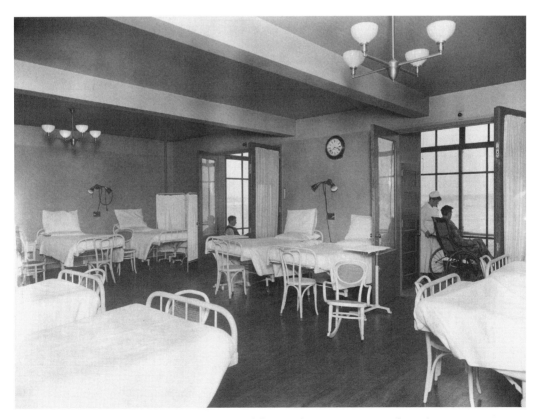

Figure 6.28. Interior of the Morgan Park hospital, 1917. Courtesy of Northeast Minnesota Historical Center, S2366B8f1, photograph 15167.

Sited at a picturesque point in Morgan Park that overlooked Spirit Lake, the hospital's expansive and formal landscape included a vegetable garden maintained by the medical staff (Figure 6.29). The garden supplied patients with "fresh and appetizing" produce during the summer and fall months.[37]

Since no direct road connection was available between the hospital and steel plant for nine months, ambulances were forced to meander along a circuitous one-mile-long route. The problem was resolved in 1917 when several "subways" were tunneled beneath the many railroad tracks that crisscrossed the steel plant grounds; later, a concrete road was constructed between the two points.[38]

By February 1917, all employees and families associated with the Minnesota Steel and Universal Portland Cement companies, as well as local workers affiliated with the Duluth, Missabe and Northern Railroad, had been assigned to the hospital. When patient numbers quickly taxed the

Figure 6.29. A view of Morgan Park, ca. 1918, looking toward the southwest from the hospital's carefully landscaped grounds. In the background from right to left are the school, the clubhouse, the office building, and the steel plant. Courtesy of Northeast Minnesota Historical Center, S2366B7af8.

hospital's capacity, plans were made to double the building's size. Before the expansion plans were initiated, an April fire, perhaps ignited by sparks from the steel plant's heating plant, destroyed the building's fourth floor and roof, and caused severe smoke and water damage throughout the remainder of the hospital. Twenty-four patients, fourteen of whom were carried out on stretchers, avoided asphyxiation by being quickly evacuated from the building. "The air in the rooms was stifling," one report noted, "and it was under the greatest difficulty that the rescuers made repeated trips." The most seriously ill and injured patients were transported to homes in Morgan Park, where they remained until their transfer to hospitals in downtown Duluth could be arranged. Tragically, just before the fire, Clarence Smith, a young laborer who recently had arrived from Birmingham, Alabama, was being readied for an operation after receiving a very serious head injury caused by a piece of dislodged metal from an exploding saw. When the surgery, termed "the only aid which could be given the sufferer"—was canceled because of the conflagration, an ambulance transferred Smith to St. Luke's Hospital, where he died a short time later. Dr. William H. Magie, Minnesota Steel's chief surgeon, insisted that "the exposure and jarring of moving Smith did not cause his death, and the outcome would have been the same even had the unfortunate fire not occurred." Smith's friends, as well as a Finnish-language socialist newspaper published in Duluth, gave a different interpretation, asserting that Smith probably died because the surgery hadn't occurred in adequate time.[39]

The hospital was repaired over the next weeks, but apparently the fire stymied any expansion plans. Just three months later, however, Morgan Park experienced its most significant tragedy when two hospital workers and two steel plant employees drowned in a single incident. The catastrophe occurred when Myrtle Hager, a twenty-one-year-old hospital laundress, plunged over a drop-off after wading into Spirit Lake. Two of Ms. Hager's female companions, both in their early twenties—Tena McLean, a laundress, and Rae Nurmi, a hospital cook who had emigrated from Finland three years earlier—drowned in their attempt to rescue the panic-stricken Ms. Hager. The same fate befell two men who tried to aid the women: Arthur Henry, a fifty-year-old finishing mill superintendent, and Melvin Olson, a twenty-eight-year-old assistant auditor for Minnesota Steel. Paradoxically, Myrtle Hager was the only survivor.[40]

The hospital would remain a fixture in Morgan Park for another decade, offering care for the employees of U.S. Steel's subsidiary operations and their families. While the general public could use the facility if beds were available, these patients were assessed a ten-dollar use charge for the operating and delivery rooms, and a one-dollar daily fee for the "care of babies." Public accident cases were not admitted, except in life-and-death situations, and then only with the understanding that a "patient shall immediately afterward be removed to a public hospital or elsewhere."[41]

When road conditions between Morgan Park and downtown Duluth improved during the 1920s, the need for a local hospital became less imperative. Therefore, after serving as a hospital for eleven years, the facility was closed in March 1927 and remodeled into an office building for Minnesota Steel's department of labor and employee relations.[42]

Churches Times Two

Church congregations in America's company towns often received monetary and moral support from their corporate sponsors. A similar situation occurred in Morgan Park, where two churches—one for Catholics, the other for Protestants—emerged in 1918 and 1922, respectively. Both were sited on lots provided by Minnesota Steel and received construction, operating, and maintenance funds from the company.

Work on the first religious facility, the Blessed St. Margaret Mary Catholic Church, commenced in August 1917 after a local priest, the Reverend Hugh Floyd, secured a $15,000 donation from U.S. Steel; the $39,000 building was dedicated in late 1918. Although the name of the architect or architects cannot be confirmed, the Duluth firm of DeWaard and Stauduhar may have been involved because they designed the nearby church rectory, also in 1917. Situated at the southeastern corner of Block 35 in Morgan Park's western neighborhood, the church was constructed of concrete blocks that were painted white some years later (Figures 6.30). A simple but well proportioned example of the Spanish Mission Revival style, a pair of three-story towers flanked the church's central entrance; wooden beams supported the interior nave and a gable roof. Some years after the church dedication several members of the parish donated funds for stained glass windows; one window facing the former steel plant depicts Christ as a worker, whereas on the other side, a window looking toward the school shows Christ as a teacher (Figure 6.31).[43]

A special census, conducted in 1919, determined that 504 Morgan Parkers over four years of age were Catholic communicants. Of these, 380 were adults, and 125 were children. Some local Catholics undoubtedly belonged

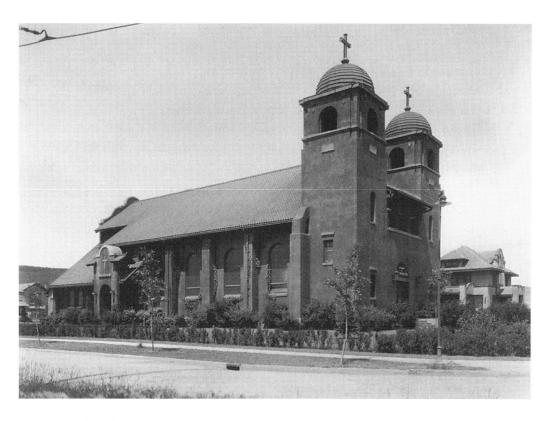

Figure 6.30. Blessed St. Margaret Mary Catholic Church, with the rectory to the right, July 1924. The church was later painted white. Courtesy of Northeast Minnesota Historical Center, S2366B8f7aa.

Figure 6.31. One of the stained glass windows in Morgan Park's Catholic church that faces the steel plant shows Christ as a worker; the opposite wall, which faces the school, includes a window that depicts Christ as a teacher. Photograph by the author, 2006.

to other parishes, but the vast majority certainly belonged to the Blessed St. Margaret Mary Catholic Church.[44]

The Protestant church would not open until 1922, but discussions about the need for such a facility were initiated six years earlier. Since Minnesota Steel officials advocated for a single Protestant congregation in Morgan Park, it was first necessary to determine which denomination would prevail in the model town. Local Episcopalians held an Easter service in one of Morgan Park's apartment buildings in 1916, but it was the Presbyterians who began conducting regular services in early 1917. By March, as discussions were taking place between representatives of various denominations and Morgan Park Company officials, there were intimations "that the Protestants may agree upon one united church for the district." Soon thereafter the Reverend H. Van Thorn, a local Presbyterian pastor, was encouraging Morgan Park's Protestants to organize "one strong church" rather than building several small and struggling churches of different denominations. The proposal initially caused some controversy, but in November 1917 seventy members voted to organize a single congregation, identified as the United Protestant Church. A group of sixteen Minnesota Steel officials and professional employees who belonged to the congregation, called the "Committee of Sixteen," was instrumental in facilitating the process.[45]

Although steel company officials had once proposed the Neighborhood House as a permanent site for Protestant services, the Reverend J. W. Kuyper, who began serving the congregation in July 1917, successfully lobbied for a separate edifice. In late October 1918, Morgan Park Company manager J. F. Davidson reported "an annual sum of four thousand dollars will be contributed by the company into the church fund for a period of two years." The congregation's building committee signed a contract with Duluth architects German and Jenssen in December 1918, requesting them to prepare preliminary studies "as to type, size, [and] arrangement of the building," including floor plans, elevations, seating, colors, and cost estimates.[46]

After the architects' proposal was completed in April 1919, Davidson questioned the $171,000 estimate for the building, interior furnishings, and site preparation. Terming the total "so much larger a sum than anyone had previously in mind," Davidson asked the building committee "to ascertain from the architects what makes it so expensive and to consider what features could be eliminated." He pointed to the proposed bowling alleys, the basement social room with its stage and dressing rooms, the clubroom, and the men's locker rooms, all of which replicated facilities found elsewhere in Morgan Park.[47]

Only limited evidence is available to document the subsequent architectural changes, but a somewhat less ambitious design was presented to the congregation in October 1920. The proposed church was in the English Gothic style, with a high nave interior, a beamed ceiling, and a single side aisle. The central bell tower that defined the main facade of the church also served as the entrance. Most of the recreational facilities that Davidson had previously criticized were eliminated, but several decorative flourishes still remained: a crenellated roof, stained glass, Gothic motifs, a covered automobile entrance or porte cochere that extended from the church to the driveway, and lancet arches on the tower. The new proposal received the congregation's "spontaneous and enthusiastic support," and was approved "without a dissenting vote." Certainly part of the reason for the enthusiasm was Minnesota Steel's offer to pay $100,000 for construction costs, with the congregation given responsibility for the provision of interior furnishings.[48]

The church began to emerge in September 1921 at the northwestern corner of the eastern neighborhood—the community's major entrance. Since the steel plant had been shut down since June, Minnesota Steel paid many of its unemployed men thirty cents per hour to work on the church and the nearby houses in Blocks 1 and 6. The concrete blocks for the church were manufactured on site, while fabrication of the wooden trim and construction forms occurred in the steel plant's carpenter and pattern shops (Figures 6.32, 6.33). The church dedication in early April 1922 was marked by morning and evening religious services that attracted nine hundred participants, and an afternoon gathering of some two hundred local temperance society members whose chaplain, the Reverend Charles Ramshaw, served as the congregation's minister—a position he would fill for the next twenty-eight years.[49]

A total of 1,130 Morgan Park residents four years of age and older were listed as Protestants in 1919. Presbyterians formed the largest denomination, followed by the Lutherans, Methodists, Episcopalians, Congregationalists, and eight smaller groups. With such a diversity of denominations, certainly not all Protestants chose to join the Morgan Park church. The congregation grew slowly during its early history, reaching a membership of 235 members by 1929, including several Minnesota Steel Company executives and supervisors. At that time, the members represented twelve different Protestant denominations.[50]

Figure 6.32. The United Protestant Church in May 1922, one month after its dedication. Courtesy of Northeast Minnesota Historical Center, S2366B8f7aa.

Figure 6.33. Interior of the United Protestant Church, about 1922. Courtesy of Northeast Minnesota Historical Center, S2366B7af9, photograph 18501.

A Bank to a Boathouse: Other Buildings and Facilities

Several structures in addition to those mentioned above were constructed in different areas of Morgan Park during its formative years: a neighborhood house, a boat club, a bank, community garages, two streetcar waiting stations, a railroad depot, a root house, and a curling rink. The Morgan Park Company managed the model town's residential areas and community buildings and provided police and fire protection, as well as water, sewer, and garbage collection services. The managers, clerks, carpenters, plumbers, and maintenance personnel who performed these duties were accommodated in several Morgan Park buildings.

A "welfare building," more commonly termed the Neighborhood House, emerged at Block 33 in 1916, just as construction of Morgan Park's first lower-rent housing units was underway. Intended as a recreational and social center for the western neighborhood, the simple exterior of the three-story building reflected the straightforward architectural character of the nearby houses (Figure 6.34). The first floor had space for a nurse's office, including "a fully equipped place to meet all of the requirements of her

Figure 6.34. The Neighborhood House, in this July 1920 scene looking north along Ninety-first Avenue West, reflected the architectural features of Block 33's multifamily residences. Courtesy of Northeast Minnesota Historical Center, S2366B7f6.

duties," a barbershop, and a small store for the sale of "special foreign goods and foods." The second floor had separate meeting rooms for men, women, and children, while the upper level had one large auditorium for lectures, dances, and recreational activities, along with a kitchen where girls gathered for cooking classes. The basement had reading rooms, classrooms, and a workshop.[51]

Because of the relatively small size of the western neighborhood, the barbershop and store were never provided. These spaces were converted into a children's playroom with an interior sandbox, and a boys' club. The Neighborhood House also accommodated Catholic and Protestant religious services until separate churches were provided for the two congregations. In June 1919 the Reverend Kuyper wrote of his hope "that for one hour all the Protestant cars will stop in front of the Neighborhood House and get enough religion for the Sunday evenings of July and August."[52]

The Morgan Park Boat Club was located along Spirit Lake and directly east of the hospital. Built by the Duluth Boat Club in 1907 and operated by the organization until 1915, the property was acquired by Morgan Park's Good Fellowship Club in late 1917. The remodeled complex provided members with a boathouse and an upper-level dance pavilion, a clubhouse, an eight-room summer camp building, two summer cottages, tent sites, tennis courts, picnic tables, swings, and croquet grounds (Figure 6.35). A toboggan run also provided wintertime recreational enthusiasts with opportunities to "slide out on to the river." Steel plant supervisors drove their automobiles to the boathouse, but most people walked to the site. The facilities were abandoned by the late 1920s, probably because of high maintenance costs.[53]

A much more long-lived institution was the venerable Park State Bank, organized by D. II. Lewis and others in 1916, and operated by Lewis family descendants all the way to the present. The bank began serving customers on the second floor of the Lake View Building and remained there until February 1919, when a new facility opened nearby. Designed by Duluth architect Anthony Puck, the thirty-by-sixty-foot bank building was constructed of brick and white stone and was graced by two neoclassical columns at its entrance (Figure 6.36). Situated inside the building were five teller's windows that served the rush of workers who descended on the bank to cash their checks every payday, two vaults, two hundred safety deposit boxes, a lobby and waiting area, and offices (Figure 6.37). On the second floor above the vaults was a small opening that provided a vantage point for an armed guard who watched as the workers cashed their paychecks on Friday afternoons. (Before getting to the bank the steelworkers picked up their checks

Plate 1. The small, parklike area situated at Beverly Street and Eighty-eighth Avenue in 2002, now the site of the Bob Stoner Memorial Garden. Located close to the major entrance into Morgan Park, the site formerly accommodated a streetcar waiting station, one of the community's most popular meeting places.

Plate 2. The former managers' houses grouped around the cul-de-sac in the eastern neighborhood are among the best-preserved residences in Morgan Park.

Plate 3. The sloped front lawns looking south along Eighty-fourth Avenue West have changed very little since these homes were constructed in 1914–15.

Plate 4. Mature trees and vegetation, as revealed by this residential lot on Arbor Street, define several areas of Morgan Park's eastern neighborhood.

Plate 5. A two-story residence located on the Eighty-seventh Avenue West cul-de-sac in the eastern neighborhood that has remained much the same as when it was built in 1917.

Plate 6. A multifamily house with six units, located at the corner of Eighty-eighth Avenue West and Edward Street in the eastern neighborhood.

Plate 7. A view of the rear facade and alley of a six-unit multifamily house located on Eighty-seventh Avenue West.

Plate 8. The concrete blocks used to construct this house on Eighty-fifth Avenue West have been covered with contemporary siding materials.

Plate 9. The multiple ownership of this four-unit residence on Eighty-fifth Avenue West is illustrated by the different building materials and colors on individual units.

Plate 10. The United Protestant Church, pictured here in 2002, serves as an anchor for Morgan Park's eastern neighborhood. The tower openings are now filled in with concrete blocks.

Plate 11. Blessed St. Margaret Mary Catholic Church in the western neighborhood borders the former steel plant property, and currently serves a congregation of some 150 families from the greater Morgan Park area.

Plate 12. A group of community garages borders one section of the eastern neighborhood along Edward Street.

Plate 13. The Park State Bank in the foreground, with the Lake View Building behind.

Plate 14. In 1982 the Morgan Park Community Building, shown at left, replaced the Good Fellowship Club Building, which had been a community institution from 1918 to 1981.

Plate 15. Looking north at an eight-unit residence along Ninety-first Avenue West in Block 34 of the western neighborhood.

Plate 16. A view to the north of the alley and rear facade of the same eight-unit residential building shown in Plate 15.

Plate 17. Looking toward the south at three houses that front on Hilton Street in Block 35 of the western neighborhood.

Plate 18. Looking south along Ninety-first Avenue West between Grace and Falcon Streets in the western neighborhood. These houses were constructed during the 1950s and 1960s.

Plate 19. The gate to the former steel plant site has remained closed for more than twenty-five years.

Figure 6.35. Three of the buildings, seen here in February 1917, which formed the Morgan Park Boat Club complex. The lower level of the main building, extending into Spirit Lake, sheltered boats, while the upper level served as a dance pavilion. Courtesy of Northeast Minnesota Historical Center, S2366B7f6.

at the pay house on the steel plant grounds, where the paymaster, who stood behind a caged enclosure, was also guarded by armed men.) Every feature of the "live and modern banking institution," from the lobby drinking fountain to the electrically powered adding machines, impressed the large crowds of people who attended the grand opening in 1919 (Figure 6.38).[54]

A streetcar line, built and operated by the Duluth Street Railway Company, began servicing Morgan Park on June 10, 1916. From then until the entire Duluth system ended in 1939, residents and steel plant workers were provided with direct access to much of the city. Just before the June 1916 opening, Railway Company officials spent seven thousand dollars each for "four handsome streetcars of the most modern type" to serve the Morgan Park run. When a shift change occurred each morning and evening at the plant, five to ten additional cars were put into service on a schedule that

Figure 6.36. Park State Bank, 1924. Courtesy of Northeast Minnesota Historical Center, S2366B8f7aa, photograph 20559.

Figure 6.37. Steelworkers lining up to cash their checks in the Park State Bank, 1920s. Courtesy of Park State Bank.

Figure 6.38. By the early 1920s, all the major buildings along Morgan Park's tree-lined boulevard were in place. Between the Lake View Building at the left front and the steel plant at the rear are the Park State Bank, the Good Fellowship Club, and Minnesota Steel's office building; at the far right is the school. Streetcar tracks ran down each side of the grassy boulevard. Courtesy of Northeast Minnesota Historical Center, S2366B7f6.

had them arriving and departing every ten minutes. The earliest streetcar appeared in Morgan Park at 5:30 A.M., while the last one departed the community about one hour after midnight. When the plant employed as many as 3,500 people from 1916 through 1918, each shift change was accompanied by a lineup of streetcars that stopped by the unheated waiting station, located just outside the steel-plant gates. Although the vast majority of workers exited and entered the streetcars in the western neighborhood, it was the eastern neighborhood that enjoyed the benefits of a substantial waiting station, situated at the intersection of Beverly Street and Eighty-eighth Avenue West (Figure 6.39). "I'll meet you at the waiting station," was a common expression of Morgan Park's children, who gathered at the building throughout the year. The octagonal concrete-block station included public restrooms that were cleaned daily; a former resident claimed that the building was steam heated by a coal-fired furnace "so management wives wouldn't get cold during winter."[55]

Figure 6.39. The streetcar waiting station that stood at the edge of the manager's district in the eastern neighborhood, early 1920s. The building also served as a popular meeting place for Morgan Park children. Courtesy of Northeast Minnesota Historical Center, S2366B7af8.

No private garages were allowed in Morgan Park until the post–World War II years, but early residents could rent one of the 230 or so automobile parking spaces that eventually were provided in thirteen community garages. (By June 1917, one-fourth of the 350 families owned an automobile.) Five garages built of concrete blocks provided 94 spaces, while eight constructed of board and frame and sheathed with metal offered 136 spaces. The largest unit, a 90-by-150-foot concrete-block structure attached to the police and fire station, was heated by a basement steam boiler; it included space for twenty-six automobiles, five motorcycles, two trucks, and dead storage for sixteen vehicles, as well as an area for servicing and repairing vehicles and a vehicle fueling station. Another steam-heated garage was built nearby in 1917, and two other community garages, designed in the form of crescents that faced each other, provided a score of heated rental spaces in the managers' housing district. The remaining garages were constructed from the 1920s to the early 1940s.[56]

Three other structures were utilized for brief periods of time before being razed or abandoned. One, a railroad passenger depot built in 1916, bordered the tracks that paralleled the St. Louis River (Figure 6.40). The widespread use of streetcars and private automobiles quickly obviated the need for railroad passenger service, and the depot was torn down in 1925. Another facility, a large community root cellar located just west of the police and fire station, served residents during the 1920s and 1930s, but it was not demolished until the 1970s. When the cellar opened in October 1920, the Morgan Park Company announced that its ninety-six bins were "easily accessible to all Park residents needing better storage facilities for winter vegetables." The structure with the briefest tenure was the curling clubhouse. It emerged in late 1916 after a group of local curling enthusiasts enlisted the help of the Morgan Park Company in constructing a 46-by-150-foot building

Figure 6.40. Workers commuted between the steel plant and Duluth on trains that stopped at the Morgan Park station depot, which was removed in 1925. The hospital is visible on the hill in the background. Courtesy of Park State Bank. Three similar photographs that form a series of depot images along Spirit Lake may be found in the collections of the Northeast Minnesota Historical Center, S2366B7Af8.

Figure 6.41. The building for Morgan Park's curling club, with its three sheets of ice, as it appeared in January 1917. The curling club was used only during the winter of 1916–17 before being torn down to provide space for the baseball field. Courtesy of Northeast Minnesota Historical Center, S2366B7f1.

Figure 6.42. By 1920, no other residential section of Morgan Park displayed a more sophisticated blending of landscape and architectural design than did the cul-de-sac at the end of Arbor Street and Eighty-seventh Avenue West. Courtesy of Northeast Minnesota Historical Center, B7af8.

that accommodated three sheets of ice (Figure 6.41). Women also pursued curling after one sheet was shortened by six feet. Constructed on the baseball field, the building was dismantled in May 1917, and, despite the curlers' wishes, it was never replaced. Nevertheless, during that one winter of 1916–17, the ice sheets in the curling building were in constant use—"stormy nights included."[57]

By late 1922 the sometimes frenetic pace of building activity that had defined life in the community since 1913 came to an end. Throughout these years, and for the remainder of the decade, Morgan Park served as a prototypical model company town. Its essential features were already evident by 1918, when Leiffur Magnusson issued his report about the community. Morgan Park, stated the U.S. Department of Labor analyst, "has been developed in an orderly and systematic manner, town-planning principles have been observed in its layout, educational and recreational facilities have been provided, and houses of a permanent and substantial character erected" (Figure 6.42).[58]

7. ENGINEERING THE GOOD LIFE

Other than a few, brief downturns, the U.S. Steel Corporation experienced remarkable financial success during the twentieth century's first three decades. Throughout this period the gigantic firm possessed sufficient monetary resources to build, manage, and maintain thousands of company houses throughout the nation. Indications of U.S. Steel's financial accomplishments certainly were evident at Morgan Park, where a model town stood next to a manufacturing plant that employed a few thousand workers, and where the smoke of prosperity billowed from large stacks outlined against the sky (Figure 7.1).

Since the severe economic restrictions that began during the early 1930s led to sharp cutbacks in many of U.S. Steel's employee benefit programs, only the first fifteen years of Morgan Park's existence overlap with the gigantic corporation's most profitable early history. Therefore, it is the period from 1916 to 1930 that most clearly illustrates what the "good life" was like in a highly managed and supervised model company town.

Managing a Community

About fifty people worked for the Morgan Park Company, a separate organization that Minnesota Steel formed in 1915 to manage the model town. The workforce maintained the streets, alleys, and lawns that formed Morgan Park's public landscape, distributed coal and fuel, collected garbage and trash, repaired the houses and buildings, changed screens and storm windows, and shoveled snow off many of the sidewalks (Figure 7.2). Other company employees served as watchmen and staffed the fire department and police force, including a law-enforcement officer who patrolled the community on horseback (Figure 7.3). Al Bothun vividly described the schedule that the Morgan Park Company followed before a family moved into a different house. "They sent the painters in; they painted everything all up and got everything all ready for you, fixed the furnace, did everything, got everything ready for you," recalled Bothun in 2001. "You moved in and you had

Figure 7.1. Overview of the steel plant and the Morgan Park community, ca. early 1920s. At the foreground of the western neighborhood (right) is the former labor camp; only the large building remains today. Courtesy of Northeast Minnesota Historical Center, S2386B14f21.

Figure 7.2. Workers employed by the Morgan Park Company delivering coal to a residence, July 1920. The men carried the conveyance to the house, where the coal was then dumped down a chute that led to a basement bin. Courtesy of Northeast Minnesota Historical Center, S2366B7af11.

Figure 7.3. Members of Morgan Park's police force and fire department stand by a new LaFrance fire truck around 1918. Courtesy of Northeast Minnesota Historical Center, S2386B14f21.

your house to live in. If you couldn't do it yourself they'd come and change your [storm] windows for you and put screens on."[1]

Another important task performed by the Morgan Park Company was tenant selection. The employees who signed up for housing were chosen "generally in the order of their application," though Magnusson pointed out that "other considerations may . . . have weight in the matter, such as the character of the applicant's services, his general desirability as a tenant, and the likelihood of his becoming a permanent employee." While the rental agreements did not limit a lease to the employment period only, the tenants could be required to vacate their properties thirty days after receiving notice. Besides rents, additional fees were also charged for vehicles parked in the community garages.[2]

The Residents: Who They Were in 1919–20

In early 1919 the Morgan Park Company conducted a population census of the new community it managed in southwestern Duluth. The survey revealed that of the 2,127 people who resided in Morgan Park, 40 percent were wage earners; the total population included 1,118 males and 1,009 females. The family dwelling units accommodated somewhat more females (862) than males (822), but men clearly outnumbered women in the boarding-houses and labor camp (187 to 56). A total of 127 people roomed or boarded in private residences. Thirty percent (644) of the community consisted of children younger than sixteen years of age.[3]

One year later, the 1920 federal census counted 1,947 people in Morgan Park. The eastern neighborhood of Morgan Park, which by then included sections that had been built from 1913 to 1915 and those built in 1917–18, was home to 1,640 residents. The western neighborhood had 306 people: 184 in Block 33 and 122 in the labor camp. (Blocks 34 and 35 had not yet been built.) The combined population of nearby Gary and New Duluth to-taled 2,840 people, while 153 residents were found in diminutive Oliver, Wisconsin.[4]

Only 17 percent (335) of Morgan Park's residents were of foreign birth in 1920; they were overwhelmingly dominated by the 315 old immigrants who came from Canada (88), Sweden (68), Britain (58), Norway (36), Germany (16), Holland (15), Ireland (14), and four other countries (14). Only 20 new immigrants—a scattering from Finland, Bohemia, Russia, Poland, and Italy—resided in Morgan Park.

In Gary and New Duluth, by contrast, more than 47 percent (1,345) of all residents had been born outside the United States. Furthermore, the compo-sition of the foreign-born population was the opposite of Morgan Park. Only 210 (20 percent) of immigrants who resided in Gary and New Duluth were old immigrants: 61 Swedes, 40 Norwegians, 38 Germans, 31 Canadians, 17 Danes, 13 Britons, and a few representatives from other nationality groups. Of the 1,135 new immigrants, the 613 South Slavs clearly predominated: 303 Slovenians, 218 Croatians, 70 Serbians, and 22 Montenegrins. Following the South Slavs were 111 Italians, 61 Poles, 56 Greeks, 54 Finns, 29 Russians, 25 Hungarians, 23 Romanians, and smaller numbers of Bohemians, Slovaks, Albanians, Bulgarians, and other nationality groups. Oliver, the small com-munity located on the Wisconsin side of the St. Louis River, served as a microcosm of Gary and New Duluth; its population of 153 people, many who had moved from the Mesabi Range to Oliver, included 43 foreign-born residents, 36 of whom were South Slavs.[5]

As noted, South Slavs predominated in Gary and New Duluth, although, as Hudelson and Ross write, they "were not welcome in Morgan Park." When interviewed by the Minnesota Historical Society in 1980, several first- and second-generation South Slavs recalled that Morgan Park's residents "always thought they were better than those [people] in New Duluth and Gary." Similar sentiments were also evident during the early history of the Morgan Park school, wrote one woman who interviewed several alumni from Gary. These students were often viewed as "foreigners," a perception that persisted for many years. Nonetheless, many South Slavs said they "didn't envy a thing" about Morgan Park. The people from Gary and New Duluth never wanted anything to do with rental housing; they wished to shun domination by a company ("too much like the old country"), and they believed there was insufficient living space in Morgan Park. Avoiding corporate policies and controls—especially those that limited opportunities to keep pigs, chickens, geese, and two or three cows—had also been very important to the earliest residents. Given the constraints of living in a company town, the South Slavs could not understand why Morgan Parkers believed the model town was superior to Gary and New Duluth.[6]

Equally striking were the racial differences that existed between Morgan Park and Gary. While U.S. Steel's official policy may have claimed that "no race segregation is attempted," African Americans were never selected as Morgan Park renters. Gary, on the other hand, was home to 110 African American residents—about 4.5 percent of the total population. (Just over 22 percent of all 495 African Americans who lived throughout Duluth in 1920 were concentrated in Gary.) The African American community in Gary had 50 adult males, 30 adult females, and 30 children under the age of sixteen. The steel plant employed 40 of the African American men. Except for one foreman, all were laborers, with most working in the coke plant, where they performed jobs considered "hot, dirty, and unhealthy." The 10 men who worked elsewhere found jobs as factory laborers, construction workers, restaurant waiters, and as a barber, a janitor, and a farmer. Only 5 of the 30 African American women worked outside the home—as a hairdresser, a cook, a restaurant helper, and laundresses.[7]

Accounts of efforts to recruit African American laborers from the South during the World War I years and employ them at the steel plant are indicated in the census. Almost 65 percent of the African Americans employed had been born in one of the twelve Southern states that stretched from Georgia, Alabama, and Kentucky to Texas and Oklahoma. Most of the remaining African Americans were from the Midwest, primarily Illinois and Minnesota.

Evidence of the clear racial divide that existed between Morgan Park and Gary is found in the few accounts that African Americans have given of their experiences in the area. Edward Nichols, who began working at the plant in 1916, reported that he and his black colleagues resided in a Gary "shantytown," whereas whites lived in "a model city made out of concrete blocks." Morgan Park's inhabitants, recalled Nichols, "had low rents, reasonable, and as long as they were orderly and obeyed their bosses . . . they were privileged to live there, and also privileged to get a higher wage than the black workers." The model town was also a place that blacks strictly avoided—especially after the infamous June 1920 lynching of three African American men in the city. Nichols's son, Charles, who was a teenager in the 1920s and 1930s, recalled that he always felt "a twinge of fear" when riding through Morgan Park on the streetcar that ran between Gary and downtown Duluth. "Never . . . get off the streetcar in Morgan Park" was the unwritten rule that Duluth's African American parents gave their children. According to young Nichols, their parents "were always concerned that if something went wrong with the streetcar and we had to get off in Morgan Park, we might be in harm's way."[8]

Pursuing the "Good Life" in Morgan Park

From 1916 to 1930, Morgan Park's citizens partook of the many opportunities that a model company town offered. Both adults and children found ample opportunity to join numerous community and service groups and to participate in social events. Thirty-six organizations—ranging from educational, musical, dramatic, and religious associations to scouting, athletic, fraternal, and medical and relief groups—were active in the community by early 1919. From October 1917 to October 1921 residents received the *Morgan Park Bulletin,* a handsome weekly magazine that informed them of the programs and events offered by these organizations and provided information about "how to garden, how to take care of their furnaces, how to manage their water supply—[and] keeping their lawns trimmed and premises neat." Physicians, teachers, nurses, pastors, and directors of various organizations and the Morgan Park Company wrote the articles (Figure 7.4).[9]

The majority of Morgan Park's activities were centered in the school, the Good Fellowship Clubhouse, the Neighborhood House, and the two churches; many occurred with either the implicit or explicit approval of Minnesota Steel and the Morgan Park Company. A number of programs, whether considering the highly organized school curriculum or the multitude of offerings in the Good Fellowship Club, revealed the pervasive and paternalistic influence of a corporate sponsor.

Figure 7.4. From 1917 to 1921, the weekly Morgan Park Bulletin *offered residents advice on numerous topics. Courtesy of Duluth Public Library.*

Morgan Park Bulletin

Volume 2.   Thursday, November 6, 1919.   No. 54

join
The American Red Cross

All you need is a ♥ -and a- $

MORGAN PARK   DULUTH, MINNESOTA.

The Morgan Park School: Work-Study-Play the "Wirt" Way

During Morgan Park's formative years, probably no single institution received more attention from both residents and nonresidents than the local school. Much interest focused on the use of the "Wirt Plan" or "Gary Plan," an educational program previously introduced at Gary, Indiana, by its superintendent of schools, William Wirt. Shortly after assuming his position in 1907, Wirt built a school system that quickly received national attention from American educators, industrialists, and the public.[10]

Students attending a Wirt school were divided into two groups or "platoons." During a part of each day, one group filled all the classrooms, where they studied traditional academic subjects. The other platoon was divided into several smaller groups, which allowed them to pursue other specialized activities. Some students utilized the playgrounds, athletic field, gymnasium, and swimming pool, while others took part in art, music, dancing, and dramatics, worked in laboratories and libraries, participated in field trips, and attended auditorium events featuring music, movies, theatrical performances, and lectures. Because the two platoons switched places later in the day, all the facilities were in constant use (Figures 7.5, 7.6). By organizing schools around a "work-study-play" program that prepared children

Figure 7.5. A girls' exercise class, conducted in a hallway of the school in 1918. Photograph by Henry Fuermann and Sons; courtesy of Northeast Minnesota Historical Center, S6080, CD 1.

Figure 7.6. As in all schools that followed the Wirt program, kindergarten and primary-age children had ample opportunities to study, play, and work throughout the year, July 1920. Courtesy of Northeast Minnesota Historical Center, S2366B7af9.

"for the social realities of the time," Wirt claimed that education would serve as a miniaturized version of adult society.[11]

In September 1915, after Minnesota Steel Vice President George Reis informed the Duluth School Board that the company would "donate grounds and equipment for a school modeled after those of Gary," city superintendent R. E. Denfeld visited the Indiana city. One month later Denfeld approved the Wirt program for Morgan Park, announcing that it might serve "in the nature of an experiment, and . . . may influence the future education in Duluth." Many local commentators expressed approval, though the wife of one Duluth educator was more skeptical: "I wonder if the 'Gary' system is not an attempt to wean ornery people away from study and make strong husky steel hands of them," she mused. Al Bothun, who began attending the school during the late 1920s, supported this observation. "I was raised to go to work in the steel plant, that was it. You didn't do nothing but go to work in the steel plant, or else you went to college and got to be a lawyer or a doctor or something—and I wasn't about to try anything like that."[12]

Members of Duluth's Socialist Club expressed opposition to the Wirt plan, claiming it was part of Minnesota Steel's attempt to gain control of the school. Ransom Metcalfe, editor of the *Steel Plant News* published in nearby Gary, quickly came to the defense of the steel company. Stating that the nation had already "devoted too much attention to the few who manage to get into the high schools and much too little to the needs of those who are compelled to leave school at an earlier age," Metcalfe viewed the Wirt plan as "an effort to do better by the many."[13]

One program that quickly brought attention to Morgan Park was the use of film as an educational tool; Morgan Park, in fact, was the first Duluth school to acquire a movie projector. "Emphasis is placed upon visual education, by means of the motion picture, the slide, and the projected picture," stated a Morgan Park educator. Among the early showings were films about life in Central Africa and sports in the United States, and others that featured wildlife, such as "Beaver Preparing for Winter" and "Feeding the Fish-Eaters." Morgan Park's teachers developed their own evaluation methods to assess the educational success of the films, eventually concluding that the use of visual imagery was "very effective," an "economical" use of the teachers' time, and something that made children "greatly interested" in what they learned. A "system of moving picture shows" was also organized for Morgan Park's residents two or three nights a week.[14]

The auditorium period, where students learned the "very important lessons for future life," was deemed the most important part of the school day.

"One day the children will listen to selections on a Victrola, and hear a talk on music; the next day the topic will be forging, or steel making or politics," explained Morgan Park Principal R. D. Chadwick, himself a former school administrator from Gary, Indiana. "Visualization, motivation, expression, appreciation of the better things are an outcome of the auditorium period, properly utilized," Chadwick reasoned.[15]

The first "gymnasium entertainment" occurred in April 1917, when Morgan Park's elementary students demonstrated their athletic and physical education accomplishments one year after the Wirt plan had been implemented. The program offerings ranged from military marches and bouncing ball, wand, and Swedish drills to Russian, Norwegian Mountain, French doll, and German clap dances. Onlookers found the "foreign dances" and the "perfect time" of the drills so well done that the students were called back for several encores. The evening program concluded with a basketball game between boys in the upper grades.[16]

The next year a school "exhibition" featured practical displays on view in the manual training and machine shops, the commercial rooms, the cooking and sewing departments, and even the laundry room. Included as part of the exhibition were tours of the student kitchen and its "up-to-date equipment," where girls were taught "family-scale cooking." One week later Elbert Gary and several of his U.S. Steel colleagues visited the school while on a trip to Duluth. After Gary briefly addressed the students about "the many ways they could help President [Woodrow] Wilson in winning the war," the smallest children sang the national anthem without the benefit of songbooks or instrumental accompaniment, which "greatly impressed the visitors."[17]

Principal Chadwick also hoped that Morgan Park adults would engage in "community gymnasium work" directed by three former collegiate athletes who had starred in basketball, boxing, and wrestling. Soon basketball games were being scheduled between different steel plant departments, while the best players formed a team that faced opponents from other areas of Duluth. The first match, in early January 1917, saw the merchant mill squad defeat the rail mill men by a 30-to-4 score. Community members watched other games with "intense interest," including one where a "magnificent" steel plant team overwhelmed the Proctor YMCA 53 to 7. Once the Good Fellowship Clubhouse opened in early 1918, all basketball games were played there.[18]

Also appearing in January 1917 were the first adult evening classes in citizenship, mathematics, drafting, metal work, sewing, and cooking (Figure 7.7). The most popular offerings, though, featured "gymnasium work": a women's

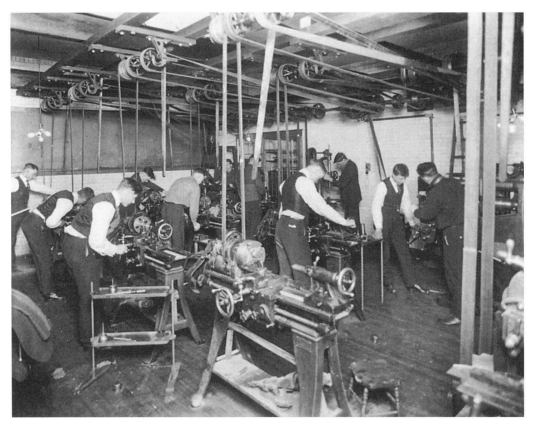

Figure 7.7. Included among the popular night school offerings at Morgan Park was this 1919 class in metal lathe work. From Morgan Park Bulletin, *February 13, 1919.*

class on Monday evenings; boxing, wrestling, and basketball for men on Tuesday, Wednesday, and Thursday; and a Friday evening gymnastics program for men offered by Max Alletzhauser, the long-time supervisor of physical training in Duluth's public schools.[19]

Local observers quickly expressed satisfaction with the number of night school participants. "The plan to make the Morgan Park schoolhouse a place for community gatherings and for community use has met with success," noted one account. "Since the auditorium was first thrown open, few nights have passed that some affair has not been held in the schoolhouse." When local citizens learned that the night school classes were scheduled to end in late March 1917, large meetings were organized in Morgan Park and Gary in protest. The patriotic fervor associated with the war was largely responsible for the successful effort that extended the program into early June. The *Duluth News Tribune* argued that foreign-born people residing in the western area of the city should avail themselves of opportunities to learn English in night school. "The immigrant should not be coaxed, he should be compelled [to attend]," exhorted the newspaper. Furthermore, the editors contended, a worker who didn't understand English could be "easily led by the agitator who speaks his language." Lulu Mae Coe, editor of the *Morgan Park Bulletin*, voiced a similar theme, writing that the war had shown "the vital need of the United States to bring the incoming alien crowds into sympathetic accord with the fundamental American idea."[20]

The Reverend J. W. Kuyper, pastor of the United Protestant Church, offered a more tempered view, writing that the country needed "to do away with every word of contempt and every word of derision and say thank God for the foreigner." Any Americanization program, Kuyper wrote, must be "strong and efficient so that the future will prove that we were wise builders."[21]

When the second school year began in September 1917, several new courses were added to the adult curriculum, including a class in steel-plant chemistry taught by R. C. Weed, a graduate of both Brown and Harvard universities. Women pursued classes in millinery, dressmaking, and clothing design, as well as basketry work. During the year, almost 30,000 visits were made to different evening events held at the school. Movies attracted 13,455 viewers; 10,065 people attended performances, dances, exhibitions, and mass meetings; classes drew 4,190 participants; and 1,380 citizens attended war meetings.[22]

In May 1919 officials also reviewed the regular day-school offerings at Morgan Park, primarily to assess the Wirt program's effectiveness. Their report affirmed that the practical aspects of the curriculum—vocational subjects, auditorium assemblies, alternating work and play periods in the primary grades, and lessons based on the "problem method"—had been carried out successfully. The review concluded that "the Morgan Park school attempts to prepare a child as adequately as possible for life after school years in order that when he or she leaves school and starts out to earn a livelihood or to manage a home, the transition will be an easy and natural one."[23]

Initially, the Morgan Park facility only served grades one through eight, with high-school students attending the Stowe school in New Duluth. Freshmen and sophomores enrolled at Morgan Park for the first time in 1917, with juniors and seniors joining them one year later. Samuel Plantz, the president of Lawrence College in Appleton, Wisconsin, spoke at Morgan Park's first graduation exercise in June 1922. Twelve students formed the class, with the two valedictorians, Lillian Karjala and Frank Draeger, receiving the highest marks in both academics and athletics—another reflection of Wirt program objectives.[24]

Athletic events were popular as soon as the school opened. Already in April 1917, Morgan Park captured the championship in a special basketball tourney organized for elementary schools in the western district of Duluth, and in 1921, Morgan Park was designated as Duluth's junior high school football champions. Once Morgan Park became a high school, students and residents alike supported its athletic teams, the "Wildcats." (During the school's early history, Morgan Park's high school teams were also called the "Steel Planters" and "Planters.") Football was a special favorite of both students and residents; Morgan Park's high school handbook of 1925 even deemed football "an essential of education."[25]

Initially the Wildcats had a difficult time competing against the other, longer-established high school teams that formed the four-team Duluth City Conference; even more challenging was the Head of Lakes Conference, which included all the public and parochial high schools in Duluth and Superior, along with individual public schools in Proctor, Cloquet, and Two Harbors. Although the Wildcats did not bring home a football championship in 1927, the "Eleven Iron Men" from Morgan Park were very competitive, defeating archrival Duluth Central for the first time. In 1929 the Wildcats barely missed capturing the Miller Trophy, awarded to the Head of Lakes Conference champions, when they lost the season's final game to the Central Trojans by a 6-to-0 score. Morgan Park's 1929 footballers did, however, qualify as tri-champions in the City Conference (Figure 7.8). The Wildcats basketball team experienced earlier success when they defeated the Trojans 13 to 12 in the 1928 district championship game.[26]

The Wirt plan remained a major part of Morgan Park's educational program throughout the 1920s. The general curriculum allowed students "to get any combination of courses [they] desired," while the industrial curriculum "had the aim of preparing boys to enter industrial fields." The girls' professional curriculum offered college prep courses, but with "the definite aim of preparing girls for the profession of home-making"; the popular stenography curriculum provided training for those students who wished to become skilled in shorthand. Also offered was a summer-school curriculum that assisted "the forward student[s] to go ahead of their classes and to help the backward student[s] keep up with their class."[27]

The economic depression of the 1930s led to a reduction in Wirt program offerings at Morgan Park, as well as throughout the nation. Subsequent studies of Wirt schools have noted that the programs often embraced two con-

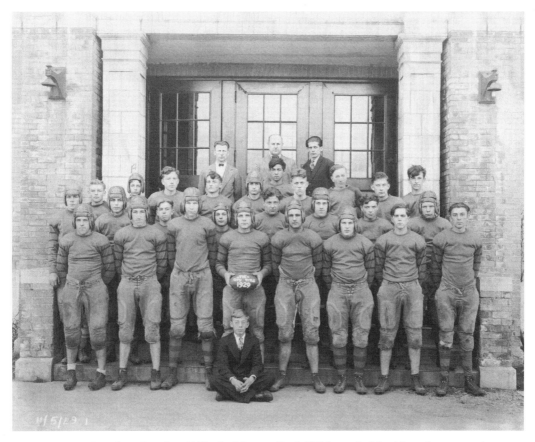

Figure 7.8. In late October 1929, the Morgan Park Wildcats finished in a three-way tie for the high school football championship of the Duluth City Conference. Courtesy of Christine Carlson and Llewellyn Ausland.

tradictory philosophies: democracy and efficiency. Progressive-era goals and reforms might have been emphasized, but Wirt also saw the schools as representing "order, self-discipline, and obedience to authority," all of which would lead to the development of students who exhibited conservative values such as "cooperation, conformity, unity, and patriotism."[28] Minnesota Steel officials certainly must have viewed Morgan Park's Wirt program in a similar light.

Good Fellowship in the Clubhouse—for Many, but Not All

Once the Good Fellowship Clubhouse opened in late 1917, Morgan Parkers had access to numerous supervised programs, many of which occurred in the gymnasium—"one of the most modern and well equipped rooms in this part of the country." (A number of the athletic events formerly conducted in the school's small gymnasium were now transferred to the clubhouse.) William Trepanier, a former Duluth hockey coach, served as the first director of physical activities. Identified as someone who had made "physical training his life work," Trepanier demonstrated his prowess by performing one-armed handstands on a taut wire. He offered athletic instruction to the club's male members, supervised the gymnasium, and oversaw all boxing and wrestling matches. A steel plant team played football in the Duluth-Superior War Industries League in 1918, bowling and tennis tourneys attracted widespread participation, and a semi-pro baseball team competed for several years. Some employees who joined the employee ranks in 1917 and 1918 were purposely recruited because of their major and minor league baseball experience, though questions were raised about the "legitimacy" of the work they performed in the plant. All baseball players needed to perform genuine work, not "straw jobs," warned the Good Fellowship Club's board of directors; if not, they faced the possibility of finding themselves in the nation's military "fight."[29]

In June 1918 Geraldine Vallier was hired to develop social and recreational classes for the community's "feminine element." The new director possessed quite remarkable credentials, having previously served as a team manager and coach in general athletics at Michigan State Normal College, where she supervised volleyball, basketball, tennis, and field hockey instruction, and also performed as a musician and dramatist. Just before assuming her new position, Vallier had organized women's gymnasium activities in the Morgan Park school, events "recalled with pleasure by those who attended the classes." Identified as an expert gymnast, swimmer, and dance instructor, the new director was introduced to the girls and women of Morgan Park as someone who could "offer an exceptional opportunity to develop a wider use of the various social and recreational facilities." Despite Vallier's obvious talents, she occasionally had some difficulty convincing women and girls to participate in the program of organized recreation. In 1919 Vallier sent out a letter listing the healthful and pleasant activities available at the clubhouse. Now was the time to learn how to swim, bowl, or dance, implored Vallier, particularly directing her comments to those women whose "daily routine of work [provides] insufficient exercise." Employing words that still resonate today, the recreation director pointed out that a woman could improve her health and vitality by following a program of "regular prescribed athletics."[30]

Minnesota Steel's employees and their families, whether residing in Morgan Park or elsewhere, could enjoy the "good fellowship" in the clubhouse, be it dancing, bowling, swimming, or reading; but only men could participate in the "get-together smokers" (Figures 7.9, 7.10). Many South

Figure 7.9. Rooms for reading, socializing, and smoking (the latter for men only) were available in the Good Fellowship Clubhouse. Shown here is one of the women's rooms in January 1918. Courtesy of Northeast Minnesota Historical Center, S2366B8f7aa.

TONIGHT

NEW YEAR'S BALL

At MORGAN PARK CLUB HOUSE

Given by the Thomas B. Shaughnessy American Legion
Post and Auxiliary.

MUSIC BY CHUCK'S NOVELTY ORCHESTRA.

Couples 75c   -   -   Extra Ladies 25c

DANCING FROM 9 P. M. TO 1925.

Figure 7.10. The Good Fellowship Clubhouse accommodated numerous social events in Morgan Park, such as the 1924 New Year's Eve dance. From Duluth News Tribune, December 31, 1924.

Slav steelworkers in Gary, however, didn't feel comfortable participating in the Good Fellowship Clubhouse activities—even if membership dues were deducted from their paychecks. Ultimately, the Gary Athletic Club, organized in 1929, would provide the community's population with a place for both sports-related and social activities.[31]

African Americans also had to pay monthly dues, but they couldn't even enter the Morgan Park Good Fellowship Clubhouse, much less participate in any of its activities and organizations. It was, according to one white retiree in 1992, "the height of unfairness." When a "colored club" from Gary wished to hold a concert in the building's auditorium in November 1923, the request was turned down for a rather lame excuse. "Due to the large number of dates now booked for Club activities," noted the organization's minutes, "[the] Committee did not see fit to grant this request." Nevertheless, the steel plant baseball team displayed no hesitancy in recruiting a star black player who reportedly had been unable to sign a major league contract because of his color. In another rather perverse form of irony, some of the most popular programs in the Morgan Park clubhouse were minstrel shows that featured white men dressed up in blackface who mimicked what they believed were African American speech and personality traits. (Similar shows also occurred in the Gary clubhouse.) In 1920 alone Morgan Park's "burnt-cork artists" performed five minstrel shows to capacity audiences in the community and elsewhere in Duluth.[32]

Good Neighbors in the Neighborhood House

U.S. Steel in 1920 identified Morgan Park's Neighborhood House as one of twenty "Practical Housekeeping Centers" that it sponsored in various mining and manufacturing communities throughout the eastern half of the nation. These facilities, the corporation reported, provided "special rooms and equipment" for carrying out various utilitarian programs such as "the preparation and cooking of foods, the care and feeding of babies, dressmaking, and many other phases of domestic science, even to the proper method of making beds." Furthermore, the housekeeping centers were intended "to furnish an object lesson for the wives and daughters of the employees by illustrating what may be accomplished in the way of convenience, comfort and attractiveness within their means." Morgan Park's Neighborhood House did, in fact, include a second-floor kitchen where young girls developed their culinary skills (Figure 7.11). Boys had access to a basement craft shop, where they often pursued woodworking projects (Figure 7.12).

Figure 7.11. One of the Saturday morning activities offered in the Neighborhood House shortly after it opened in 1916 was this girls' cooking class. From U.S. Steel Corporation, Bureau of Safety, Sanitation, and Welfare, Bulletin No. 9 (December 1924).

Figure 7.12. The Neighborhood House had a basement workroom, where boys could pursue woodworking projects. From U.S. Steel Corporation, Bureau of Safety, Sanitation, and Welfare, Bulletin No. 9.

Figure 7.13. In 1920 members of Morgan Park's Boy Scout and Forestry and Engineering Corps worked to develop trails and campgrounds at the edge of the community. Courtesy of Christine Carlson and William Satterness.

In 1920, shortly after a local "Boy Scout and Forestry and Engineer Corps" had been organized in Morgan Park, the troop began developing trails and campgrounds by opening up some of the heavily wooded, "nearly impenetrable" places that bordered the community (Figure 7.13).[33]

The majority of activities associated with the Neighborhood House were intended for residents of the western neighborhood, though some programs, especially those for children, attracted participants from throughout Morgan Park. (Gary had a similar facility, called the Little Gray House.) One resident later recalled that residents of the western neighborhood "controlled" the Neighborhood House, unlike the Good Fellowship Clubhouse, which was run by the community's "upper people." In addition to cooking and craft classes, children could take part in numerous activities: plays, phonograph concerts, sewing instruction, and story hours. Social events, community meals, parties, dances, and Red Cross meetings were organized for their parents. The Model City Rebecca Lodge also met in the building, as did the Women's Benefit Association of Maccabees.[34]

The building housed a social worker, Phyllis Dacey, who served as "a good neighbor to all." Dacey, the first woman to fill the position, had two years of experience in Boston's Lincoln Settlement House and had also worked in an Ohio infants' hospital. "Miss Dacey's work is not to be considered a matter of charity," reported the Morgan Park Company shortly after her arrival in April 1917. "She will do no private nursing, or care for the sick, but her duties will be confined to giving suggestions and instruction in the care of the sick, and the prevention of the spread of disease." Sometime in 1918 Dacey volunteered to serve in an evacuation hospital operated by the American Expeditionary Forces in France. "It has been a great satisfaction to have been here and I am mighty glad to have been able to stay until the end [of the war]," she informed readers of the *Morgan Park Bulletin* late that year. It appears that Dacey did not return to Morgan Park, but her successors would address the needs of thousands of steel company employees and family members for fifty more years.[35]

Among the events that social workers and members of the Child's Welfare League of Morgan Park organized in the Neighborhood House were "infant welfare demonstrations" or baby clinics. Some 400 people attended the first clinic in June 1918, when 112 babies were weighed and measured by the Morgan Park hospital staff. The mothers also viewed a model nursery, observed demonstrations in a feeding and clothing booth, read literature about infant care, and heard lectures on such topics as "Poliomyelitis," "Care of Teeth and Mouth," and "Conservation of Childhood."[36] The baby clinics continued, often on a weekly basis, throughout most of the 1920s.

Certainly to many Morgan Park families the most important features of the Neighborhood House were the children's playrooms, where supervised activities occurred (Figure 7.14). Duluth's director of recreation reported that the Neighborhood House permitted "mothers to get away from home for a few hours without 'dragging the kids' along—better for the children, and a boon to mothers." A Civic Pride Club that also met in the Neighborhood House asked the children of Block 33 "to keep a supervisory eye over the back yards," and encouraged them to pick up scrap paper and to refrain from walking across lawns and gardens. A note in the *Morgan Park Bulletin* later thanked the children for protecting the "green velvet carpet" of the Neighborhood House lawn.[37]

Community-oriented activities occurred within the Neighborhood House until 1927, when the building was donated to Morgan Park's Catholic congregation and converted into Blessed St. Margaret Mary Parochial School. The school subsequently served a large contingent of elementary students from Morgan Park and its surrounding area for more than thirty years until it was replaced by a new building.[38]

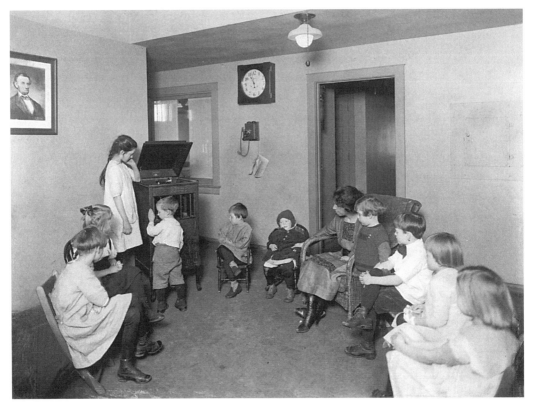

Figure 7.14. Children could participate in many activities in the Neighborhood House, including listening to records played on a "Victrola," as shown here in 1919. Courtesy of Northeast Minnesota Historical Center, S2366B7af9.

Playgrounds: Being Happy and Safe throughout the Day

Certainly among Morgan Park's most popular features were its playgrounds. The Morgan Park Child's Welfare League supervised the development of the community's first playground, located in a relatively quiet corner of the school grounds (Figures 7.15, 7.16). By 1920, three "infant playgrounds," all supervised by high school girls, were serving children under nine years of age in different areas of Morgan Park; almost two thousand visits were made by children to all of the community's playground facilities during just one July week of that year. (Children over the age of nine used the school playground, as did adults.) Emma Ghering, who had studied playground direction at Columbia University and acquired previous experience in New England and in Duluth's school system, oversaw the development of the program during its formative phase. By 1923, the number of playgrounds had expanded to eight.[39]

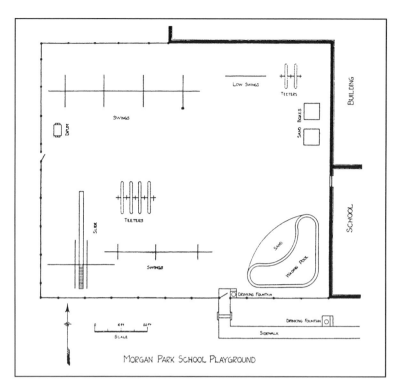

Figure 7.15. The plan for Morgan Park's first playground, sponsored by the local Children's Welfare League and developed on a section of the school grounds in 1917. From J. R. Batchelor, "Making Play an Asset," in R.D. Chadwick, ed., The Value of Play: Know Your School Series *(Duluth), no. 2, 1918. Courtesy of Northeast Minnesota Historical Center, Pamphlet 1200.*

Figure 7.16. Infants and young children had a clear view of the steel plant when their playground opened in 1917; a combined wading pool and sandbox were included as part of the playground. Courtesy of Northeast Minnesota Historical Center, S2366B7af11.

Equipped with swings, sand tables, building blocks, teeter-totters, and tables, the playgrounds were termed children's "resorts," and touted as productive substitutes for the "street and alley time" that otherwise might have consumed a child's day (Figure 7.17). "Fair-play is taught; games are organized; physical efficiency is developed; opportunity is given for the child to use his own initiative; and his play is directed as it should be," claimed Morgan Park's recreation director. The *Morgan Park Bulletin* reported that many parents were happy to see "their boys and girls go on summer mornings to the infant playgrounds, to be happy, safe, and contented throughout the day." With the children engaged in playground activities, Morgan Park's housing districts were quieter, which pleased the night-shift men who slept during daytime hours.[40]

Each playground supervisor saw that the "children are directed, their speech and actions are watched, their possibilities enhanced, and their every moment happy." A local policeman even claimed that the children's language improved because of the supervised play, and that there had been

Figure 7.17. Three more supervised playgrounds, in addition to the one located by the school, were available in Morgan Park by 1921. Photograph by Albert Solomon; courtesy of Northeast Minnesota Historical Center, S2366acc6417, photograph 44.

a reduction in complaints about "ruthlessly destroyed gardens, lawns, and flowers." Other reports pointed to the children's efforts to create and act out their own games, all of which allowed for "self-expression and the power of thought," and an ability to put "into action thoughts that probably otherwise would float about in a nebulous haze."[41]

For Every Home a Garden

Lawn and garden contests were commonplace in many early twentieth-century company towns. These competitions not only encouraged residents to improve the aesthetic attributes of their communities, but lawn and garden maintenance was also seen as a way to organize the workers' free-time hours. A busy worker was, after all, less likely to engage in activities the company deemed inappropriate, whether spending time in saloons or engaging in union activities and labor agitation. In 1991, Einar Bjork still remembered Morgan Park as it was in the 1920s: "no pets, no garbage in the lawn; there were no garages, no sheds. Everyone had pretty green lawns."[42]

The Morgan Park Company conducted annual lawn and garden contests from 1916 through the 1920s (Figure 7.18). The 1916 contest awarded a total of $425 in prizes for "lawns and general particulars about the house"; three years later the program had expanded to include rear-lot vegetable gardens, flowers, window boxes, porch decorations, play areas, and birdhouses. The judges noted the "wonderful" development that had occurred at Morgan Park within the span of just five years, especially the transformation of the townsite from a "wooded wilderness" into a place with "beautiful, green, velvety lawns" (Figure 7.19). Nevertheless, residents were also reminded that the remaining wooded areas within and around Morgan Park "should be looked upon by everyone as a public park, and every effort made to protect the trees from injury."[43]

The *Morgan Park Bulletin* offered numerous critiques of the residents' lawns and gardens. The failure of some people to mow their lawns in a timely manner was deemed "very regrettable," given that any lack of attention could "disfigure" an entire street. Some lawns were reported as being "marred by clothesline poles not vertical, not painted a desirable color, not of standard pattern, or not in standard location; by dog houses made of scrap lumber and unpainted; by unsightly piles of material, and the like." When pointing out that fences and gardens should display a unified appearance, the Morgan Park Company called for olive green posts (a common color throughout the model town) that had a smooth wire or wooden rail at

Figure 7.18. A 1918 award-winning garden situated at the backyard of a residence along Eighty-eighth Avenue West in the eastern neighborhood. From Morgan Park Bulletin, *September 12, 1918.*

Figure 7.19. A view of the gardens planted at the rear of the multifamily residences located along Eighty-seventh Avenue West, around 1918. Courtesy of Northeast Minnesota Historical Center, S2366B7af8.

the top. Another "good taste" recommendation suggested that staining the clothes poles, also olive green, would allow them to "commingle" with the fence posts, thereby permitting both of them to "sink into the landscape and become inconspicuous." When a clothes pole was missing or "untidy," the Morgan Park Company charged residents only ninety cents for a replacement. Acknowledging this was considerably below the actual cost for an eight- or nine-foot-long cedar or tamarack pole, the company reported that it wished "to meet the residents half way in their efforts to preserve the attractiveness of their yards."[44]

In 1917, the Morgan Park Company designated ten acres of vacant land that was divided into garden plots that residents could rent for a nominal sum. A model garden at the center of the acreage, tended by the company's gardener, was intended "to demonstrate the possibilities of making a garden picturesque as well as productive."

One year later, when World War I Victory Gardens were commonplace throughout the nation, 260 Morgan Park families paid one dollar each to rent the forty-by-fifty-foot patches of ground (Figure 7.20). Another garden area was provided next to the cement plant. (Overall, Duluthians planted

Figure 7.20. From 1916 to 1918 the Morgan Park Company provided land on the outskirts of the community for residents to plant Victory Gardens. From U.S. Steel Corporation, Bureau of Safety, Sanitation, and Welfare, Bulletin No. 7.

10,500 gardens in 1918.) The gardens usually grew potatoes, rutabagas, carrots, cabbages, onions, and other crops that didn't require daily care and cultivation. One observer noted that while the women of Morgan Park gave "careful attention" to their household gardens, the men were responsible for tending the gardens located at the edge of the community. For several years the Morgan Park Company also maintained a nine-acre potato field, a three-acre demonstration garden, and a three-acre truck garden. When making a brief Morgan Park visit in June 1918, Elbert Gary was "greatly impressed" by the war gardens that residents had established.[45]

Eighty-three percent (358) of Morgan Park's houses with backyards had rear-lot gardens in 1920. During that year the retail value of the produce from the allotment gardens, the small hospital garden, and the fifteen acres cultivated by the Morgan Park Company was estimated at $30,000.[46]

School gardens were also popular at Morgan Park, to such an extent that for a brief time in the spring of 1917, gardening became a required course in the curriculum. The program, proposed by Principal Chadwick, followed the plan of gardening previously employed in the schools of Gary, Indiana. One year later, Morgan Park's "soldiers in the U.S. School Garden Army"

Figure 7.21. Beginning in 1917, and continuing for several years thereafter, children were encouraged to maintain garden plots on land donated to the community school by the Morgan Park Company. From U.S. Steel Corporation, Bureau of Safety, Sanitation, and Welfare, Bulletin No. 7.

were encouraged to spend time tending the plots and contribute their "bit toward winning the war" (Figure 7.21). The clubs existed well into the 1920s. Gardens made Morgan Park "a paradise of beauty," enthused some observers, and could even provide "a supply of food material sufficient to feed the whole population."[47]

Socializing, Entertaining, and Celebrating

Most residents who remained in Morgan Park for any length of time apparently were satisfied with their life in a model company town. Morgan Park, after all, had numerous facilities and services that few, if any, other communities and neighborhoods of similar size could offer.

Announcements of Morgan Park events and activities appeared on a regular basis in the society pages of Duluth's newspapers after late 1916, and continued for about two more years. Birthday parties, wedding showers, illnesses, card parties, and the comings and goings of residents and visitors were most typically reported, although mention was also made of the first Morgan Parker who bagged a deer during the November 1916 hunting season.[48]

Community-wide celebrations were popular in Morgan Park for many years, especially two annual events organized by the Good Fellowship Club: the summer picnic and the Christmas party. The occasions that attracted the largest number of people, however, were the Fourth of July celebrations that occurred during Morgan Park's formative years. Organizers of the 1917 event, proclaimed an "old-fashioned celebration," raised one thousand dollars to cover the costs of organizing a parade, purchasing fireworks, securing a band, decorating the streets, and constructing a dance pavilion (Figure 7.22). Also featured was a group of "colored singers" who sang "plantation and jubilee songs." The 1918 festivities, attended by an estimated five to six thousand people, began with the launching of a small warship in the nearby Riverside shipyards. Following this was a "magnificent" parade that featured numerous local groups: Red Cross workers in uniforms; representatives from six Morgan Park community organizations and eleven steel plant units; the Italian, Serbian, Greek, Croatian, and African American societies of Gary-New Duluth; and schoolchildren, under the direction of Geraldine Vallier, who demonstrated a series of "Roman games" that included athletics and military dances. After the parade concluded at the Morgan Park baseball field, "decorated and fixed up in true carnival style," there were baseball games and track events, as well as pie eating, tug-of-war, and greased pole competitions.[49]

Figure 7.22. The Independence Day parade on July 4, 1917, made its way along Morgan Park's major roadway, Eighty-eighth Avenue West. Courtesy of Northeast Minnesota Historical Center, S2366B8f7aa.

No early occasion ever attracted more people to the community than did Independence Day in 1921, when Morgan Park was designated as the official venue for Duluth's Fourth of July activities. Proclaimed as "the most comprehensive program of features ever presented in the state for an Independence Day celebration," thousands of people came to Morgan Park, where they saw a three-and-a-half-mile-long parade with "floats costing hundreds of dollars," and five to six thousand marchers from seventy civic and military organizations. Games and contests took place later in the day, including the "turning loose and catching of a cub bear." During the evening people danced on streets lit by Japanese lanterns, while "water fireworks" in the form of flying fish and sea serpents shot over Spirit Lake concluded the festivities. Immediately thereafter "the most complete jam of automobiles" ever seen in Duluth occurred when some one thousand vehicles became "tangled" as they attempted to depart Morgan Park. Traffic jam notwithstanding, Morgan Parkers were commended for their "delightful hospitality" and willingness to extend "open arms . . . open hearts and open welcome to everybody."[50]

Numerous social events also took place at the Neighborhood House. The festivities that occurred on Labor Day in 1919, for example, included a luncheon for the residents of Block 33, an afternoon play, "My Aunt from California," a girls' dance exhibition, a picnic supper, and a "pavement dance," which continued until midnight.[51]

Discordant Notes

Morgan Park, as described by Duluth realtor C. R. Stowell in 1916, was a "beautiful" place. But Morgan Park was of even greater interest, according to Stowell, because of its residents. "To live in Morgan Park is to be a distinct type of citizen of Duluth," Stowell avowed, "with a different viewpoint toward civic affairs as far as they relate to the neighborhood." Its citizens, Stowell insisted, demonstrated a "community spirit" encouraged by the Morgan Park Company's actions—namely, the organization's belief that employees deserve "something more than wages—that it owes them an opportunity to live healthfully and wholesomely, and its return comes in the added efficiency that such living conditions generate."[52]

Undoubtedly many, if not most, early Morgan Park residents enjoyed the amenities and services that gave them opportunities "to live healthfully and wholesomely." Nonetheless, some dissonance was certainly evident within the community. And people who found the regulations excessively onerous obviously chose not to live in Morgan Park, or they departed after a brief period of residence. Although Stowell insisted that no "sociological meddling" occurred in the model town, company officials monitored both steel hearth and home hearth closely. "If you had a faucet leak you would just call over there for a plumber in the maintenance building," stated one eighty-nine-year-old resident in 1991, "but yes they had rules."[53]

Maintaining the moral principles of a model town meant that Morgan Park was designated as an alcohol-free zone. Early observers predicted that the absence of saloons would "keep the standard of the community high," while others reported that "Morgan Park has neither saloons nor slums; everybody who lives in it is prosperous." In fact, alcoholic beverages could not be purchased legally in Morgan Park until the 1940s, when they were made available for a brief period of time in the American Legion hall. Therefore, it was the taverns and saloons of nearby Gary and Oliver that became the favored destinations of thirsty Morgan Parkers and others affiliated with the community. Included in this group was a Morgan Park police lieutenant who spent time in a West Duluth jail in January 1917 for being "drunk and disorderly . . . and in a quarrelsome frame of mind." One of his colleagues, less than two months later, was also relegated to the same jail after being arrested for assaulting his wife.[54]

The neighboring Wisconsin settlement of Oliver proved to be the greatest concern to Duluth officials and citizens. To Duluth congressman Clarence Miller, Oliver was a place that had been organized for nothing other than "booze purposes"; furthermore, Oliver was also responsible for the "demoralized conditions" that existed on the streetcars running between Duluth and the steel plant. John L. Morrison, a "teetotaling, straitlaced Midwesterner" who served as the muckraking editor of the *Duluth Rip-Saw* from 1917 to 1919, also mounted a vigorous campaign against Oliver, which he termed a place of "drunkenness, fornication, debauchery, robbery and about all the filthiness in the devil's calendar." Receiving the brunt of his bitter criticism and sarcasm was Mayor H. L. Pryor, along with the chief of police and the community's aldermen, all of whom, Morrison maintained, benefited financially from the illicit activities (Figure 7.23). In September 1918 congressman Miller, with the support of three U.S. senators from Minnesota and Wisconsin, introduced a resolution, signed by President Wilson, that would "close up Oliver"—the steel plant district's "moral pest hole."[55]

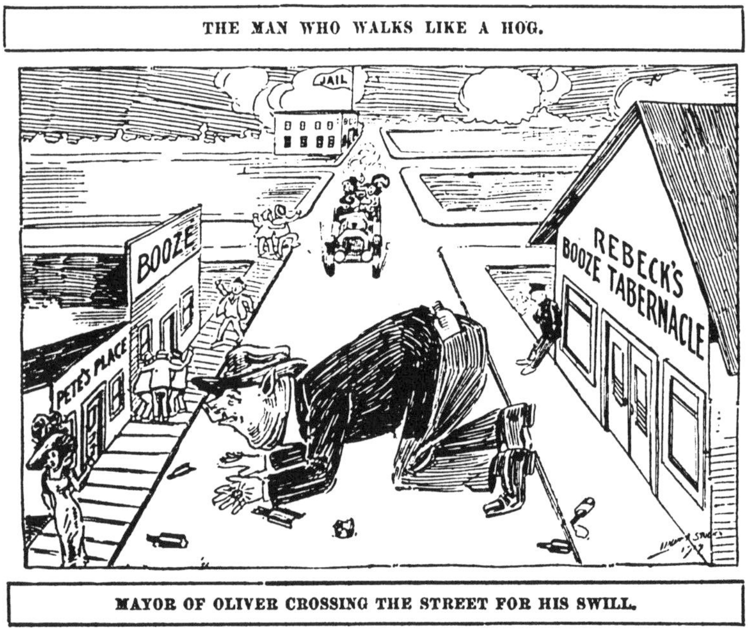

THE MAN WHO WALKS LIKE A HOG.

MAYOR OF OLIVER CROSSING THE STREET FOR HIS SWILL.

Figure 7.23. A cartoon in the muckraking newspaper the Duluth Rip-Saw *depicted H. L. Pryor, the mayor of Oliver, Wisconsin, as benefiting from the vice and graft in the small community located close to the steel mill. From* Duluth Rip-Saw, *June 28, 1919.*

One year later, passage of the Eighteenth Amendment to the Constitution was seen by its advocates as a way to end the manufacture, sale, import, and export of intoxicating liquors throughout America; nevertheless, the subsequent production and distribution of illicit spirits quickly shifted to homes and numerous sequestered sites. Shortly thereafter, Oliver and Gary became infamous for their many "blind pigs"—places where illegal alcoholic beverages were sold or consumed on the premises. One long-time Morgan Park resident recollected that after his family attended Sunday Catholic church services during the 1920s, they drove to Gary or Oliver, where homemade wine, beer, and "moonshine" could be purchased from various residents. In 1927 alone, federal agents arrested twenty-five Oliver bootleggers, destroyed twelve stills, and burned or padlocked numerous buildings where moonshine was produced. The next year an Oliver house was the site of a "drunken brawl" where two men were stabbed to death, including an off-duty Duluth police officer.[56]

Other issues involving company policies and practices could be minor and even petty, such as the failure of Morgan Parkers to clear their sidewalks of snow in a timely manner. Also problematic to company officials were children who engaged in "dangerous practices and misbehavior." According to Al Bothun, "the police department knew everything; they knew whose kids belong to who and who did what, and who was the one liable to be in trouble." Parents received reports noting the inappropriate behavior of their children, and they might even be given a bill for any damages that ensued. Insisting that they had no intention of "knocking" the children, company officials claimed they only had "the deepest interest in them and enjoy seeing them have the finest kind of time always—[but] in the right way."[57]

More serious was the charge, again issued by Morrison of the *Duluth Rip-Saw,* claiming that Minnesota Steel had illegally removed four pieces of equipment from the school machine shop in 1918. Company officials acknowledged that they had taken the equipment, but asserted the machines were needed for war-related activities. Soon, Minnesota Steel received notice from Duluth's Board of Education that the firm had "no proprietary interest" in the machines. "The Minnesota Steel Company has no more right to take machinery from the Morgan Park school than any other concern," charged Board of Education President J. R. McGiggert.[58]

Another charge leveled by the *Rip-Saw* insisted that Morgan Park had been the site of serious voting irregularities during the July 1918 Board of Education election. Minnesota Steel officials, who maneuvered to have residents and employees vote for Fred Knight, one of the company's managers, incensed Morrison. Steel plant employees had been allowed to leave work and canvass for votes, and many workers were driven to the polls in company vehicles—a violation of election laws. Apparently the company's efforts were successful, for 791 of 825 local voters supported Knight, and more than 600 marked their ballots only for him—even though three school board positions were open. The *Duluth News Tribune* was equally infuriated over Minnesota Steel's practices: "It was straight, fair notice to Duluth that they had no interest in Duluth's schools as a whole, in the school system nor the city's children outside their own 'private property,'" declared the newspaper's editorial page. Knight failed to garner enough votes elsewhere in Duluth to win the election, but this was not the last time that conflicts would emerge between city officials and those representing Minnesota Steel.[59]

Morgan Park definitely was a company town, recalled one resident who spent most of his life in the community, "and the feudal system was in full force." Einar Bjork, a Swedish immigrant who later became a labor leader and president of the local steel plant union, also reported on the partisan politics that characterized life in Morgan Park. Before voting, residents "had to call for a ballot," which meant they were forced to announce their political preference. "And if you lived in Morgan Park, and you call[ed] for a Democratic ticket," Bjork stated, "you got in trouble. Damn right." When Bjork began working at the steel plant in late 1922, he initially resided in West Duluth. When a foreman ordered him to move into the company-operated Nenovan Club in Morgan Park, Bjork refused. The foreman immediately gave him an "open transfer," which meant the company could fire him at any time. Eventually, however, Bjork married and moved into one of Morgan Park's family residences.[60]

Few other critical commentaries about Minnesota Steel's paternalistic practices have been preserved to the present, and even fewer current residents can recall the company-town era that ended during the early 1940s. Some, however, do have memories of the pervasive company controls that once regulated life in Morgan Park:

> If you didn't shovel your sidewalk in a certain time the company came and did it, but then it was deducted from your check. The same with mowing the lawn; you had to maintain the outside of your house, and if you didn't it was done for you and it was deducted. If there were marital problems that disturbed the neighborhood and it was reported, then the man got called into the office; if

it happened again, you were put on leave, and, of course, if you were terminated, you also lost your house.[61]

One person who directly experienced the operations of both the Minnesota Steel and Morgan Park companies was the Reverend J. W. Kuyper, the Oberlin College graduate and former football player who served as pastor of Morgan Park's United Protestant congregation from July 1918 to August 1919. When the influenza pandemic of late 1918 led to the closing of the church for several weeks, Kuyper went to work in the steel plant's open-hearth section. The *Duluth Herald,* impressed with Kuyper's physical strength, noted that he was the only religious leader in the city who pursued "hard labor" during the wartime era. Despite the rigors of a steel plant job, Kuyper insisted that he would not be deterred from preaching "good sermons."[62]

It was the management practices of the Morgan Park Company, which Kuyper witnessed firsthand while advocating for the construction of a church, that he found most frustrating. In his October 1918 farewell sermon to the congregation, a presentation heavily laced with sarcasm, Kuyper called Morgan Park Company manager J. F. Davidson the community's "King." Kuyper questioned how Davidson and his assistants could claim universal competency when supervising the community's services and activities. Not only did they believe in their ability to administer a village and sponsor a school system, retorted Kuyper, but they simultaneously acted as authorities "on running a club for the social and general welfare of the people," and in selecting and employing "unregistered nurses to take care of the sick."[63]

Most galling to Kuyper were Davidson's attempts to exert power over Morgan Park's ecclesiastical matters, which the Protestant minister claimed were even greater "than the Pope of Rome in the height of his glory in the days of the past." Kuyper steadfastly refused to worship any "King or Kaiser"—especially one who "sat on the throne in Morgan Park." He acknowledged, nonetheless, that because so many residents worked for Minnesota Steel, they had "sworn complete allegiance to the King," and would "come at his beck and call." Voicing strong beliefs "in a democratic church where the truth can be spoken," it is not surprising that Kuyper and his family had already departed Morgan Park by the time he offered the sermon.[64]

In their brief 1992 overview of Morgan Park, Nash and Silberman commented on the contrasts between living in a "fish bowl," on the one hand, and having a company that enforced community "standards" on the other.

"But for all of Morgan Park's positive aspects, there were negative ones as well," they observed. "Behind the air of generosity and harmony was a system of social control no less absolute simply because it was not immediately visible. Yet as in any small town, what may be regarded as stifling closeness and enforced conformity by some will be seen as neighborliness and the expression of shared values by others."[65]

PART III

From Despair to Prosperity, 1930–1945

The steel plant at Morgan Park is going full blast and with so many men out fighting, they've now got nearly 500 women working, doing everything from piling steel to feeding some of the blast furnaces.

—*Duluth News Tribune*, August 22, 1943

The residential suburb of Morgan Park, a development built twenty-eight years ago to house workers at the steel plant, has been sold to an Ohio purchaser in a deal made public in Duluth today.

—*Duluth Herald*, December 18, 1942

8. STRUGGLING FOR WORK DURING THE 1930S

Minnesota Steel's employees had endured cutbacks and even a brief shutdown at the manufacturing plant during the 1920s, but these were minor events compared to what transpired throughout much of the 1930s. The "hot side" of the plant was shut down for more than five years, and one of the two blast furnaces was totally dismantled at mid-decade. Only the mills composing the "cold side" of the facility operated whenever small contracts were received from manufacturers. No wonder that steel plant employees felt fortunate if they found even part-time work during the Depression.

The "Bitter Years" of the Early Thirties

Kenneth Warren has described the overall condition of U.S. Steel during the early 1930s as "terrible." A comparison of figures from 1929 and 1930 reveals how quickly the economic fortunes of the corporation plummeted. U.S. Steel's total output fell from a record high of 24.5 million tons in 1929 to 18.8 million tons in 1930, the operating capacity of its plants declined from 90 percent to 67 percent, and profits plunged from $197.5 million to $104.4 million. By the latter months of 1930 the entire American steel industry was displaying noticeable symptoms of the nationwide economic malaise. "Current reports of steel ingot production are not reassuring," was the *New York Times'* somber assessment in November. Although the declines were severe, it is doubtful that anyone realized the situation would only worsen over the following years.[1]

Despite the uncertain national conditions, Minnesota Steel officials remained positive throughout much of 1930 (Figure 8.1). Louis Reis, who had replaced Samuel Sheldon as president and general manager of Minnesota Steel early in the year, reported in May that a number of new orders allowed the plant's one operating blast furnace to run at 80 percent of its capacity. Duluth's residents viewed the steel products on display in the windows of the Northern National Bank throughout much of the summer, and participated in steel plant tours. The cement plant also operated at close to 100

Figure 8.1. Even though the dire circumstances of the economic depression were evident by the end of 1930, the Minnesota Steel Company bravely advertised its manufactured products to the public. From Duluth Herald, *December 31, 1930.*

MINNESOTA STEEL COMPANY

SUBSIDIARY OF UNITED STATES STEEL CORPORATION

MORGAN PARK, DULUTH, MINNESOTA

---MANUFACTURERS OF---

Specially Designed Steel Posts

of Various Sizes and Weights for Snow Fences, Highway Signs, Railroad Crossing Signs, Right-of-Way Fences and

THE NATIONAL DIRT-SET END AND CORNER POSTS

Embodying a new principle which avoids the cost of concrete setting—well adapted to light soil.

We Also Manufacture

HOG POULTRY AND CATTLE FENCING—MERCHANT BAR PRODUCTS, ROUNDS, SQUARES, FLATS, ANGLES—REINFORCING BARS, WIRE RODS, MATERIAL FOR BOLTS, NUTS, SPIKES, AND OVER 900 VARIETIES OF NAILS.

The Minnesota Steel Co.

SUBSIDIARY OF UNITED STATES STEEL CORPORATION

Operating Right Here in Your Own City and Built to Serve This Great Northwest, Extends to Its Many Friends and Patrons

A HAPPY NEW YEAR

percent of its capacity during the summer months of 1930. When a November *Wall Street Journal* article reported on a $10-million steel-manufacturing mill that was proposed for the vicinity of Morgan Park, the *Duluth Herald* noted that the New York newspaper was an "authority for . . . industrial and other investment concerns," but cautioned that a similar announcement made by the *Wall Street Journal* in September 1929 had never been realized. "Just what the [1930] plan is, is uncertain," stated the *Herald*—a prescient warning, given that the entire Morgan Park facility would be shut down in just a few months.[2]

In northeastern Minnesota, the first signs of the impending economic malaise were reports of significant declines in the overall demand for the state's iron ore. About thirty-one million tons of ore were shipped from the state's mines to America's steel mills in 1930, some fourteen million fewer tons than the record total of forty-five million tons established just one year earlier. And in Duluth itself, census figures reported that with 5,700 people out of work by April 1930, the city's unemployment rate was higher than that of any other urban area in the nation. Two years later the number of unemployed in Duluth had burgeoned to 11,715, almost 27 percent of the working population. Mayor Samuel Snively attempted to develop municipal projects that would provide some financial resources for the city's most needy residents. Already on one November day in 1931, some 4,500 "youths and greyhaired men" had appeared at city hall, hoping to find employment on a few public works projects.[3]

The situation became increasingly dire for the entire American steel industry throughout 1931 and 1932. U.S. Steel's mills turned out only 11.3 million tons of product in 1931, and a paltry 5.5 million tons in 1932; the corporation also lost $71.2 million in 1932—the first loss in the firm's history and the largest it would experience until the early 1980s. Despite these calamitous conditions, U.S. Steel president Farrell, who retired in 1932 after serving in the position for twenty-one years, put on a brave face when describing the early Depression. Admitting that he could not predict when the nation might emerge from the economic predicament, Farrell still believed there was "no doubt that we will come out of it stronger and better than we were before."[4] Farrell, who died in 1943, lived long enough to see the Depression end, though the slump certainly spanned many more years than he had envisioned.

The demand for steel products fell so quickly and precipitously at Morgan Park that during the transition from 1930 to 1931, both of its blast furnaces, five of ten open-hearth furnaces, and half of the coke ovens were shut down completely. With the hot side of the plant now termed "dormant capacity," only the merchant, rod, and wire mills operated on a part-time basis over the subsequent seven years.[5]

As many as 250 part-time laborers also worked on an intermittent basis at the Universal-Atlas Cement Company plant during the early 1930s. (The Universal Company, a U.S. Steel subsidiary with a nationwide network of cement plants, changed its name to Universal-Atlas in early 1930, after acquiring the Atlas Cement Company.) When the Minnesota Highway Commission announced that the facility had received contracts to supply almost one million barrels of cement for northern Minnesota's 1931 road-paving program, local residents were elated. With every 400,000 barrels of cement estimated to provide three months of full-time work for 210 employees, both Mayor Snivley and Minnesota Governor Floyd B. Olson attempted to funnel public contracts toward Universal-Atlas.[6]

From Minnesota Steel to American Steel and Wire

As if the economic depression hadn't already created enough havoc at Morgan Park, a dramatic management change occurred at the steel plant in 1932. In June, the American Steel and Wire Company (AS&WC), a U.S.

Steel Corporation affiliate based in Cleveland, leased the Morgan Park plant from its parent organization. This transfer meant that Minnesota Steel now functioned simply as a holding company, not as an operating entity. Ironically, the new leasing arrangement went into effect almost exactly on the twenty-fifth anniversary date of Minnesota Steel's founding in 1907. Recommended by U.S. Steel president William Irvin for reasons of "economy and efficiency," Kenneth Warren described the transfer as an "indignity" to Minnesota Steel since the firm lost its separate identity. In 1937 U.S. Steel chairman Myron Taylor even admitted that the corporation had "not been entirely fair with the [American Steel and] Wire Company because, when we wanted to dispose of some of our property in Duluth, we dumped it onto them."[7]

Nationwide, U.S. Steel and its affiliates now operated with little more than a skeletal workforce. In 1932, only 14 percent of all U.S. Steel employees were full timers, while 68 percent of the pre-Depression labor force was relegated to a twenty-five-hour workweek. Wages and salaries were also reduced by 15 percent, which meant that an average employee now earned just $15.50 per week—one-half of what had been paid in 1929. Hundreds of steelworkers throughout Duluth were laid off permanently, while others felt fortunate if they got hired occasionally for part-time work. Einar Bjork, who later became a leading union activist at Morgan Park, observed "it was pretty much seniority" that determined who stayed in the labor force during these years; furthermore, anyone laid off for more than two continuous years lost all privileges of seniority. Similarly, an eighty-one-year-old retired steelworker from Gary who was interviewed in 1975 recalled that workers living in Morgan Park during the 1930s were "assured of a job—[or] at least the last to be laid off"; those living elsewhere were not as fortunate.[8]

No wonder that Morgan Park general manager Louis Reis wished to put 1932 behind him as the year drew to a close. "The less said about what we have done in 1932, or rather, failed to do, because of lack of orders, the better," wrote Reis in a brief report. In a somewhat uncharacteristic remark for a business executive, Reis viewed the election of Democratic President Franklin D. Roosevelt, which had occurred two months earlier, as reason to "look forward, with hope, to the future." Reis reasoned that "hope for the future may be soon realized if the thousands of voters of Minnesota and other Northwestern states, who registered their confidence in the advent of better conditions, will back up that expression of confidence by even a moderate, but sustained, ordering of the merchandise we manufacture and which they need."[9]

After 1932, America's steel industry posted very slight production gains. U.S. Steel's output grew from 5.5 million net tons in 1932 to 9.0 million tons in 1933, and then to 9.7 and 12.5 million tons in 1934 and 1935, respectively; the increases, nevertheless, were so minimal that the corporation's finances continued to hemorrhage. From 1932 through 1935, U.S. Steel experienced a cumulative net loss of $128 million, a figure so massive that only a business conglomerate with its vast financial resources could have avoided bankruptcy.[10]

If U.S. Steel can be described as enduring a very severe cold during the early 1930s, then the Morgan Park plant suffered from a case of chronic pneumonia. The hot side of the facility was still classified as dormant capacity in 1935, and one of the two inactive blast furnaces was even dismantled during the year. The off-and-on production activities that did occur during these years were totally dependent on whatever small orders arrived at the mills, but these facilities were also shut down for several months at a time. Since the individual orders could be for as little as five hundred pounds of steel products, the manufacturing and fabricating equipment demanded constant changing—all of it "done at considerable loss."[11]

Manufacturing operations may have been in the doldrums during the 1930s, but the environmental quality of the St. Louis River channel environment improved noticeably. John Wilson, the former Duluth city engineer, noted that as production at the plant slowed, "green life replaced the blackened fringe and normal conditions were reestablished" along the river.[12]

In late 1934, when limited production activities resumed at the merchant, wire, and rod mills after a typical five-month-long hiatus, H. H. Lumley, the new general manager, expressed hope about the forthcoming year. But, as he admitted, when considering the future "there really is nothing one can say." The stress of supervising Morgan Park's facilities may have even contributed to the health problems experienced by Reis, who had retired as general manager in November 1934 at the age of fifty-four. Less than a year later Reis was dead of a heart ailment. No wonder that a *Duluth News Tribune* staff writer termed the early 1930s the "bitterest period" in Morgan Park's history—"a period which old timers hope will never come again."[13]

Coping with "Chicago Plus"

During the decade, many of Duluth's civic and business leaders still believed that conditions could be improved by changing the basing point system used to determine transportation charges for steel manufactured at Morgan Park.

Duluthians had hoped the system would improve in 1924 when the Federal Trade Commission (FTC) ruled in favor of removing Pittsburgh Plus; but U.S. Steel only expanded the number of base point cities very slightly. Even after Chicago replaced Pittsburgh as Duluth's basing point, steel manufactured at Morgan Park in 1934 was still assessed an average surcharge of $6.60 per ton over the Illinois price.[14]

Hearings conducted by the National Recovery Review Board (NRRB), headed by famed attorney Clarence Darrow, featured the experiences of Otto Swanstrom, who had founded the Duluth-based Diamond Calk Horseshoe Company in 1908. The inherent unfairness of the pricing system was noted by the *New York Times*, which reported that Swanstrom had paid an extra Chicago-based freight charge for steel bars produced at Duluth— even though "the bars never had seen Chicago." In a letter to the *Washington Post* that appeared shortly after the hearings, Swanstrom contended that further "discrimination against us and in favor of Chicago will, within a short period of time, force us to close our plant and confiscate the greater part of our investment."[15]

In late May 1934, Swanstrom received word that Duluth would soon be made a basing point for steel products. Nevertheless, few changes were made to the system—even after a 1935 FTC report pointed out that the price for manufacturing steel at Duluth had been raised well above the Chicago figure. "When the new Duluth base became effective [a year ago], the base price applicable there was arbitrarily placed at a considerable differential over the Chicago base price," noted the FTC. "This case illustrates how inadequate may be the relief which attends the mere establishment of an additional basing point." Despite the damning evidence, Duluth would not be free of such restrictions until three more years had passed.[16]

Unionizing a Workforce

Several New Deal programs intended to lift the country out of the depths of the economic depression were initiated in early 1933 by President Roosevelt's administration. Several proposals sought to better conditions for industrial workers, such as the National Recovery Administration (NRA), which called for the provision of an eight-hour workday and the establishment of a minimum rate of pay for common laborers. Nationwide, wage rates ranged from thirty-five cents to forty cents per hour, with the Duluth figure set at thirty-seven cents.[17]

One major New Deal program that had an immediate impact at Morgan

Park was the National Labor Relations Act, or Wagner Act. Passed by the U.S. Congress in 1935, the measure authorized the development of a National Labor Board to supervise the efforts of workers engaged in union organization and collective bargaining. U.S. Steel continued to oppose most of the Wagner Act's provisions, primarily the closed shop, which limited employment to members of an officially sanctioned union. Instead, the corporation sought to develop employee representation plans or company unions, a concept that many workers at Morgan Park and elsewhere rejected because they were construed as being little more than labor councils that represented corporate interests. "These organizations," according to labor historian Robert Zieger, "designed primarily to undercut true labor unions, operated under company auspices and usually under tight managerial control."[18]

In 1936 U.S. Steel president Irvin once again called for the establishment of "open shops"—unions that did not restrict employment to members of the labor organization only. During that year Irvin wrote the following to his employees:

> The United States Steel Corp. has always stood for the open shop and will continue to do so. It will never require employees to belong to any union to gain employment. On the contrary, it will defend their rights to work, free from outside interference and coercion. . . . No man in our employ has to join any organization in order to work for us. His progress in his work depends upon individual merit and effort and not upon his influence with some outside organization.[19]

Despite Irvin's opposition, the Steel Workers' Organizing Committee (SWOC), an offshoot of the Congress of Industrial Organizations (CIO), began unionizing American steel laborers during the summer of 1936. SWOC's regional director, Van Bittner, asked Morgan Park steelworker Earl Bester to organize a local union at the plant in August. On a Sunday afternoon in September, Bester, who eight years earlier had led an unsuccessful drive to organize a group of Morgan Park crane operators, met secretly with seventeen of his fellow steel plant colleagues in the basement of the Clyde Pease Tavern in West Duluth. "The local [union] flowered out from the seventeen," Bester later recalled, and led to the formation of Local 1028 of the Amalgamated Association of Iron, Steel and Tin Workers. Local 1028, which had four hundred members by September 1936, received its charter on November 8, 1936, the first CIO union in the Duluth area. Workers at the nearby Universal-Atlas plant would later form Local 1210 of the Cement Workers Union.[20]

The nascent union movement also had to cope with the "spy system and other channels" used to monitor organizational activities. Many workers believed the most insidious aspect of these practices was the "dollar a day man"—an employee who received an extra dollar per day from the company for spying on his fellow workers. Such men were "the worst thing" about working at the steel plant, exclaimed a retired worker in 1991, while Bester noted "they had a stool pigeon on every job, almost next door to you." U.S. Steel tried to appease its union-minded workforce by offering all employees an immediate 6.5 cents per hour wage increase in 1936, but the action "did not slacken activity of union-minded men in the [Morgan Park] plant." After SWOC's national membership had grown to 125,000 steelworkers, negotiations with five of U.S. Steel's largest producing units—including American Steel and Wire—were initiated. The contract between union and industry representatives, signed in March 1937, granted employees a ten-cent-per-hour pay increase, a forty-hour workweek, time and a half for overtime, and a one-week paid vacation for workers who had at least five years of seniority.[21]

Membership in Local 1028 was considered a sacred right to many workers. "Unionism is like a religion with me," commented Leonard Wegmiller in 1943. "It's something I always believed in." Likewise, an immigrant laborer who started working in the steel plant workforce in 1913 praised the improvements that unionization had brought to Morgan Park. "We used to work six days [a week], 12 hours a day and we earned less than now when we work 5 days, 8 hours a day," he affirmed. "We've got seniority rights. No more bosses' pets on the best jobs. We've got rights." Many years later Ernest "Bucky" Johnson recalled how grateful he was for the job security provided by the union:

> Before the unions, like when you went to work, you didn't know if
> you were going to have a job or not, you know. They could lay you
> off just like that, for no reason at all. If they didn't like you, well. . . .
> We got the union in, then they couldn't do that. The union helped
> you out. The union did a lot.[22]

Union numbers grew so rapidly that by mid-1937, Local 1028 had 1,500 members—close to 85 percent of all eligible employees. Meanwhile, Earl Bester, who had played the key role in forming the union, organized iron-ore miners on Minnesota's Mesabi Range and the mining districts of northern Wisconsin and Michigan.[23]

From 1937 to 1940, employee grievances were of great concern to Local 1028's leaders and members. If former workers were either inadvertently or "conveniently . . . forgotten by the company" when positions at the plant were being filled, the union's stewards noted the oversights and had the workers reinstated. The committee also checked into claims that the company was "attempting to chisel on vacations" and gave considerable attention to seniority issues. "The grievance committee of the union," said Local 1028's recording secretary Ervin Drill in October 1939, "will go to bat for any former union member who contacts us and gives us necessary information to establish his record of employment." Since the union's members could not hold meetings in any of Morgan Park's buildings, they initially conducted their business in West Duluth's Redman Hall (Figure 8.2).[24]

In late 1937, *Midwest Labor* reported that Local 1028 had filed a complaint with Duluth's Superintendent of Schools, alleging that a New Duluth elementary school teacher was questioning students in a way that was "calculated to poison their minds against the union activity of their fathers who are in the main employees of the steel plant." The complaint alleged that the teacher

BEST WISHES FOR A MERRY CHRISTMAS
AND A HAPPY NEW YEAR

—From the—

Steel Workers Organizing Committee

LET'S ALL GET BEHIND THE CIO
NATIONAL LEGISLATIVE PROGRAM

—FOR—

3,000,000 WPA JOBS
PROTECT CIVIL LIBERTIES
PUT TEETH IN THE WAGNER ACT
KEEPING AMERICA OUT OF WAR

HENRY A. BURKHAMMER

District Director, SWOC, Duluth

Figure 8.2. The Minnesota Steel Company sent out season's greetings to newspaper readers at the beginning of the 1930s, but at the end of the decade the recently organized Steel Workers Organizing Committee (SWOC) announced its presence. From Midwest Labor *(Duluth), December 22, 1939.*

had suggested the union was "unreasonable, full of radicals, and responsible for the lay-offs at the plant" and inferred that the students' fathers were "a greedy, ungrateful group of whiners."[25] Apparently the issue was resolved because *Midwest Labor* reported no further complaints thereafter.

During that year a reporter for the same newspaper, who called herself "Calamity Jane," interviewed the wives of several steel plant workers in New Duluth, asking what they would do "with a bigger pay envelope"—something the union was working to provide. One respondent replied that if her family only had a little more money, "we wouldn't have to board with our in-laws—we'd have our own place . . . maybe our own little home." Another woman noted that after her son lost his job, he and his new wife moved into the family residence, which expanded the number of people in the household to seven. Remarking that she had recently suffered a nervous breakdown and had trouble breathing, the woman answered the question with a pragmatic wish: "If I had a little money I would take it easy and get well." One respondent mentioned that extra money would allow her to "go and see a dentist and have all these teeth pulled, and plates put in," as well as "paint the house up a little and buy a new rug." The woman's dreams extended beyond such mundane concerns, however, for her utmost yearning was an opportunity to travel. "People should have a little trip before they get old and tired," she exclaimed. "When you get too old you don't care any more. It isn't right for people to live and die in one place. Life gets too monotonous!" But the very most modest hopes were especially poignant. "Well, I'd really like a permanent wave," stated one woman whose husband always told her that any hairdo had to "wait 'till next payday." Looking toward the future, she responded wistfully: "Oh, I hate to get old . . . never having had a permanent wave!"[26]

A Prelude to War

The efforts of Morgan Park's union leaders to improve the lives of steel plant employees during the latter half of the 1930s coincided with a gradually improving economic outlook throughout the city and the nation. Most heartening to Duluthians was the reopening, in 1936, of the steel plant's single blast furnace, along with two open-hearth furnaces and several coke ovens. Although initial expansion plans called for the hiring of no more than 250 additional employees, the *Duluth Herald* greeted the news enthusiastically. "The blast furnaces and ovens have been cold since 1930," noted the newspaper, "and the reopening will put back into use a portion of the plant that in former years was the scene of great activity." With both the hot and cold sides of the Morgan Park plant now operating on a limited basis, a modest fifty thousand tons of steel and steel products were shipped to a few markets in 1937.[27]

More positive news arrived in June 1938, when city officials finally achieved what they had been seeking for over twenty-five years: the implementation of a Duluth-based pricing system for steel products. Especially pleased was Julius H. Barnes, the former president of both the Duluth Board of Trade and the U.S. Chamber of Commerce, who twenty years earlier had led the group that unsuccessfully lobbied Elbert Gary to eliminate the Pittsburgh Plus system. Barnes believed that because of the "injustice" Duluth had experienced over the previous two decades, the city's progress as a great industrial center had been severely impeded. "It was especially unjust to Duluth in that it [Pittsburgh Plus] took away half of the advantage of its cheap water transportation advantage, its great natural advantage," Barnes wrote in a statement prepared for local business leaders. "Duluth has a right to feel that it would have been today a larger more active industrial center if the leaders of the steel industry held a quarter century ago the views of today's younger leadership. Perhaps it may not be too late now to recover some of the ground lost, and some of the rights of which this community was deprived over all these years." Barnes then expressed his hopes for the future, a future that would include the development of "plants that manufacture fencing for Western farms, pipes for Western oil mills and water mains, sheets, and boxes for Western products."[28]

A limited version of Barnes's dream was realized almost immediately when U.S. Steel announced that the local plant would serve as the sole manufacturer of all steel posts produced by the corporation. Despite the designation, company executives were less than sanguine when asked whether the city's new status as a basing point would attract new industries to Duluth. "Basing point or no basing point," they observed, "competition is so keen that any big user of steel is able to get prices from far-away mills that make the local mills scratch to meet them, regardless of freight costs. Larger volume in bigger mills accounts for the difference in costs."[29]

U.S. Steel's national output experienced an overall decline in 1938 (a recession year within the Depression), but the figure at Morgan Park actually doubled, with 100,000 tons of steel being produced during the year. The increase was attributed to a steady demand for rods, billets, and fence posts in several eastern states, along with orders from some South American countries. Operating at 40 percent of its capacity in October, the plant employed close to 1,400 workers, who received an average hourly wage of 84.5 cents for thirty-eight hours of work per week. The cement plant, which had been shut down since September 1937, started operating with one shift of 150 workers in April 1938.[30]

During the last year of the decade, America's steel production system rebounded; from 1938 to 1939, the output for all of U.S. Steel's facilities rose from 10.5 million tons to 17.6 million tons. When U.S. Steel President Benjamin Fairless visited Duluth and the Morgan Park plant in July 1939, he confirmed that business conditions for the corporation had improved markedly. Several factors were responsible for the improvements, including congressional authorization of an American rearmament program that began in 1939 and requests from European nations for supplies and armaments that would be employed in the battle against the Nazi juggernaut. Numerous American manufacturers, anticipating that the issuance of federal permits for huge orders of war munitions would restrict their ability to make regular purchases in the future, were also stockpiling steel by 1939.[31]

The Morgan Park plant participated fully in the nationwide expansion. By late 1939 the facility often operated day and night, employing 1,800 laborers.[32] While the gains experienced at Morgan Park and elsewhere in America were tied to the demands of an ever-widening European conflict, few people could have predicted the massive amounts of steel that the war effort would require from 1940 through 1945.

9. GETTING BY AND MAKING DO

Morgan Park's company town status may have been maintained through the precarious years of the Great Depression, but several management changes foreshadowed the much more dramatic transitions of the 1940s. The first change occurred in 1930 when Morgan Park's street names and numbers were altered and integrated with those of Duluth.[1] Three years later, responsibility for most of Morgan Park's community services was transferred to the City of Duluth, and by mid-decade, non-steel-plant employees were permitted to rent housing in Morgan Park and preliminary plans were being made to sell the residences.

Affiliations with Duluth

U.S. Steel's drastic financial losses of the early 1930s led to significant modifications, and even the elimination of many services and employee-benefit programs that the corporation offered in its steel plants and towns. Morgan Park certainly was no exception. In March 1933, less than a year after responsibilities for manufacturing operations had been transferred to the American Steel and Wire Company, the Morgan Park Company submitted a letter to the Duluth City Council requesting that it accept the deed for the model town. Although U.S. Steel would retain ownership of Morgan Park's buildings, the petition called for the transfer of all community services to the City of Duluth. The council's members reluctantly considered the proposal, even if they saw "no alternative but to accept the deed to the property from the Morgan Park Co."[2]

The council debated the issues after Duluth's engineer and planning commission members inspected the community and approved the transfer. Duluth Finance Commissioner Clarence A. Williams, who adamantly opposed the exchange, called the community a "white elephant" and questioned whether the Morgan Park Company had any right to "saddle the city with property it could not afford to maintain." The company's attorney offered a rejoinder, pointing out that even if the city refused to accept the deed, it still had responsibility to furnish police protection since Morgan Park was located within Duluth's boundaries.[3]

Following a series of negotiations that stretched out for seven weeks, the Morgan Park Company agreed to place "the plat in perfect condition" by expending more than $130,000 on donations and the upgrading of services. The resolution, accepted by the City Council in late August 1933, included numerous provisions: to improve Morgan Park's streets, sidewalks, and storm sewers; to rewire the street lighting system; to pay for police services through the end of 1935; to transfer Morgan Park's fire engine to the city; and to donate 9.5 acres of property along the St. Louis River for a park. The estimated annual expenditure of $22,000 needed for community maintenance was acceptable to Council members since U.S. Steel had been making annual tax payments of $30,000 to $60,000 for its Morgan Park holdings.[4]

Limited Work, Empty Houses

The federal population census of 1930 revealed that 1,980 people resided in Morgan Park—33 more than in 1920. The eastern neighborhood experienced a small population decline, whereas the western neighborhood grew slightly. (The construction of Blocks 34 and 35 in 1921–22 provided more housing in this neighborhood, but most of the resulting population gain was offset by the closing of the labor camp later in the decade.) The shutdown of Morgan Park's blast furnaces in late 1930 and early 1931, however, ushered in a steady erosion of population numbers that continued over several subsequent years. Only 15 of Morgan Park's 510 family dwelling units were vacant in early 1932, but the number grew to 68 in 1934, and then to 112 in 1935. Assuming that each vacant dwelling formerly housed an average of four residents, Morgan Park lost some 460 residents between 1930 and 1935. Almost 20 percent of all houses in the lower-rent western neighborhood (20 of 125 units) were vacant in 1935, while close to 25 percent of the eastern neighborhood's dwellings (92 of 395) were unoccupied; however, only 3 of 30 houses in the managers' district stood empty.[5]

The population losses and vacancy rates almost certainly would have been greater had Morgan Park's residents not benefited from the hiring preferences that the company followed whenever the plant operated for brief periods of time. One long-time steel plant employee recalled, in 1991, that most employees knew there would be "much less chance for you to be laid off if you were living in Morgan Park and attending to the company, than if you lived elsewhere." The experience of Vito Di Mele, a West Duluth resident who joined the steel plant workforce in 1916 but did not work one day over a four-year period from 1931 to 1935, was probably quite typical. "I had my own home away from Morgan Park," reported the father of eight in 1946, "and they were then keeping only those [workers] renting company houses." But some who lived in Morgan Park, such as Elief Bothun, were not assured of steady employment either; a community resident since 1922, Bothun worked only thirty-two days during one grim year of the Depression.[6]

The high vacancy rates led Morgan Park Company superintendent J. C. MacDonald to announce, already in 1933, that the housing gradually would be "thrown open for occupancy by residents other than employees of the Minnesota Steel plant." It was not until early March 1936, however, that an advertising campaign was launched that featured Morgan Park's "affordable" monthly rents—$17.50 for a four-room row house, $24.50 for a five-room single-family residence, and $36.50 for a nine-room dwelling (Figure 9.1).

Figure 9.1. Because of the limited number of jobs available at the steel plant during the early to mid-1930s, many residents departed Morgan Park in their search for work elsewhere. In 1936, people not affiliated with steel plant operations were able, for the first time, to rent the housing units. From Duluth News-Tribune, March 1, 1936.

The new renters could also become associate members of the Morgan Park clubhouse, thereby giving them access to movies, the swimming pool, the gymnasium, and the physical education instructor. Within a brief period of time, about 10 percent of the houses were occupied by people not affiliated with American Steel and Wire.[7]

For these new renters, Morgan Park provided relatively attractive, inexpensive residential accommodations. This fact was reflected in a survey of American planned communities, conducted in 1936 by two Harvard University city planning and landscape architecture faculty members, who gave high marks to Morgan Park's appearance, terming it "especially good." The concrete blocks, considered an "intelligent" use of construction materials, also gave the community "a harmonious although somewhat drab appearance." Furthermore, Morgan Park's mature plantings and landscape features, along with its "consistently well-maintained" residential lots, were described as "highly effective, although somewhat heavy in places"; overall, it was the vegetation that "relieve[d] the drabness of the grey concrete."[8]

When the blast furnace, two open hearths, and several coke ovens gradually went on line later in 1936, a number of steel plant workers started moving back into Morgan Park. By early 1937, only twenty-seven of Morgan Park's houses stood empty, and most of the remaining units were filled relatively quickly.[9]

Among those who returned to Morgan Park were Fritz and Hilda Friederici. Born in Germany, Friederici earned a mechanical engineering degree from the University of Cologne before immigrating to the United States in 1907. In 1910 he and his brother Max were among the first engineers that Minnesota Steel hired to work on the design of the Duluth steel plant. The brothers resided in an apartment on Duluth's near east side until 1914, the year that Fritz Friederici married Hilda Isaacson, the daughter of Finnish immigrants who lived in the rural community of Sawyer, located about twenty miles west of Morgan Park. Two years later the couple and their infant son moved into one of the managers' houses in the eastern neighborhood. Friederici was a member of the "Committee of Sixteen," which facilitated the establishment of Morgan Park's United Protestant Church congregation in 1917, and he also performed violin solos at community programs. The family resided in Morgan Park until 1928, when they journeyed to the Chicago area, where Friederici accepted employment as a chief engineer with the Taylor Pipe Works Company. In 1935, when Friederici was rehired by American Steel and Wire, the couple moved back to the Morgan Park manager's district, but into a different house than the one they had inhabited earlier.[10]

Building Losses and Gains

The overall inventory of buildings in Morgan Park experienced a decline during the 1930s, although some new construction did occur. The most noticeable loss was the building that, from 1916 to 1927, initially served as a hospital, and then as a steel company employment and labor relations office for seven years. Since the size of the Morgan Park workforce fell so appreciably during the Depression, little need existed for an employment office, and the building was demolished in 1934. Two other structures were razed in the eastern neighborhood at this time, both by early 1936: the smallest of the four Nenovan Club buildings, and a duplex—the only residential dwelling ever removed from Morgan Park.[11]

The western neighborhood also experienced significant changes when the East View and West View boardinghouses were demolished. From 1934 to 1939, the former North View boardinghouse served as a school "annex" that accommodated Morgan Park elementary students enrolled in grades three and four. The North View was razed in late 1939, following the completion of a project that expanded the original school building by adding six classrooms, a music room, industrial arts facilities, a new gymnasium, "and a science department, adapted to teaching physics, chemistry, and biology." The federal Public Works Administration (PWA) provided almost half of the $180,000 expended on the addition and remodeling.[12]

The single new building that emerged during the period was the Morgan Park Auto Sales and Service Filling Station, opened by the Standard Oil Company in 1938 at a site located one block north and across the street from the Lake View Building (Figure 9.2). Its development led to the eventual closing of a nearby automobile service and gasoline station that had been operated by the Morgan Park Company since the 1920s.[13]

Throughout the 1930s, the Lake View Building typically housed a grocery store, a department store, the post office, one or two physicians, a dentist, a barber, a beauty salon, a tailor, a shoe repair shop, the Morgan Park Company office, and two fraternal lodges. By the end of the decade, however, the former company-run grocery and department stores had been leased out to private operators. Elsewhere, the Morgan Park Company managed the Nenovan Club and restaurant until 1936, when the largest of the three buildings was converted into a hotel.[14] Clearly, corporate control of Morgan Park's commercial and institutional buildings was beginning to change by mid-decade.

Figure 9.2. This automobile service station, constructed along Eighty-eighth Avenue West in 1938, was the only major new building that emerged in Morgan Park during the decade of the Great Depression. Portrayed here in a 1992 nighttime view, the building's physical appearance has changed very little over time. Photograph by John Gregor; courtesy of John Gregor.

Passing Time

Because work at the steel plant was so limited during most of the 1930s, many Morgan Park families were forced to make do with very limited monetary resources. After deductions were made for rent and grocery charges at the company store, most residents who worked on an irregular basis "never saw a paycheck." As a Morgan Park teenager during the Depression, Al Bothun recollected that his family "didn't have hardly enough money to buy food," and even less to purchase fuel for heat; to get by, the children would dig out pieces of coal buried in the mud at the steel plant's "coke flats." James Aird, one of the first children born in Morgan Park and a resident of the community for his entire life, remembered how "life became a struggle to survive."[15]

A report by the New Deal's Works Progress Administration (WPA), which surveyed almost 3,300 of Duluth's young people (seventeen to twenty-four years of age) in 1938, revealed just how dire the overall economic situation appeared at the time. The survey director declared that since many young adults didn't dare "to look into the future for more than a few months at most," it often was "a case of [the] worried marking time." The most common complaint, quite understandably, was the dismal shortage of employment opportunities, compounded by the fact that many individuals had already spent months, if not years, in unsuccessful job searches. Some of Duluth's unemployed were put to work on short-term projects funded by the WPA, including the construction of a western road entrance to Morgan Park in January 1938. To offer "the greatest possible amount of hand labor" for the 150 men who removed about 3,500 cubic yards of earth from the two-block-long right-of-way, only shovels, picks, and wheelbarrows were allowed on the job.[16]

Since the single commodity that most young people possessed during the Depression was "spare time," their lives often evolved around "movies, the neighborhood poolroom, an uncle's farm, reading, hitch-hikes to other cities, tinkering with an old car, helping mother with the housework, nursing a sick friend, [and] painting and repairing the house." Their parents, at the same time, devoted more time to family and community activities. Gardening assumed the importance it had achieved at Morgan Park during World War I, with residents once again spending considerable hours tending their backyard plots, as well as other gardens located on company land situated by the baseball field. (Nationwide in 1932, U.S. Steel employees cultivated 80,475 garden plots on some twenty square miles of land, which provided an estimated $1.2 million in produce.) School activities such as the annual minstrel show continued to take place, but it was Morgan Park's athletic teams that received the greatest attention from students and residents alike.[17]

Sometime during the 1930s Duluth's recreation department assumed responsibility for the supervision of Morgan Park's nine small playgrounds, although the Morgan Park Company was in charge of maintenance. In 1938 Duluth's recreation directors noted that the high unemployment rates

Figure 9.3. Local moviegoers could see Minnesota's Iron Range, Duluth's ore docks, and the steel plant at Morgan Park in this 1938 documentary, Steel—Man's Servant: The Story of Steel. *From* Duluth News-Tribune, *September 23, 1938.*

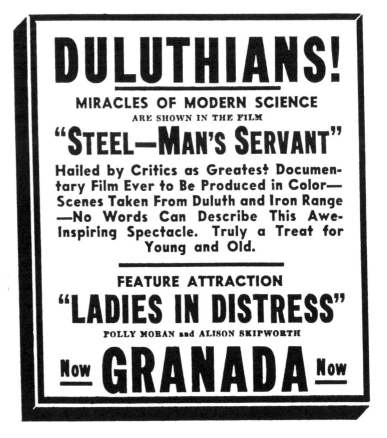

experienced in Morgan Park, Gary, and New Duluth contributed to the record numbers of people who participated in or observed organized recreational activities, some of which included contests and competitions. Babies received prizes for being the jolliest, the most outstanding, the youngest, the fattest, or for having the curliest hair, whereas boys and girls engaged in dodgeball, softball, and track events, and adults played baseball and softball. The annual July "Community Night" events held in Morgan Park and several other areas of Duluth awarded prizes to children who paraded through the playgrounds with their doll buggies, coaster wagons, and bicycles in tow. Because manufacturing operations ran at minimal levels during the Depression, the different steel plant units no longer fielded separate ball teams; now the squads consisted of single and married men who competed against each other.[18]

At this time the Good Fellowship Club began inviting nonmembers from the greater Morgan Park area to "open house programs," where free bowling, basketball, swimming, cards, and dancing were offered. The Club's "stag smokers," however, were members-only events attended by five hundred or so men. Summertime classes for both adults and children were also offered in the community, and a bicycle club was organized in 1939.[19]

Morgan Park played a role in the state political election of 1938, when Harold Stassen, the Republican candidate for governor, spoke to a "record audience" of more than three hundred people in the school auditorium. On that mid-October day, the crowd heard Stassen castigate the progressive Farmer-Labor Party and its incumbent governor, Elmer Benson, as a "gang of political bosses and petty politicians." Stassen was specifically critical of governmental officials for purchasing blacktop at "fancy" prices rather than operating the nearby cement plant, which had been idle from September 1937 to April 1938. Stassen handily won the statewide election in November, thereby becoming the "Boy Governor" of Minnesota at the age of thirty-one. Although Stassen carried Morgan Park by a vote of 592 to 398, Benson was the clear favorite in Gary-New Duluth, where he garnered 702 votes to Stassen's 209.[20]

Dances were very popular in Morgan Park and Duluth during the Depression; an "Unemployment Ball" held at the Duluth Armory in February 1931 was among the earliest of many inexpensive, citywide, leisure-time activities that people pursued. Movies shown in the Good Fellowship Clubhouse and in Duluth's four theaters were also heavily attended. One film that received attention in September 1938 was the documentary *Steel—Man's Servant*, which accompanied the feature-length movie, *Ladies in Distress*, playing at the Granada Theatre (Figure 9.3). Produced by Hollywood Industrial Films, the color documentary began with a portrayal of mining activities on the Mesabi Range, and then traced the subsequent path of iron ore to Duluth's docks and steel plant before most of it arrived in the mills and manufacturing facilities of the eastern United States. During its one-week-long run in Duluth, the documentary's "awe-inspiring spectacle" was advertised as "a treat for young and old." To Morgan Park's residents, however, the most "awe-inspiring spectacle" must have been the "feverish night and day activities" that, by the late 1930s, were becoming ever more visible at the nearby steel plant.[21]

10. MORE STEEL FOR ANOTHER WAR

The United States did not officially declare war against the Axis powers until late 1941, but the nation's manufacturing firms clearly were on an increasingly active wartime footing as the 1940s began. U.S. Steel Corporation plants throughout the nation produced twenty-three million tons of steel in 1940, the highest figure since 1929, and then manufactured close to thirty million tons annually from 1941 through 1944, all record totals for the firm.[1]

The virtually insatiable national and global appetite for steel was also reflected in notable production gains at Morgan Park during the wartime years. The situation contrasted sharply with plant superintendent Louis Reis's rather poignant pleas for steel orders in 1932, when he announced that the manufacturing facility was "fully equipped and manned, ready to do the bidding of our customers." Twenty-five U.S. Steel executives inspected the steel plant and the Mesabi Range in June 1940, and as fall gave way to winter, Morgan Park's single blast furnace was producing close to its annual capacity of 300,000 tons of steel, and the open hearths and merchant and wire mills were operating at a fast pace. Local observers commented that the round-the-clock production activities reminded them of the "record years" of World War I. Although Duluth's citizens received no information about what sort of manufacturing might be occurring at the plant, it was understood that "important war orders are being filled here for Eastern manufacturers." In April 1942, when close to two thousand workers were employed, a War Production Board official reported that the facility was "keeping up with the rest of the industry."[2]

Expanding a Steel Plant

That the plant was successfully "keeping up with the rest of the industry" can be credited, in no small part, to the local steelworkers' union. In November 1941, some weeks before the United States officially entered World War II, Local 1028 adopted a resolution that called for expansion at the steel plant; the proposal was then forwarded to President Franklin D. Roosevelt and the federal Office of Production Management (OPM). When

Minnesota's Republican U.S. Senator Joseph Ball informed the union that no steel company had expressed an interest in the request, the entire CIO Council of Duluth threw its support behind the local steelworkers' resolution. The union continued to press U.S. Steel for a new furnace, arguing that such an addition would allow the manufacturing plant "to fill orders without delay and to guard against the possibility of curtailed production in the event that the blast furnace now in operation should be put out of commission."[3]

On December 27, 1941, three weeks after the Japanese attack on Pearl Harbor, local steel plant representatives from both labor and management formed the Victory Production Committee (VPC), which lobbied for the blast furnace. Before the VPC presented its case to the OPM at a Minneapolis meeting in February 1942, Local 1028 representative Anton Westerhaus offered a vivid image of how the future output of a new furnace could be measured. "The additional steel tonnage our plant would produce in one year would be enough for a line of twenty-two tanks which would stretch from here [Duluth] to the Twin Cities," Westerhaus claimed. On February 20, VPC representatives received the welcome words, "we have our blast furnace." The *Duluth News-Tribune* informed its readers that the arrival of a second furnace was good news "for a surprised and mightily pleased citizenry."[4]

The replacement furnace, built by the Illinois Steel Company for its Joliet plant in 1904, was dismantled in 1942 and moved 450 miles north to Duluth. The decision to go with a reconstructed furnace rather than building an entirely new unit was made so production could get underway at Morgan Park as quickly as possible. The federal government's Defense Plant Corporation, which maintained ownership of the furnace throughout the war, provided the $7,601,555 that was needed to purchase, transport, and renovate the unit. It was then "rebuilt on modern lines" by two hundred employees from the Bates and Rogers Construction Company of Chicago. The majority of coke ovens at Morgan Park, dormant since the early 1930s, were also refurbished. All of the revamped facilities were dedicated at a ceremony on February 24, 1943, attended by more than 150 company, union, railroad, engineering, construction, military, newspaper, and government representatives. The event concluded when a silver dollar was thrown into the white molten pig iron produced by the furnace. Although the *News-Tribune* had expressed hope that an additional furnace might serve as "the forerunner of other plants of similar or kindred types, with payrolls and prestige such as they bring with them," the speakers attending the opening stressed its role in America's war effort. "Pig iron will help attain victory," predicted

B. E. Pheneger, who had been named steel plant superintendent two and a half years earlier."[W]e are now all fighting for the same end."[5]

Once full production was achieved, the plant's annual output expanded from 300,000 to 655,000 net tons of steel (Figure 10.1). While Mesabi iron ore still served as the primary material for steel making, scrap metal was also used. One of the largest sources for local scrap was Duluth's abandoned streetcar tracks. In February 1941 laborers employed by the federal Works Progress Administration (WPA) started removing steel rails from the Lake Avenue viaduct in downtown Duluth. By November 1942, when workers were still "tearing up trolley tracks all over town," 1,500 tons of rails had been transported to the Morgan Park facility.[6]

Superintendent Pheneger also implored Duluthians to donate metal household objects and items for shipment to steel mills in the eastern United States (Figure 10.2). Donors were assured that everything they provided would be converted into "bullets, tanks and guns" that would support Allied efforts "to bury Hitler and Hirohito beneath piles of discarded metal." The list of possible items for donation included old radiators, plumbing fixtures, steel shovels, and discarded furnace and grates, along with "beds made of brass or iron; electric cords . . . electric toasters, irons, heaters, fans, electric

Figure 10.1. Beginning during World War II and continuing thereafter for several years, the steel and cement plants worked at full capacity. Photograph by Fred J. Roleff, 1940s; author's personal postcard collection.

JUNK needed for War

Scrap Iron and Steel

Needed for tanks, ships, guns—all machines and arms of war.

Other Metals · Rubber—Rags —Manila Rope—Burlap Bags

Needed to make bombs, fuses, binoculars; planes; tires for jeeps; gas masks; barrage balloons; parachute flares; sandbags.

HOW TO TURN IT IN

Sell to a Junk dealer . . . Give to a charity . . . Take it yourself to nearest collection point . . . or consult your Local Salvage Committee—

Phone:

Melrose 4230	Melrose 2621	Melrose 4717
Melrose 2135	Melrose 7703	Melrose 2801

If you live on a farm, phone or write your County War Board or consult your farm implement dealer.

WASTE FATS—After they have served maximum cooking use. Strain into a large tin can and sell to your meat dealer after you have collected a pound or more.

TIN CANS—Wanted only in areas close to detinning plants, as announced locally.

WASTE PAPER—Needed only as announced by local committees.

Figure 10.2. As part of their contribution to the war effort, Duluth residents were asked to donate many types of "junk," especially scrap iron and steel, which would be melted down at the Morgan Park steel plant and at similar facilities elsewhere in the nation. From Duluth News-Tribune, *July 21, 1942.*

appliances; door knobs, hinges, keys, locks, trim springs; old knives, pots, pans, scissors; lamps and lighting fixtures made of brass, copper or iron; metal ash trays, bowls, statues, vases; porch and garden furniture made of metal; radio parts containing metal; screens made of brass or copper; sleds, ice skates, roller skates, and broken parts of vacuum cleaners containing metal." Residents were also encouraged to scour their cellars, garages, and yards for old stoves, fire extinguishers, bathtubs, automobile parts, batteries, lawn mowers, bicycles, tricycles, logging chains, playground equipment, wheelbarrows, and many other items.[7]

One major collection drive in September 1942 generated 750 tons of scrap, including a hundred-pound relic shell from World War I donated by a Morgan Park resident. Even some of Duluth's historic icons were considered for the scrap heap. In November 1942, the city's school board approved a bid of $65.50 from the Northwestern Iron and Metal Company to remove and melt down the Spanish-American War cannon that had stood in front of Central High School since 1900. Also considered was the possibility of raising and salvaging as many as ninety-four shipwrecks from the floor of Lake Superior, including the *Thomas Wilson*, which sank in Duluth's ship canal in 1902.[8] The proposal was never pursued, and the *Wilson,* now listed in the National Register of Historic Places, remains at the bottom of the canal.

The Morgan Park plant set eighty-one production records in 1943, and two years later it received an Army-Navy Production Award of Excellence for the manufacture of war materials. The April 1945 award ceremony, attended by company and union representatives, allowed American Steel and Wire to fly a large "E pennant" atop one of its buildings.[9]

The record production figures, however, did not come without significant personal costs, for at least three steelworkers—Peter Parendo, Ford Sheridan, and George Stetich—were killed on the job from 1940 through 1945. Untold numbers of workers also suffered a wide range of injuries during these years.[10]

Men and Women Working during Wartime

Unlike the 1930s, when American manufacturing jobs were very scarce, the early years of the 1940s posed a quite different dilemma: how to find a highly trained workforce among a population whose technical skills had not advanced or had been used very little for many years. Among the early efforts to address the problem was a federal program in early 1940 that provided funds for the expansion of the industrial arts and trades classes offered in the nation's junior and senior high schools. The first classes offered at Morgan Park, initially limited to male enrollees, provided instruction in welding and electricity.[11]

By 1942 Duluth's schools were offering subjects "tied in either directly or indirectly to preparing students for service to their country." Pre-induction programs familiarized older students with military service, while other students could choose classes ranging from aeronautics and naval navigation to home nursing and social studies courses that emphasized "a better understanding of our American democracy, its institutions, laws and functions." In early 1943 Morgan Park's high school was one of thirteen in Minnesota that offered female students a class in "aero-mechanics glider construction." Although none of the enrollees had previous mechanical experience, those female students who displayed sufficient skills were quickly allowed to use power tools, such as band saws, when assembling the wing ribs for the gliders.[12]

It was the Vocational Training for War Production Workers Program of 1940 that had the most immediate and wide-ranging impact on both the national and local workforce. Between October 1940 and December

1941, more than 1,500 Duluth workers were trained for industrial jobs. In Morgan Park, hundreds of adult men attended late afternoon sessions at the steel plant, where they either acquired or upgraded their skills in acetylene welding, as well as jig tool and die making. Others enrolled in mathematics and steel technology classes at the high school. With 52 former steel plant workers serving in the armed forces in late 1941, a figure that grew to as many as 1,500 by September 1943, experienced steelworkers—including some of the 37 men who had been employed at the plant since it opened in 1915—trained the new workers with great urgency. Before this training took place, the experienced employees enrolled in night school classes to learn "the art of instructing new steel workers." One group of trainees attending a thirteen-week welding class included four young Ojibwe men from the Mille Lacs Indian Reservation at Onamia, Minnesota. All four had departed school just before the eighth grade and were reportedly highly pleased with the "opportunity for trade and mechanical training," which included five hours of instruction seven days a week. To them, Morgan Park was a "swell" place.[13]

Once Duluth went on a full-scale wartime footing in 1942, thousands of people found work in numerous manufacturing enterprises, including the Riverside shipyards, located about one mile north of Morgan Park. By the summer of 1944, the labor shortage at the steel plant and other factories had become so acute that the firms were unable to fill all their contracts. At this time, American Steel and Wire officials introduced a practice seldom seen since the World War I years: placing advertisements for workers in local newspapers. The ads featured the good pay and high quality of the work environment—"a friendly, pleasant place"—but strongly emphasized the plant's role in "helping the war effort" (Figure 10.3). Most of the ads included individual photographs and brief biographies of local steel workers, along with personal statements that appealed to the prospective employees' patriotism (Figures 10.4, 10.5). Sam Balach, a steel plant employee since 1915 and the father of four sons serving in the armed services, believed his work was linked to America's future military success: "I feel that everything I can do to maintain the flow of materials to the battle lines is going to help those four boys get home sooner," reported Balach. Albin Anderson noted that with victory in sight, "we must produce more than ever before to give our boys all they need for the final knockout blow to the enemy," while Herman Ewald reminded potential workers about the prospects for continued employment with a company that will "go on in the steel and wire business long after this war is over."[14]

Figure 10.3. With so many men serving in the armed forces by 1944, American Steel and Wire collaborated with the U.S. Employment Service to locate and hire new steelworkers. From Duluth News-Tribune, *August 15, 1944.*

To Men Not Employed In Vital War Industry

More men are needed in one of Duluth's largest industries—steel. Without production in this most basic and vital industry very little war could be carried on.

For years the American Steel & Wire Company has operated a steel plant in Duluth where at the present time materials are being made for the war effort. Among its workers are two generations of many families. Every effort is being made to provide good, steady jobs for hundreds of men and women after the war in the manufacture of peacetime products.

Right now, there is a shortage of men in many of the departments at the Morgan Park plant. It is a friendly, pleasant place to work. The pay is good. You don't have to have previous experience to get a job. You don't have to go out of town.

The American Steel & Wire Company invites men who are not in vital war industry to apply for work at its plant in Duluth, through the United States Employment Service, 212 Bradley Building, Duluth, Minnesota. If you are successful in obtaining a job, you will earn good wages, be helping the war effort, and more tons of steel and steel products will be shipped every day from which products going into the war effort will be made.

Workers Now Employed in Agriculture or Essential Activity Should Not Apply!

Ask for Company Representative

War Manpower Commission

UNITED STATES EMPLOYMENT SERVICE
Second Floor, Bradley Bldg.

10 East Superior Street, Corner Lake Avenue

But it was women who most clearly changed the complexion of the wartime workforce in Duluth and throughout America. When the United States entered the global conflict in late 1941, just 11,550 of the nation's women had completed federally sponsored training programs; by April 1943, almost 740,000 had been or were enrolled in programs that emphasized wartime production occupations.[15]

Only 175 women worked in Duluth's industries before the war, but by the summer of 1942, they were entering the labor force in large numbers. Later in the year Duluth employers attending a "Women in Industry" conference heard about the federally funded vocational programs being offered at the War Production Training Center at 4832 Grand Avenue. Here, women from northeastern Minnesota received instruction for "essential" jobs, including positions at the steel plant. The sight of so many "gals" engaged in "men's work" was initially greeted with amazement by observers, such as Ray Sicard, who wrote a weekly "Letter to Your Soldier" column for the *Duluth News-Tribune*. "Imagine women cab drivers," Sicard exclaimed in one of his early letters of October 1942, picturing "cute little girls running around in Western Union and Postal Telegraph uniforms, not to mention girls work-

Figure 10.4. In September 1944 American Steel and Wire launched an intensive advertising campaign that used veteran steelworkers, such as William Bester, to attract new workers to the plant. From Duluth News-Tribune, *September 22, 1944.*

Figure 10.5. African American steelworker George A. Cox, born in Mississippi in 1900, began working at the wire mill in 1923; he was one of several family members who eventually were employed at the steel plant. From Duluth News-Tribune, *September 14, 1944.*

ing as auto mechanics in garages, filling tanks with gas, changing tires and doing lots of jobs you fellows had to worry about before Pearl Harbor." Less than a year later, however, Sicard was describing conditions quite differently. Duluth's female industrial workforce, which peaked at 2,050 women, included almost 500 at the steel plant who worked side by side with men, "doing everything from piling steel to feeding some of the blast furnaces" (Figure 10.6). The columnist admitted that "where just a year ago it was considered an unusual sight to see a woman board a bus in overalls with a lunch bucket under her arm, it's so common nowadays that folks don't even give it a second thought."[16]

Among the contingent of women laborers was Alfreda Mattson Berg, who secured a steel plant job in 1944 (Figure 10.7). A resident of Morgan Park since 1922, the year her husband started working in the wire mill, Berg became a thirty-nine-year-old widow and the single parent of two teenage sons in 1942. Deciding there was "more honor" in working for U.S. Steel than as a domestic, she started her eighteen-year career in the fence-post manufacturing plant by sweeping floors. Eventually Berg performed many other jobs, including lifting heavy bundles of fence posts into railroad cars.[17]

Figure 10.6. Men and women worked side by side in the steel plant during much of World War II. Courtesy of Robert Berg.

Figure 10.7. Alfreda Mattson Berg, at the back far right, with several of her female co-workers by the fence-post fabrication unit in the mid-1940s. Courtesy of Robert Berg.

A few women who were interviewed almost a half-century after the war's end recalled the difficult work their cohorts had performed in the steel plant. "A lot of women worked right on the line and they drew the wire and they made the nails," stated one woman, while a long-time office and laboratory employee commented on women who performed "dirty nasty jobs" that often required them to "carry heavy loads and work in the ovens." On the other hand, a male respondent reported that two men always worked "out in the open" with two women so as to reduce the likelihood of "hanky panky"; nevertheless, he admitted, "a lot of it went [on] anyway." Others noted that with everyone working long shifts that could extend over sixteen continuous hours, both men and women needed "iron backs" to carry out the hard labor. Some men had more caustic comments, such as one who exclaimed that in "no way" were women suited for steel plant work. Another even asserted that men resented the presence of women because they did "eighty percent of the work for one hundred percent of the pay."[18]

The excessive work burden faced by many women in Duluth and the nation received considerable attention by 1943. When visiting Duluth in September, Florence Williams, national director of the YWCA, pointed out that besides working six days a week for forty-eight to sixty hours, many women also had to take care of their families and homes. Williams reported that women often worked "in poorly ventilated, badly lighted factories, where the machines were made for men and have not been adjusted to women's reach," and that many didn't have "adequate restrooms, rest periods or food." Without the cooperation of management, labor, and communities, Williams warned, "the fatigue problem of women may well result in a serious labor shortage."[19]

Two years later, similar findings were reported in a YWCA survey of Duluth's female workers and fifty of their employers. The published survey results did not differentiate between women who worked in the steel plant and in other industries, but with so many employed in steel manufacturing, the overall findings very likely reflected the situation at Morgan Park.[20]

The average woman who worked in Duluth's manufacturing industries in 1945 was thirty-one years old. Fifty percent of the women filled jobs formerly held by males; 80 percent of the employers believed the quality of their work was equivalent to that of the men. Females may have had a higher rate of job absenteeism, but the survey also revealed that the most common cause for missing work was illness—primarily because of colds and respiratory problems caused by personal fatigue and inadequate ventilation at job sites. Also contributing to the women's health problems was the excessively heavy work they encountered when placed in inappropriate jobs demanded by the war emergency. (Very limited information is available about the health problems encountered by female workers at the Morgan Park steel plant, but during just one week in February 1944, at least two women were hospitalized, one in a nearby tuberculosis sanitarium.) To reduce the stress encountered by women, the YWCA report called for the implementation of an eight-hour workday, a forty-eight-hour and six-day work week, two fifteen-minute rest periods each day, and a thirty-minute lunch break.[21]

Several programs were developed to assist the city's female workforce. From mid-1943 to early 1946, scores of women volunteers participated in a program, organized by the Duluth Civilian Defense Council, that provided daycare for some seven hundred children of working mothers. An "Industrial Center" that offered recreational facilities and social programs was provided at the West Duluth YWCA, but it did not open until just shortly before the war ended in August 1945. One offering was a club that provided opportunities for "girls from large industrial concerns [to] meet each Tuesday for fun and relaxation." The programs began with a six o'clock dinner, followed by activities such as "a song fest, travel motion pictures, what's news in the world, square dancing, volleyball, baseball, or badminton"; the program concluded with a nine o'clock "plunge" in the YWCA pool.[22]

Duluth's newspaper editors occasionally took time from their thoughts and comments about the war effort to reflect on the present and future role of women in the workforce. A 1942 *News-Tribune* editorial stated that while there were some worries "about how the women are to be lured back into the homes when the war is ended," it also pointed out the necessity for caution when evaluating postwar conditions, which might not be "a reasonably accurate facsimile of the pre-war world." By 1944, however, the editorial page had adopted a more traditional line. With industries employing large numbers of "married women and women willing to accept matrimony," the newspaper predicted "they will return to their homes, most of them willingly, as soon as the opportunity affords." The 1945 YWCA survey confronted the issue directly by asking the female respondents a key question: "What are the postwar plans of the woman in industry?" Despite the difficult conditions they often encountered in industrial jobs, almost three-quarters of Duluth's employed women hoped to remain in the workforce after the war concluded. Most employers, on the other hand, echoed the *News Tribune's* assessment, believing "that the majority of jobs now open to women will be filled by returning servicemen." According to the newspaper's editorial page, the future was clear—quite simply, "women who went into industry as a wartime expedient will have to be replaced by family heads." The YWCA's survey investigators addressed the issue directly, concluding that "only under conditions of full production and full employment" would the working women of Duluth have an opportunity "to maintain and strengthen the gains and the inroads they have made."[23]

Union Advances

In early 1940, Steelworkers Local 1028 submitted an application to American Steel and Wire, requesting permission to use the Morgan Park clubhouse for union meetings. The company refused, citing provisions of the Wagner Act that banned corporate endorsement of or interference in labor organizations. Local 1028's membership contended that the act applied only to illegal company unions, and reminded corporate officials that the clubhouse, following its completion in 1916, had been "turned over to the workers to pay for the upkeep." When the union's argument failed, Local 1028 began occupying rented quarters in West Duluth's Dormedy Hall on Central Avenue in March 1941. Three years later the union purchased its own building, located four miles from the plant, for $6,000. A $70,000 remodeling of the "Union Home," financed in part with $13,650 in donations provided by 1,100 members of Local 1028, was completed in September 1945. Union activities obviously occurred within the building, but it also was a place "where papa and mama can have a quiet beer and a spin around the dance floor."[24]

The local union made a number of significant gains throughout the wartime years. Among its major accomplishments was the successful lobbying effort that led to the construction of a second blast furnace at Morgan Park in 1942. During that same year, the steelworkers, along with miners on the Iron Range, voted to cut their ties with SWOC, choosing instead to affiliate with the United Steelworkers of America (USWA). Also in 1942, national union officials successfully negotiated a 5.5 cent-per-hour wage boost for all laborers employed by U.S. Steel and its affiliates; the agreement meant that a typical Morgan Park steelworker now received 78 cents for an hour of labor. More than one hundred of the steel plant's clerical staff also joined the national union in 1944 as members of Local 3391.[25]

Local 1028's committees maintained a busy schedule throughout the war years. Among the most active was a grievance committee, which invited all workers with job-related issues or problems "to come up and talk over your troubles." Also formed during the war years were salvage drive, legislative, labor management, housing, safety, and U.S. Savings Bond sales committees. The legislative committee, headed by veteran labor organizer Earl Bester, evaluated policies under consideration by the national union's leadership group and lobbied in the Minnesota Legislature. The safety committee reviewed numerous "hazardous conditions" that employees previously had chosen not to report because of the fear they might lose their jobs.[26]

In 1940, the sick and entertainment committee's provisions, along with recently enacted federal Social Security measures, were deemed sufficient to end several of the voluntary benefit programs provided by the Good Fellowship Club's former relief committee. (The Club continued to offer its members group insurance programs, credit union services, fuel purchases at reduced prices, and access to a blood bank.) By September 1943 the sick and entertainment committee had sponsored visits to hundreds of members confined to hospitals or their homes because of illness or injury, organized numerous dances and parties, and offered an annual summer picnic that attracted as many as one thousand people to a park in Fond du Lac. The July 1940 picnic, termed a "rousing success" by *Midwest Labor*, awarded 187 prizes to attendees, who participated in numerous games and competitions. The event concluded with a baseball game that saw the wire mill employees defeat the hot rolling mill team by a 2-to-1 score. A year later the wire mill team was victorious once again, this time beating the rolling mill team in a tug-of-war competition.[27]

America's steelworkers flexed their union muscles in April 1941, when they threatened to strike if U.S. Steel did not offer them a package of improved employee benefits, including a ten-cents-an-hour wage increase and improvements in vacation programs and seniority rights. The strike threat ended when U.S. Steel agreed to several of the requests, an action that added an annual $450,000 to the Morgan Park plant payroll.[28]

Three years later, when the national USWA failed in its efforts to secure another wage increase, the National War Labor Board (NWLB) appointed a fact-finding panel to investigate the issues that separated the two protagonists. The NWLB issued its report to President Roosevelt about one year later, but it was not until August 1945, shortly after the Japanese surrender in the Pacific, that President Harry S. Truman replaced wartime wage stabilization policies with collective bargaining procedures. In September 1945 the USWA asked for a two-dollar-per-day wage increase, which the companies turned down one month later. Following this action, steelworkers throughout the nation voted to strike by a five-to-one margin. The workforce at the Morgan Park steel plant was even more adamant in its strike commitment, supporting the proposal by a vote of 2,160 to 166, a thirteen-to-one margin. Soon, local steelworkers would participate, albeit briefly, in a strike that commenced in January 1946.[29] This action may have been the first walkout in the thirty-year-long history of the steel plant, but it certainly would not be the last.

11. NO MORE COMPANY HOUSING

As the 1940s dawned, radio and newspaper accounts provided Morgan Parkers with information about military and political crises in Europe and Asia. America's formal entry into the global conflict would not occur until the end of 1941, but the round-the-clock production activities at the steel plant that began in 1940 gave residents front-row access to the earliest preparations for war. And then, during the early 1940s, Morgan Park's inhabitants were forced to confront an issue that further compounded their already hectic lives—U.S. Steel's decision to sell most of its properties in the community, including all of the dwelling units. Within a short period of time, Morgan Park would no longer be called a company town.

Crowded Houses, Busy Lives

Morgan Park's population reached 2,100 residents in 1940, and almost every house was quickly occupied; spare rooms in some dwellings were also rented to new steelworkers who needed accommodations. Even some houses in the managers' district had roomers, including the one occupied by Beverly Street residents Fritz and Hilda Friederici. Mrs. Friederici expressed frustration over the hectic schedule she experienced during the war years. "I have so little time," she wrote to friends in early 1943. "Everything in the house needs repair and with the things I do for my parents, my two roomers and my stint at the Red Cross . . . there is really very little time."[1]

Despite the frenetic wartime situations they often encountered, Morgan Park's citizens still sought to maintain the typical flow and rhythms of daily life. Local PTA members took time to attend meetings, such as one that discussed "the influence of forces in everyday life on the social life of youth," while high school girls sewed clothing items for the Junior Red Cross. Clubhouse and school athletic events also received considerable attention from students and residents. A basketball team, organized in October 1941 and dubbed "Steel Plant Union No. 1028," finished with an undefeated record in Duluth's Senior League and went on to win the city tournament in February 1942, first by nosing out the Family Loan quintet 28–26 in overtime, and then by concluding with a 44–14 rout of the Young and Hursch team. The team finished the season with an exhibition game against the Harlem Globetrotters. A high school basketball game between the Morgan Park Wildcats and the Two Harbors Agates, scheduled for the evening of December 8—the day following the bombing of Pearl Harbor—also went on without interruption, as did the season's remaining contests. Once the United States entered the war, a labor-management committee made plans to select land in the steel plant district that could be plowed and allocated to steelworkers for their victory gardens.[2]

The Finale to Company Housing

Residents of the model village had been able to purchase their rental units since 1933, and non-steel-plant employees could rent a Morgan Park house as of 1938. Because the sales program was not promoted very intensively, only two dwellings had been sold by early 1942. Recognizing that a more organized and aggressive sales campaign was needed, U.S. Steel officials decided "to utilize real estate tactics in disposing of the property." John W. Galbreath, a Columbus, Ohio, businessman who had recently begun converting large groupings of company houses "into cash or profitable properties" for corporate owners, was invited by U.S. Steel to submit a bid for its Morgan Park holding. All of U.S. Steel's holdings, other than the manufacturing facility and clubhouse, were placed on the sales docket: 509 residences in 245 buildings, the community garages, the Lake View Building, and the buildings that once housed the Nenovan Club dormitories. U.S. Steel's decision was based on the increasing maintenance problems associated with a thirty-year-old community, and what officials claimed was a growing tax burden.[3]

Galbreath Company employees spent the spring and early summer months of 1942 inspecting and appraising the properties. Many residents were "shocked" and "very disturbed" upon receiving word that their houses would be sold to a real estate firm before being made available for purchase by the current renters. Perhaps even more unsettling was the possibility that anyone who did not buy quickly might be "compelled [to leave] in order to make room for those who will purchase." In early July, American Steel and Wire representatives attending a meeting arranged by Local 1028 of the steelworkers union heard from residents who argued, "this was no time to make workers worry when they were engaged in winning the war." The union's executive committee then forwarded letters to President Roosevelt and Congressman William Pittenger, asking them to intervene and delay the sale. *Midwest Labor* echoed a similar theme, stating that steelworkers did not deserve such treatment "when they were giving all that they had to increase production and to purchase bonds and support the war." The Morgan Park Community Club, an organization formed in 1936 that typically advocated for school, road, bus line, and other improvements, also registered its displeasure, pointing out that being turned over "to the tender mercies of a real estate office doesn't exactly appeal to us."[4]

Despite these concerns, the sales program moved forward. In late summer 1942, Morgan Park's renters were given one year to consider whether to purchase their homes. The prices were set at one-half the original construction costs when they had been built twenty to thirty years earlier. The Galbreath Company finalized the acquisition from U.S. Steel in early January 1943, and assumed responsibility for rent collections. Engineer Fritz Friederici summarized the transition that occurred at the time. "The houses here have been sold to an Ohio company," he wrote in February, "but the status is quo until 6 months after the war so far as the tenants are concerned. We pay the rent at the [Galbreath] company now instead of having it taken out of our pay, but it still hurts!"[5]

Reporter Ray Sicard also wrote about the sale in one of his weekly newspaper letters to Duluthians serving in the military:

> Did you fellows know that the suburb of Morgan Park, with the exception of the steel plant, that clubhouse out there and other plant properties has been sold to an Ohio man? Yes, and he's now going to turn around and sell those homes out there to the folks who are working in the plant. Chances are that when the folks own their own home out there, it'll make that suburb even more attractive. And by the way, that deal was probably one of the biggest real estate jobs put over in the Northwest in a long time.[6]

A year and a half later, the Galbreath Company would petition the federal government's Office of Price Administration for permission to raise rents by 30 percent, basing the request on the claim that U.S. Steel's charges had been substantially less than prevailing rates for a considerable period of time. Local 1028's executive committee quickly noted that it strongly opposed any increase.[7]

Morgan Park's residents received another letter from the Galbreath Company in early July 1943, telling them about the advantages of home ownership. Pointing out "that it is foolish to pay rent year after year when you could just as well OWN your home in the same length of time without additional cost or effort," the company reminded Morgan Park's renters "the opportunity to buy your own home STARTS NOW" (Figure 11.1). The question of whether or not to purchase was an agonizing decision for many residents who had grown accustomed to as many as thirty years of corporate largesse. After hearing that his family's residence, part of a four-unit apartment on Eighty-seventh Avenue West, had been put up for sale, Edward Olson asked incredulously, "Who is going to pay that kind of money for this house?" But when another party purchased the dwelling, Olson was "devastated." Eventually, however, the family moved into one section of a duplex they purchased on Eighty-sixth Avenue West.[8]

In September 1943, the general public was informed that any houses

John W. Galbreath & Co.
MORGAN PARK
1076 88th AVENUE, WEST
DULUTH, MINN.

June 7, 1943.

It will take you only two minutes to read this letter, but it brings you an opportunity which will provide life-time benefits for yourself and family.

Of course, you agree that it is foolish to pay rent year after year when you could just as well OWN your own home in the same length of time without additional cost or effort. One Morgan Park tenant, for example, told us the other day that he had spent $10,500 for rent and today he has nothing to show for all that money except a lot of receipts which are not worth a penny. In the same time, that man could have paid in full for a nice home and had a substantial amount of savings in the bank. It is the same way with every family that keeps on paying rent. Rent money is SPENT money—all gone with the wind.

You do not have to rent the home in which you now live any longer. You can arrange with us to BUY it with a small cash payment and monthly payments which will represent savings instead of wasted rent money. This is true of your home and every other dwelling in Morgan Park—including the apartments—they are all for sale to the occupants.

In bringing you news of this home-ownership opportunity, we have no intention, however, of asking you or anyone to move immediately. Regardless of whether you buy or not, you can stay in the house you now occupy as long as the war lasts and for at least six months after it is over. We would not willingly do anything to disturb your war effort, or to cause you any worry about shelter when the big job is to defeat the enemies of our country.

Nevertheless, the opportunity to buy your own home STARTS NOW, and why should you keep on paying rent when you can begin at once to build an estate which will provide happiness for your family and security for the future!

We suggest that you drop into our office and see Mr. Holman, our manager. He can give you all the information you desire as to the sale price of your house or any other houses in Morgan Park in which you might be interested. He can also give you the monthly payments you will be required to make after you have once made a down payment and have purchased your house.

We do not need to point out to you the advantages of owning your own home in Morgan Park. Our community is favored with fine schools and fine people. It is the kind of a neighborhood in which you want your wife and children to live—one in which property values are protected.

We know that buying a home is something that requires careful consideration. The opportunity is now yours, and we can only suggest that you drop into our office so that we can talk thinks over. You will like the plan and be surprised to find how easily you can stop paying rent and live the happier way as the OWNER of your own home.

Sincerely yours,

Figure 11.1. In June 1943, five months after acquiring the Morgan Park property from U.S. Steel, the John W. Galbreath Company encouraged renters to purchase their residences. Courtesy of Northeast Minnesota Historical Center, S2366b2f19.

not purchased by current Morgan Park residents would be placed on the open market. While new purchasers could not move into their new homes immediately, they did become instant landlords, which allowed them "to collect the rent for the duration of the war." The Galbreath Company, now ensconced in the former Morgan Park Company office in the Lake View Building, initiated a forceful advertising campaign, which claimed that the houses' "double [wall] construction" made them "better today than newly built homes . . . selling for twice as much" (Figure 11.2). The reasonable prices—ranging from $1,000 for the smallest unit in a multifamily row-house, to $1,925 for one section of a duplex, and $7,500 for the largest single-

Figure 11.2. Nine months following its purchase of U.S. Steel's Morgan Park holdings in early 1943, the Galbreath Company began selling the houses and other buildings in the residential district to individual buyers. From Duluth News-Tribune, *September 19, 1943.*

family house—were touted as "a golden opportunity to get ahead that will never come again." Sixty-eight houses were purchased during the first two weeks of the sales campaign.[9]

In December 1945, returning military servicemen were informed that Morgan Park's unsold houses had been approved for low-interest GI loans, and could still be purchased at 1942 prices. "Even though prices have skyrocketed [elsewhere], the prices have not been raised," exclaimed an advertisement for Morgan Park.[10]

The Galbreath Company sold 364 houses between early 1943 and early 1945. All together, the same people occupied 90 of the purchased dwellings at both the beginning and end of the two-year period. A total of 123 houses remained as rental units in 1945, with one-half of these residences being inhabited by the same renters in 1943. In other words, the occupants of 315 dwellings—254 of the recently purchased units and 61 of the rental properties—changed over the two-year period. The remaining 22 houses were vacant in 1945.[11]

The Galbreath Company continued to receive complaints from members of the Morgan Park Community Club throughout 1945. Now the issues ranged from increasing rental costs, to a lack of heat and light in the garages, to the company's failure to clear the sidewalks of snow.[12] By the end of the year, however, Morgan Park's transition from company town to typical neighborhood was virtually complete. Although the community was no longer under corporate control, one vestige of the past still dominated life in Morgan Park: the residents' virtually complete economic dependence on the nearby steel plant.

PART IV

Closing a Steel Plant but Preserving a Community, 1946–2006

U.S. Steel spokesmen emphasize the corporation has no present plans to shut down its Duluth Works, but they do not foresee a program to modernize or expand the facility due to insufficient market.

—Einar Karlstrand, *Duluth Herald*, April 27, 1970

Morgan Park is a good place to live—if you're old or young.

—Comment by a seventy-two-year-old resident in 1975

12. SIX STRIKES TO SHUTDOWN

The nation's post–World War II steel demands, which included the Korean War years of 1950–53, were responsible for limited expansions and upgrades at the Morgan Park plant. Likewise, the record steel-production figures achieved throughout the early and mid-1940s were quickly exceeded, albeit relatively modestly, during the 1950s. For the labor force employed at Morgan Park, however, the most important events were six nationwide strikes that took place from 1946 to 1959, most of which resulted in significant wage, vacation, pension, and other gains for steelworkers.

Despite these seemingly favorable events, the future of the steel plant appeared increasingly uncertain by the early 1960s. The facility was becoming ever more outmoded and antiquated, and it could not compete with the newer basic oxygen furnaces emerging elsewhere in America. Then, in 1971, Duluthians heard the dreaded news that proved more painful than anything they had faced during six previous decades of manufacturing history—U.S. Steel would shut down its Morgan Park facility. Throughout the remainder of the decade, the corporation disposed of its holdings, first the steel manufacturing facility and mills, and then the cement and coke production units.

Making Steel to the End

In October 1944, the federal government's Defense Plant Corporation had begun making plans to dispose of the Morgan Park blast furnace it had financed two years earlier. In late 1946 American Steel and Wire purchased the furnace, which it had operated since the early 1943 opening. Although the federal government had expended $7,601,555 to purchase, move, and rehabilitate the furnace in 1942, its "appraised economic and utilization value" was placed at $2,025,575 in 1946. The actual sale price was for $1,835,400— 90 percent of the appraised value—but a figure deemed satisfactory by the government since it was considered "impossible" that any other company could operate the plant.[1]

As many as 3,600 workers—one in thirteen of all jobholders in Duluth— found employment at the Morgan Park plant by the late 1940s and early

1950s. (U.S. Steel's total workforce reached a record high of 340,000 employees in 1953.) Unlike the last years of World War II, only relatively few women now worked in steel manufacturing activities at Morgan Park, though most of the main office remained a female domain. Included among the women in the steel plant's manufacturing area were some who still performed difficult and demanding jobs. One male worker recalled the physical strength of a woman in the nail mill "who could carry more kegs than any guy in the [entire] steel plant," while another was impressed by a woman "who could work along side any man," and was able to lift rolls of wire that weighed as much as 150 pounds. When payroll clerk Barbara Isaacson East gathered time cards from men working in the plant's manufacturing areas from 1951 to 1956, she found that the steelworkers behaved respectfully. Even forty years after departing the plant, East recalled, "the men always treated me special."[2]

Modest Hopes, Modest Gains

The postwar increases in steel output occurred when two open-hearth furnaces, removed from service during the 1930s, were replaced in 1949–50. All ten of the original furnaces that first operated in 1916 were also available once again. Most of the ninety coke ovens were upgraded, and by 1951 steel manufacturing at the Morgan Park plant reached a record annual high of 915,000 gross tons of steel.[3]

A new mill, built in 1955–56, began using the plant's wire to manufacture welded steel mats employed in interstate highway construction. The mill emerged on the site of the former keg and cooperage shop that had closed in 1954 when "attractive Minnesota-made corrugated fiberboard cartons" were first used to package nails. Lieutenant Governor Karl Rolvaag attended the mill's June 1955 groundbreaking, while Governor Orville Freeman, whose 1954 campaign had included a pledge to make "a complete study" of steel mat-production possibilities, participated in the March 1956 grand opening. After pushing the new mill's "on button," Freeman stated that the new facility "adds to Minnesota's wealth, increasing the state's tax base." The wire mill also produced 70 percent of the tiny valve springs used in the manufacture of new automobiles in America.[4]

A two-day-long October 1956 open house celebrated the 125th anniversary of steel wire manufacturing in America. Steelworkers at Morgan Park spent considerable time in September constructing "the equivalent of a miniature city—with new roads, new walkways, shining wire fences, ramps and refreshment stands," all intended to facilitate the movement of the 51,000 people who would tour the plant's buildings and grounds over a three-day period (Figure 12.1). Bulldozers prepared "smooth" roads for buses that transported people around the plant site; the installation of additional lighting ensured that "no corner . . . [was] hidden from view" and that the facility would be visible after dark. Workers who climbed high ladders used pressure hoses that probed "into every nook and cranny of the girders and roof-rafters to put the mills at their shining best." And 3,000 signs were painted, all intended to provide visitors with factual information about the plant's annual production of 5 million fence posts, its weekly output of 150 million nails and 21 thousand miles of steel wire, and its daily consumption of 65 million gallons of water (Figure 12.2). Morgan Park's entrance road, lined

Figure 12.1. More than fifty thousand people toured American Steel and Wire's manufacturing operations during the three-day open house of October 1956. They departed Morgan Park in buses, which then transported them to different sites on the steel plant grounds. Courtesy of Northeast Minnesota Historical Center, S2366B790f11, photograph 105528.

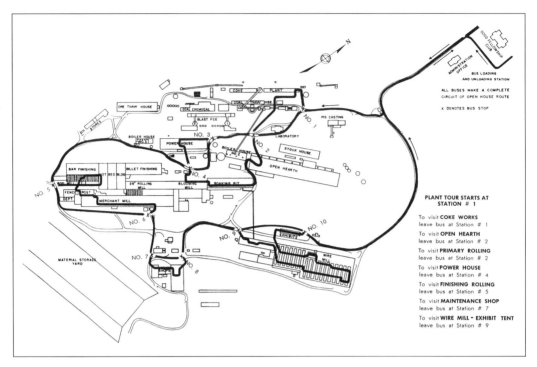

Figure 12.2. A slightly modified version of the tour map for visitors to the October 1956 steel plant open house. Courtesy of Northeast Minnesota Historical Center.

with colored flags, greeted the onlookers who "poured" into the community to watch "the exciting spectacle of steel making."[5]

Certainly no one attending the gala open house realized that this was the final public celebration of steel-making activities at Morgan Park. Never again would the plant be available for observation by hundreds, much less tens of thousands of people. Indeed, by 1959 a local writer was warning that "within the industry the Duluth plant is regarded as a 'marginal operation' because of its comparatively high manufacturing costs"—virtually the same argument that U.S. Steel officials had often used since 1907.[6]

Six Strikes, Fourteen Years: Reaping the Benefits of Unionization

During the rather brief period from 1946 through 1959, the workforce employed at Morgan Park, along with hundreds of thousands of other members of the United Steelworkers of America (USWA), participated in six strikes—in 1946, 1949, 1952, 1955, 1956, and 1959—the duration of which ranged from twelve hours to 116 days. Most resulted in wage and benefit increases that made steelworkers among America's best-paid blue-collar laborers.

In December 1945, Local 1028's members had voted overwhelmingly to strike if the USWA's request for a twenty-five-cent-per-hour pay increase were not granted. The actual walkout began on January 21, 1946, but involvement by Duluth's steelworkers—their first opportunity to participate in a strike action—was delayed because of a Minnesota labor-relations law that mandated a waiting period of up to thirty days, during which time a fact-finding commission weighed the potential statewide consequences of the walkout. On February 1, a three-man panel appointed by Governor Edward Thye presented its report, which offered an obvious conclusion, namely that the state of Minnesota had no power to resolve a strike that "would have to be settled on a national basis." The workforce employed at Morgan Park joined the strike on February 8, but the action ended just one week later, when U.S. Steel agreed to a one-year contract that guaranteed an 18.5-cents-per-hour wage increase. A local observer complimented the strikers' behavior, declaring that no army "ever had better discipline, better morale and a willingness to serve for the good of all."[7]

When the initial group of employees returned to the plant immediately after the strike ended and began tapping one of the blast furnaces, an explosion of slag and molten metal killed laborer Nick Palumbo and injured three other workers (Figure 12.3). Superintendent Pheneger's understated evaluation of the tragedy was typical of most assessments

NICK PALUMBO
WEST DULUTH

"I was in the last war and I am happy to have a part in producing the steel that is helping to win this war. I have made a good living at the American Steel & Wire Company since 1922 and I expect to be here after the war is won, when we swing back to peace-time production. If you are looking for work, why not apply today at the Steel Plant?"

Apply at
U. S. Employment Service
212 Bradley Building, Duluth
or
American Steel & Wire
Employment Office, Morgan Park
All hiring in accordance with WNC regulations.
—Advertisement.

Figure 12.3. Nick Palumbo expressed satisfaction with steel plant conditions in September 1944, and also encouraged others to apply for jobs. Tragically, a blast furnace explosion just over a year later would kill Palumbo. From Duluth News-Tribune, *September 29, 1944.*

made by company officials following a steel plant fatality. "The first cast of a furnace after a shutdown is always a ticklish affair," intoned Pheneger, "and it often offers quite a difficult problem."[8]

Soon after the one-year contract terminated in early 1947, another strike was avoided when union and company representatives ratified a two-year agreement that provided steelworkers with an average pay hike of one dollar per day. In August 1949, however, when the USWA's initial request for improved pension and insurance benefits was turned down, its membership voted to strike. (The union claimed that U.S. Steel retirees were receiving less than six dollars per month.) The steelworkers who worked at the Morgan Park plant concurred, again voting overwhelmingly (2,384–144) to support the walkout that began on the first day of October. Unlike in 1946, however, it was now clear that employees would be out of work for an appreciably longer period of time than a single week; therefore, the county's welfare department quickly began preparing for an increase in relief assistance, which grew by 41 percent over three weeks. Union officer Earl Bester, a tireless and ubiquitous presence in every major labor action that affected the workforce from the late 1920s through the 1960s, served as the local counselor, a position that allowed him "to enable local unions to utilize fully [the] services of community welfare and relief organizations in the event of a continued strike." Local 1028 also provided picketers with warm food prepared in a soup kitchen at the union hall.[9]

The national strike ended on November 12, following an agreement brokered between USWA leaders and steel company executives. The union was quite successful in achieving its goals, which included guarantees of a minimum monthly pension of $100 for workers who retired at age sixty-five with at least twenty-five years of service. The benefits were estimated as being worth $15,000 per worker.[10]

All was not harmonious within the ranks of steel plant unionists, however. After Henry Olsen and Ervin Drill published two issues of an underground newspaper, *Rank and File Duluth Steelworker*, in early 1951, Local 1028's officials "tried" the two men at the Steelworkers Hall. Both were charged with circulating a nonauthorized publication that had "false reports, and misrepresentations," although it was the Communist sympathies of Olsen and Drill that were really on trial.[11] This was, after all, the height of McCarthyism in American history.

Negotiations on the next national contract stalled in April 1952, whereupon President Harry Truman "seized" America's steel plants and thereby averted a strike; however, after the U.S. Supreme Court overturned Truman's action in early June, the union initiated an immediate work stoppage. The ensuing fifty-five-day shutdown ended when steelworkers received an hourly wage increase of sixteen cents, along with improved fringe benefits.[12]

The USWA called its subsequent strike in July 1955, but the impasse ended within twelve hours when the steel industry agreed to an hourly wage increase of fifteen cents. This was followed, one year later, by an industry request for a five-year no-strike agreement from the union. In refusing the offer, labor leaders called for wage and benefit gains that steel executives claimed would cost the companies an additional sixty cents per hour per worker. When the petition was turned down, the union approved a strike that began on July 1. The ensuing shutdown was described by the *Duluth News-Tribune* as providing steelworkers with unpaid summer "vacation time," which they used for "painting their houses, weeding gardens, washing cars and playing with their children." When the strike concluded five weeks later, the union had secured a three-year contract that provided improved pension, unemployment, and hospitalization benefits for steelworkers, along with minimum hourly wage guarantees that would reach $1.96 by 1959—a gain of forty-six cents over the three-year period.[13]

It was the 116-day shutdown of 1959 that most clearly tested the mettle of all steelworkers in America. When the Morgan Park plant closed in mid-July, several strikers' wives exhibited both stoicism and concern over what they correctly envisioned would be a lengthy standoff. While some women reported that their husbands got "crabby" when they couldn't work, most were concerned about stretching finances to meet family needs. By the time the stalemate entered its second month, several strikers were pursuing part-time jobs, working as farmhands, carpenters, weekend musicians, or blueberry pickers. During September, when numerous unemployed steelworkers (and Mesabi miners) could not pay their rent, utility, and heating bills, the county welfare department experienced a 77 percent increase in relief assistance requests. In early November, however, the strikers returned to their jobs when the U.S. Supreme Court upheld President Dwight Eisenhower's request to invoke a back-to-work injunction under the Taft-Hartley Act, a 1947 Congressional action that severely restricted the power of unions. The court's decision mandated that contract negotiations continue for as many as eighty more days, during which time the steel mills were to remain open. Steelworkers at Morgan Park were generally pleased that they could once again return to the plant, but many were upset with the forced injunction, preferring instead that "they would have settled and got us a contract." The negotiated agreement, finally achieved in January 1960, provided employees with wage increases, cost-of-living adjustments, and a lump sum payment of $1,500 at the time of retirement.[14] The workforce employed at Morgan Park would benefit from other contracts signed during the 1960s, but the 1959 walkout marked their last strike action.

Leading up to Closure

Throughout the 1960s, steel production at the Morgan Park plant both waxed and waned, with significant fluctuations often occurring during a single year. When favorable conditions prevailed, seven of the ten open hearths and both blast furnaces operated, but when production plummeted, only three open hearths and a single blast furnace functioned. Employee numbers varied considerably during the decade, ranging from 1,700 to 3,000 workers. In 1964, when U.S. Steel merged seven of its general operating divisions into a single organizational unit, the Morgan Park plant was renamed the "Duluth Works." While the facility served as U.S. Steel's sole producer of fence posts and steel wool, wire fabrication continued to be the primary activity. Nevertheless, only 20 percent of all locally produced steel was converted into finished products at the plant. As a Duluth reporter noted in 1964, what with "depression, business dropoffs, layoffs, and occasionally a rumor—happily always false—that U.S. Steel would close the plant," the fifty-year history of the facility had been anything but "smooth."[15]

When rumors of a total shutdown circulated during the mid-1960s, Duluth Mayor George D. Johnson and Minnesota Governor Elmer L. Andersen contacted U.S. Steel officials, asking for information about the plant's future. U.S. Steel President Roger Blough replied that the corporation had "absolutely no plans" to close the facility, but warned that "the Duluth plant must rely on the demand for wire products, and that demand in recent years has been severely plagued by heavy foreign imports." In 1966, when U.S. Steel planned a massive expansion of several plants, most in the Chicago area, Duluth officials were concerned that no assurance was given about the fate of the local facility. Blough once again warned how necessary it was that each steel plant remain competitive. "It has to have the economies to support it in the market it serves," he commented, also noting that U.S. Steel could best "serve the very large and growing Chicago market from Chicago."[16]

Pollution Problems

Not only market limitations defined the Duluth steel plant during the 1960s, for now there also was increasing recognition of the harmful air and water emissions that occurred as part of the manufacturing process. Pollution had been evident from the time the first steel was produced in late 1915, but for many decades the plant's "smoke and noise" were typically regarded as a sign of economic progress (Figure 12.4). When a regional organization that advocated for improved fishing and hunting habitat filmed the St. Louis River in 1949, the movie portrayed the industrial effluents, many from the steel plant, that drained into the water—"tar, paint, animal blood, sewage, oil, acid, dyes, chemicals and other contaminating materials."[17] Despite the damning evidence, it would not be until the 1960s and the emergence of a nationwide environmental movement that widespread attention began to be focused directly on the Duluth Works' pollution discharges.

The first actions were local, as in 1966 when a Morgan Park Pollution Control Committee was organized to protest the air pollution discharges emitted by the Universal-Atlas Cement Company plant. After securing the signatures of one thousand Morgan Park, Gary, New Duluth, Smithville, and Riverside residents—who signed petitions that called for a solution to involve the "combined action" of federal, state, county, and city governmental

Figure 12.4. Harmful chemical discharges from the steel plant, as shown in 1958, contributed significantly to the despoliation of the St. Louis River. Photograph by Warren D. Kress; courtesy of Donald Kress.

agencies—the requests were forwarded to several agencies. Two years later the Minnesota Pollution Control Agency (MPCA) began enforcing recently enacted state and federal air and water pollution laws. The agency requested information from U.S. Steel concerning the corporation's "intention[s] regarding abatement of the air and water pollution resulting from its Duluth facilities." In June 1970 U.S. Steel's environmental division replied that the corporation would attempt to meet the air and water quality mandates, but only if "economic studies indicate the feasibility of continuing steel and cement operations at the Duluth locations." The MPCA gave U.S. Steel until July 1973 to make its assessment, and an additional two years thereafter to comply with pollution guidelines. U.S. Steel officials noted their willingness to cooperate in satisfying the timetable and regulations.[18]

Rather than waiting three years, U.S. Steel officials announced, already in September 1971, their plans to shut down the hot side of the plant in two months (Figure 12.5). When reporting on the decision during an October visit to Duluth, U.S. Steel Board Chairman Edwin Gott reiterated a theme that corporation executives had often made in the past, namely "the absence of a steel market in this area of sufficient size to provide both the volume of business and economic potential necessary to justify a large investment for a modern integrated steel production unit." The magnitude of U.S. Steel's decision became strikingly evident on November 13, when the furnaces were shut down and 1,600 of 2,500 employees received discharge notices. Some unemployed workers found work outside the steel industry, typically for much less financial remuneration, but the majority either retired or took positions in U.S. Steel operations located in northeastern Minnesota and elsewhere.[19]

Gott made another trip to Duluth in January 1972, when he confirmed that the hot side of the Duluth Works would never again reopen. He also reported that operations at the merchant and rod mills, as well as the coke and cement plants, were planned to continue. A year and a half later, however, notice was given that the mills would close in October 1973, an action that displaced another 700 employees. (For the next few years, four small metals industries employing about 165 laborers were located in several steel plant buildings.) The coke ovens and cement plant were to remain open, but only if the MPCA did not impose expensive environmental control measures on the operations.[20]

After two years of often rancorous litigation with the MPCA, U.S. Steel officials declared that the cement plant, which employed 145 workers, would close in January 1976. Unlike the sentiments that prevailed when the steel

Figure 12.5. A view of the one blast furnace that still operated at the steel plant in September 1971, just two months before the entire facility was shut down. Photograph by the author.

plant closed, the vast majority of Morgan Park and Gary–New Duluth citizens welcomed the news that the severe air pollution problems caused by cement manufacturing were ending. "I hate the cement plant," one Morgan Parker exclaimed a few months before the closing. When a Michigan firm proposed to reopen the plant in 1978, a Gary–New Duluth Community Club member pleaded with MPCA officials "to not again make us hostage to the cement dust." Soon after the MPCA turned down the application, the plant was razed. Finally, in May 1979, following U.S. Steel's announced unwillingness to meet federal air quality regulations, operations at the coke plant were also terminated. With this action the last group of 250 U.S. Steel employees lost their jobs.[21]

Although the abandoned manufacturing complex would loom over the community for more than another decade, U.S. Steel's once pervasive presence in Duluth and Morgan Park was gone (Figure 12.6). And, as Hudelson and Ross have written, the demise of U.S. Steel and other local industrial operations led to the loss of all former CIO unions in Duluth. "With the

Figure 12.6. In 1989, the smokestacks of the abandoned steel plant were still visible from the Morgan Park community, as shown in this photograph taken from the roof of the United Protestant Church. Photograph by the author.

decline of the unions," they report, "working-class families lost much of the economic security that had been won by their parents and grandparents."[22]

The Economics–Environment Equation

Although it was pollution that highlighted the debate at Morgan Park from 1968 through 1979, the plant's deficiencies were not necessarily excessive when compared to other U.S. Steel facilities. Complying with pollution control regulations certainly would have reduced the profit margin of the Duluth Works, but these standards alone were not sufficient to end steel-making operations. Other factors were of greater importance in the decision that ultimately led to the closing.

The overarching issue, as always, was the limited market demand for steel produced and fabricated in Duluth. In addition, by the early 1970s Morgan Park's blast and open-hearth furnaces were dilapidated and obsolete when compared to the modern basic oxygen furnaces that characterized one-half of the American steel industry at the time. Replacing the existing Morgan Park plant with a new or renovated basic oxygen unit would have required an expenditure of well over $100 million (1971 dollars)—a significantly greater amount than the $10 to $20 million estimated to implement pollution control measures. The restrictions posed by market shortfalls and the outmoded condition of the plant were too much to overcome by the latter third of the twentieth century. Quite simply, the environmental concerns that emerged in the late 1960s only "brought the years of neglect into clearer focus and provided a convenient 'rationale' for closing the facility."[23]

The circumstances at Duluth also presaged similar events that would subsequently define the "deindustrialization" of America's "Rust Belt." Beginning during the late 1970s, and then after gaining momentum throughout the 1980s, numerous steel mills and other manufacturing operations in Pennsylvania, Ohio, West Virginia, and elsewhere were shut down, leaving behind decayed factories, abandoned towns, and bewildered and disillusioned people. Even U.S. Steel's Homestead Works, once the world's most famous steel-making center and a place that had employed as many as 10,000 workers, closed in 1986. In his poignant lament about Homestead's demise, former *New York Times* reporter William Serrin termed the situation an example of the "old game" that has characterized much of American history—"use things up, people and places, then discard them."[24]

Aftermath

A survey of 341 Morgan Park residents conducted three and a half years after the shutdown revealed that 62 percent believed U.S. Steel had treated the community fairly, 28 percent termed the corporation's treatment unfair, and 10 percent had no opinion. When asked whether the steel plant should have remained open even if there had been an increase in pollution output, 80 percent said yes, 11 percent believed it was better to discontinue operations, and 9 percent were unsure. "When the people moved out here they knew it was company houses, and they should have put up with the pollution," replied one woman, a resident of Morgan Park for thirty-five years. One of the dissident voices, an attorney who had lived in the community for twenty years, hoped that someday he could "find out what the true attitude of the corporation was; they never really told us their true attitude." Another respondent was disappointed with both protagonists: "The government should have let up some on its pollution control[s]," he said, "and the steel plant should have complied with more." When 112 Gary residents were asked the same question about the pollution issue, they expressed attitudes that closely mirrored those of the Morgan Parkers: 78 percent believed the plant should have remained in operation, 16 percent were of the opinion that shutting down was the best option, and 6 percent had no opinion or were unsure.[25]

Almost 20 percent of the Morgan Park respondents believed the quality of the environment had improved following the steel plant closing, 73 percent said conditions had remained the same, and 7 percent actually felt that environmental quality had deteriorated. Gary's respondents, on the other hand, were even more positive when evaluating the results: 36 percent felt that environmental quality had improved (a figure that exceeded the Morgan Park findings by 16 percent), 52 percent saw no change, and 7 percent reported a decline.[26]

Thirteen years later, in 1988, U.S. Steel began razing the abandoned buildings that covered much of the abandoned 640-acre property. Included in these activities was the disposal of the hazardous building materials, primarily asbestos, found in many structures (Figure 12.7). Despite the conditions he had encountered, one contractor who conducted some of the work

Figure 12.7. Demolition of the steel plant was completed during the 1990s. Photograph by John Isle in 1992; courtesy of John Isle.

in 1992 was nostalgic as he looked back at the demolition project fourteen years later—"ahh, the diesel smoke and the explosions; life was good," he wrote in 2006. A "spectacular blaze" also resulted in the complete destruction of one remaining building in 1997.[27]

The most dangerous pollutants, however, were those that contaminated the water; in fact, the pollution was so serious that the Environmental Protection Agency listed the former steel plant property as a Superfund site in 1984. One of the most hazardous areas, a coke-settling pond situated along a creek that feeds into the St. Louis River, included 20,000 cubic yards of coal tar contaminated with ammonia, cyanide, phenols, and heavy metals. Remediation was carried out on-site in 1997, when the wastes were solidified with concrete stabilizers. The former wire mill–settling basin, described as "full with solids," was also excavated and planted with wetland vegetation.[28]

In August 2003, the MPCA deemed several sections of the property tentatively suitable for redevelopment, but with the caveat that "the shallow waters of Spirit Lake and polluted bottom sediments remain unsafe." One year later, Duluth's Economic Development Authority purchased the "lightly polluted" cement plant property for $232,000, intending eventually to convert its sixty-five acres into a business and industrial park. No development has occurred as of 2007. Various proposals have also been made to transfer the remaining 535 acres that remain in U.S. Steel ownership "back into productive use." The site certainly has numerous attributes, especially its railways, highways, and utilities, as well as scenic views of the river and the wooded Wisconsin shoreline; but it remains unclear whether future developers will choose to invest in a property that still has so many long-term questions regarding contaminants and pollutants.[29]

Today, the former steel plant district at Morgan Park no longer shows any immediately visible evidence of the more than six decades of heavy manufacturing activity that occurred on the site. Unfortunately, insidious remnants of those activities remain immersed in the land and water. At Morgan Park, the past still casts a shadow over both the present and the future.

13. PRESERVING THE MODEL TOWN

Morgan Park's residential district underwent numerous transitions from 1946 onward. The community's future appeared assured when more than one hundred new dwelling units were built from 1952 to the early 1960s, but conditions changed dramatically when the steel plant closed in late 1971. Over time, housing values declined, although it was income loss that most directly impacted Morgan Parkers. Several nonresidential buildings were razed from the 1950s on, but new citizens interested in rehabilitating and preserving Morgan Park's historic homes started moving into the community during the 1970s. Since then, however, the preservationists' objectives have not always meshed with the views of all long-time residents, as well as the views of other recent arrivals who look at Morgan Park as an interim stop in their search for housing in the Duluth area.

The Beginning of the End

Virtually all of Morgan Park's residences had been purchased by 1947, at which time the Galbreath Company closed its local sales office. John Galbreath reported that he was "proud" of what the company had accomplished at Morgan Park and elsewhere; the company was "doing something for the country," he declared in 1951. Once the sales were completed, Morgan Park became much more like other Duluth neighborhoods; nonetheless, the enclave was still a company town in one important sense—its singular economic dependence on the steel plant.[1]

Housing, Streets, and Utilities

Because the United States faced a serious housing deficit following the Depression and the war, numerous government programs were quickly developed to alleviate the problem. One 1946 act, which authorized the Federal Public Housing Authority to transfer barracks from decommissioned military sites to American cities, offered temporary living quarters at seven different Duluth locations for 174 military veterans and their families. An undeveloped area in Morgan Park's western neighborhood (Block 31) accommodated five poorly insulated, round-roofed Quonset buildings, each with eight units. Forty families typically resided in the Quonsets until they were razed between 1953 and 1955.[2]

Immediately after the war ended, the three Nenovan buildings were converted into apartments, along with some second-floor offices in the Lake View Building. With more new housing available throughout the greater Duluth area, housing densities decreased in Morgan Park, from 4.1 persons per unit in 1940 to 3.3 in 1950. Therefore, Morgan Park's total population figure declined from 2,100 people to 1,870 during the decade. The median family income of Morgan Park's residents ($3,490) was somewhat higher than the figure for all of Duluth ($3,010), while the average value of a house in Morgan Park ($7,715) and the city ($7,840) differed only slightly.[3]

A few new dwellings emerged at scattered sites in Morgan Park during the immediate postwar period, but a housing boom occurred between 1952 and 1958, when 110 new single-family units were built on six undeveloped blocks in the western neighborhood (Figure 13.1). Several of these houses,

Figure 13.1. More than one hundred frame houses similar to these units located along Ninetieth Avenue West were built in Morgan Park during the 1950s and 1960; most emerged in the western neighborhood. Photograph by the author, 1971.

including three on display at 1338, 1348, and 1354 Ninety-first Avenue West in Duluth's 1953 "Parade of Homes," were constructed and marketed by a Duluth firm, Anderson Enterprises, Inc. The new residences reflected postwar preferences for one-story and one-and-a-half-story houses, and displayed a number of contemporary features intended to entice prospective homeowners. With 850 to 1,100 square feet of living space, the two- and three-bedroom houses came with "custom hardware and kitchen cabinets, ventilating fans in the kitchen and weather stripped windows," as well as sliding doors on wardrobe closets, tiled bathroom showers, living-room picture windows, storm windows, built-in clothes chutes, basement fruit rooms with temperature controls, forced-air heating, and concrete steps with ornamental wrought-iron railings. Prices ranged from $11,000 to $13,450. During the late 1950s and early 1960s, another thirty houses were constructed on other sites located throughout the community.[4]

By the 1950s, the carefully maintained landscapes that had characterized Morgan Park were no longer reflected by the entire community (Figure 13.2). Private garages also began appearing along Morgan Park's alleys at this time.

Figure 13.2. By 1958, the once well-maintained streets, terraces, and yards were no longer evident in some sections of the western neighborhood. Photograph by Warren D. Kress; courtesy of Donald Kress.

Nowhere was the influence of the automobile more visible than in the western neighborhood, where the interior garden and play areas of Blocks 33, 34, and 35 were filled with garages. Some of the former community garages were torn down, though many were converted into storage units.

Despite the new houses that appeared in Morgan Park during the 1950s, the population density declined from 3.3 persons per household in 1950 to 3.0 in 1960. As a result, the overall population count of 1,840 in 1960 represented a slight decline of thirty people over the decade. The downturn was reversed during the 1960s, albeit slightly, when the population count registered a gain of fifty people. Despite the relatively limited gain, Morgan Park was the only older neighborhood in Duluth that experienced some population growth and very little decline in the number of younger families. In 1959, the median family income figure for Morgan Parkers ($6,350) exceeded that of Duluthians ($5,875), but a decade later, the order had changed ($8,530 for Morgan Park, $9,315 for Duluth). The median value of a Morgan Park residence in 1959 ($9,700) trailed the figure for Duluth ($11,100), but this was reversed in 1969 ($16,000 for Morgan Park, $14,300 for Duluth).[5]

A few nonresidential buildings, most quite small, were constructed in Morgan Park from the mid-1950s to 1972. They were the community's second automobile service station and a commercial concrete-block building, both located north of the Lake View Building; the Morgan Park Medical Center, situated south of the Park State Bank; and a group home in the western neighborhood, which eventually became a crisis shelter for women and children. The only major building was the new Blessed St. Margaret Mary Catholic School. Designed by the Duluth and Minneapolis architectural firm of Maguolo and Quick, the 1960 building replaced the school that had been located in the former Neighborhood House since 1927. The new brick and masonry school, which housed grades one through eight in four classrooms and several ancillary rooms, served students from the greater Morgan Park area. The major facilities in the building, also utilized by Morgan Park's Catholic parish, were a multipurpose room and a stage, along with an adjacent kitchen equipped with facilities that could serve five hundred people.[6] Although the school closed during the 1990s, the multipurpose room and kitchen are still used by the parish.

Three venerable structures disappeared from the Morgan Park landscape prior to the late 1972 steel plant closing. The first was the water tower, razed in 1952—exactly forty years after it had emerged along the southern edge of the western neighborhood (Figure 13.3). Removed when the steel

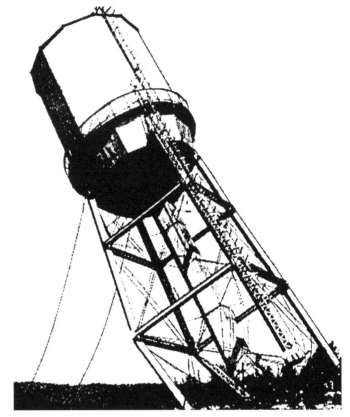

Figure 13.3. The first structure removed from postwar Morgan Park was the water tower, torn down in May 1952. From Duluth News-Tribune, May 9, 1952.

plant started drawing all of its water from Duluth's city wells, the ninety-three-foot-high tower was converted into 130,000 pounds of scrap, reportedly to assist in meeting "civilian and defense needs." The former Neighborhood House was demolished during the summer of 1961, shortly after the dedication of the new Catholic school. Two years later, the Beverly Street streetcar waiting station was demolished. This one-time favorite meeting place for children had remained vacant and poorly maintained after the termination of streetcar service in 1939; and the neglected building was criticized by members of Morgan Park's Community Club for several ensuing years. The former waiting station was eventually converted into a small grocery store in 1948, but it closed nine years later. Immediately following the building's removal in 1963, the land parcel was converted into a small triangular area of open space.[7]

Many Duluth streets, including several in Morgan Park, were so deteriorated by the late 1940s that residents often called them "foxholes." Visitors also complained about the "general state of disrepair" of streets and sidewalks throughout southwestern Duluth. Nevertheless, Morgan Park voters defeated a June 1948 petition that called for the repair of the community's worst streets, but only because all homeowners would have been assessed equally for the repairs, not just those residents who lived along the upgraded roadways.[8]

In 1948, when Morgan Park's underground electric lines were described as "overburdened," above-ground poles and lines appeared in the community for the first time. In addition, Morgan Park's untreated sewage still flowed directly into the St. Louis River, even as residents complained that the city assessed them for sewer services not received. Duluth officials retorted that the fees paid by Morgan Parkers were justified. "Everybody benefits from a clean water supply and everybody should pay," was the official response. It would not be until 1960 that Morgan Park was connected to a recently built sewage treatment plant in the nearby neighborhood of Smithville.[9]

Always the School, but the Clubhouse, Too

Both the school and the clubhouse continued to play a central role in the lives of local residents following World War II. People from throughout the Morgan Park area utilized both facilities, though participation in most clubhouse activities was limited to steel plant employees and their families.

The high school's first group of postwar graduates, the class of 1946, received attention when twelve of thirty-one male seniors enlisted en masse in the U.S. Marine Corps. Probably no school events attracted greater interest than did football games, especially those during the early 1950s, when the Wildcats were undefeated over three seasons and captured four Duluth high-school championships. The 1963 and 1970 football teams also emerged as undefeated city champions, with the 1970 squad receiving designation as the best team in Minnesota's medium-sized school division.[10]

But school-related activities were not limited to athletic accomplishments. One event, quite anachronistic by today's standards, was the annual Morgan Park minstrel show, which occurred from 1925 to 1948. Popular with many American schools and other organizations throughout the period, minstrel shows typically featured several "endmen"—whites who carried on comedic and musical routines by employing "an exaggerated form of Black English vernacular"—along with a more sophisticated "interlocutor," who bantered with the endmen. The final 1948 show, with forty-four Morgan Park male and female students in blackface, was replaced in subsequent years by musical variety and comedy programs such as the 1950 offering, "Sister Susie Swings It." The often-offensive racial stereotypes portrayed by minstrel shows were eliminated in much of the United States by the late 1940s and early 1950s.[11]

Another musical event generated attention in May 1955, when Morgan

Park's high-school band director, Wayne Samskar, dedicated his recently completed musical composition, "Study in Steel," to the community. The band performed the composition's three movements—"Blast Furnace," "Nail Mill," and "Open Hearth"—all symbolizing "the cascade of molten steel, the rumbling of machinery, the clang of bells, the rumbling of locomotive, the clanking of massive cranes, and the vast expanse of the building and the general activity." A local reviewer commented that because of Samskar's former experiences as a steel plant laborer, the musical work was no "delicate" piece that featured "birds and flowers and fountains"; instead, it interpreted "the tension and magnitude of the steel industry."[12]

A 1965 city bond referendum, which authorized $250,000 for the construction of an addition to the Morgan Park school, resulted in an unexpected clash between the executive committee of the local Parent-Teachers Association (PTA) and the Duluth Board of Education. When architects for Perkins and Will Associates of Chicago recommended a two-story addition that would demolish the school's central doorway entrance and replace it with a two-story brick addition, the executive committee, led by its president, Mrs. Julius Cherra, immediately opposed the proposal. Cherra noted that if it were implemented, the Perkins and Will design would interrupt two of the three rows of uniform windows that defined the building's front facade. Despite Cherra's insistence that the committee was "going to do something about it," the school board approved the addition and the resulting facade alteration. One of the board members justified his vote, saying that in this case, "the aesthetic must yield to the educational." Soon the school had a large library, counselors' offices, and more classrooms.[13]

In March 1970 the school faced the most serious crisis in its history when an arsonist caused $250,000 in damage to the building. Although the facility was closed for only a single week, the cleanup and rehabilitation of the school stretched out over subsequent months and years. The most time-consuming task was the restoration and replacement of more than a half-century of school records and memorabilia.[14]

Often paired with the school was the Good Fellowship Club building and its programs, which continued to receive accolades from residents and nonresidents alike, including an August 1957 community celebration that marked the fortieth anniversary of the organization. Five years later, when commenting on the low rates of juvenile delinquency in Morgan Park, Duluth's police chief and probation officers stated that the Good Fellowship Club's numerous programs were responsible. A total of 2,300 members, including several three-generation families, utilized the club's offerings, primarily the programs overseen by an athletic director and a visiting nurse. Monthly dues of $1.50 per member generated an annual income of more than $40,000 that supported the programs, while U.S. Steel paid for the building's taxes, fuel bills, and half the maintenance costs.[15]

By 1968, with the club's membership numbers in decline, the City of Duluth assumed ownership of the building. When 1971 financial projections indicated that subsequent dues would generate annual revenues of only $16,000, the membership ranks were opened to anyone residing in southwestern Duluth. The response, nonetheless, was insufficient to replace U.S. Steel's former subsidy.[16] The steady deterioration of the clubhouse that occurred during the 1970s would eventually result in the removal of this distinctive community icon.

Even as U.S. Steel relinquished management of the clubhouse, vestiges of the old paternalism remained. Shortly before the plant closed, a soon-to-be-retired U.S. Steel employee was designated as the clubhouse manager. After two Morgan Park women questioned him about one of the club's programs, the manager immediately informed a steel plant supervisor about their inquiry. The next day the husbands of both women were called into the administrative office of the Duluth Works, where it was insinuated that both men could be fired from their jobs if they "didn't keep their wives quiet." To these two women, U.S. Steel's final operations at Morgan Park still included some supervisors who were "the old guard, or left over from the old guard."[17]

Economic Change and Historic Preservation, 1972–2006

The 1971 steel plant closing obviously sent shock waves throughout Morgan Park and much of Duluth. Because the primary economic foundation for Morgan Park and nearby neighborhoods ended with the shutdown, many laid-off workers accepted employment with U.S. Steel operations located on Minnesota's Iron Range and elsewhere. Some, nevertheless, chose to remain in the Duluth area. Of the 371 respondents who were surveyed in 1975, fully 87 percent replied that Morgan Park's desirability as a place to live had influenced their decision to stay either somewhat or very much. When informed that jobs were available in Gary, Indiana, one Morgan Parker exclaimed, "My God, who wants to live there?" Likewise, another former steelworker who lived outside Morgan Park said he simply could not consider moving to Gary, "where a strip of trees is called a forest and a catfish is a prime fishing target."[18]

Demographic Transitions

There was no appreciable increase in housing vacancies after the steel plant closed. Twenty-nine residential units stood empty in 1971, and the annual figure never exceeded thirty-three during the remainder of the decade (Figure 13.4). The 1975 survey revealed that about 12 percent of the respondents had moved into Morgan Park during the three and a half years following U.S. Steel's shutdown of the plant. This was somewhat but not inordinately higher than the turnover rates experienced during the two three-year periods preceding the closing (8.3 and 8.5 percent respectively). Almost 70 percent of the respondents replied that they intended to remain in Morgan Park for ten years or more.[19]

When asked to compare the former model village with nearby neighborhoods such as Gary, New Duluth, and Smithville, 85 percent of Morgan Parkers expressed a clear preference for their community. "It's away from the city, kinda country-like and quaint," said one long-time resident, while a seventy-two-year-old man noted that "Morgan Park is a good place to live—if you're old or young." A sixty-eight-year-old widow who had lived in

Figure 13.4. The original rear porches for this six-unit row house on Eighty-eighth Avenue remained relatively unchanged in 1972. Photograph by the author.

Morgan Park fifty years summarized the attitudes of many citizens: "I just like the whole thing, everything about it."[20]

Length of residence within Morgan Park was strongly correlated with the results. Some 94 percent of residents who had made Morgan Park their home for more than twenty years preferred the community to any other district of Duluth, whereas 56 percent of the respondents who had resided in Morgan Park for three or fewer years expressed similar sentiments. Likewise, 86 percent of the retirees believed the quality of housing in Morgan Park was superior to what could be found in adjoining neighborhoods; only 58 percent of the lower-income residents were of a similar mind, but most, of course, were relegated to the community's poorest and least expensive dwelling units.[21]

On the other hand, Gary's residents, as they had done throughout history, continued to prefer their community to Morgan Park. Only 6 percent believed that the model town was a more desirable place to live than Gary; 47 percent termed the two places similar, whereas 46 percent believed that Morgan Park was "worse" than their community. "Too many houses too close together," was a common criticism of Morgan Park, although some respondents had additional observations. There "isn't enough air to breathe" in Morgan Park, claimed one Gary resident, while another replied that the houses in Morgan Park "are all the same—cement blocks; in Gary each house is individual—all different." Another Gary denizen preferred a population of "mostly industrial workers" to the "mixed element of people" found in Morgan Park.[22]

The total population of Morgan Park declined by more than four hundred people during the decade, falling from 1,890 in 1970 to 1,450 in 1980. Again, a significant portion of the loss was caused by a reduction in the average household size—from 2.9 to 2.2 persons. The decline would have been even greater, but the opening of the new Spirit Lake Apartments for senior citizens in 1978 added 81 new dwelling units to the housing inventory. Quite remarkably, the median family income figures for Morgan Parkers ($15,015) and Duluthians ($15,230) remained virtually equal in 1979, with only a small differential existing between the median housing values for both places ($37,600 in Morgan Park and $39,200 in Duluth).[23]

A schism between Morgan Park's owners and renters was clearly evident by the mid-1970s, and probably had been emerging since the 1950s. The "welfare people are coming," said one forty-seven-year-old, lifelong respondent disapprovingly in 1975, whereas a retired wire-mill worker opined that some people had "bought up houses here and rented [them] to undesirable people." Another resident with thirty years of experience in the community had an even more universally negative impression; to him, Morgan Park was "going downhill as far as people keeping up property."[24]

Population numbers continued to fall during the 1980s, reaching an all-time low of 1,435 people in 1990. The 1980s were also characterized by a growing socioeconomic gap between Morgan Parkers and Duluthians. Since more than one-half of Morgan Park's dwelling units had five or fewer rooms, the smallest residences served as magnets for lower-income people in search of affordable rental housing. An area of subsidized housing, termed the Morgan Park Town Houses, was also constructed in the formerly un-developed northwestern quadrant of the community during the early 1980s. Overall, the proportion of Morgan Park's population living below the pov-erty line grew from 10 to 18 percent between 1979 and 1989. (The respective figures for Duluth were 8 and 10 percent.) Most tellingly, the 1989 median family income for Morgan Parkers was but $22,000—almost $15,000 less than the figure for Duluth.[25]

During the 1990s, however, both the population count and socioeconomic conditions improved somewhat. By 2000, Morgan Park served as home to 1,510 residents—a gain of 140 people over 1990. The poverty rate declined to 11 percent, exceeding Duluth's figure by only 2.5 percent. Median family incomes also improved during the decade, growing by close to 40 percent to $36,250; nevertheless, this was still some $10,000 under the figure registered by Duluth. The difference in median housing values was even greater—$64,500 for Morgan Park and $81,600 for Duluth.

Preserving What and for Whom?

In 1972, Bill and Sue Majewski purchased a former manager's house on sale in the eastern neighborhood of Morgan Park. Although they were initially impressed by the ample size and reasonable price of the house, the couple quickly grew to appreciate the high quality of construction and its inherent historical qualities. Initially bothered by the changes that some residents had made to the exteriors of their houses, the Majewskis became two of Morgan Park's first "preservation pioneers." As they and others would learn, however, rehabilitating a Morgan Park house built of concrete block walls and cement floors is a demanding task—never more so than when trying to upgrade electrical and plumbing systems.[26]

Almost two decades later, Nancy Thompson purchased a house in the western neighborhood; since then, the political activist and preservation advocate has been coping with the "charm and challenge" of rehabilitating a Morgan Park residence (Figure 13.5). Employing her own labor as "sweat equity," Ms. Thompson replaced many of her home's missing interior furnishings with original Morgan Park fixtures, some of which she tracked down in other communities by placing advertisements in Duluth newspapers.[27]

Ever since 1974, when it declared Morgan Park eligible for inclusion in the National Register of Historic Places, the Minnesota Historical Society (MHS) has been a major player in the local preservation scene. The actual nomination of Morgan Park as a National Register district, nevertheless, was quickly shelved when residents questioned the restrictions that might accompany such a designation—a phenomenon that mirrors what has occurred in other historic lower-income communities and neighborhoods in America. As Alison Hoagland observed in 1999, owners of former company houses often wish to individualize and personalize their residences, unlike many preservationists, who focus on aesthetic features "expressed in architectural uniformity." To local preservation champion Bill Majewski, a city planner by profession, the architectural uniformity of Morgan Park's

Figure 13.5. Nancy Thompson, one of Morgan Park's ardent historic preservationists, with her two golden retrievers, Bruce and Butter, in 2001. Photograph by the author.

housing was appealing—even if many other residents didn't find it charming. Likewise, a Duluthian whose family had formerly lived in Morgan Park for several decades, commented on the "charm and beauty [that] lie in the sameness of the cement-block look of its streets."[28]

When homeowners in lower-income communities such as Morgan Park applied for federally assisted rehabilitation grants to upgrade and weatherize their dwellings, they were required to satisfy the Secretary of the Interior's (SOI) Standards for Rehabilitation. This meant that historically compatible materials and styles were required whenever residents replaced visible exterior features, such as windows or siding. On the other hand, residents who had sufficient personal funds to install new windows or to apply vinyl or metal siding to their houses were able to bypass the standards. Gary Doty, Duluth's mayor from 1996 to 2002 and seldom a friend of preservation, sided with the less financially advantaged homeowners. "To consign lower-income Duluthians to live in homes with old windows, inadequate siding, and, in some cases, a near total lack of insulation, for the sake of historic preservation makes no rational sense," said Doty in 1999.[29]

These and other issues have also caused many Morgan Parkers to question the benefits of historic preservation. In 2001, long-time resident Al Bothun termed the National Register "the dumbest thing, [because] you've got to go through somebody. If you only had to go to one person, fine, but you've got to go to about ten organizations. . . . It's a terrible situation." Because so many house roofs, porches, and exteriors had been modified by 2001, former Morgan Park resident Sally Solomon confessed that she had "mixed thoughts" about historic preservation. "Man, it's not as pretty as it was when I was [living] out there," she observed. But John Howden, a resident of Morgan Park since 1918, considered much of the discussion and controversy irrelevant. "All this historic business," said the ninety-two-year-old in 2001, less than a year before his death, "is little more than signing a paper." According to Howden, "you alone have jurisdiction over your own house; nobody tells you how you can run your home."[30]

Losing a Clubhouse, Changing a School, Saving a Church

As Morgan Parkers have mulled National Register designation from the 1970s to the present, the community has experienced numerous physical changes (Figure 13.6). While much of the transition is exhibited in the form of relatively superficial changes to the exteriors of Morgan Park's concrete-block houses, it is the removal of several nonresidential and institutional

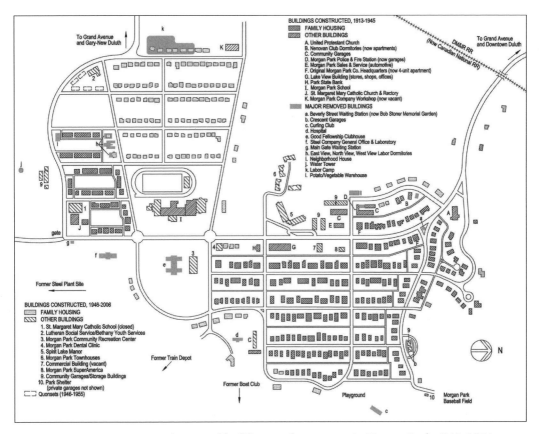

Figure 13.6. Existing and removed buildings and structures in Morgan Park, 1913–2006. Derived from aerial photographs, historic maps, building and demolition permits, resident interviews, and author's field notes; cartography by Kassie Martine.

buildings that causes many residents to ask whether too much has already been lost. The company office building that had stood in the western neighborhood since 1915 came down during the mid-1970s, while the eastern neighborhood's distinctive pair of crescent-shaped garages was removed one decade later. The demise of no building, however, generated more controversy and community angst than did the razing of the Good Fellowship Clubhouse in late 1981.

Shortly after U.S. Steel surrendered control of the clubhouse to the City of Duluth in 1968, the deteriorating condition of the structure, coupled with increasing utility costs and declining membership revenues, eventually led to calls for its removal; the recommendation also called for the replacement of the clubhouse with a new, albeit much smaller and less elaborate, energy-efficient community building. In 1980 city officials submitted their combined demolition and new construction proposal, which was to be accomplished by using more than a half million dollars of Duluth's federally supplied community development funds. "It's the end of the era of the steel plant," lamented the club's vice president.[31]

The Minnesota Historical Society temporarily delayed the demolition steamroller in late 1980 when staff members in its historic preservation office identified the clubhouse as a key component in "an extremely well-preserved company town" that had national historical significance. (Although Morgan Park was not listed in the National Register of Historic Places, the MHS review occurred because federal funds would be used in a community declared eligible for the register.) In May 1981 the MHS preservation office turned down the city's demolition request because of the "adverse effect" it would have on the entire Morgan Park community. Soon, nine hundred residents of Morgan Park and nearby neighborhoods signed petitions that called for the MHS to rescind its decision, while the *Duluth News-Tribune* fanned the flames by terming the clubhouse an "albatross," an "oversized, antiquated facility," and "a financial drain and an aesthetic blight." Despite this local opposition, MHS staff members forwarded the antidemolition resolution to the National Advisory Council on Historic Preservation, which approved the request in June 1981.

One month later, however, the process took a sudden turn after MHS director Russell Fridley wrote a letter to the Advisory Council that contradicted his staff's decision. Calling attention to the fact that the building had not yet been listed in the National Register of Historic Places, Fridley said that if the clubhouse had either "state or national importance, we'd be fighting to preserve it." Instead, he requested that the council not "hamstring" the city's wishes to demolish the building and replace it with a new structure, a recommendation that the *Duluth Herald*'s editorial page termed "sage counsel." The Advisory Council approved the demolition in mid-October 1981, and after Fridley and Mayor Fedo signed a memorandum of agreement one month later, the building was quickly reduced to rubble (Figure 13.7).[32]

The memorandum also called for a new building design that would be "architecturally compatible with the Morgan Park Historic District." After the new community center was completed in late 1982, the *News-Tribune* praised its "sleek, modern architecture," its "bright and open spaces," and its "warmth, [generated] from the hearts of the people who use the building." About a decade later, however, the newspaper used quite different words when describing the sentiments of local residents, many who now claimed that removal of the old clubhouse was "a shame," that the new

Figure 13.7. The Good Fellowship Club, portrayed here in September 1981, was closed and boarded up in November 1980 and torn down one year later. Photograph by the author.

building failed to serve as a "social magnet" for the community, and that there was "no comparison" between the two structures. Tearing down the old clubhouse was "the worst thing they could've done," mourned one long-time Morgan Parker in 1991.[33]

Morgan Park's school also received considerable attention during the post-steel-plant era, but at least the building was not demolished. Events soon after the plant closing appeared quite favorable when the Duluth School Board, in 1975, approved a one-million-dollar swimming pool for Morgan Park, which opened the next year. In 1979 the Wildcats basketball team, for the first and only time in school history, advanced to the state tournament in the Twin Cities. Although the squad lost in the first round, students and residents expressed great pride in the team's accomplishments, even if their enthusiasm was tempered by news that the high school might close. Questions about its future had emerged one year earlier, when the Duluth School Board expressed concern over the small size of the student body (about three hundred pupils, or some seven hundred to a thousand fewer then the city's other high schools), as well as projected enrollment declines. In early 1981 the board presented its plan to eliminate Morgan Park's high school and to close twelve elementary and junior high facilities elsewhere in Duluth. Morgan Park's students expressed their displeasure in April by walking out of classes and engaging in a brief protest march, and local residents simultaneously prepared themselves "to go to almost any length[s] to keep the high school open." Despite several rancorous meetings and threats of lawsuits, Morgan Park's high school was consolidated with the Denfeld facility during the summer of 1982. The Morgan Park building was then converted into a junior high school for western Duluth, and a middle school in 1990.[34]

While many residents still bemoan the loss of the clubhouse and the high school, the United Protestant Church serves as an example of a successful preservation project. Despite the congregation's relatively small size, its 140 members made plans to raise $325,000 for the exterior repair of their seriously deteriorated building in 2002. Donations, pledges, and special events quickly generated $202,000, which allowed the congregation to secure a loan that covered the remaining amount. Soon, leaking windows, crumbling concrete blocks, and the decaying porte cochere were repaired, missing mortar and parapets were replaced, and the entire exterior was painted. One feature of the historic church could not be restored: eight damaged openings in the church tower, which were enclosed with concrete blocks. When summarizing the congregation's activities in 2003, the congregation's pastor proclaimed: "They've done so much in a year and a half!"—an apt accolade for the accomplishments of his flock.[35]

It Takes a Village

As the 1990s transitioned into a new century and a new millennium, only a minority of Morgan Park residents were directly involved in the rehabilitation and preservation of the community's historic homes and buildings. Ironically, however, it was the legacy of the past, but now in a totally unexpected and nonwelcome manner, that sparked significant resident involvement and action throughout Morgan Park. Even though the issue was seemingly mundane—the breakdown of the community's sewer and water lines—the ensuing emergency threatened the safety, health, and financial well-being of numerous residents.

Duluth's Department of Public Works had devoted considerable resources to the repair of Morgan Park's utilities since the early 1990s, but a crisis occurred in 2000 when sewage started gushing into the basements of many homes. Streets and alleys collapsed, and two residents almost drowned when they were temporarily trapped by sewer line cave-ins. In the wake of the emergency in late 2001, a number of concerned citizens formed a grassroots organization, the Morgan Park Sewer Task Force, which focused on strategies that would help lower-income citizens pay for the high costs of utility replacement. Led by local activist Debbie Isabell Nelson, whose own post–World War II house had suffered tens of thousands of dollars in damages since 1993 because of sewer backups, the task force publicized its efforts by adopting the theme, "It Takes a Village to Build a Sewer" (Figure 13.8).[36]

Groundbreaking for the project began on eight blocks of Morgan Park's streets in June 2003 and continued throughout the remainder of the community over subsequent years. The depth of the utility lines, which had been placed as many as eighteen feet beneath Morgan Park's narrow alleyways during the early twentieth century, exacerbated the costs. The sewer task force quickly assumed the lead in assisting the many residents who were concerned about the expenses they would incur for utility improvements. Task force members worked closely with Duluth officials to obtain a low-interest loan from the Minnesota Public Facilities Authority that paid for much of the water-line replacement costs; they also applied for federal Community Development block grants that covered a significant proportion of the homeowners' increased assessment costs. In 2006, with the project all but completed, Morgan Parkers could cheer the significant accomplishments

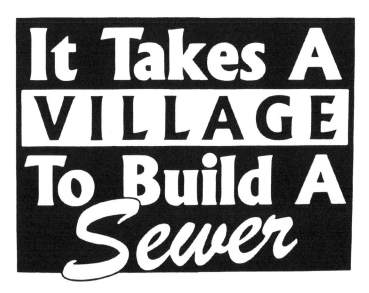

Figure 13.8. Morgan Park's residents came together to work on the community's serious utility problems during the early 2000s. Image from photograph by the author, 2003.

of an $11.5 million effort—reportedly the most expensive residential public works project in Duluth history.[37]

Restoring the Model City

On New Year's Day 2006, the *Duluth News-Tribune* published a brief letter from Bob Stoner, a former Morgan Park native who had attended his fifty-fifth high school class reunion a few months earlier. According to the one-time resident, the area that had served as his home environment during the Depression and World War II years was now "a slum," complete with "junk, junked cars, trash and dilapidation." Terming the situation "a shame," the Beloit, Wisconsin, citizen asked: "What happened?"[38]

Almost immediately the indefatigable Debbie Isabell Nelson, now president of the Morgan Park–Smithville Community Club, responded to the writer, informing him that some of the disarray was caused by the massive amount of utility and street construction work then under way. Nonetheless, she also agreed that Morgan Park "suffered from the lack of some property upkeep, which has contributed to the dilapidated look of our neighborhoods." Pointing out that the club had made the beautification of Morgan Park its 2006 goal, Isabell Nelson predicted that current residents would recapture "the spirit of community" that was clearly evident when Bill Stoner lived in the town.[39]

Just one month later, in February 2006, community club members adopted a new slogan, "Restore the Model City," to publicize the organization's activities. By May the group had produced its first newsletter, which announced an ambitious agenda for the organization: "to build bridges between our residents, landlords, businesses, churches, sport groups, school and city leaders, and to develop a revitalization plan for our wonderful, historical community." Over the summer the club organized a citizens patrol, a flower fest, a "One Lawn at a Time" beautification program, ice-cream socials, a community picnic, and the distribution of forty-two flats of bedding plants to residents.[40]

Especially noteworthy was the designation of the Bob Stoner Memorial Garden in August 2006 at the intersection of Beverly Street and Eighty-eighth Avenue West—a key location close to Morgan Park's main entrance and the site of the former streetcar waiting station (Figure 13.9). Although Stoner did not live to participate in the dedication ceremony, his words were recognized for providing the inspiration that sparked public interest in en-

Figure 13.9. The message on the bench in the recently dedicated Bob Stoner Memorial Garden reflects the growing community awareness of Morgan Park's unique origins and legacy. Photograph by the author, 2006.

hancing Morgan Park's appearance and public face. Other projects will follow, including the eventual placement of "a large U.S. Steel plant artifact" somewhere in the community.[41]

Many of these programs are similar to those provided in Morgan Park decades earlier. What differs, of course, is that in the past many of the offerings were organized, supported, and funded by the paternalistic largesse of an employer and landlord. The activities that occur in Morgan Park today are truly of a grassroots nature, indicative of a democratic and egalitarian social structure far different from its paternalistic past.

U.S. Steel has left as its legacy in Morgan Park a collection of sturdy concrete-block dwellings, gently winding streets, and landscaped yards and terraces—taken together, an attractive and unique residential environment. But beyond that, Morgan Park's single- and multifamily houses, open spaces, and church buildings still provide a view of what life was like for steel plant employees and their families in a company-controlled town. Despite the loss of its original economic underpinnings, Morgan Park persists, tenaciously so, as a pleasant, appealing, and viable community, as well as a remnant of America's rapidly disappearing industrial heritage. To ensure that the model town remains as such, it is essential that local residents, as well as the larger Duluth community, continue to remember, interpret, celebrate—and most important, preserve its past.

NOTES

Preface

1. *Polk's Duluth City Directory, 1950* (St. Paul: R. L. Polk and Co., 1950), 9; here-after these sources will be referred to as the Duluth city directory, or Duluth city directories.

2. Arnold R. Alanen, "Sixty Years of Transition in a Planned Company Town, with a Portrayal of Current Resident Evaluations," in *The Behavioral Basis of Design, Book 1: Selected Papers*, ed. Peter Suedfeld and James A. Russell (Stroudsburg, Penn.: Dowden, Hutchinson and Ross, Inc., 1976), 185–92; Arnold R. Alanen, "The Rise and Demise of a Company Town," *Professional Geographer* 29 (February 1977): 32–39. See also Arnold R. Alanen, "Morgan Park: U.S. Steel and a Planned Company Town," in *Duluth: A Bicentennial Collection*, ed. Rick Lydecker and Lawrence J. Sommer (Duluth: American Revolution Bicentennial Commission, 1976).

3. Arnold R. Alanen, *Pines, Mines, and Lakes: A Field Guide to the Architecture and Landscapes of Northeastern Minnesota* (Madison: Department of Landscape Architecture, University of Wisconsin-Madison, and Vernacular Architecture Forum, 2000).

Introduction

1. Margaret Crawford, *Building the Workingman's Paradise: The Design of American Company Towns* (London: Verso, 1995), 12–26.

2. Michael Chevalier, cited in *The Anglo American Suburb*, ed. Robert A. M. Stern and John Montague Massengale (London: Architectural Design, 1981), 50; John S. Garner, *The Model Company Town: Urban Design through Private Enterprise in Nineteenth-Century New England* (Amherst: University of Massachusetts Press, 1984), xi–xii.

3. Crawford, *Building the Workingman's Paradise*, 29–31.

4. Ibid, 37.

5. Stanley Buder, *Pullman: An Experiment in Industrial Order and Community Planning, 1880–1930* (New York: Oxford University Press, 1967), 42–43. Stern and Massengale, *Anglo American Suburb*, 52; Richard Ely, "Pullman: A Social Study," *Harper's New Monthly Magazine* 70 (February 1885), 464.

6. Almont Lindsey, *The Pullman Strike: The Story of a Unique Experiment and of a Great Labor Upheaval* (Chicago: University of Chicago Press, 1967), 343–44.

7. Arthur C. Comey and Max S. Wehrly, "Planned Communities," Part 1 of *Urban Planning and Land Policies, Volume II of the Supplementary Report of the Urbanism Committee to the National Resources Committee* (Washington, D.C.: U.S. Government Printing Office, 1939), 47–49; Crawford, *Building the Workingman's Paradise*, 52, 79; Anne E. Mosher, *Capital's Utopia: Vandergrift, Pennsylvania, 1855–1916* (Baltimore: The Johns Hopkins University Press, 2004), 74–93.

8. John W. Reps, *The Making of Urban America: A History of City Planning in the United States* (Princeton, N.J.: Princeton University Press, 1965), 427–28; Raymond A. Mohl and Neil Betten, "The Failure of Industrial City Planning: Gary, Indiana, 1906–1910," *Journal of the American Institute of Planners* 38 (July 1972): 212; U.S. Census of Population, 1960–2000.

9. Stuart D. Brandes, *American Welfare Capitalism, 1800–1940* (Chicago: University of Chicago Press, 1976), 5–6, 10.

10. Crawford, *Building the Workingman's Paradise*, 48; Gwendolyn Wright, *Building the Dream: A Social History of Housing in America* (Cambridge, Mass.: MIT Press, 1981), 177–82; Christopher J. Cyphers, *The National Civic Federation and the Making of a New Liberalism, 1900–1915* (Westport, Conn.: Praeger, 2002), 41–63; Richard Hudelson and Carl Ross, *By the Ore Docks: A Working People's History of Duluth* (Minneapolis: University of Minnesota Press, 2006), 142.

11. Crawford, *Building the Workingman's Paradise*, 77.

12. Ibid., 59; Jon A. Peterson, *The Birth of City Planning in the United States, 1840–1917* (Baltimore: The Johns Hopkins University Press, 2003), 118; William H. Wilson, *The City Beautiful Movement* (Baltimore: The Johns Hopkins University Press, 1989).

13. Ebenezer Howard, *Garden Cities of Tomorrow*, updated ed. (London: Blackwell Publishers Ltd., 1996); Mervyn Miller, *Letchworth: The First Garden City*, 2d ed. (Chichester, West Sussex, England: Phillimore and Co., Ltd., 2000), 38–75.

14. Crawford, *Building the Workingman's Paradise*, 75; Mel Scott, *American City Planning since 1890* (Berkeley and Los Angeles: University of California Press, 1969), 90; John Nolen, "Industrial Village Communities in the United States," *Garden Cities and Town Planning* 11 (January 1921): 6–7.

15. George H. Miller, "Fairfield: A Town with a Purpose," *American City* 9 (September 1913): 213–19; Crawford, *Building the Workingman's Dream*, 84–89; Reps, *Making of Urban America*, 430; Comey and Wehrly, "Planned Communities," 27.

16. "The Housing Development for the Chickasaw Shipbuilding Co. at Chickasaw, Alabama," United States Steel Corporation: Bureau of Safety-Sanitation and Welfare, *Bulletin No. 7* (December 1918): 83.

17. V. H. Jensen, *Heritage of Conflict: Labor Relations in the Nonferrous Metal Industries up to 1930* (Ithaca, N.Y.: Cornell University Press, 1950), 273.

18. *Mining Magazine* 7 (1856), 311.

19. Arnold R. Alanen and Lynn Bjorkman, "Plats, Parks, Playgrounds, and Plants: Warren H. Manning's Landscape Designs for the Mining Districts of Michigan's Upper Peninsula," *Journal of the Society for Industrial Archeology* 24, no. 1 (1998): 50.

20. C. T. Rice, "Labor Conditions at Calumet and Hecla," *Engineering and Mining Journal* 92 (December 23, 1911): 1235.

21. Larry Lankton, *Cradle to Grave: Life, Work, and Death at the Lake Superior Copper Mines* (New York: Oxford University Press, 2001), 263; U.S. Census of Population, 1910 and 2000.

22. William G. Mather, "Some Observations on the Principle of Benefit Funds and Their Place in the Lake Superior Mining Industry," *Proceedings of the Lake Superior Mining Institute* 5 (1898): 12.

23. W. H. Moulton, "The Sociological Side of the Mining Industry," *Proceedings of the Lake Superior Mining Institute* 14 (1909): 91; Harlan Hatcher, *A Century of Iron and Men* (Indianapolis: Bobbs-Merrill Company, Inc., 1950), 244–50.

24. Katherine Eckert, *Buildings of Michigan* (New York: Oxford University Press, 1993), 499, citing Manning; Warren H. Manning, "Villages and Homes for Working Men," *Western Architect* 16 (August 1910): 85; *Detroit Free Press*, March 15, 1908; Alanen and Bjorkman, "Plats, Parks, Playgrounds, and Plants," 41–44.

25. *Daily Mining Journal*, Marquette, Mich., February 12, 1908, 9.

26. Arnold R. Alanen, "Gwinn: A Model Town 'Without Equal,'" *Michigan History* 78 (November/December 1994): 35; U.S. Census of Population, 1910–2000.

27. Arnold R. Alanen and Barbara Wyatt, "National Register of Historic Places Registration Form for the Gwinn Model Town Historic District" (Lansing: Michigan State Historic Preservation Office, 2001).

28. *Duluth News Tribune*, June 9, 1904, 4; *Itasca Iron News* (Bovey, Minn.), February 2, 1906, 8, and March 9, 1906, 4; Donald L. Boese, *John C. Greenway and the Opening of the Western Mesabi* (Bovey, Minn.: Itasca Community College Foundation, 1975), quotation on 139.

29. Mary Ann Nord, *The National Register of Historic Places in Minnesota: A Guide* (St. Paul: Minnesota Historical Society Press, 2003), 111–14.

30. Eckert, *Buildings of Michigan*, 499.

1. The Economics and Politics of Iron Ore and Big Steel

Separate editions of some newspapers, primarily the *Duluth News Tribune*, were published for different geographic locations in northeastern Minnesota and northern Wisconsin. Therefore, some articles occasionally appeared on different pages or dates in certain editions, or did not appear at all. Some issues in the microfilm collection at the University of Minnesota Duluth, for example, differ from those held by both the Duluth Public Library and the Minnesota Historical Society.

1. *Duluth Evening Herald*, April 2, 1907, 8.

2. Kenneth Warren, *Big Steel: The First Century of the United States Steel Corporation, 1901–2001* (Pittsburgh: University of Pittsburgh Press, 2001), 28, 65; Hudelson and Ross, *By the Ore Docks*, 41–42; Bill Beck and C. Patrick Labadie, *Pride of the Inland Seas: An Illustrated History of the Port of Duluth-Superior* (Afton, Minn.: Afton Historical Society Press, 2004), 130.

3. Warren, *Big Steel*, 8, 9; Ida Tarbell, *The Life of Elbert H. Gary: A Story of Steel* (New York: D. Appleton-Century Company, 1933), citing Schwab, 112.

4. Warren, *Big Steel*, 27–28, 32–33, 42–43; Tarbell, *Life of Elbert H. Gary*, 135.

5. Warren, *Big Steel*, 106–17.

6. Ibid., 32–33.

7. Ibid., 65.

8. Ibid.; Arnold R. Alanen, "Years of Change on the Iron Range," in *Minnesota in a Century of Change: The State and Its People Since 1900*, ed. Clifford E. Clark, Jr. (St. Paul: Minnesota Historical Society Press, 1989), 165; Lake Superior Iron Ore Association, *Lake Superior Iron Ores* (Cleveland: The Association, 1938), 257.

9. Clarke Chambers, "Welfare on Minnesota's Iron Range," *Upper Midwest History* 3 (1983): 4, 7, 8, 37; Alanen, "Years of Change," 165.

10. Warren, *Big Steel*, 65.

11. *Duluth Evening Herald*, April 8, 1889, 3; *Duluth News Tribune*, May 25, 1904, 7; August 25, 1962, 1; *Skillings Mining Review* 36 (February 14, 1948): 1; Langdon White and George Primmer, "The Iron and Steel Industry of Duluth: A Study in

Locational Maladjustment," *Geographical Review* 27 (January 1937): 82; Dwight E. Woodbridge and John S. Pardee, *History of Duluth and St. Louis County Past and Present* (Chicago: C. F. Cooper and Company, 1910): 521–25, quotation on 521; Lawrence J. Sommer, "Forgotten Industries of Duluth," in *Duluth: A Bicentennial Collection,* ed. Rick Lydecker and Lawrence J. Sommer (Duluth: American Revolution Bicentennial Commission, 1976), 196.

12. Warren, *Big Steel,* 68; Herbert Casson, *The Romance of Steel: The Story of a Thousand Millionaires* (New York: A. S. Barnes and Company, 1907), 354–55.

13. *Duluth News Tribune,* March 1, 1902, 1, 3; March 6, 1902, 1.

14. *Duluth Evening Herald,* February 23, 1907, 2; Minnesota House of Representatives, *Journal of the House of the Thirty-Fifth Session of the Legislature of the State of Minnesota,* vol. 1 (St. Paul: McGill Warner Co., State Printer, 1907), 51, 52, 70; White and Primmer, "Iron and Steel Industries of Duluth," 82.

15. Warren, *Big Steel,* 71, citing U.S. Steel Finance Committee minutes of January 22, 1907.

16. *Duluth News Tribune,* February 15, 1907, 6; "Celebrating the Opening of the Steel Mills of Duluth," *The Zenith* (published by the Marshall-Wells Hardware Company of Duluth), November 1915, 116–17 (copy on file in the Duluth Public Library; hereinafter referred to as DPL).

17. *Duluth Evening Herald,* February 23, 1907, 2, citing Jefferson; White and Primmer, "Iron and Steel Industry of Duluth," 83.

18. *Duluth News Tribune,* February 5, 1907, 2; Minnesota House of Representatives, *Journal of the House of the Thirty-Fifth Session,* 320.

19. *Minneapolis Tribune,* February 6, 1907, 4; *Duluth News Tribune,* February 8, 1907, 4.

20. *Duluth News Tribune,* February 16, 1907, 5; February 21, 1907, 1, 3; February 23, 1907, 1, 3, citing Bliss; February 24, 1907, 5; February 25, 1907, 1, 3.

21. *Duluth News Tribune,* February 26, 1907, 1, 6, citing an anonymous state senator; March 1, 1907, 1, 7, citing U.S. Steel Finance Committee; March 8, 1907, 1, 3; March 9, 1907, 1, 7; *Leader-Chronicle* (Superior), March 2, 1907, 1, 4; Warren, *Big Steel,* 71, citing U.S. Steel Finance Committee minutes of January 22, 1907; Minnesota House of Representatives, *Journal of the Thirty-Fifth Session,* 541, 592–94.

22. Warren, *Big Steel,* 71; *Duluth News Tribune,* April 2, 1907, 1, 5; *Duluth Evening Herald,* April 1, 1907, 1; April 3, 1907, 1, 7, citing Jefferson, Rockne, and Saari; *Minneapolis Journal,* March 26, 1907, 4; Minnesota House of Representatives, *Journal of the House of the Thirty-Sixth Session of the Legislature of the State of Minnesota,* vol. 1 (St. Paul: McGill Warner Co., State Printer, 1909), 62, citing letter to Johnson (the 1907 letter was not entered into the legislative journal until 1909).

23. *Duluth News Tribune,* April 23, 1907, 1, 5; *Leader-Chronicle,* April 6, 1907, 1; *Engineering and Mining Journal* 84 (September 14, 1907): 508.

24. *Duluth News Tribune,* February 15, 1907, 6; *Leader-Chronicle,* April 6, 1907, 1; *Minneapolis Journal,* October 13, 1907, 4; *New York Times,* April 4, 1907, 12; April 5, 1907, 13; White and Primmer, "Iron and Steel Industry of Duluth," 83; letter from C. R. Rusk to T. F. Cole, April 9, 1907, Materials Relating to the Oliver Iron Mining Co. 1863–1972, James S. Steel, comp. (on file in Minnesota Historical Society Archives; hereinafter referred to as MHS Archives); *Iron and Coal Trades Review* 12 (July 1, 1910): 12.

25. *Duluth Evening Herald,* March 1, 1907, 10; April 4, 1907, 8; *Labor World* (Duluth), April 6, 1907, 1.

26. *Duluth Evening Herald,* March 10, 1907, 10; March 15, 1907, 1; April 8, 1907, 7; *Duluth News Tribune,* March 13, 1907, 3, citing Cullum.

27. *Duluth Evening Herald,* April 6, 1907, 1.

2. Building a Steel Plant

1. *New York Times,* June 13, 1907, 11.

2. *Duluth News Tribune,* June 24, 1907, 1, 6; *Index and Outline Map of the City of Duluth, St. Louis County, Minn., and Vicinity,* with *July 1893 Supplement* (Philadelphia: Fred K. B. Roe, 1890), n.p. (copy on file at Northeast Minnesota Historical Center; hereinafter referred to as NEMHC); *Minneapolis Journal,* May 13, 1913, 5.

3. Delegation from St. Louis County, *Brief Against the Tonnage Tax Bill* (St. Paul: The Delegation, 1909), 47; *Duluth Evening Herald,* January 2, 1909, 1, 7; Leiffur Magnusson, "A Modern Industrial Suburb," *Monthly Review of the U.S. Bureau of Labor Statistics* 6 (April 1918): 3.

4. Warren, *Big Steel,* 71–72, citing U.S. Steel, *Annual Report for 1907*; *Iron Age* 92 (September 18, 1913): 603; *Engineering and Mining Journal* 84 (September 14, 1907): 508.

5. Warren, *Big Steel,* 80; Lake Superior Iron Ore Association, *Lake Superior Iron Ores* (Cleveland, Ohio: The Association, 1938), 308; *Duluth Weekly Herald,* February 19, 1908, 7, citing Reis.

6. *Duluth News Tribune,* October 25, 1908, 1–2; October 27, 1908, 1; *Duluth Evening Herald,* October 14, 1908, 12; November 4, 1908, 1, 15; Roy O. Hoover, *A Lake Superior Lawyer: A Biography of Chester Adgate Congdon* (Duluth: Superior Partners, 1997), 89.

7. Minnesota House of Representatives, *Journal of the House of the Thirty-Sixth Session of the Legislature,* vol. 1 (St. Paul: McGill Warner Co., State Printer, 1909), 62, 228–29; *Iron and Coal Trades Review* 12 (July 1, 1910), 12.

8. Delegation from St. Louis County, *Brief,* 55–56.

9. Hoover, *Lake Superior Lawyer,* 91–92; *Duluth News Tribune,* March 26, 1909, 14; March 31, 1909, 1, citing Range Mayors Committee.

10. Hoover, *Lake Superior Lawyer,* 93; *Duluth News Tribune,* April 1, 1909, 1, 4; April 2, 1909, 1, 9; April 3, 1909, 1.

11. *Duluth News Tribune,* April 7, 1909, 1; April 8, 1909, 1, 6, citing Congdon; Hoover, *Lake Superior Lawyer,* 93–94.

12. *Duluth News Tribune,* April 17, 1909, 1, 10; April 18, 1909, 1-A, 4-A, 11-A; April 19, 1909, 1, citing Harmon and Coyle; April 20, 1909, 1, citing Morrison.

13. Minnesota House of Representatives, *Journal of Thirty-sixth Session,* vol. 2, 1893–97, citing Governor Johnson, on 1894.

14. *Duluth News Tribune,* April 21, 1909, 1, 8.

15. *Leader-Clarion,* April 24, 1909, 3; Winifred G. Helmes, *John A. Johnson: The People's Governor* (Minneapolis: University of Minnesota Press, 1949), 305; *Iron and Coal Trades Review* 12 (July 1, 1910): 12.

16. *Duluth Evening Herald,* January 2, 1909, 1, 7; October 3, 1909, 14-A.

17. Warren, *Big Steel,* 72, citing U.S. Steel finance committee minutes of September 29, 1909; *Iron and Coal Trades Review* 12 (July 1, 1910), 12.

18. Congdon in *Duluth Evening Herald*, October 12, 1909, 1, citing Corey; *Duluth News Tribune*, December 23, 1909, 11.

19. *Duluth Evening Herald*, November 20, 1909, 2; *Duluth News Tribune*, December 10, 1909, 5; January 16, 1910, D-2.

20. Congdon in *Duluth Evening Herald*, October 12, 1909, 1; *Iron Age* 88 (November 30, 1911), 1198; *Iron Age* 92 (September 18, 1913), 603–4; *Duluth News Tribune*, December 23, 1909, 11; March 24, 1910, 10; March 26, 1911, 7-C; James Aird, "Beds Never Got Cold," *Duluth News-Tribune*, September 30, 1956, 2.

21. *Duluth News Tribune*, January 16, 1910, 2-B; January 24, 1910, 10; *Duluth Evening Herald*, January 18, 1910, 3; February 5, 1910, 6.

22. *Duluth News Tribune*, March 25, 1910, 1; March 26, 1910, 15, citing Reis; *Duluth Evening Herald*, March 26, 1910, 2.

23. *Duluth News Tribune*, March 26, 1910, 15; *Superior Telegram*, March 26, 1910, 2, 7.

24. *Duluth Weekly Herald*, April 13, 1910, 4.

25. *Duluth Weekly Herald*, May 11, 1910, 10; July 27, 1910, 3; *Duluth News Tribune*, March 24, 1910, 10; March 25, 1910, 1; July 31, 1910, B-9; September 2, 1910, 1; September 11, 1910, D-1; *Duluth Herald*, August 24, 1910, 1, 11; August 27, 1910, 1, 6, 2, 3; Walter van Brunt, ed., *Duluth and St. Louis County, Minnesota: Their Story and People*, vol. 1 (Chicago and New York: American Historical Society, 1921), 311, citing comments in 1912 by William Sargent and James Bardon.

26. *Duluth Herald*, August 25, 1910, 8.

27. *Duluth Weekly Herald*, January 4, 1911, 3; *Duluth Herald*, January 14, 1911, 1, 11; *Duluth News Tribune*, January 29, 1911, C-1; March 26, 1911, C-7.

28. *Duluth News Tribune*, March 3, 1911, 1, 3; March 8, 1911, 1, 7; March 17, 1911, 1, 10; *Labor World*, March 18, 1911, 6.

29. *Duluth Herald*, May 24, 1911, 2; May 25, 1911, 5.

30. *Iron Age* 88 (September 21, 1911), 626, citing Farrell; *Duluth Herald*, September 8, 1911, 1, 13, citing Buffington.

31. *Iron Age* 88 (November 30, 1911), 1198; *Duluth News Tribune*, March 26, 1911, C-7.

32. *Duluth News Tribune*, April 14, 1912, C-1, C-2, citing Farrell; *Duluth Herald*, April 12, 1911, 6, citing McGonagle; August 12, 1912, 7; *Duluth Weekly Herald*, April 10, 1912, 8; *New York Times*, June 12, 1912, 13.

33. *Duluth News Tribune*, February 15, 1915, 10; Aird, "Beds Never Got Cold," 2; author's interview with Paul and Sally Solomon, June 1, 2001.

34. *Duluth News Tribune*, February 1, 1913, 1–2; February 7, 1913, 1–2; February 14, 1913, 1–2; February 18, 1913, 1, citing Range Ministers Association; February 19, 1913, 1–2; February 20, 1913, 8.

35. *Duluth News Tribune*, Febuary 27, 1913, 11; February 26, 1913, 1, citing an unnamed Minnesota Steel official; *Duluth Herald*, April 11, 1913, 14, citing Eberhart; July 8, 1913, 1.

36. *Duluth Herald*, May 26, 1913, "Duluth: The City of Industry," n.p., citing Rockwell.

37. *Superior Telegram*, August 23, 1913, 16; September 1, 1913, 5; *Duluth News Tribune*, August 30, 1913, 4; August 31, 1913, 12; June 21, 1914, 10-A; *Duluth Herald*, February 22, 1914, 16-A; June 22, 1914, 6; *Minneapolis Journal*, May 13, 1913, 5.

38. *Duluth Herald*, September 29, 1913, 5; October 7, 1913, 2; *Duluth News Tri-*

bune, September 29, 1913, 1–2; September 30, 1913, 9; October 2, 1913, 8; October 8, 1913, 8; November 2, 1913, Magazine Section, 1.

39. *Engineering and Mining Journal* 97 (January 10, 1914): 79–80; Francis N. Stacey, "Pittsburgh Moving West: The Significance of the New Steel Plant at the Head of Lake Superior," *World's Work* 27 (January 1914): 328–29.

40. *Duluth News Tribune,* May 24, 1914, B-10; *Iron Age* 95 (April 8, 1915): 819.

41. *Duluth News Tribune,* February 15, 1915, 10; March 23, 1915, 7; April 1, 1915, 1; April 3, 1915, 7; April 8, 1915, 12; *Duluth Herald,* April 10, 1915, 4; April 12, 1915, 5; *New York Times,* April 8, 1915, 17; *Iron Age* 95 (April 8, 1915): 819.

42. *Duluth Herald,* April 30, 1915, 7, citing Hammond; July 20, 1915, 8; *Duluth News Tribune,* July 10, 1915, 1, 4; July 12, 1915, 3, 6; July 14, 1915, 8; July 15, 1915, 8; July 17, 1915, 1, 8; July 29, 1915, 9; July 30, 1917, 5, citing John Brennen.

43. *Duluth News Tribune,* July 16, 1915, 1–2; July 17, 1915, 1, 8; July 18, 1915, 9-A; July 21, 1915, 3; July 27, 1915, 9.

44. *Duluth News Tribune,* August 13, 1915, 3.

45. *Duluth News Tribune,* July 10, 1915, 1, 4; July 11, 1915, 6-A; July 13, 1915, 4; July 19, 1915, 4; August 19, 1973, 17-B, citing Don Hawkings.

46. *Duluth News Tribune,* August 3, 1915, 4; August 10, 1915, 4; August 31, 1915, 4; September 21, 1915, 4; September 27, 1915, 4; October 17, 1915, 4-A; October 26, 1915, 4; November 5, 1915, 6; November 7, 1915, 11; *Superior Telegram,* November 6, 1915, 7.

47. *Superior Telegram,* October 13, 1915, 20, citing Erhart; November 5, 1915, 8; March 23, 1916, 9; April 1, 1916, 10; April 12, 1916, 12; November 24, 1916, 3; *Duluth News Tribune,* August 31, 1915, 5; January 6, 1916, 4; July 17, 1917, 4; *Duluth Herald,* May 2, 1916, 11.

48. *Duluth News Tribune,* October 17, 1915, 4-A; October 21, 1915, 4; November 12, 1915, 4.

49. *Duluth Herald,* November 24, 1915, 1, 5; *Wall Street Journal,* November 25, 1915, 1.

50. *Duluth News Tribune,* November 25, 1915, 1, 6, citing Reis; *Duluth Herald,* November 25, 1915, 8.

51. *Duluth News Tribune,* December 2, 1915, 4; *Duluth Herald,* December 2, 1915, 17.

52. *Duluth Herald,* December 2, 1915, 17; December 3, 1915, 16; December 16, 1915, 1; *Duluth News Tribune,* December 11, 1915, 1-A, 4-A, 10-A; *Superior Telegram,* December 11, 1915, 1; American Iron and Steel Institute, *Directory of the Iron and Steel Works of the United States and Canada: Nineteenth Edition Corrected to May 1st, 1920* (New York: The Institute, 1920), 238.

3. Neighborhood Housing from Gary to Oliver

1. Information about the dates and locations of all plats is from the St. Louis County Recorder's office in Duluth. Also see "The Village of New Duluth," undated newspaper article, c. 1919, from the *Duluth Rip-Saw,* in the Vertical File for New Duluth, NEHMC; *Index and Outline Map of the City of Duluth,* with *July 1893 Supplement; Minneapolis Journal,* May 13, 1913, 5.

2. C. E. Lovett, "Early History of West Duluth, New Duluth and Their Environs" (undated and unpublished 11pp. manuscript, SA File, NEMHC).

3. Ibid.

4. Ibid.; *Duluth Daily Tribune,* October 26, 1890, 3; October 27, 1890, 2; December 17, 1939, 1-A, 17-A; *Duluth Herald,* August 22, 1928, 11; "Village of New Duluth"; *Index and Outline Map of the City of Duluth,* with *July 1893 Supplement.*

5. *Duluth News Tribune,* August 28, 1907, 7; *Duluth Evening Herald,* January 31, 1910, 11; *Duluth Herald,* May 10, 1916, 11; Aird, "Beds Never Got Cold," 2.

6. T. W. Wahl and Co., *Spirit Lake, Minnesota: The Site of the New Steel Plant of the United States Steel Corporation,* 1908 (Pamphlet 1420, NEMHC); *Eveleth News* (Eveleth, Minn.), December 2, 1909, 5; *Virginia Enterprise* (Virginia, Minn.), December 17, 1909, 12.

7. The advertisements began appearing in Duluth's newspapers in August 1910, and were evident on the Iron Range one year later; *Sosialisti* (Duluth), January 13, 1916, 4.

8. *Duluth Herald,* May 17, 1913, 27; May 26, 1913, "Duluth: City of Industry," n.p.; *Duluth News Tribune,* June 1, 1913, 9-A; *Duluth Weekly Herald,* December 10, 1913, 3; "Celebrating the Opening of the Steel Mills of Duluth," 118.

9. *Duluth Herald,* May 17, 1913, 27, citing Barnes.

10. Ibid., citing Moore and Volk.

11. *Duluth News Tribune,* April 14, 1912, C-3; November 4, 1913, 9; May 29, 1914, 7; September 13, 1915, 4; October 1, 1915, 4; October 3, 1915, 6; November 4, 1913, 4; *Duluth Herald,* September 19, 1913, 9; October 4, 1913, 7; October 31, 1913, 7; July 7, 1914, 11.

12. *Labor World,* November 4, 1911, 4; *Duluth Weekly Herald,* June 18, 1913, 3; *Duluth Herald,* July 1, 1913, 3; *Duluth News Tribune,* August 28, 1913, 8; September 27, 1913, 9; October 2, 1913, 9, citing Webster; July 11, 1916, 17.

13. *Duluth Herald,* August 27, 1913, 4; August 28, 1913, 4, 12; October 4, 1913, 7; *Duluth Weekly Herald,* September 3, 1913, 3; *Duluth News Tribune,* August 28, 1913, 8; October 2, 1913, 9.

14. *Duluth News Tribune,* August 28, 1913, 7; May 12, 1914, 9.

15. *Duluth Herald,* April 7, 1913, 2, citing Kuehnow; August 28, 1913, 4; September 2, 1913, 2; August 22, 1914, 17; *Duluth News Tribune,* April 7, 1913, 12, citing Kuehnow; June 13, 1915, 8; October 12, 1915, 4.

16. *Duluth Herald,* May 17, 1913, 27; August 17, 1913, 4; September 11, 1913, 18; October 4, 1913, 7; December 15, 1913, 2; *Duluth News Tribune,* October 11, 1913, 9; January 3, 1915, A-8; October 5, 1915, 4; November 26, 1915, 5; *Mesaba Ore and Hibbing News* (Hibbing, Minn.), August 12, 1911, 2.

17. Norris Dickey, "History of Billings Park and the Steel Plant," 1941, W.P.A. Project #11068 (Superior Public Library, hereafter referred to as SPL); *Duluth News Tribune,* May 6, 1917, 13-A; August 26, 1917, 12-A; July 5, 1936, 6-A.

18. Dickey, "History of Billings Park"; *Leader-Clarion,* October 19, 1907, 2; January 18, 1908, 5. The dates for Billings Park and the other Wisconsin plats are from the Douglas County Recorder's office in Superior.

19. *Keep Your Eye on the Steel Plant and Belt Line Acres,* c. 1910, 13 (SPL); *Duluth Herald,* May 26, 1913, "Duluth City of Industry," n.p.; June 8, 1917, 4; November 19, 1915, 3.

20. *Duluth Herald,* December 31, 1910, 11; August 3, 1912, 7; *Eveleth News,* April 28, 1910, 4; Great Northern Land Company of Duluth, *Carnegie* (fold-out ad-

vertisement), c. 1911 (53150, 1:41, NEMHC); "Superior: The City of Opportunities," published by the *Superior Telegram*, 1912 (SPL).

21. Great Northern Land Company of Duluth, "Carnegie."

22. Ibid.

23. *Duluth News Tribune*, March 27, 1910, 10-C; May 8, 1910, B-14; April 5, 1913, 9; October 7, 1915, 12; *Superior Telegram*, April 12, 1910, 4; April 13, 1910, 7; August 29, 1913, 9.

24. Parkside and Sunnyside Gardens advertisements, c. 1914 (NEMHC); *Duluth Herald*, August 26, 1916, 9.

25. *Duluth News Tribune*, April 14, 1912, 4-C; November 25, 1917, 15-A; *Superior Telegram*, March 24, 1910, 5; May 19, 1917, 14.

26. *Duluth Evening Herald*, February 8, 1904, 5; *Duluth Herald*, May 26, 1913, "Duluth the City of Industry," n.p.; *Virginia Enterprise*, June 27, 1913, 9; *Superior Telegram*, November 20, 1915, 6; *Duluth News Tribune*, April 14, 1912, 4-C; November 2, 1913, 13; August 29, 1915, 9-B; October 8, 1915, 11; Douglas County Schools, "History Stories about the Towns and Villages of Douglas County," 1948 (mimeographed document in SPL); D. W. Van Vleck, "Map of the Proposed Village of Oliver," 1916 (53150, 1:42, NEMHC); U.S. Census of Population, 1920–2000.

4. The Emergence of a Model Company Town

1. *Duluth Evening Herald*, January 2, 1909, 7; *Duluth News Tribune*, March 24, 1910, 10.

2. *Duluth Herald*, May 13, 1913, 1, 4.

3. *Iron Age* 92 (September 18, 1913), 604; Magnusson, "Modern Industrial Suburb," 2.

4. Gregory Kopischke, "Morell, Anthony Urbanski," and "Nichols, Arthur Richardson," in *Pioneers of American Landscape Design*, ed. Charles Birnbaum and Robin Karson (New York: McGraw-Hill, 2000), 253–57.

5. Ibid.; Morell and Nichols, Inc., "Partial List of References and Work," c. 1946, manuscript copy in Morell and Nichols Papers, Northwest Architectural Archives, University of Minnesota (hereinafter referred to as NWAA).

6. Kopischke, "Morell," and "Nichols," 253–57; Arthur R. Nichols, "Summary of Events and Trips of Arthur R. Nichols," 1968, and "Guide to the Morell & Nichols Papers," both in Morell and Nichols Papers (NWAA).

7. *New York Times*, April 27, 1913, S-6; May 14, 1913, 13; *Duluth Herald*, May 13, 1913, 5; May 14, 1913, 10; June 24, 1914, 4.

8. C. R. Stowell, "Industrial City of the Steel Workers of Duluth," *Realty* 4 (March 1918), 27; Wilson, *City Beautiful Movement*, 2; Arthur Nichols, undated lecture notes in Morell and Nichols Papers (NWAA); *Duluth News Tribune*, July 1, 1913, 9.

9. U.S. Steel Corporation, Bureau of Safety, Sanitation and Welfare, *Bulletin No. 7* (December 1918), 67–68; "Morgan Park, Minn. An Industrial Suburb for the Minnesota Steel Company—Dean & Dean, Architects," *American Architect* 113 (June 1918), 747; Magnusson, "Modern Industrial Suburb," 3; *Duluth News Tribune*, November 2, 1913, Magazine Section, 1.

10. R. V. Sawhill, "'Model City' Near New Steel Plant," *Iron Trade Review* 57 (September 30, 1915), 648; U.S. Steel Corporation, *Bulletin No. 7*, 68.

11. Al Bothun, in a February 24, 2007, communication to Morgan Park resident Nancy Thompson, identified "the other." Several long-time residents still recall using the terms "Hunkyville" and "Pig Pen." Also see Raymond A. Mohl and Neil Betton, *Steel City: Urban and Ethnic Patterns in Gary, Indiana, 1901–1950* (New York: Holmes and Meier, 1987), 267.

12. Sawhill, "Model City," 648; Magnusson, "Model Industrial Suburb," 5–6; *Duluth News Tribune*, November 2, 1913, Magazine Section, 1. The depth of the original utility lines was confirmed by Morgan Park resident Nancy Thompson, who observed the sewer and water lines as they were being replaced in 2003.

13. U.S. Steel Corporation, *Bulletin No. 7*, 67; *Iron Age* 97 (January 6, 1916), 48.

14. *Duluth Herald*, July 23, 1913, 3; July 26, 1913, 24; August 1, 1913, 1; *Duluth News Tribune*, August 8, 1913, 9; September 18, 1913, 9.

15. *Duluth Herald*, April 17, 1915, 3; April 22, 1915, 5; May 29, 1914, 5; *Duluth Weekly Herald*, May 16, 1914, 4; *Duluth News Tribune*, October 24, 1915, 10-A; Universal Portland Cement Co., *Concrete Roads* 3 (April 1916): 51–52.

16. George D. McCarthy, "Morgan Park—A New Type of Industrial Community," *American City* 14 (February 1916): 152; U.S. Steel Corporation, *Bulletin No. 7*, 70.

17. A. R. Nichols, "Highway Design: Its Relation to Landscape Objectives," *Proceedings of the Seventeenth Annual Meeting of the Highway Research Board* (December 1937), 271.

18. Morell and Nichols, "Morgan Park, Duluth, Minnesota: Industrial Town for United States Steel Corporation," memorandum, c. 1918, and "Planting Plan for Morgan Park," c. 1914, both items available in Morell and Nichols Papers (NWAA); Nichols, "Highway Design," 271; U.S. Steel Corporation, *Bulletin No. 7*, 68.

19. *Duluth Herald*, April 22, 1915, 5; April 26, 1915, 2; *Duluth News Tribune*, July 28, 1915, 4.

20. Charles Frederick Carter, "The Latest in Steel Towns," *Illustrated World* 25 (April 1916): 181; Sawhill, "'Model City,'" 647–48; Charles Henry MacKintosh, "Morgan Park—A Model Village," *The Minnesotan* 2 (November 1916): 27.

21. James Alexander Robinson, *The Life and Work of Harry Franklin Robinson, 1883–1959* (Hong Kong: Hilross Devel. Ltd., 1989), 24 (donated copy on file at NEMHC); Christopher Meyers, "Gary—America's Magic Industrial City: From Sand Hills to Urban Decay," http://ww2.metnitco.net/users/chameyer (accessed December 15, 2005); "Obituary" (George Dean), *American Architect* 116, no. 2 (1919), 821; *New York Times*, November 12, 1949, 15; Frank Lloyd Wright, "In the Cause of Architecture," *Architectural Record* 23 (March 1908), 156.

22. Meyer, "Gary—America's Magic Industrial City"; "George Robinson Dean," *Western Architect* 29 (January 1920): 4; Robinson, *Life and Work of Harry Franklin Robinson*, 24.

23. *Duluth Herald*, May 31, 1913, 4; *Duluth News Tribune*, August 24, 1913, 10-A; Sawhill, "'Model City,'" 647–48; Charles Nelson, "National Register of Historic Places Inventory—Nomination for Morgan Park, 1977," State Historic Preservation Office, Minnesota Historical Society (hereinafter referred to as MHS-SHPO).

24. Sawhill, "'Model City,'" 648; Meyers, "Gary—America's Magic Industrial City"; *Duluth Herald*, August 1, 1913, 8.

25. Pamela H. Simpson, *Cheap, Quick, and Easy: Imitative Architectural Materials, 1870–1930* (Knoxville: University of Tennessee Press, 1999), 11–16.

26. Ibid., 23, 27.

27. *Duluth Herald,* March 10, 1905, 14; *Duluth Weekly Herald,* January 17, 1912, 3.

28. *Duluth Herald,* August 21, 1913, 4; August 23, 1913, 24; *Duluth News Tribune,* August 24, 1913, 10-A.

29. Harvey Whipple, ed., *Concrete Houses: How They Were Built* (Detroit: Concrete-Cement Age Publishing Co., 1920), 11.

30. Simpson, *Cheap, Quick, and Easy,* 13; letter from Richard Phillip to W. J. Kohler, March 8, 1916 (Kohler Company Archives, Kohler, Wisc.).

31. Whipple, *Concrete Houses,* 11; "Morgan Park," *American Architect,* 743; Carter, "Latest in Steel Towns," 184.

32. *Duluth Herald,* August 23, 1913, 24; December 6, 1913, 29; January 3, 1914, 28; March 31, 1914, 3; *Duluth News Tribune,* September 15, 1913, 2; May 24, 1914, B-10; December 4, 1914, 9; September 8, 1916, 4.

33. Magnusson, "Modern Industrial Suburb," 13.

34. Robinson, *Life and Work of Harry Franklin Robinson,* 79.

35. Carter, "Latest in Steel Towns," 184; U.S. Steel Corporation, *Bulletin No. 7,* 69; "Warm Air Heating in a Northern City," *Metal Work* 85 (May 15, 1916), 607.

36. Magnusson, "Model Industrial Suburb," 12.

37. Morgan Park Company, *The New Houses in Morgan Park* (Duluth: Morgan Park Company, c. 1917), 6–7 (MHS-SHPO); Nelson, "National Register Nomination."

38. Robinson, *Life and Work of Harry Franklin Robinson,* 83–84; Dean and Dean, *New Houses in Morgan Park,* 12–13; Nelson, "National Register Nomination."

39. Dean and Dean, *New Houses in Morgan Park,* 19, 21, 22; Nelson, "National Register Nomination."

40. Nelson, "National Register Nomination."

41. Ibid.

42. Ibid.; Magnusson, "Modern Industrial Suburb," 18; author's interview with Isobel Olson Rapaich, April 14, 2001.

43. *Duluth News Tribune,* August 19, 1915, 4; August 31, 1915, 4; Magnusson, "Modern Industrial Suburb," 14–15; U.S. Steel Corporation, *Bulletin No. 7,* 72.

44. Dormitory demolition permit, December 2, 1935 Duluth City Hall (hereafter referred to as DCH).

45. Magnusson, "Modern Industrial Suburb," 14–15; U.S. Steel Corporation, *Bulletin No. 7,* 72; Stowell, "Industrial City of Steel Workers," 28; *Morgan Park Bulletin,* November 7, 1918, 8.

46. *Duluth News Tribune,* July 28, 1915, 4; August 10, 1915, 4; August 19, 1915, 4; October 13, 1915, 4.

47. *Duluth News Tribune,* September 13, 1915, 4; October 13, 1915, 4; October 20, 1915, 4.

48. Aird, "Beds Were Never Cold," 2; *Duluth Herald,* March 31, 1914, 3; familial information about Morgan Park's earliest residents was derived from the manuscript schedules for the 1920 U.S. Census of Population.

49. *Duluth Herald,* May 29, 1914, 5; *Duluth News Tribune,* May 24, 1914, B-10; October 21, 1915, 4; October 24, 1915, 10-A.

50. *Duluth News Tribune,* June 11, 1915, 1; August 20, 1915, 3; August 26, 1915, 9; August 27, 1915, 9, 14.

51. *Duluth News Tribune,* August 28, 1915, 4; October 24, 1915, 10-A.

52. *Duluth News Tribune,* June 11, 1915, 1; August 28, 1915, 4; "Celebrating the Opening of the Steel Mills in Duluth," 118.

5. Stability and Prosperity for U.S. Steel

1. *Duluth Herald,* January 28, 1916, 21; *Duluth News Tribune,* February 20, 1916, A-5; April 20, 1916, 4; *Iron Age* 97 (January 6, 1916), 48. Joseph Pennell (1857–1926), an American artist, was a prolific book illustrator during his career.

2. *New York Times,* March 3, 1916, 13; American Iron and Steel Institute, *Directory of the Iron and Steel Works of the United States and Canada: Nineteenth Edition Corrected to May 1st, 1920* (New York: The Institute, 1920), 238; *Duluth News Tribune,* February 20, 1916, A-5; February 21, 1916, 4; February 22, 1916, 4; March 15, 1916, 4; May 1, 1916, 10.

3. *Duluth Herald,* May 4, 1916, 4; May 18, 1916, 4; June 21, 1916, 13; *Duluth News Tribune,* July 4, 1916, 4; November 20, 1916, 4; *Washington Post,* July 18, 1915, R-5; *Skillings Mining Review* 6 (February 16, 1918): 1.

4. *Duluth Herald,* January 29, 1916, 2, citing Huey; September 9, 1916, 4; *Duluth News Tribune,* April 21, 1916, 4; May 1, 1916, 10; October 3, 1916, 4, citing Huey; December 18, 1942, 9.

5. *Duluth Herald,* June 25, 1916, 15; July 19, 1916, 18.

6. *Duluth Herald,* June 4, 1917, 4; *Duluth News Tribune,* July 19, 1917, 4; November 25, 1917, 15-B.

7. *Duluth Herald,* January 28, 1916, 21.

8. Ibid.

9. Michael Fedo, *The Lynchings in Duluth* (St. Paul: Minnesota Historical Society Press, 2000, originally published in 1979), 4, 13; *Twin City Star* (Minneapolis), June 3, 1916, 2; *Duluth Herald,* February 17, 1917, 4; *Duluth News Tribune,* March 10, 1917, 4.

10. *Duluth News Tribune,* July 22, 1917, 4-A, citing T. Monson; November 5, 1917, 4.

11. *Duluth News Tribune,* December 8, 1917, 1; Duluth Board of Education Report, 1918, on file in the Duluth Public Library (hereafter referred to as DPL).

12. *Duluth News Tribune,* October 1, 1918, 1; October 7, 1918, 6.

13. Fedo, *Lynchings in Duluth,* 4; Hudelson and Ross, *By the Ore Docks,* 121–28, quotation on 127.

14. Carl H. Chrislock, *Watchdog of Loyalty: The Minnesota Commission of Public Safety During World War I* (St. Paul: Minnesota Historical Society, 1991), 89, 323.

15. *Duluth News Tribune,* May 6, 1917, 4-A; May 19, 1917, 10.

16. *Duluth News Tribune,* February 16, 1917, 1, 4; February 17, 1917, 3; February 20, 1917, 3; June 5, 1917, 4.

17. *Duluth News Tribune,* February 17, 1917, 3; April 16, 1917, 4; May 21, 1917, 4; letter from Elise Braun Alletzhauser to Elsa Alletzhauser, 1936 (provided by Karin Hertel McGinnis).

18. Warren, *Big Steel,* 73.

19. *Duluth News Tribune,* August 10, 1917, 1, citing Duluth Real Estate Exchange; October 20, 1917, 3; October 23, 1917, 7.

20. *Duluth News Tribune,* November 8, 1917, 3; November 23, 1917, 3; June 13, 1918, 10; *Iron Age* 101 (June 20, 1918): 1632, citing Gary.

21. *Iron Age* 101 (June 20, 1918): 1632, citing Gary; Warren, *Big Steel*, 73–74, citing U.S. Steel Finance Committee minutes of July 16, 1918.

22. Warren, *Big Steel*, 74; *Iron Age* 103 (February 13, 1919), 434, citing Duluth manufacturer; *Duluth News Tribune*, July 27, 1924, 11-A.

23. Warren, *Big Steel*, 74, citing U.S. Steel Financial Committee minutes of October 8, 1918; the last quotation, from an unnamed newspaper account of October 21, 1918, is in the "Mines/Minerals Scrapbook 1903, 1910–1928," State Auditor, Land Department files (MHS Archives).

24. *New York Times*, April 24, 1919, 18, citing Gary; *Wall Street Journal*, April 25, 1919, 8; *Duluth News Tribune*, April 24, 1919, 3, citing Reis; *Skillings Mining Review* 7 (May 10, 1919): 7.

25. Warren, *Big Steel*, 74–75.

26. Ibid, 74; *Duluth News Tribune*, December 23, 1919, 1; December 29, 1919, 1, 4.

27. *Duluth Herald*, June 30, 1916, 25.

28. Warren, *Big Steel*, 117; Hudelson and Ross, *By the Ore Docks*, 133–35; *Labor World*, September 27, 1919, 1: *New York Times*, January 9, 1920, 1, citing Strike Committee.

29. Warren, *Big Steel*, 117, citing Gary.

30. *Duluth News Tribune*, September 20, 1919, 14; September 21, 1919, 1; *Duluth Herald*, September 22, 1919, 1; *Wall Street Journal*, September 23, 1919, 10.

31. *Labor World*, September 27, 1919, 1; Carney in *Truth* (Duluth), October 10, 1919, 3; Richard Hudelson, "Jack Carney and the *Truth* in Duluth," *Soathar: Journal of the Irish Labour History Society* 19 (1994): 129–39.

32. *Labor World*, September 18, 1920, 8.

33. Hudelson and Ross, *By the Ore Docks*, 206–7; *Morgan Park Bulletin*, March 10, 1921, 7; *Duluth Herald*, June 27, 1921, 1; author's interview with John Howden, June 1, 2001.

34. *Morgan Park Bulletin*, August 26, 1920, 11; *Duluth Herald*, August 28, 1920, 2; March 6, 1923, 8, citing Tarbell; see also Ida M. Tarbell, *The History of the Standard Oil Company* (New York: McClure, Phillips, 1904); interview with Earl Bester by Jack Spiese, October 26, 1967, Earl Bester Papers (MHS Archives).

35. Good Fellowship Club, *40th Anniversary Program*, 1957 (NEMHC); U.S. Steel Corporation, *Bulletin* no. 7, 64.

36. *Duluth News Tribune*, February 23, 1916, 4; May 21, 1916, 8; *Duluth Herald*, May 29, 1916, 15; July 17, 1916, 16; December 11, 1916, 2.

37. "Minutes of the Good Fellowship Club," December 18, 1917, citing Clark (S2366 B2f19, Box 1, NEMHC); U.S. Steel Corporation, *Bulletin* no. 7, 64.

38. "Minutes of the Good Fellowship Club," December 22, 1917; January 29, 1918.

39. *Morgan Park Bulletin*, December 26, 1918, 8; *Duluth News Tribune*, July 27, 1919, 12-A; December 29, 1919, 3; July 21, 1922, 12; August 12, 1928, B-6.

40. "Minutes of the Good Fellowship Club," August 6, 1920.

41. "Minutes of the Good Fellowship Club," January 10, 1918; February 9, 1918; October 24, 1922; November 21, 1922.

42. *Wall Street Journal*, January 30, 1919, 8; April 24, 1919, 8; April 25, 1919, 7; *Duluth News Tribune*, August 1, 1920, D-2; *Skillings Mining Review* 7 (May 10, 1919): 7; Warren, *Big Steel*, 74–75.

43. Warren, *Big Steel*, 363; *New York Times*, December 5, 1920, 28; April 11, 1921, 23; *Duluth News Tribune*, May 13, 1921, 5; October 31, 1921, 5.

44. *Duluth Herald*, June 30, 1921, 2; *Duluth News Tribune*, July 10, 1921, 4-A.

45. *Duluth Herald*, February 21, 1917, 4; March 16, 1917, 10; *Duluth News Tribune*, September 20, 1919, 1, 14; January 6, 1921, 5, citing Preuss; March 11, 1921, 1–2; April 8, 1921, 1–2; April 21, 1921, 1; Warren, *Big Steel*, 75.

46. *Duluth Herald*, January 3, 1923, 1, 4.

47. *Duluth Herald*, January 3, 1923, 1, 4; *Duluth News Tribune*, December 26, 1926, 1-E; American Iron and Steel Institute, *Directory of the Iron and Steel Works of the United States and Canada* (New York: The Institute, 1930), 231.

48. *Duluth News Tribune*, July 16, 1924, 1; August 21, 1924, 1; October 1, 1924, 1; November 23, 1924, 16-B; December 26, 1926, 1-E; *Skillings Iron Review* 14 (June 20, 1925): 20.

49. Warren, *Big Steel*, 75–76.

50. Ibid., 47–50; *New York Times*, September 18, 1924, 1, 8; *Duluth News Tribune*, August 20, 1924, 1; November 15, 1924, 6; August 24, 1938, 1.

51. *Duluth News Tribune*, April 29, 1920, 3; *Duluth Herald*, January 3, 1923, 1, citing Samuel Sheldon; *New York Times*, November 23, 1929, 21.

52. Warren, *Big Steel*, 75, citing August 31, 1925, letter from Sheldon to C. L. Close.

53. Author's interview with Al Bothun, March 25, 2001; Rapaich interview; *Duluth News Tribune*, September 25, 1944, 2; *Midwest Labor* (Duluth), November 26, 1943, 1; additional biographical information about Cox and Wiley came from the manuscript schedules for the 1920 and 1930 U.S. Census of Population.

54. Agnes Murray, a longtime steel plant office secretary, termed Sheldon the "Wild Bull of the Pampas" in a December 29, 1971, interview; memoranda from Sheldon to Minnesota Steel Company department superintendents, February 18, 1926; December 9, 1927, and February 26, 1929 (given to the author by Murray).

55. *Labor World*, September 27, 1919, 1; Carney in *Truth*, July 8, 1921, 4.

56. "Biographical Material on Earl T. Bester, Director, District 33"; interview with Earl Bester and Joseph Paszak by Jean Johnson, 1980, in "20th Century Radicalism in Minnesota Oral History Project," both items in Earl Thomas Bester Papers (MHS Archives). Members of the Communist Trade Union Education League also attempted to organize a steel plant union during the latter 1920s by appealing to South Slav and Italian workers; see Hudelson and Ross, *By the Ore Docks*, 186–87.

57. *Wall Street Journal*, July 22, 1927, 8; *Duluth News Tribune*, September 14, 1928, 1, citing Farrell.

58. *Duluth Herald*, July 11, 1929, 1; November 17, 1930, 1; *Wall Street Journal*, April 16, 1929, 13; July 13, 1929, 7; September 24, 1929, 6.

59. John Wilson, "The Safe Guarding of Duluth's Water Supply: An Unfinished Story," *Duluth Publicity*, January 18, 1941, 2; *Duluth Herald*, November 13, 1930, 3.

60. *Duluth News Tribune*, November 22, 1929, 1; November 23, 1929, 9, citing W. McGonagle; *New York Times*, November 23, 1929, 29.

6. The Complete Company Town

1. "Universal Portland Cement Co: Cleanliness and Health Follow Extensive Use of Concrete," *Concrete Roads* 3 (April 1916): 51–52, citing League of Municipalities; *Duluth News Tribune*, August 28, 1915, 4; January 4, 1916, 1; *Duluth Herald*, June 21, 1917, 7; Stowell, "Industrial City of the Steel Workers of Duluth," 27.

2. *Duluth News Tribune*, June 20, 1916, 14; June 21, 1916, 1, 4, citing Close.

3. *Duluth News Tribune*, April 6, 1916, 4; October 4, 1916, 4; May 27, 1917, 7-B; *Duluth Herald*, April 7, 1916, 20.

4. *Duluth News Tribune*, April 6, 1916, 4; May 10, 1916, 4; September 8, 1916, 4; May 27, 1917, 7-B; *Duluth Herald*, August 5, 1916, 6; March 20, 1917, 15.

5. Site plan for Block 33 prepared in 1916, Morell & Nichols Papers (NWAA); *Duluth News Tribune*, May 18, 1916, 4; February 5, 1917, 4; April 9, 1917, 4; April 19, 1917, 4; *Duluth Herald*, August 5, 1916, 6; March 20, 1917, 15; June 25, 1917, 2.

6. Magnusson, "Modern Industrial Suburb," 15.

7. Ibid.; *Duluth News Tribune*, February 26, 1910, 9.

8. Magnusson, "Modern Industrial Suburb," 15; Nelson, "National Register of Historic Places"; Robinson, *Life and Work of Harry Franklin Robinson*, 79.

9. Magnusson, "Modern Industrial Suburb," 13, 15, 19.

10. Ibid., 17, 19; Robinson, *Life and Work of Harry Franklin Robinson*, 79; Magnusson "Model Industrial Suburb," 19; *American Architect*, "Morgan Park, Minn.," 753.

11. Magnusson, "Modern Industrial Suburb," 21; Robinson, *Life and Work of Harry Franklin Robinson*, 79.

12. *Duluth Herald*, June 2, 1920, 21; *Duluth News Tribune*, April 2, 1922, 4-C.

13. Magnusson, "Modern Industrial Suburb," 7.

14. Ibid., 7–11; *Duluth News Tribune*, April 19, 1917, 4; April 30, 1917, 4; *Morgan Park Bulletin*, December 5, 1917, 15; John Howden used the term "Mexican houses" in his interview.

15. *Duluth News Tribune*, April 30, 1917, 4; C. B. Stowell, "Industrial City of Steel Workers of Duluth," *Realty* 4 (March 1918): 27.

16. Robinson, *Life and Work of Harry Franklin Robinson*, 79; *Morgan Park Bulletin*, January 2, 1918, 5.

17. Morgan Park Company, *New Houses in Morgan Park*; *Duluth News Tribune*, March 26, 1917, 4; *Duluth Herald*, March 20, 1917, 15; John Howden used the term "Silk Stocking Row" in his interview.

18. Robinson, *Life and Work of Harry Franklin Robinson*, 19–23; "Harry Robinson," http://www.prairiestyles.com/index.htm, 1999–2003 (accessed on July 26, 2006).

19. Robinson, *Life and Work of Harry Franklin Robinson*, 23–24; "Harry Robinson."

20. Morgan Park Company, *New Houses in Morgan Park*, 3.

21. *Duluth News Tribune*, May 6, 1916, 4.

22. *Duluth News Tribune*, January 4, 1916, 1–2.

23. *Duluth News Tribune*, January 4, 1916, 1; January 5, 1916, 1, citing Freimuth.

24. *Duluth News Tribune*, July 18, 1916, 4; July 19, 1916, 4; May 17, 1917, 4; *Duluth Herald*, July 18, 1916, 11.

25. *Duluth News Tribune*, July 19, 1916, 4; July 20, 1916, 4; May 10, 1917, 4; *Morgan Park Bulletin*, April 24, 1919, 10–13.

26. *Duluth Herald*, July 19, 1916, 18; *Morgan Park Bulletin*, November 7, 1918, 9.

27. *Duluth News Tribune*, December 11, 1915, 4; January 8, 1916, 4; January 21, 1916, 4.

28. *Duluth News Tribune*, February 11, 1916, 4; March 15, 1917, 5; list of specifications from J. C. Bush to Duluth Board of Education, January 2, 1917 (Board of Education files).

29. *Duluth Herald*, March 15, 1917, 5; March 16, 1917, 23; *Duluth News Tribune*, March 16, 1917, 4; Elise Braun Alletzhauser letter to Elsa Alletzhauser, 1936.

30. *Duluth News Tribune*, May 10, 1916, 4; *Duluth Herald*, January 26, 1917, 16; Magnusson, "Modern Industrial Suburb," 6.

31. *Duluth Herald*, January 25, 1918, 8; Magnusson, "Modern Industrial Suburb," 6–7.

32. *Duluth Herald*, January 25, 1918, 8; untitled and undated article about the Good Fellowship Club (S4491B1f2, NEMHC).

33. *Duluth Herald*, January 25, 1918, 8; *Duluth News Tribune*, November 18, 1917, A-6; Magnusson, "Modern Industrial Suburb," 7.

34. *Duluth Herald*, January 25, 1918, 8; *Morgan Park Bulletin*, January 2, 1918, 5; January 23, 1918, 7.

35. *Duluth News Tribune*, October 13, 1915, 4; *Duluth Herald*, February 17, 1917, 4.

36. Magnusson, "Modern Industrial Suburb," 7; comments by Llewellyn Ausland, written on the back of a Morgan Park hospital photograph in possession of Christine Carlson.

37. *Morgan Park Bulletin*, September 19, 1918, 16; Magnusson, "Modern Industrial Suburb," 7.

38. *Duluth Herald*, July 29, 1916, 30.

39. *Duluth News Tribune*, March 23, 1917, 4; April 22, 1917, 1, 4; April 23, 1917, 4, citing Magie; *Duluth Herald*, February 17, 1917, 4; April 23, 1917, 2; *Industrialisti* (Duluth), April 24, 1917, 4.

40. *Duluth News Tribune*, April 28, 1917, 4; July 17, 1917, 1, 4; *Duluth Herald*, July 17, 1917, 6. One month earlier, Edward Clancy, the head plumber for the Morgan Park Company, drowned while working at the boathouse; see *Duluth News Tribune*, June 10, 1917, 4-A.

41. "Morgan Park Hospital: Regulations as to Admissions of Patients," included as part of *Hospital Patients Record*, 1920s (S2440, NEMHC).

42. Hospital remodeling permit, March 19, 1927 (DCH).

43. *Duluth News Tribune*, August 28, 1917, 15; September 9, 1917, 4-C; November 11, 1917, 4-C; *Duluth Herald*, March 21, 1917, 21.

44. *Morgan Park Bulletin*, February 13, 1919, 2.

45. *Duluth News Tribune*, March 31, 1916, 4; January 11, 1917, 6; January 19, 1917, 4; April 18, 1917, 4; April 20, 1917, 4, citing Van Thurn; May 16, 1917, 4; May 17, 1917, 4; September 22, 1917, 4; November 6, 1917, 4; December 23, 1917, 5-A; *Duluth Herald*, March 21, 1917, 21; April 21, 1917, 5; United Protestant Church, *Fiftieth Anniversary* (Morgan Park: The Church, 1972), n.p.

46. Building Committee minutes of December 14, 1918, republished in United Protestant Church, *United Protestant Church: History of Its Very Beginnings* (Morgan Park: The Church, 2004), 4–5; *Morgan Park Bulletin*, October 31, 1918, n.p., citing Davidson.

47. Davidson to Building Committee, minutes of May 22, 1919, republished in United Protestant Church, *United Protestant Church: History of Its Very Beginnings*, 9–12.

48. *Morgan Park Bulletin*, November 11, 1920, 1–2; Building Committee minutes of October 24, 1920, republished in *Fiftieth Anniversary*, n.p.

49. *Duluth News Tribune*, April 3, 1922, 5; Scalise, "When We Built the Church," in United Protestant Church, *Fiftieth Anniversary*, n.p.

50. *Morgan Park Bulletin*, February 13, 1919, 2; *Duluth News Tribune*, October 29, 1929, 10-A.

51. *Duluth Herald*, March 20, 1917, 15; Magnusson, "Modern Industrial Suburb," 21.

52. Magnusson, "Modern Industrial Suburb," 21–22; *Morgan Park Bulletin*, June 26, 1919, 25, citing Kuyper; Howden interview.

53. Untitled and undated article about the Good Fellowship Club (S4491B1f2, NEMHC); *Duluth News Tribune*, November 18, 1917, A-6; Howden interview.

54. *Duluth Herald*, July 10, 1916, 11; *Morgan Park Bulletin*, February 13, 1919, 7; February 20, 1919, 14; Paul and Sally Solomon interview; letter from Sally Solomon to author, August 4, 2001.

55. *Duluth Herald*, May 16, 1916, 3; May 25, 1916, 17; June 12, 1916, 21; *Duluth News Tribune*, June 11, 1916, 12; interview with Donald Grubb by Patty O'Leary and Steve Salmi, October 22, 1991. This interview is a product of undergraduate writing assignments for classes supervised by Professor Eleanor Hoffman at the University of Minnesota Duluth from 1990–93. Professor Hoffman sought out stimulating subjects that would engage the students in writing; local history was the subject matter for the classes, with Morgan Park as the focus. The interview, and others used in this book, are on deposit as a collection in the Northeast Minnesota Historical Center; hereinafter, the interviews will be referred to as "Writing for the Social Sciences," S4491, NEMHC; written statement by Llewellyn Ausland on the back of a waiting station photograph in possession of Christine Carlson; Sally Solomon interview.

56. Magnusson, "Modern Industrial Suburb"; *Duluth Herald*, June 11, 1917, 5; *Morgan Park Bulletin*, August 7, 1919, 7; June 10, 1920, 4.

57. *Duluth Herald*, November 22, 1916, 17; *Duluth News Tribune*, December 15, 1915, 4; January 21, 1917, 1-C; April 16, 1917, 4; *Morgan Park Bulletin*, January 30, 1919, 7–9; October 21, 1920, 4–5.

58. Magnusson, "Modern Industrial Suburb," 1.

7. Engineering the Good Life

1. Bothun interview.

2. Magnusson, "Modern Industrial Suburb," 22–23; quotation on 22.

3. *Morgan Park Bulletin*, February 13, 1919, 1–2.

4. All information in this paragraph and those following is from the microfilmed manuscript schedules of the 1920 U.S. Census of Population. Christine Carlson confirmed the count of African Americans listed in the census.

5. Ibid.; Douglas County Schools, "History Stories about the Towns and Villages of Douglas County."

6. Hudelson and Ross, *By the Ore Docks,* 95; interviews by Marjorie Hoover in the "Duluth: Miscellaneous South Slav" file (1980) for the Ethnic History Project Papers (MHS Archives); Gloria Collad De Smedt, "Seek the Truth—MPHS: Our First 55 Years," c. 1971 (typewritten manuscript in Morgan Park school archives).

7. Magnusson, "Modern Industrial Suburb," 5; Hudelson and Ross, *By the Ore Docks,* 206; manuscript schedules of the 1920 U.S. Census of Population.

8. Interview with Edward Nichols by David Taylor, June 17, 1972, Minnesota Black History Project (MHS Archives); Chris Julin and Stephanie Hemphill,

"Postcard from a Lynching," *Minnesota Public Radio Newsletter,* June 2001, citing Charles Nichols.

9. *Morgan Park Bulletin,* January 23, 1919, n.p.; Magnusson, "Model Company Town," 24.

10. Ronald D. Cohen and Raymond A. Mohl, *The Paradox of Progressive Education: The Gary Plan and Urban Schooling* (Port Washington, N.Y.: Kennikat Press, 1979), 5–6.

11. Ibid.; *Duluth News Tribune,* January 21, 1916, 4; *Duluth Herald,* December 2, 1916, 8.

12. *Duluth News Tribune,* September 14, 1915, 4; October 9, 1915, 4, citing Denfeld; Elise Braun Alletzhauser letter to Elsa Alletzhauser, 1936; Bothun interview.

13. *Labor World,* December 11, 1915, 6, citing Metcalfe in *Steel Plant News.*

14. *Duluth News Tribune,* December 15, 1916, 4; December 21, 1916, 4; December 23, 1916, 4; September 22, 1918, 6-D; *Duluth Herald,* March 1, 1917, 11; *Morgan Park Bulletin,* February 27, 1918, 6.

15. *Morgan Park High School Handbook, 1925,* 18 (Morgan Park school archives); *Duluth Herald,* August 2, 1916, 4; March 15, 1917, 5, citing Chadwick.

16. *Duluth News Tribune,* April 22, 1917, 4-A; April 26, 1917, 4; April 27, 1917, 4.

17. *Duluth News Tribune,* June 6, 1918, 4; June 13, 1918, 5; information about the kitchen is from an undated newspaper item on the 1916–26 display panel at the Morgan Park school.

18. *Duluth News Tribune,* December 23, 1916, 4; January 5, 1917, 4; January 11, 1917, 4; January 25, 1917, 4; *Duluth Herald,* January 4, 1917, 28.

19. *Duluth News Tribune,* January 18, 1917, 4; January 22, 1917, 4; January 29, 1917, 4.

20. *Duluth News Tribune,* April 6, 1917, 6; April 7, 1917, 4; May 17, 1917, 4; May 31, 1917, 4; Cole in *Morgan Park Bulletin,* July 15, 1920, 2.

21. Kuyper in *Morgan Park Bulletin,* October 31, 1918, 2.

22. *Morgan Park Bulletin,* November 21, 1917, 3; February 27, 1918, 5–6; "First Annual Exhibit: Morgan Park School Program, June 4, 1918," 1 (copy in possession of Christine Carlson).

23. *Morgan Park Bulletin,* May 29, 1919, 1–7, quotation on 2.

24. *Duluth News Tribune,* September 2, 1917, 6-A; September 10, 1917, 4; June 11, 1922, 6-A; June 14, 1922, 8; *Duluth Herald,* June 12, 1922, 4.

25. *Morgan Park High School Handbook, 1925,* 39; *Duluth News Tribune,* April 15, 1917, 4-A; *Morgan Park Bulletin,* December 15, 1921, n.p.

26. *Duluth Herald,* March 4, 1928, 16; October 20, 1929, B-1; October 29, 1929, 24; *Duluth News-Tribune,* October 20, 1929, B-1; November 24, 1929, 4-B; display panels for 1927–29 at the Morgan Park school.

27. *Morgan Park High School Handbook, 1925,* 6–7; *Duluth News Tribune,* May 31, 1917, 4.

28. Cohen and Mohl, *Paradox of Progressive Education,* 7, 10, 87–88.

29. *Duluth News Tribune,* April 16, 1917, 4; May 5, 1917, 4; November 18, 1917, A-6; April 7, 1918, 7-B; October 7, 1918, 5; March 1, 1919, 9; *Morgan Park Bulletin,* November 14, 1917, 4; February 20, 1919, 2; *Superior Telegram,* October 2, 1918, 9; Good Fellowship Club minutes of July 27, 1918 (S2366B2f19, Box 1, NEMHC).

30. *Morgan Park Bulletin,* June 5, 1918, 6; December 26, 1918, 4; April 3, 1919, 11; citing Vallier.

31. *Duluth News Tribune*, June 18, 1917, 4; Hudelson and Ross, *By the Ore Docks*, 109.

32. Interviews with George and Marian Orescanin and Dan Bastie, by Marjorie Hoover, 1980, for *They Chose Minnesota: A Survey of the State's Ethnic Groups*, ed. June Drenning Holmquist (St. Paul: Minnesota Historical Society Press, 1981); the interview transcripts may be found in the MHS Archives; Good Fellowship Club minutes, November 13, 1923 (S2366B2f19, Box 1, NEMHC); *Duluth News Tribune*, June 4, 1917, 4; February 26, 1920, 6; September 27, 1992, 1-E, citing Jim Harper; Hudelson and Ross, *By the Ore Docks*, 206.

33. U.S. Steel Corporation, Bureau of Safety, Sanitation and Welfare, *Bulletin No. 8* (December 1920), 50–51; *Morgan Park Bulletin*, August 26, 1920, 12–14.

34. Bothun interview; *Duluth News Tribune*, May 5, 1919, 3; *Wisconsin Sunday Times* (Superior), June 3, 1923, A-1.

35. *Duluth News Tribune*, April 8, 1917, 2-C; April 9, 1917, 4, citing Morgan Park Company; *Morgan Park Bulletin*, January 9, 1919, 5, citing Dacey.

36. *Morgan Park Bulletin*, June 19, 1918, 14–15; *Duluth Herald*, June 15, 1918, 25; *Wisconsin Sunday Times*, May 20, 1923, 5-A.

37. R. D. Chadwick, "The Value of Play," *Know Your School Series*, no. 2 (1918), 40, citing J. R. Batchelor (Pamphlet 1200, NEMHC); August 28, 1919, 4; *Morgan Park Bulletin*, September 4, 1919, 13; May 20, 1920, 13.

38. Duluth city directories, 1927 and 1928.

39. *Morgan Park Bulletin*, June 3, 1920, 7–8; July 29, 1920, 6–7; *Duluth News Tribune*, June 14, 1917, 4; June 19, 1917, 4; June 26, 1917, 4; *Wisconsin Sunday Times*, June 24, 1923, A-4.

40. *Morgan Park Bulletin*, July 25, 1918, 9, citing Geraldine Vallier; October 28, 1920, 1–2; *Wisconsin Sunday Times*, July 22, 1923, 4-A.

41. *Morgan Park Bulletin*, October 28, 1920, 2–4.

42. Interview with Einar Bjork by Stacey Dunk and John Hawkins, May 31, 1991 ("Writing for the Social Sciences," S4491, NEMHC).

43. *Duluth News Tribune*, October 25, 1916, 4; *Duluth Herald*, April 4, 1919, 25; *Morgan Park Bulletin*, July 31, 1919, 2; August 14, 1919, 1–2, 10.

44. *Morgan Park Bulletin*, October 31, 1917, 5; April 3, 1918, 8; June 12, 1919, 4; August 14, 1919, 12; letter from Morgan Park Supply Company to Marcus Nelson of Tamarack, Minn., August 30, 1915 (provided by Robert Harder).

45. *Morgan Park Bulletin*, September 12, 1918, 17–19; October 10, 1918, 2–4; April 3, 1919, 9–10; August 14, 1919, 16; September 10, 1920, 3; *Duluth News Tribune*, March 25, 1917, 3-A, 12-B; June 19, 1917, 4; November 26, 1917, 4; June 29, 1918, 1.

46. *Morgan Park Bulletin*, September 10, 1920, 1–3.

47. *Morgan Park Bulletin*, June 19, 1918, 6–7; *Duluth News Tribune*, March 26, 1917, 4; April 8, 1917, 4; May 17, 1917, 4; May 31, 1917, 4, *Duluth Herald*, March 20, 1917, 15; *Wisconsin Sunday Times*, June 3, 1923, A-1.

48. *Duluth News Tribune*, November 12, 1916, 4-B.

49. *Duluth News Tribune*, June 18, 1917, 4; June 26, 1917, 4; July 5, 1918, 4; *Duluth Herald*, July 3, 1917, 5; *Morgan Park Bulletin*, July 11, 1918, 1–5.

50. *Duluth Herald*, June 20, 1921, 3; July 2, 1921, 2; July 4, 1921, 1; July 5, 1921, 20.

51. *Duluth News Tribune*, August 31, 1919, 9-A.

52. Stowell, "Industrial City of the Steel Workers of Duluth," 27–28.

53. Ibid., 28; Bjork interview with Dunk and Hawkins.

54. Van Brunt, ed., *Duluth and St. Louis County, Minnesota*, 313; *Duluth News Tribune*, November 2, 1913, Magazine Section, 1; January 24, 1917, 4; March 2, 1917, 4.

55. Morrison in *Duluth Rip-Saw*, December 8, 1917, 1; July 13, 1918, 1; August 24, 1918, 1; *Duluth News Tribune*, September 7, 1918, 3; September 10, 1918, 3, citing Miller; September 13, 1918, 3; Fred W. Friendly, *Minnesota Rag: The Dramatic Story of the Landmark Supreme Court Case That Gave New Meaning to Freedom of the Press* (New York: Vintage Books, 1981), 7.

56. Howden interview; *Duluth News-Tribune*, January 9, 1928, 1–2; January 10, 1928, 1–2, 16; January 11, 1928, 1–2; January 13, 1928, 17; January 25, 1928, 11.

57. *Morgan Park Bulletin*, March 24, 1921, 1–2; Bothun interview.

58. Morrison in *Duluth Rip-Saw*, November 16, 1918, 3; *Duluth News Tribune*, November 9, 1918, 3, citing McGiggert.

59. Morrison in *Duluth Rip-Saw*, July 27, 1918, 4; *Duluth News Tribune*, July 22, 1918, 1, 6.

60. *Duluth News-Tribune*, September 27, 1992, 1-E, citing Jim Harper; interviews with Einar Bjork by Martin W. Duffy, March 5, 1977 (MHS Archives); and Dunk and Hawkins.

61. Rapaich interview.

62. *Morgan Park Bulletin*, July 25, 1918, 9; *Duluth Herald*, November 2, 1918, 10; United Protestant Church, *1957 Yearbook* (Duluth: The Church, 1957), 2 (copy in possession of Christine Carlson).

63. Comments by Kuyper (archives of the United Protestant Church of Morgan Park).

64. Ibid.

65. Anedith Nash and Robert Silberman, *Morgan Park: Continuity and Change in a Company Town* (Minneapolis: University of Minnesota, Department of Art History, 1992), n.p.

8. Struggling for Work during the 1930s

1. Warren, *Big Steel*, 144, 363; *New York Times*, November 6, 1930, 42.

2. *Skillings Mining Review* 19 (May 24, 1930): 15; *Duluth News-Tribune*, August 29, 1930, 10; *Wall Street Journal*, November 17, 1930, 1; *Duluth Herald*, November 17, 1930, 1.

3. *Duluth News-Tribune*, May 19, 1930, 10; July 2, 1930, 3; September 19, 1932, 2; *Duluth Free Press*, November 13, 1931, 1; *New York Times*, September 5, 1930, 14; Alvin H. Hansen, Dreng Bjornaraa, and Tillman M. Sogge, *The Decline of Employment in the 1930–1931 Depression in St. Paul, Minneapolis, and Duluth* (Minneapolis: University of Minnesota Press, 1932), 32–33.

4. Warren, *Big Steel*, 365; *Duluth News-Tribune*, December 31, 1931, 1-A, citing Farrell.

5. American Iron and Steel Institute, *Directory of the Iron and Steel Works of the United States and Canada* (New York: The Institute, 1935), 36.

6. *Duluth News-Tribune*, January 11, 1930, 11; December 10, 1930, 1; September 22, 1931, 9; December 4, 1931, 13; July 4, 1934, 1.

7. *Skillings Mining Review* 21 (May 14, 1932): 3; *Duluth Herald*, June 1, 1932, 1; *New York Times*, June 21, 1932, 31; *Washington Post*, June 21, 1932, 16; Warren, *Big Steel*, 76, citing Myron Taylor.

8. U.S. Steel Corporation, *Annual Report, 1932* (New York: The Corporation, 1933); interview with Bjork by Dunk and Hawkins. The comment by the anonymous, retired steelworker is from a telephone interview conducted in 1975; for further information refer to endnote 21, chapter 12.

9. *Duluth News-Tribune,* December 31, 1932, 2, citing Reis.

10. Warren, *Big Steel,* 363.

11. American Iron and Steel Institute, *1935 Directory,* 36; letter from G. Zeller to author, November 2, 1977; *New York Times,* November 23, 1934, 31; September 10, 1935, 21; G. Nordin in *Duluth News-Tribune,* May 13, 1934, 1-C; December 5, 1934, 1.

12. Wilson, "Safeguarding of Duluth's Water Supply," 2.

13. *New York Times,* November 23, 1934, 31; September 10, 1935, 21; G. Nordin, in *Duluth News-Tribune,* May 13, 1934, 1-D; December 5, 1934, 1, citing Lumley; September 9, 1935, 1.

14. *New York Times,* May 21, 1934, 1, 3.

15. *Duluth News-Tribune,* May 21, 1934, 1, 3; March 15, 1935, 1, 6; August 5, 1945, 1-A; *New York Times,* May 21, 1934, 1; Swanstrom in *Washington Post,* March 24, 1934.

16. *Duluth News-Tribune,* May 31, 1934, 1, 4; March 15, 1935, 6, citing the FTC; August 24, 1938, 1; *New York Times,* March 14, 1935, 31.

17. *Duluth News-Tribune,* August 21, 1933, 1, 3.

18. Warren, *Big Steel,* 165; Robert H. Zieger, *American Workers, American Unions, 1920–1985* (Baltimore: The Johns Hopkins University Press, 1986), 48.

19. *Duluth News-Tribune,* June 4, 1936, 5, citing Irvin.

20. "Biographical Background on Earl T. Bester"; Earl T. Bester interview; *Midwest Labor* (Duluth), July 28, 1939, 5; December 13, 1939, 4; December 18, 1942, 2, citing Bester.

21. *Midwest Labor,* September 17, 1937, 2; July 28, 1938, 5; *New York Times,* March 4, 1937, 1, 2; March 18, 1937, 1, 6; Zieger, *American Workers,* 48–49; interview with Earl Bester and Joseph Paszak by Jean Johnson for "20th Century Radicalism in Minnesota Oral History Project," 1980 (MHS Archives).

22. *Midwest Labor,* August 20, 1937, 3, citing unnamed steelworker; March 12, 1943, 3, citing L. Wegmiller; interview with Ernest Johnson by Mary Terpstra and Gina Malander, April 16, 1991, in "Writing for the Social Sciences" (S4491, NEMHC).

23. *Midwest Labor,* August 20, 1937, 3; "Biographical Background on Earl T. Bester."

24. *Midwest Labor,* August 18, 1939, 1, 2; August 25, 1939, 1; October 1, 1939, 3; October 20, 1939, 1, citing Drill.

25. *Midwest Labor,* November 19, 1937, 1.

26. *Midwest Labor,* October 1, 1937, 4.

27. *New York Times,* September 2, 1936, 36; *Duluth Herald,* August 29, 1936, 1; *Duluth News-Tribune,* September 2, 1936, 14; October 12, 1938, 1-B.

28. *Duluth News-Tribune,* August 24, 1938, 1, 5, citing Barnes.

29. Warren, *Big Steel,* 363; *Duluth News-Tribune,* September 26, 1938, 8, citing AS&WC officials.

30. Warren, *Big Steel,* 363; *Duluth News-Tribune,* March 29, 1938, 1; October 12, 1938, 1-B.

31. Warren, *Big Steel,* 363; Zieger, *American Workers,* 63; *Duluth News-Tribune,* July 22, 1939, 1, 3; *Duluth Herald,* October 5, 1939, 1.

32. *Duluth Herald,* October 5, 1939, 1.

9. Getting By and Making Do

1. *Rearrangement of Street Names and House Numbers in Morgan Park,* 1930 (3150, 4:66, NEMHC).

2. *Official Proceedings of the City Council of the City of Duluth for 1933* (Duluth: The City, 1933), 535 (DCH); *Duluth News-Tribune,* June 14, 1933, 3; June 15, 1933, 9; *Duluth Herald,* June 15, 1933, 4.

3. *Duluth News-Tribune,* July 4, 1933, 3, citing Williams.

4. *Official Proceedings of City Council, 1935,* 535–36; *Duluth Herald,* August 28, 1933, 2; *Duluth News-Tribune,* August 26, 1933, 1; August 29, 1933, 9.

5. Manuscript schedules for the U.S. Population Census of 1930; Duluth city directories, 1930–36.

6. Interview with Jim Harper by Tracey Garver and Cheryl Pietila, April 10, 1991, in "Writing for the Social Sciences" (S4491, NEMHC); *Midwest Labor,* January 11, 1946, 8, citing Di Mele; Bothun interview.

7. *Duluth News-Tribune,* June 15, 1933, 4, citing MacDonald; March 1, 1936, 8-A; April 19, 1936, 6-A; Arthur C. Comey and Max S. Wehrly, Morgan Park Company response to "Harvard School of City Planning Questionnaire to Public Officials on Model Community Developments," 1936 (Frances Loeb Library, Graduate School of Design, Harvard University).

8. Arthur C. Comey and Max S. Wehrly, "Morgan Park. Duluth, Minn," unpublished summary included as part of "Harvard School of City Planning Questionnaire," 1936.

9. *Duluth Herald,* August 29, 1936, 1; Duluth city directories, 1930–39.

10. Biographical information about Friederici is from microfilmed manuscript schedules of the U.S. Census of Population for 1910, 1920, and 1930; Duluth city directories, 1910–36; *Duluth News-Tribune,* December 22, 1948, 11; *Duluth Herald,* December 20, 1948, 23; communications to the author from Barbara East Johnson, January 6, 2006, and Karin Hertel McGinnis, April 5, 2006.

11. Demolition permits for the hospital, December 12, 1935, and duplex, December 11, 1935 (DCH).

12. Demolition permits for East View, January 2, 1934, and North View boardinghouses, August 29, 1939 (DCH); "Dedication Program: Morgan Park School," October 23, 1939 (S4412, 57, NEMHC); *Duluth News-Tribune,* September 12, 1939, October 1, 1939, 17-A; October 15, 1939, 15-A; October 23, 1939, 10-A.

13. Filling station building permit, April 12, 1938 (DCH); Bothun interview.

14. Duluth city directories, 1932–39.

15. Bothun interview; *Duluth News-Tribune,* February 4, 1979, Outlook Section, 63, citing Aird.

16. *Duluth News-Tribune,* January 10, 1938, 10; October 2, 1938, 7-A, citing E. R. Stearns.

17. *Duluth News-Tribune,* March 15, 1938, 10; October 2, 1938, 7-A; October 7, 1938, 4; Howden interview; U.S. Steel Corporation, *Annual Report, 1932* (New York: The Corporation, 1933).

18. *Duluth News-Tribune,* July 21, 1934, 9; July 1, 1936, 10; July 10, 1938, 7-A; October 7, 1938, 4.

19. *Duluth News-Tribune,* February 1, 1936, 9; January 14, 1938, 10; August 11, 1939, 6.

20. *Duluth News-Tribune,* October 14, 1938, 1, 4, citing Stassen; November 10,

1938, 3; *Proceedings of the City Council of the City of Duluth* (Duluth: The City, 1938), 262.

21. *Duluth News-Tribune*, February 28, 1931, 2; September 23, 1938, 8; *Duluth Herald*, August 16, 1937, 14; October 5, 1939, 1.

10. More Steel for Another War

1. Warren, *Big Steel*, 363–64.

2. *Duluth Herald*, October 29, 1940, 1; *Duluth News-Tribune*, December 31, 1932, 2, citing Reis; June 9, 1940, A-11; April 1, 1942, 1, citing W. E. Hauck.

3. *Midwest Labor*, January 2, 1942, 1; February 26, 1943, 3.

4. *Midwest Labor*, January 2, 1942, 1; February 6, 1942, 2; citing Westerhaus; February 26, 1943, 3; *Duluth News-Tribune*, March 23, 1942, 10.

5. *New York Times*, August 17, 1941, F-5; *Duluth News-Tribune*, February 21, 1942, 1; August 9, 1942, B-6; February 20, 1943, 1; *Duluth Herald*, February 20, 1943, 2; February 24, 1943, 1; February 25, 1943, 2, citing Pheneger; December 21, 1946, 8.

6. *Midwest Labor*, February 13, 1941, 1; *Duluth Herald*, August 21, 1942, 2; August 29, 1942, 3; *Duluth News-Tribune*, September 6, 1942, Cosmopolitan section, 4; September 24, 1942, 1, 3; November 6, 1942, 8; Sicard on November 22, 1942, Cosmopolitan section, 9.

7. *Duluth News-Tribune*, September 25, 1942, 9; September 28, 1942, 1, 3.

8. *Duluth Herald*, August 23, 1943, 5; *Duluth News-Tribune*, November 7, 1942, 1; March 31, 1943, 7.

9. *New York Times*, February 1, 1944, 25; March 6, 1945, 15; *Minnesota Labor*, April 6, 1945, 6.

10. *Duluth News-Tribune*, March 8, 1940, 4; May 22, 1942, 8; *Minnesota Labor*, February 2, 1945, 3.

11. *Duluth News-Tribune*, March 31, 1940, Cosmopolitan Section, 2.

12. *Duluth Herald and News-Tribune*, December 31, 1942, Annual Industrial and Business Edition, 2; May 15, 1943, Pictures Section, 2.

13. *Duluth News-Tribune*, January 12, 1941, Cosmopolitan Section, 2; August 17, 1941, 8-A; December 19, 1941, B-6; December 28, 1941, 3; July 12, 1942, Cosmopolitan Section, 2; October 16, 1942, 9; November 8, 1942, 10-A; *Midwest Labor*, September 2, 1943, 8.

14. *Duluth News-Tribune*, August 15, 1944, 2; September 11, 1944, 10; September 22, 1944, 2; September 24, 1944, 6, citing Ewald; September 25, 3, citing Balach; September 29, 1944, 4, citing Anderson.

15. "Answering the Call to Duty," *Techniques* (February 2002), 29.

16. Industrial Committee of the Young Women's Christian Association of Duluth, Minnesota, *Women at Work: A Survey of Industrial Women Workers in Duluth* (Duluth: YWCA, 1945), 5; *Duluth News-Tribune*, September 6, 1942, 6-A; September 20, 1942, Pictures Section, 3; Sicard on October 4, 1942, Cosmopolitan Section, 10; November 7, 1942, 4; Sicard on August 22, 1943, Cosmopolitan Section, 10; *Duluth Free Press*, December 11, 1942, 1.

17. Letter from Bob Berg to author, July 26, 2006.

18. *Duluth News-Tribune*, February 4, 1990, 1-E, 5-E, citing Evaristo Del Zotto. The information in the paragraph was also based on the following interviews, prepared for "Writing for the Social Sciences," S4491, NEMHC: Jeanette Hunt, by Jenny Gerwing and Sherri Hobbs, November 11, 1991; Anne Sandstrom, by Patti

Reichert and Lisa Sylvester, April 25, 1991; Ernest Johnson, by Mary Terpstra and Gina Melander, April 16, 1991; Jim Harper, by Tracey Garver and Cheryl Pietila, April 10, 1991; Bruno Busch, by Julie Honkanen and Kim Woessner, November 11, 1991.

19. *Duluth News-Tribune*, September 19, 1943, 7-C, citing Williams.

20. Industrial Committee, *Women at Work*, 2.

21. Ibid., 9–12; *Midwest Labor*, February 11, 1944, 3.

22. *Duluth News-Tribune*, July 8, 1945, 1-C; March 10, 1946, 1-C.

23. *Duluth News-Tribune*, May 16, 1942, 12; September 12, 1944, 12; *Minnesota Labor*, October 26, 1945, 3; Industrial Committee, *Women at Work*, 2.

24. *Midwest Labor*, February 2, 1940, 1; March 20, 1941, 1; *Minnesota Labor*, September 21, 1945, 7; February 11, 1949, 3; *Duluth News-Tribune*, June 8, 1947, Cosmopolitan Section, 3.

25. *Duluth News-Tribune*, August 11, 1942, 1; August 26, 1942, 1; September 24, 1944, B-3; *Duluth Herald and News-Tribune*, December 31, 1942, Annual Industry and Business Edition, 18.

26. *Midwest Labor*, July 26, 1940, 2; July 9, 1943, 1; September 3, 1943, 8.

27. *Midwest Labor*, January 19, 1940, 2; July 19, 1940, 2; July 26, 1940, 2; July 18, 1941, 3; September 3, 1943, 8; *Duluth News-Tribune*, November 19, 1944, Cosmopolitan Section, 3.

28. *Duluth News-Tribune*, April 5, 1941, 1, 5; April 15, 1941, 1.

29. *Duluth News-Tribune*, November 30, 1945, 4; *Duluth Herald*, November 29, 1945, 1; *New York Times*, January 20, 1946, 63; Zieger, *American Workers*, 89.

11. No More Company Housing

1. U.S. Census of Population, 1940; letter from Hilda and Fritz Friederici to Elsa and Leo Hertel, February 13, 1943 (provided by Karin Hertel McGinnis).

2. *Duluth News-Tribune*, March 9, 1940, 4; March 3, 1941, 5; December 9, 1941, 10; February 20, 1942, 14; February 25, 1942, 8; *Midwest Labor*, October 24, 1941, 2; March 26, 1943, 1.

3. Memorandum from J. G. MacDonald to Morgan Park Community Club, August 19, 1942 (S2366B2f19, NEMHC); author's interview with Marlin Rastello, December 29, 1971; *Duluth Herald*, December 18, 1942, 1; *Range Facts* (Virginia, Minn.), November 11, 1943, 1; *Duluth News-Tribune*, December 19, 1942, 3; January 7, 1951, Cosmopolitan Section, 6.

4. Memorandum from Morgan Park Community Club to J. G. MacDonald, August 29, 1942 (S2366B2f19, Box 2, NEMHC); *Midwest Labor*, July 10, 1942, 3.

5. Friederici letter to Hertels, February 13, 1943.

6. Sicard in *Duluth News-Tribune*, January 17, 1943, Cosmopolitan Section, 10.

7. *Minnesota Labor*, August 11, 1944, 8.

8. Letter from John Galbreath Company to Morgan Park residents, July 17, 1943 (S2366B2f19, Box 2, NEMHC); Rapaich interview.

9. *Duluth News-Tribune*, September 3, 1943, 6-A; September 12, 1943, 18-A; September 19, 1943, 6-A; September 26, 1943, 6-A; October 3, 1943, 6-A.

10. *Duluth News-Tribune*, December 3, 1945, 10.

11. Duluth city directories, 1943–45.

12. Memoranda from Morgan Park Community Club to J. W Galbreath Co., January 16, 1945, and January 20, 1945 (S2366B2f19, Box 2, NEMCH).

12. Six Strikes to Shutdown

1. *Duluth Herald,* October 19, 1944, 5; *Duluth News-Tribune,* December 21, 1946, 1.

2. Communications to the author from Don Long, March 19, 2006, and Barbara East, December 28, 2005; Dunk and Hawkins interview with Bjork.

3. *Skillings Mining Review* 39 (December 10, 1949), 2; *Duluth News-Tribune,* January 1, 1952, B-3; Warren, *Big Steel,* 364.

4. *Duluth News-Tribune,* October 26, 1954, 9, citing Freeman; June 3, 1955, 1, 7; March 28, 1956, 1, citing Freeman; September 19, 1956, 16; *Duluth Publicity,* June 5, 1959, 1.

5. *Duluth News-Tribune,* September 16, 1956, 16-A; September 21, 1956, 4; September 23, 1956, Feature Section, 41; September 28, 1956, 2; September 29, 1956, 5; September 30, 1956, AS&W Open House Section, 1–12; October 4, 1956, 1; *Duluth Herald,* September 13, 1956, 1, 9; October 1, 1956, 1, 3; October 3, 1956, 1; *Duluth Publicity,* September 14, 1956, 1; September 28, 1956, 1; *Steel Plant News* (Gary, Minn.), September 21, 1956, 1.

6. Walter Eldot in *Duluth News-Tribune,* January 12, 1959, 15.

7. *Duluth News-Tribune,* January 21, 1946, 1; February 8, 1946, 2; February 16, 1946, 1, 4; February 18, 1946, 1, 3; *Minnesota Labor,* Febrary 22, 1946, 8; *Duluth Herald,* January 22, 1946, 1, 3; February 2, 1946, 1; February 7, 1946, 1, 3; *New York Times,* February 2, 1946, 1, 8.

8. *Duluth News-Tribune,* February 19, 1946, 1, citing Pheneger; *Minnesota Labor,* February 22, 1946, 8.

9. *Duluth News-Tribune,* April 21, 1947, 1, 4; August 3, 1949, 5; August 31, 1949, 1; October 1, 1949, 1, 9; October 5, 1949, 1, 3, citing Bester; October 26, 1949, 1, 5; *Minnesota Labor,* October 21, 1949, 1–2; *Duluth Herald,* October 1, 1949, 1, 3.

10. *Duluth News-Tribune,* November 12, 1949, 1, 4; *Minnesota Labor,* November 18, 1949, 1–2.

11. Hudelson and Ross, *By the Ore Docks,* 269–70. Because of space limitations, this account does not discuss the internal divisions that occurred within the ranks of Local 1028; however, see Hudelson and Ross, chapter 10.

12. *New York Times,* April 13, 1952, F-1; July 25, 1952, 7; *Duluth News-Tribune,* July 27, 1952, 1-A.

13. *Duluth News-Tribune,* July 2, 1955, 1–2; July 8, 1956, 1, 8; *New York Times,* July 1, 1956, 34; *Minnesota Labor,* August 10, 1956, 1–2.

14. *Labor World,* July 16, 1959, 3; *Duluth News-Tribune,* July 19, 1959, 1, 11; July 22, 1959, 1, 12; August 16, 1959, 1-A, 2-A; November 1, 1959, 1; November 8, 1959, 1–2, 15; January 5, 1960, 1; January 6, 1960, 1; *New York Times,* November 8, 1959, 1, 54–55; January 5, 1960, 1, 19. The Duffy interview with Einar Bjork provides further information about the 1959 strike (MHS Archives).

15. *Duluth Herald,* September 9, 1964, 1; September 21, 1964, 1; December 10, 1964, 1; January 5, 1966, 1; *Duluth Budgeteer,* December 9, 1965, 1, 3; R. Skophammer in *Duluth News-Tribune,* September 13, 1964, 1, 2; March 28, 1965, 15; October 23, 1965, 1; February 19, 1966, 1.

16. *Duluth News-Tribune,* February 13, 1964, 6, citing Blough; *Duluth Herald,* January 31, 1964, 1; August 30, 1966, 1, citing Blough; *Duluth Budgeteer,* January 6, 1966, 1.

17. Alanen, "Rise and Demise of a Company Town," 36–37; *Duluth News-Tribune,* February 10, 1949, 16.

18. *Duluth News-Tribune,* October 13, 1966, 2; letter from Herbert Dunsmore to John Badalich, June 17, 1970 (Minnesota Pollution Control Agency files).

19. *Duluth News-Tribune,* September 10, 1971, 1; October 9, 1971, 1, citing Gott; November 5, 1971, 1, 9; February 17, 1972, 1, 4; January 16, 1974, 1; *News-Tribune Herald* (Duluth), May 10, 1983, 1-A, 6-A; *Milwaukee Journal,* May 19, 1974, 1, 4.

20. *Duluth News-Tribune,* January 29, 1972, 1, 3; July 21, 1973, 1, 3; August 23, 1973, 1; Minnesota Attorney General's Office, "Memorandum to Minnesota Pollution Control Agency," December 18, 1973 (MPCA files).

21. *Duluth News-Tribune,* September 25, 1975, 8; July 16, 1977, 3-B; July 21, 1977, 2-A; April 29, 1978, 1, citing Spehar; September 30, 1978, 2-A; *Duluth Herald,* April 3, 1979, 1-A. The comment about hating the cement plant came from an anonymous respondent interviewed in a 1975 telephone survey of Morgan Park and Gary residents, conducted with the assistance of the Wisconsin Survey Research Laboratory as part of a project I supervised with research funding from the Graduate School, University of Wisconsin-Madison; hereinafter the results will be referred to as "author's survey of Morgan Park and Gary residents, 1975."

22. Hudelson and Ross, *By the Ore Docks,* 272.

23. Alanen, "Rise and Demise of a Company Town," 35.

24. William Serrin, *Homestead: The Glory and Tragedy of an American Steel Town* (New York: Times Books, 1992), 441. For examples of three other books that describe the deindustrialization of America, see the following: Barry Bluestone and Bennett Harrison, *The Deindustrialization of America: Plant Closings, Community Abandonment, and the Dismantling of Basic Industry* (New York: Basic Books, 1982); David Bensman and Roberta Lynch, *Rusted Dreams: Hard Times in a Steel Community* (New York: McGraw-Hill Book Co., 1987); John Hoerr, *And the Wolf Finally Came: The Decline of the American Steel Industry* (Pittsburgh: University of Pittsburgh Press, 1988).

25. Ibid.; author's survey of Morgan Park and Gary residents, 1975.

26. Alanen, "Rise and Demise of a Company Town," 36–37; author's survey of Morgan Park and Gary residents, 1975.

27. *Duluth News-Tribune,* June 5, 1997, 1-A; communication from John Isle to author, September 2, 2006.

28. Minnesota Pollution Control Agency, "St. Louis River—U.S. Steel Superfund Site," 2002, http://www.pca.state.mn.us/cleanup/sites/ussteel.html (accessed December 20, 2006); *Duluth News-Tribune,* January 2, 1997, 1-A, 6-A; April 24, 1998, 1-A.

29. *Duluth News-Tribune,* July 23, 1999, 1-B; July 1, 2002, 1-A, 4-A; Will Munger on November 17, 2003, 9-A; April 16, 2004, 1-B; Don Jacobson, "Officials Foresee Development at U.S. Steel Superfund Site," *BusinessNorth.com,* August 18, 2003.

13. Preserving the Model Town

1. *Duluth News-Tribune,* January 7, 1951, Cosmopolitan Section, 6, citing Galbreath.

2. *Duluth News-Tribune,* May 19, 1946, 12-A; Duluth city directories, 1947–60.

3. U.S. Censuses of Population and Housing, 1940, 1950; Duluth city directories, 1950, 1960. Since the Morgan Park census tract covers a somewhat larger area than the original community, I sought to determine a more exact population figure by taking the average household size for Morgan Park revealed in the 1940 and

1950 censuses, and multiplying this figure by the number of occupied households listed in the 1940 and 1950 city directories. I followed the same procedure when determining the population of Morgan Park in subsequent census years: 1960, 1970, 1980, 1990, and 2000.

4. *Duluth News-Tribune,* April 12, 1953, Parade of Homes Section, 26; January 3, 1954, Outlook for Tomorrow section, 30; Duluth city directories, 1952–63.

5. U.S. Censuses of Population and Housing, 1960, 1970; City of Duluth, Department of Research and Planning, "Community Renewal Program: Population Profile," 1969.

6. *Duluth Herald,* December 1, 1960, 27; Duluth city directories, 1954–75.

7. *Duluth News-Tribune,* May 8, 1952, 7; May 9, 1952, 1; Neighborhood House demolition permit, July 14, 1961 (DCH); Duluth city directories, 1957–63.

8. *Duluth News-Tribune,* June 1, 1947, 1-A, 4-A; August 29, 1947, 20, citing Harlen Olafson; June 10, 1948, 6.

9. *Duluth News-Tribune,* September 23, 1948, 6; November 21, 1948, 8-B; January 28, 1949, 4; February 11, 1949, 6; communication to author from Duluth city engineering office, May 13, 2004.

10. *Duluth News-Tribune,* May 26, 1946, 1-A; October 24, 1953, 6; October 31, 1953, 8; October 23, 1954, 6; *Parktorian,* 1964, 1971 (Morgan Park school archives).

11. *Parktorian,* 1948, 1950; "Minstrel Show," *Wikipedia* (accessed December 8, 2005).

12. Dora MacDonald in *Duluth News-Tribune,* May 1, 1955, Cosmopolitan Section, 4.

13. *Duluth Herald,* January 25, 1966, 13, citing Cherra and R. Bye; *Duluth Budgeteer,* July 27, 1977, 22.

14. *Duluth Herald,* March 30, 1970, 1–2; *Duluth Budgeteer,* July 27, 1977, 22.

15. *Duluth News-Tribune,* August 11, 1957, 7; October 21, 1962, Cosmopolitan Section, 10; March 3, 1972, 2.

16. *Duluth News-Tribune,* March 3, 1972, 2.

17. Rapaich interview.

18. Alanen, "Sixty Years of Transition in a Planned Company Town," 4–5; author's survey of Morgan Park and Gary residents, 1975; *Minneapolis Star,* February 28, 1972, 1-B, citing Mrs. Clarence Dzuck; *Milwaukee Journal,* May 19, 1974, 1, citing Richard Closson.

19. Duluth city directories, 1970–1980; Alanen, "Sixty Years of Transition," 4–5.

20. Alanen, "Sixty Years of Transition," 5; author's survey of Morgan Park and Gary residents, 1975.

21. Alanen, "Sixty Years of Transition," 5–6; author's 1975 survey of Gary and Morgan Park residents.

22. Author's 1975 survey of Gary and Morgan Park residents.

23. Duluth city directories, 1970–80; U.S. Censuses of Population and Housing, 1970, 1980.

24. Author's 1975 survey of Gary and Morgan Park residents.

25. U.S. Censuses of Population and Housing, 1980, 1990; Duluth city directory, 1983.

26. Author's interview with Bill and Sue Majewski, November 9, 2002; *Duluth News-Tribune,* December 25, 1999, 1-E.

27. Author's discussions with Nancy Thompson, 2001–07.

28. *Duluth News-Tribune,* April 9, 1978, B-9; letter from Bob Berg on January 15, 1996, 5-A; *Duluth Herald,* November 14, 1978, B-1; Alison K. Hoagland, "Industrial Housing and Vinyl Siding: Historical Significance Flexibly Applied," in *Preservation of What, for Whom: A Critical Look at Historical Significance,* ed. Michael A. Tomlan (Washington, D.C.: National Council for Preservation Education, 1999), 120, 122; Bill Majewski interview.

29. *Duluth Herald,* June 1, 1977, 1; *Duluth News-Tribune,* October 6, 1998, 1-B; February 1, 1999, citing Doty.

30. Bothun, Solomon, and Howden interviews.

31. *Duluth Herald,* December 12, 1978, B-1; April 1, 1980, B-1, citing Paul Siciliano.

32. *Duluth Herald,* January 27, 1981, B-1, citing Charles Skrief; June 9, 1981, B-1; July 16, 1981, 6-A; *Duluth News-Tribune,* January 31, 1981, B-8; October 29, 1981, 10-A; Advisory Council on Historic Preservation, "Memorandum of Agreement," November 1981 (MHS-SHPO).

33. *Duluth Herald,* July 14, 1981, citing Fridley; "Memorandum of Agreement"; letter from Jordan E. Tannebaum, Advisory Council on Historic Preservation, to John Fedo, December 17, 1981 (MHS-SHPO); *Duluth News-Tribune,* February 28, 1983, 9-A; July 21, 1991, A-4, citing Evelyn Stewart.

34. *Duluth Budgeteer,* July 27, 1977, 22; *Duluth News-Tribune,* October 13, 1978, C-5; *Duluth Herald,* April 1, 1981, A-1; April 13, 1981, A-1; April 28, 1981, B-1; *Parktorian,* 1979, 1982, 1983, 1990, 1991.

35. *Duluth News-Tribune,* October 5, 2002, 4-B; August 30, 2003, 1-B, 3-B, citing Peter Bagley.

36. *Duluth News-Tribune,* March 18, 2002, 1-A, 3-A; September 13, 2002, 1-B and 2-B; September 25, 2002, 3.

37. *Duluth News-Tribune,* June 25, 2003, 1-B, 3-B; January 7, 2004, 2-C; October 13, 2004, 1-B, 2-B; "Positively Minnesota," Minnesota Department of Trade and Economic Development News Release, June 16, 2003.

38. Stoner in *Duluth News-Tribune,* January 1, 2006, 20-A.

39. Isabell Nelson in *Duluth News-Tribune,* January 7, 2006, 6-A.

40. "Morgan Park Newsletter," vol. 1, May 1, 2006.

41. John Strongitharm in *Budgeteer News* (Duluth), January 28, 2007, 12.

INDEX

Compiled by Denise E. Carlson

ARNOLD R. ALANEN, a landscape historian, is professor in the Department of Landscape Architecture at the University of Wisconsin–Madison. Among his many publications are the award-winning books *Main Street Ready-Made: The New Deal Community of Greendale, Wisconsin* (with J. Eden) and *Preserving Cultural Landscapes in America* (edited with R. Melnick).

CHRIS FAUST lives in St. Paul, Minnesota. His photographs, which are collected and exhibited throughout the country, are featured in the book *Nocturnes* (Minnesota, 2007).